CW01666321

THE ART AND ARCHAEOLOGY OF VENETIAN SHIPS AND BOATS

NUMBER FIVE
Studies in Nautical Archaeology
Cheryl A. Ward, General Editor

THE ART AND ARCHAEOLOGY OF VENETIAN SHIPS AND BOATS

Lillian Ray Martin

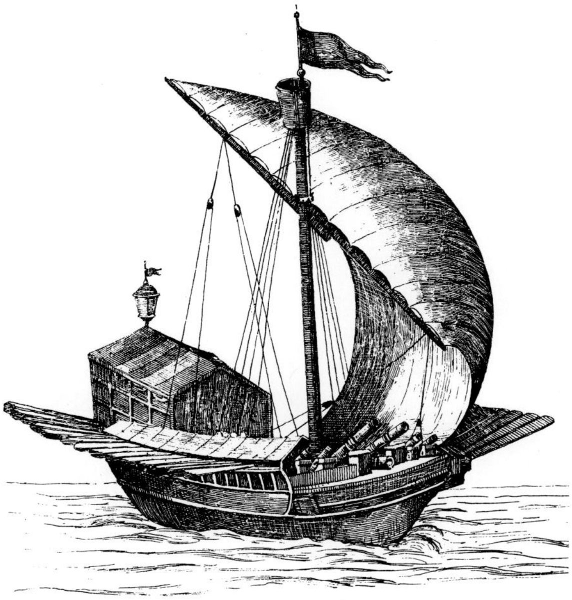

TEXAS A&M UNIVERSITY PRESS • COLLEGE STATION

CHATHAM PUBLISHING
LONDON

Copyright © 2001 by Lillian Ray Martin
Manufactured in the United States of America
All rights reserved
First edition

Published in Great Britain in 2001 by
Chatham Publishing
99 High Street
Rochester
Kent ME1 1LX

Chatham Publishing is an imprint of
Gerald Duckworth & Co Ltd

The publication of this book was made possible in part by the generous support of the Samuel H. Kress Foundation

The paper used in this book meets the minimum requirements of the American National Standard for Permanence of Paper for Printed Library Materials, z39.48-1984. Binding materials have been chosen for durability.
∞

LIBRARY OF CONGRESS CATALOGING-IN-PUBLICATION DATA

Martin, Lillian Ray, 1961–
The art and archaeology of Venetian ships and boats / Lillian Ray Martin.—1st ed.
p. cm.—(Studies in nautical archaeology ; 5)
Includes bibliographical references and index.
ISBN 1-58544-098-1
1. Ships in art. 2. Art, Italian—Italy—Venice. 3. Art, Medieval—Italy—Venice. 4. Art, Early Renaissance—Italy—Venice. 5. Navigation—Italy—Venice—History. 6. Venice (Italy)—History—697–1508. I. Title. II. Series.
N8230.M425 2001
623.8'21'094531—dc21 00-011472

BRITISH LIBRARY CATALOGING IN PUBLICATION DATA
A catalog record of this book is available from the British Library
Chatham ISBN 1-86176-173-2

To my adventuresome and loving family,

Paul, Shawn, and Kitanna

To my adventuresome and loving family,

Paul, Shawn, and Kitanna

CONTENTS

FOREWORD

RECENT ARCHAEOLOGICAL research in the Mediterranean region, both underwater and on land, has yielded an amount of information on ancient ships that would have seemed incredible only a few decades ago. Our knowledge of the ships and shipping of the Middle Ages, on the other hand, has not seen similar progress, because, for the most part, sources are limited to pictorial and literary documents, as well as linguistic and traditional data. Connections and developments in the study of these sources have made it necessary to revise previous attempts at collecting information on medieval Mediterranean vessels, to classify the information available and correct mistakes; in other words, to compile reasonably organized corpora for specific geographical areas.

I am glad to have had the opportunity to follow this research on the Venetian documentary evidence since its beginning as a master's thesis entitled "Medieval Venetian Ship and Boat Representations," 1992.

One almost obvious fact regarding the study of iconographic sources is that published drawings or photographs are sufficient only at a superficial level; one should "feel" the original documents, examine them with one's own eyes or under a lens or microscope, because lines, curves, shades and details can disappear in their reproductions. In the case of the present work, first-hand analysis was difficult due to logistical and bureaucratic obstacles, but it has been carried out with patience and determination by Lillian Ray Martin. A first result is the correction of evident and, in some cases, incredible mistakes and misunderstandings found in previous works, such as those of Jal (1840), Levi (1892) and Vocino (1950); secondly, the number of documents made available for our studies is greatly increased by this compilation.

Attempts to study the large amount of written documents date from the time of Du Cange (1868) or even Jal (1840) and some good progress was accomplished by A. Guglielmotti (1889). For some time, however, there were no outstanding developments, until the "key" to the language of Venetian shipbuilders was completely understood by Chiggiato (1987).

To date, archaeological evidence has been limited to a few wrecks in the area between the mouths of the river Po and the city of Ravenna. These wrecks cannot, in themselves, give definitive answers to questions such as those regarding the large lateeners of the Crusades, but their study tends to confirm the relationship between medieval craft and recent Adriatic boat building traditions, a relationship that is suggested by the mosaics of San Marco in Venice, or by the frescoes of Giusto de Menabuoi in Padua. We also find strong connections between the words still spoken in local dialects (mainly of the Veneto) and the terms used in written documents, an important fact considering our limited knowledge of, for example, sailing with lateen sails in the Adriatic.

The above considerations point to the significance of the present book, which demonstrates the value of art as a source for the nautical archaeology of an area with the historical significance of medieval Venice. As in other corpuses and atlases compiled in recent years, types and relationships are conceived as filing boxes, in the sense that they are not rigid classifications like those of the previous century but categories that provide the tools for classifying the findings of future research.

As the author states in her concluding paragraph [of chapter 3], this work is intended to serve as a springboard for further research in selected geographical areas. I would like, then, to suggest that Tuscany be chosen for the next area of research. The large amount of medieval and Renaissance Tuscan pictorial documents also calls for further collection and classification. In addition to the basic information covering another important area of Italian nautical history, a work on Tuscan images will exhibit by contrast the merit of the two main styles of ship drawings in the Renaissance: the Venetian one versus the Tuscan one, color and shade versus line and relief.

—*Marco Bonino*
Bologna

PREFACE

ROTUND MERCHANT ships. Sleek warships. Humble fishing boats and sturdy lighters. Pleasure craft and gondolas. The harbor of medieval and Renaissance Venice thronged with watercraft. Ships and boats were unquestionably vital to the Venetian Maritime Republic, and her ships were of extreme importance historically. Many details as to the nature of these watercraft, however, have yet to be well understood. How many and what types of watercraft did the Republic employ? What were their characteristic features? Which sails, rigging, rudders, and anchors were used? What is known of construction techniques? Three lines of evidence may elucidate these issues: archaeological remains of ships or boats, written documents concerning vessels, and artistic representations of watercraft.

Iconographic material is an indispensable source of data for the study of nautical archaeology. It will never be fully utilized, however, unless such material is completely cataloged and analyzed. The pictorial images concerning Venetian ships and boats have never before been adequately studied. This study therefore focuses on the art of Venetia prior to the high Renaissance period in order to present a catalog and analysis of the extant Venetian ship and boat representations.

The history of Venice and the style and media of her art are inextricably interwoven. As entrepôt between East and West, Venice adopted and fused into her own the artistic styles and media of both the Byzantine and European worlds. Not surprisingly, maritime images occupy a great deal of Venetian art. This fact reflects quite simply her reliance on seafaring.

It was a great pleasure to work in Venice, thanks to the kindnesses I encountered, both from scholars and institutions as well as friends. I would like to thank the following individuals and institutions for their assistance during my research, and for their permission to photograph or reproduce their materials: Procuratoria of San Marco (Dr. Maria Da Villa Urbino and Monsignor Antonio Meneguolo, administrators of St. Mark's Cathedral), Museo Storico Navale (Admiral Carlo Gottardi, director of the Naval History Museum), Fondazione Querini-Stampalia, Biblioteca Nazionale Marciana (Dr. Marino Zorzi, director, National Library of St. Mark), Museo Correr (Dr. Giandomenico Romanelli, director of the Correr Museum), Fondazione Giorgio Cini (Tessie Vecchi), Galleria dell'Accademia (Academy Picture Gallery), Seminario Patriarchale (Don Sandrini, priest), and, outside of Venice, the Bodleian Library, Oxford University (Mrs. Mary Clapinson), Gemäldegalerie Staatliche Museum (Dr. Henning Boch, director), Princeton Art Index, Yale University Beinecke Rare Book and Manuscript Library, and the Houghton Library of Harvard University (Mrs. Jennie Rathbun).

Scholars of naval architecture living in Italy proved to be exceptionally generous both with their time and resources. For the numerous courtesies extended to me by Dr. Ennio Concina, and for our frequent conversations and correspondences on Venetian technical treatises and manuscripts concerning ship construction, I am most grateful. Likewise, I am indebted to Mario Marzari, and to Alvise Chiggiato, for copies of Chiggiato's reconstruction plans and articles. I am also appreciative of the helpful correspondences of Dr. Barbara Kreutz and Dr. John Dotson, and especially of Dr. Marco Bonino, for his continual generosity and scholarly inspiration.

For advice and beneficial criticism upon reading the manuscript, I am indebted to Dr. Bruce Dickson, Professor J. Richard Steffy, Dr. Vivian Paul, Dr. Henry Graham, Dr. Marco Bonino, Dr. George Bass, Dr. Frederick van Doorninck, Dr. Fred Hocker, Dr. Sigrid Knudsen, and my editor, Dr. Cheryl Ward.

Finally, I appreciate my family and friends, for their help with translations, editing, drawings, and computer work, but above all, for their support: Elisabetta Ravagnan, Rossella Peressini, Consolata Auxilia and the Buzzi family, Mrs. Vera Gunter, Captain Tom Ray, Dr. and Mrs. Ed Fann, Mrs. Mary Moore, Roxani Margariti, Tom Oertling, Mike Fitzgerald, Wayne Smith, Georgia Fox, Maria Jacobsen, Diana Thornton, Rob Barras, Nicolle Hirschfeld, Patricia Fann, Eddie Fann, Dawn and Kelly Kidd, Caryn MacDonald, Helen C. Dewolf, Paul Martin, and again, Cheryl Ward, I thank you.

There are many images in this book, and some of them may have copyrights of which I am not aware, though I do not think so from my research. I specifically do not intend to infringe on anyone's copyright. If I have inadvertently done so, I apologize. Where not otherwise identified, photographs and drawings are by the author.

THE ART AND ARCHAEOLOGY OF VENETIAN SHIPS AND BOATS

INTRODUCTION

PICTORIAL DOCUMENTS constitute a unique corpus of data, invaluable information for anyone studying the history of ships and boats, yet these documents are rarely adequately studied. As so aptly put by Farrel (1979: 244), representational or iconographic source material "is of undoubted value to ship-archaeology but its value will only be realized if the material is recorded and discussed in its entirety." This study does just that for the early Christian, medieval and early Renaissance maritime art of Venice. It surveys the art of the Venetia region in northeast Italy and presents a catalog and analysis of the ship and boat representations from that region dating through the fifteenth century.

Venice, settled in the fifth century in the lagoons of the Adriatic Sea, was always a maritime nation. Enduring for more than a millennium as a dominant sea power, the Maritime Republic of Venice had a marked effect on the history of seafaring as well as trade. Three factors gave Venice advantages over other medieval trading city-states: the city's location, governmental policies, and the skills of her inhabitants. By the twelfth century, Venice had become the prime trading center between the eastern Mediterranean and Europe. The geographical situation of Venice, as a series of islands in the northwest Adriatic, offered protection from military attack. It also made Venice an ideal location from which her merchants could import both luxury and essential goods from the east and export them to Europe. Venice became a key trading agent between the European and Mediterranean world market; her citizens made a fortune.

The *Signoria*, the senate of the Venetian government, made trade a priority. Its policies resulted in communally controlled capitalism. By the beginning of the thirteenth century, the Maritime Republic of Venice had established the Venetian Arsenal, initially to make and store military supplies, but where, within a hundred years, a formidable military fleet was built and maintained (Concina, 1987: 11–12). Venetian policy on the ownership and operation of the merchant marine fluctuated between extremes: merchant galleys were either communally or privately owned and operated. In 1314, for example, state-subsidized and regulated galley voyages ran regularly to the North Sea (Lane, 1963: 180 and 185). Before the fourteenth century, however, the private sector controlled merchant galleys, though even then the republic regulated their construction and imposed various laws concerning their safety. Beginning in 1329, policy became more consistent: all merchant galleys were part of the state-maintained mercantile fleet, and voyages were auctioned to the highest bidder (Lane, 1973: 129). Venetian law dictated that all merchant galleys be designed so that they could be used as warships should the need arise. The government encouraged, facilitated, and protected trade.

Nearly the entire population of Venice was involved in maritime trade one way or another; their shipbuilding, navigational, and mercantile skills made Venice highly competitive in the

Mediterranean marketplace. Ships and boats were an integral part of Venetian life, and her astute merchants, mariners, and shipbuilders gained fame throughout the known world. During medieval and Renaissance times, the Maritime Republic of Venice defined state-of-the-art warships and merchant vessels (Concina, 1987: 15), and these developments significantly influenced later ships of exploration. The Venetian technology of ship construction thus offers an indication of the contemporaneous technology employed throughout the Mediterranean, and also provides insights into the design of ships that made possible the discovery of the New World.

All too little is known about the early vessels of Venice. Medieval ship remains are scant, in fact, throughout the Mediterranean. Those vessels that have been discovered are rarely complete, and often have not been properly excavated and published. In the Veneto and adjacent Emiglia-Romagna region, only three ships have been discovered and investigated thus far: the thirteenth- and the sixteenth-century merchant ships at Contarina (Contarina I and II), and a fifteenth-century galley at Lazise (Lake Garda). In addition, remains of five smaller boats from Cervia, Pomposa, Pontelagoscuro, Logonovo, and Ravenna have been excavated and published. Clearly these few examples can do no more than begin to define the broad range of regional vessel types that were used during this period.

Written records concerning ships or boats are also rare and often not specific. The earliest available Venetian ship construction treatises date to the fifteenth century, though there is one mercantile manuscript concerning ships dating to the fourteenth century. Because the technical treatises were written for masters in the shipyards, the "obvious" was often left out, making their interpretation today problematic. Four Venetian mercantile manuscripts or ship construction treatises are pertinent to this study as they provide illustrations of contemporaneous ship types.[1] Other legal documents, such as shipping contracts and maritime laws are likewise informative.[2] The inherent problems of archaeological remains and the documentary evidence, however, lead us to look beyond these sources for additional clues concerning Venetian vessels.

Artistic representations of watercraft offer other clues about ships and boats, and the evidence gleaned from them supplements the archaeological record and written accounts. Despite their limitations, artistic portrayals of ships and boats are, in fact, the closest thing we have to photographs of ancient watercraft. With varying degrees of accuracy, ship and boat representations visually describe general and technical features often not explicated by the other two forms of evidence. For example, details of rigging and superstructure are rarely preserved in the archaeological record, yet these are usually depicted in artistic representations of watercraft.

Nautical archaeologists have not paid sufficient attention to representational data from Venice or most other areas. Consideration of this body of evidence is essential to attain a more complete picture of watercraft. Scholars of northern Italian ships and seafaring to date, including Jal (1840), Casoni (1847), Lane (1934 and 1973), Bonino (1978a and 1978b) and Chiggiato (1987, 1991), have done formative work but have concentrated primarily on archaeological remains and written records. This study will instead focus on the pictorial evidence, creating a catalog that fills a gap in the current research. Because Venetians were a people dependent on seafaring, they naturally included representations of watercraft frequently in their art. Studying their art teaches us about the ships and boats they employed.

The period under study includes a very significant shift in Venetian seafaring. From the sixth through the eighth century, Venetians traded throughout the lagoons of northeast Italy and along the nearby rivers providing access to the mainland of northern Italy. Beginning in the ninth century, Venetians traveled across the Mediterranean, reaching far abroad for better trading prospects. This expansion overseas brought them great wealth but also frequently led them into armed conflict (Lane, 1973: 1–11). This shift in the trading and warring patterns of Venice must have triggered the development of new, seagoing ship types. The literary record attests to a proliferation of distinct ship types, including both military and mercantile ships. It documents the change from craft primarily suited to lagoons and rivers to seagoing vessels by the turn of the millennium. Surprisingly, the artistic record does not reflect these trends. Instead, there seems to have been a bias toward the representation of the mercantile round ship, a beamy, high-sided sailing ship with two to three decks, adapted for the transport of bulky merchandise over all other types (see graph, fig. 155).

Referring to a series of innovations in Mediterranean ship technology that occurred from 1250 to 1400, the Venetian scholar Lane spoke of a "Nautical Revolution of the Middle Ages" (1973: 118–24 and 1987: 238). The lateen-rigged ship, characterized by a triangular-shaped sail and two quarter rudders, gradually was replaced by the square-rigged (and then mixed-rigged) ship, equipped with a single stern rudder. The change in rig and steering was accompanied by a development in ship construction as well: the shell-first method evolved to a frame-first technique (Bonino, 1978b: 22), a development some scholars believe occurred sometime between the seventh and eleventh century (Pryor, 1992: 27). These improvements eventually led to the building of ships capable of ocean navigation and thus to the discovery and exploration of the New World. Lateen-rigged ships and boats with side rudders built before the major technological change make up the majority of the catalog. Square-rigged ships with side rudders begin to appear in fourteenth-century Venetian art, and mixed-rig ships with stern rudders become common by the fifteenth century. Smaller craft, when rigged, are continuously depicted as lateen-rigged.

The fact that so few early ship remains have been discovered and studied in northeast Italy makes any extant representational evidence involving early Venetian ships all the more significant. Depictions are not photographs; they are not always precise or easy to interpret. Yet, Venetian artists saw ships and boats daily, and their renditions of vessels are bound to reflect the technical development of ships and boats with a greater degree of accuracy than maritime images made by inland artists. When interpreting artistic representations, one must consider such art historical questions as: Did the artist trouble himself to be accurate in detail? To what extent did stylistic or formal conventions or limitations of the medium dictate the final product of the work? What was the purpose of the ship or boat illustration? What areas of the picture have been subjected to deterioration or restoration, and how has that affected the maritime image? These questions will be addressed generally in chapter 1, and specifically, as necessary, with each image presented in the catalog of chapter 2. Another difficulty in interpreting the artistic evidence for ships and boats is the statistical frequency with which one or another ship type or piece of equipment was depicted may at times be misleading. On the other hand, this statistical frequency can indicate what Venetians envisioned when they conceptualized "ship" or "boat," and is thus still of interest. Each vessel representation offers unique evidence for details of particular ship types, their rigs and equipment; however, only when nautical details are corroborated by appearing repeatedly in the art can one reasonably conclude that feature is meaningful. Considering the representations in aggregate, then, is the value of studying this large corpus of images.

Methodology

A systematic survey of the museums, churches, libraries, and the walls and architectural decoration of public buildings was undertaken in Venice to collect all known representations of watercraft in early Christian, medieval, and early Renaissance art. Other cities of the Venetia were also surveyed (see appendix 1). Library research augmented the on-site visits to fill in additional Venetian maritime art, particularly the portable art forms such as manuscripts and polyptychs. Experts on specific locations, such as museum directors, curators, administrators, or priests, were consulted whenever possible. The most fruitful locations for artistic representations of ships or boats proved to be mosaics and frescoes decorating church walls, predella panels (paintings that originally decorated the base or sides of large altarpieces, that today are often part of museum collections), and manuscript illuminations (in libraries and private collections). Graffiti are particularly common at the main entrances of churches, either on columns or on the portal itself, or near windows, and on the walls of quarantine locations or prisons.[3] Less fruitful locations for maritime representations included church sacristies and architectural sculpture.

Venice is a city of museums and churches. It is therefore probable that some ship or boat representations have been overlooked, particularly images in museum storage, or in libraries and manuscript collections, which were impossible to survey completely. Also, some medieval churches have been destroyed, permanently closed, temporarily closed for restoration or are now private property, and were therefore inaccessible. (Appendix 1, listing the church sites visited, also specifies those inaccessible or lost.) Nonetheless the catalog of images resulting from this research is fairly exhaustive for Venice, and it gives an adequate sample of the maritime art of Aquileia, Belluno, Bologna, Bolzano, Padua, Ravenna, Rimini, Verona, and Vittorio Veneto.

Each ship or boat image was photographed with a Nikon FM2 camera and a 60mm Micronikkor lens, using Ilford FP4 black and white film (exposed with flash at 125 ASA), Kodak TMax black and white film (exposed under natural lighting, rated at 1600 or 3200 ASA, as necessary), Kodachrome slide film (exposed with flash at 64 ASA) or Kodak Ektachrome 160 Professional Tungsten color slide film (exposed with flash and an 85b filter at 100 ASA), and 3M Scotchchrome 1000 color slide film (exposed under natural light, rated at 1000, 2000, or 3000 ASA, as necessary). When it was not possible to make original photographs of the maritime art, line drawings were made, photographic images were purchased from the museum, church, or photographic agencies, or images were reproduced, with permission as necessary, from published sources.

Further documentation included full site descriptions, and sketches or rubbings in cases where more detail could be recorded. Measurements of the maritime images are of little value to this study. Diverse media and modes of representation in Venetian art often disregard realistic proportions. Therefore, comparing measurements of different pictures is not instructive. Furthermore, ship or boat images were often physically inaccessible (as, for example, most wall mosaics).

Relevant historical, economic, and art historical factors are discussed in chapter 1. (See appendix 2 for a chronology.) Representations of the ships and smaller vessels located during this survey are cataloged and discussed in detail in chapter 2. Features of each vessel, including construction details, the stern configuration, rigging, and anchors, are topics for discussion, and are clarified when possible by comparison with other representations, written documentary evidence, and archaeological remains. Chapter 3 presents general conclusions about the characteristics of Venetian watercraft, including analysis of construction techniques, common stern designs or configurations, steering devices and their mounts, and anchors. In this final chapter, after considering the textual evidence, a typology of Venetian ships and boats is further developed by placing the represented ships and boats into recognizable categories based on size, design, and function. In this way, an indicative cross section is attained of the range of types employed in the region, from small coastal and lagoonal craft to the larger merchant ships and galleys. As Venetian ships are likely to reflect the contemporaneous Mediterranean nautical technology, this study not only reveals specific aspects of Venetian ship and boat types, but also contributes to the general understanding of ship design, rigging, hull construction, and the late medieval iron anchor used in the Mediterranean at this time.

Chapter One

A BRIEF OVERVIEW OF VENETIAN HISTORY AND ART

The lagoons of Venice were first settled by refugees fleeing from a series of invasions that devastated the cities of northeast Italy. The Goths and Attila the Hun invaded in the fifth century, the Lombards in A.D. 568. These refugees gradually inhabited numerous islands of the Venetian lagoon, and a rudimentary system of self-government evolved. The city's location within the lagoonal system provided some measure of security from attack, as well as a means of livelihood for the inhabitants.

Initially the economy of Venice was based on trade in fish and salt, commodities that the Venetians marketed in the territories of Ravenna and the Pentapolis along the Adriatic coast, and later, up the rivers of northeast Italy (Luzzato, 1961: 3–4). By the eighth century, Venice had gained control of the Veneto plains (Fasoli, 1978: 592–95), and, at least until the end of the tenth century, she monopolized trade along the Po River, one of the primary trade routes to trans-alpine Europe.[1] Venetian traders supplied the inland inhabitants not only with locally produced salt and fish paste, but also with exotic merchandise that they obtained from eastern merchants, including spices, silk, ivory, precious furs and stones, and purple-dyed cloth. Venetians must have always employed a variety of ship types, but as long as they were primarily river and lagoonal traders they depended especially on barges, leaving the Mediterranean traffic to foreigners. As it went upstream, a cargo was frequently transshipped to the type of vessel best adapted to the demands of regional navigation (Fasoli, 1978: 566).

Venice was ideally located for trade and became the essential link for the maritime and land-river commerce between the Byzantine empire and Europe. Venetian citizens grew rich by providing a marketplace for exchange between east and west. The economy of Venice was further strengthened around the turn of the millennium as Venetian mariners and merchants traveled seaward and into the eastern Mediterranean. *Zinzibar, sandali, piper, canella, zambelloti*—ginger, salt, pepper, cinnamon, and camel hair clothing—and other exotic luxuries of the east drew Venetian traders "beyond the seas." Soon they were traveling across the Adriatic to trade closer to the source of their wealth. The Venetians' superior supply of wood, from the mainland of the Veneto as well as from her colonies along the Dalmatian coast, provided their primary means of exchange (Lane, 1973: 8). This abundant wood supply was also essential for the building of the larger and stronger seagoing ship types they needed for traveling beyond the Adriatic Gulf and the riverine system of northeast Italy. By the tenth century, Venetian merchants were trading directly with the peoples of the Levant, Black Sea, Crete, and Alexandria for the luxury goods from the Far East, as well as for slaves and necessary staples, including iron, copper, tin, mercury, soap, leather goods, coarse textiles, grain, oil, wine, fruit, live animals, and slaughtered meat. By the twelfth century, the economy of Venice had peaked (Lane, 1963: 179).

The strength of Venice's economy was further enhanced by the fact that throughout most of her history, Venice succeeded in arranging advantageous trade agreements not only with both Latin and Byzantine Christians but also with "the infidels," the Fatimids of North Africa and, later, the Ottoman Turks. Thus, despite severe competition at different times with Genoa and Pisa, as well as competition with the Arabs, her versatile economy remained strong. Foremost among these relationships was a long-standing affiliation with Byzantium, which afforded her trading privileges throughout the Byzantine empire in exchange for Venetian naval support of the empire. A treaty between Charlemagne and Byzantium in 812 ensured additional trading advantages for Venice in northern Italy (Lewis, 1951: 107 and 217). But by the mid-ninth century, Venice exerted her independence by trading with Syria and Egypt, despite Byzantine regulations against such transactions (Lewis, 1951: 116). Despite papal interdicts against it, the state continually traded with Muslims in Sicily, North Africa, Syria, and Egypt (Norwich, 1982: 28; Bragadin, 1978: 407).

A renewed agreement with Byzantium in 992 imparted to Venice a virtual monopoly of the west-bound trade in the eastern Mediterranean, while the trade policy of Otto III of Lombardy in 996 effectively created a Venetian monopoly of the eastern trade from northern Italy as well (Lewis, 1951: 218). Venice was the only state that actually succeeded in establishing and maintaining trade relations with all sides, an enterprise that required much diplomacy and some military aggression.

At the beginning of the thirteenth century, the Arsenal served as a storage area for the growing Venetian navy. It evolved into an important maintenance center for ships, and, by the fourteenth century, was functioning as the public yards for the assembly-line building of navy ships (Concina, 1987: 11–12). The Venetian government not only developed a mighty navy but also regulated the construction of merchant galleys to ensure that these merchant ships would not be too unwieldy to serve as effective warships when necessary. Like their Byzantine predecessors, Venetian galleys were slender (with a length to beam ratio of about 8:1), had only one deck, and relied primarily on oared power. Other governmental policies were designed to keep capital in the hands of the people, thus facilitating their mercantile activities, and to provide Venetian merchants with the safest shipping and cheapest freight rates possible (Lane, 1973: 125; 1963: 197 and 202). Such policies and the support of her navy made Venice the strongest mercantile state of the Middle Ages in the Mediterranean. Maintaining both colonies and trading stations throughout the Adriatic and eastern Mediterranean, she became a virtual maritime empire.

The Crusades proved to be another great source of wealth for Venice. Many pilgrims preferred to book passage on a ship rather than to risk the slower and more dangerous land route. Venice's relatively convenient location to much of Europe made the city one of the most popular ports of departure. Because of Venice's maritime fame, European leaders often ordered their ships to be built in Venice. Louis IX did so in 1268, as did the organizers of the Fourth Crusade earlier in that century.

The Fourth Crusade brought more profit to Venice than all the other Crusades combined. During the winter of 1201, Geoffrey de Villehardouin, the marshal of Champagne, France, and five other envoys for the counts of Flanders, Champagne, and Blois, contracted Venice to carry 33,500 crusaders for a total sum of 85,000 marks of silver (Villehardouin, 1204: Book 5, 21; in Marzials's translation, 1965: 6). A large part of the 300-fleet flotilla, which included 100 *usserii* or horse transports and 62 galleys, was specially built for the campaign. Forty merchant ships were appropriated and converted for use as transports. Venetian trade came to a standstill as citizens prepared to meet their part of the agreement. By the departure date, however, less than a third of the anticipated crusaders had actually appeared in Venice, and they were able to deliver only about half of the huge sum due. Rather than breaking the contract, which would have been a financial disaster for Venice, the Doge Dandolo renegotiated with the crusaders, who agreed to sack Zara and Constantinople en route as partial payment for their passage (Queller, 1977: 52). Venice reaped payment fourfold: the fares were eventually fully paid; she regained control of her unruly colony, Zara; she obtained a chain of colonies stretching all the way between Venice and the Black Sea; and she received half the booty from the seizure of Constantinople in 1204 (Lane, 1973: 36–41).

The last two boons, the additional colonies and the plunder, had other long-term effects on Venice. Until this time, the Byzantine government had carefully regulated Black Sea trade: all ships passing through the Bosphorus were required to unload in Constantinople and offer their wares for sale. The Byzantine motive had been, quite simply, to keep the city supplied with essential grain, critical since the seventh century loss to the Arabs of its previous sources of grain, Egypt and Sicily (Lewis, 1951: 82 and 109). After the Fourth Crusade, however, Venice had free access to the Black Sea, and her trading ventures in the area increased.[2] The timing was ideal, for the final stop of caravans from China had shifted from the trading centers along the Levantine and Egyptian coasts to Trebizond, along the southeastern shore of the Black Sea (McNeill, 1974: 35–36). By the mid-thirteenth century, Venetian trade was flourishing in the Black Sea.

The spoil from Constantinople indirectly brought Venice further gain: reliquaries and other art objects only increased Venetian prestige and made the city an even more popular pilgrimage center. Venice eventually came to possess relics of the saints Matthew, Mark, Luke, John, Peter, and Bartholomew (six of the apostles), Anianus (Mark's disciple, and Bishop of Alexandria), Helena (mother of Constantine) and other, less famous popes, patriarchs, bishops, doctors of the Church, and saints, including Cornelius, Cyprianus, Hippolytus, Cyrillus, Stephen, Clement, Blaise, Sergius, Bacchus, Isidore, and Mark's disciples, Hermagoras and Fortunatus of Aquileia (Demus, 1988: 2–3).

During the late thirteenth century, Venice expanded her trading influence even further abroad, north as far as Flanders and England, and as far east as China. Marco Polo's famous journeys to China occurred between 1271 and 1292. No doubt this expansion was partially a result of rapid progress in techniques of navigation and shipbuilding. Lane refers to this period as the "Nautical Revolution of the Middle Ages," beginning in about 1250 (1973: 118–24; 1987: 238). Port books were conceived in the thirteenth century. These listed various bits of useful information essential for dead-reckoning navigation, including the distances and directions between ports. By circa 1250, a port book covering the entire Mediterranean had been compiled. Within twenty years, four additional innovations made winter sailing feasible in the Mediterranean: portolan marine charts, the magnetic compass, the traverse table, and the hourglass. Portolans, the first marine charts, graphically presented the information of port books, and formed, with strictly mathematical methods, a visual map of coastlines and the positions of ports. The compass rose, with its radiating rhumb lines on the charts, enabled a mariner to plot a course and follow a compass bearing. The traverse board helped reduce zigzag course lines to a straight line. Once able to measure time with an hourglass, mariners could navigate by dead reckoning. At the end of the century, portolan charts, compasses, hourglasses, and traverse tables were already in common use. The resulting improvement in navigation meant that two trips to the eastern Mediterranean were possible within the sailing season, instead of just one.

The introduction of pulleys in about 1300 facilitated the use of both steering devices and rigging. The square sail and stern rudder, innovations adapted from the cog (a northern European ship type appearing in the previous century), were introduced into the Mediterranean at about the same time. A single rudder, attached with iron pintles and gudgeons to the stern, gradually replaced the two quarter rudders.

Another important development also occurred around 1300. The trireme, or merchant galley, a new enlarged type of oared galley with more sail power and designed specifically for commerce, supplanted both the light bireme galley used to transport precious cargo, as well as some of the round ships employed for the more bulky merchandise (Lane, 1934: 14). In about 1320, the merchant galley was enlarged further. This great merchant galley had a fuller, more spacious hold than normal galleys. Her oars and armed men almost guaranteed a speedy and safe delivery of both luxury and bulky goods. As an excellent compromise between long ship and round ship, merchant galleys became the most important cargo carrier. After 1314, regular state-subsidized and state-regulated convoys of merchant galleys were sailing westward and northward to trade in the North Sea ("Flanders galleys" e.g., fig. 66), and east to Syria or Cyprus, Romania (Black Sea), and Alexandria (Lane, 1963: 180; 1973: 125). Individual merchantmen continued to travel to self-determined destinations, but they joined convoys when possible for safety. Venice, by now one of the largest cities in Europe, was in her prime.

In the early part of the fourteenth century, Venice eliminated her dependence on imported food by gaining control of Padua and Treviso on terra firma. But the fourteenth century also brought a series of devastating hardships. An earthquake damaged much of the city in 1347. The plague followed; it reached Venice in 1347 and decimated more than half of the population within the next year and a half (Lane, 1973: 19). The total population of Europe was reduced by at least one-third, resulting in a dramatically shrunken market (Kedar, 1976), and the immigrants who replenished the population were more craftsmen than seamen.

Almost immediately thereafter, a renewed war with Genoa (the first of which had occurred in 1257) brought continued suffering that finally abated with Venetian victory at Chioggia in 1381. This victory established Venetian control of the Levantine trade and reaffirmed her dominion over the Hellespont and the Black Sea trade. Venice now held strongholds all along the Dalmatian coast, the Peloponnese, on Crete, Corfu, and the Cyclades and Dodecanese islands, as well as in Constantinople.

By the fifteenth century, Venice was firmly established on terra firma and controlled territories extending all the way inland to Lake Garda.

When the Ottoman Turks began to vie for control of Aegean trade, this threat prompted the Venetians again to war. The war endured through the seventeenth century, although it culminated with the Battle of Lepanto in 1571. Venice was nominally victorious, but the losses and costs of the war were severe. Worse still, Venice failed to follow up on her victory, so by the seventeenth century, she had in fact lost control of most of her colonies to the Ottomans.

Thus, Venetian influence began to diminish dramatically in the sixteenth century. A combination of factors caused her eclipse. Most important, of course, were the expanding naval powers of the Ottoman and Spanish empires (Lane, 1973: 248), but other influences included a shortage of oak timber in Venetian domains, so essential for shipbuilding, and competition from the Portuguese expansion in the spice trade. Finally, Dutch acquisition of the Spice Islands early in the seventeenth century was more ruinous to the Venetian economy than Portuguese expansion had ever been (Lane, 1973: 294).

The later history of Venice, with the exception of its continually profitable tourist trade, is a history of decline. Venice in the seventeenth and eighteenth century gained fame as a pleasure city, and she began to flourish again with an influx of tourists. Aristocracy from all over Europe and especially Englishmen, engaged in the grand tour, and the numbers of visitors swelled each year. They came to have their portraits made, to enjoy opera and concertos, the theater, the carnival, prostitution, and gambling, to buy products of Venice such as lace, glass, and books, and to appreciate the exceptional beauty and festive spirit of the water city.

Despite its mercantile decline, the city remained independent and functioning as a center of shipping until Napoleon's occupation in 1797, when he systematically plundered the city between May and October. Many monasteries and churches were closed, their valuable art moved to Paris, while works of "lesser" merit were destroyed. In October of 1797, Napoleon placed Venice temporarily under Austrian control until 1805, when he reoccupied the city. French occupation lasted for another decade (Lane, 1973: 421 and 436). By the time she regained her independence, Venice had lost a good deal of her art and was completely ruined as a center for shipping.

The city today, though still magical, is overpopulated, and completely devoid of any industry other than glassmaking and tourism; it is a city living on its past, with overwhelming problems in the present. The nearby mainland city of Mestre provides the only other source of employment, primarily in the chemical, petroleum, and plastics industries. However, these industries have caused extreme pollution problems in the lagoon and the city. In the 1930s, electric pumps were introduced to pump water from the subsoil for industrial and agricultural purposes on the mainland. As a result, Venice is gradually sinking and has become subject to periodic flooding. This seriously threatens her buildings and the art they contain. At present, plans are being implemented to improve or control these problems, and to preserve the unique city of the Republic of Venice.

Venetian Art

The earliest surviving truly Venetian art dates to approximately the tenth century, although earlier Roman art, such as the fourth-century early Christian floor mosaics in the Cathedral of Aquileia, exists in the region. Although some of the art of Venice has been lost or relocated, the extant churches, monasteries, libraries, and public buildings of Venice, still retain a wealth of valuable images.

Stylistically, the art of Venice was greatly influenced by the Byzantine style, which in turn continued the artistic traditions of late antiquity. Early Byzantine art inherited its primary medium, mosaic, from the Roman tradition, but Byzantine artists employed it in a style that was more symbolic than naturalistic (L'Orange, 1966: 12). The primary function of Byzantine art was religious: artists concentrated their efforts on ecclesiastical decorations, votive offerings, or dedicatory images commissioned by private individuals or guilds. Artistic images were both didactic and decorative.

Byzantine religious art was therefore far from being *ars gratia artis;* artistic creation was an act of piety, and a spark of the divine essence was believed to be present within the material image. Icons were intended as

> a means of creating conditions of interior life favourable to meditation, indeed to a state of illumination conducive to "truth." Hence those great gold grounds, empty, uniform and glittering, veritable sheets of light upon which are projected figures that are impassive and serene. The figures have no individual characteristics, and the devices used to portray them are rhythmical line, symmetry, elongation of the silhouette, two-dimensionality and a conventional treatment of drapery; they have no real relation one to another or to inanimate objects (Christe et al., 1982: 131).

The tendency toward simplification and stylization of subject matter that occurs in mosaic was particularly appropriate for the medieval artists' purpose. Art within the place of worship was intended to intensify religious feeling, to heighten one's awareness of the spiritual world. Realism was neither desired nor expected. Byzantine artists represented biblical figures and saints stiffly upon a gold background, which totally divorced them from earthly reality. Likewise, in all Byzantine media, artists depicted inanimate objects such as ships and boats in a stylized, simplified manner: curved hulls with voluted ends reveal little about actual vessels. Such images where "symbolic intent can displace realism completely" (Farrel, 1979: 237), were statically repeated over time.

Venice was one of the most important centers for the diffusion of the Byzantine style in the West (Christe et al., 1982: 131 and 256), but even when most strongly influenced by Constantinople, Venetian art was never completely Byzantine. It was a unique synthesis of both Byzantine and Western stylistic traditions, combined with completely Venetian characteristics. While modeling techniques, formulaic compositions, and the style of figural representation show the impact of Byzantium, medieval Venetian representations are even further simplified and generalized. Venetian qualities include "a subtle colorism, a sense of rhythmic composition . . . and the penchant for the decorative, for splendor and sumptuousness, the striving for harmonious beauty" (Demus, 1988: 200). The eventual appearance of true perspective, the interest in emotion, and the sculptural rendering of form derive from Western Renaissance influences.

In the thirteenth and fourteenth centuries, narrative subjects, well exemplified by the art of Giotto, commonly appear in Italian art. Rendered in a completely new vernacular way, human figures exhibit a fascination with the real world (Folda, 1976: 40). In contrast to the stiff figural representations of the early medieval world, humans and saints now appear in motion, and their faces reveal their emotions. The biblical, hagiographical (concerning the lives and miracles of the saints), and liturgical (portraying rites of the liturgy) cycles were expanded with new episodes, including radical new themes, the portrayal of people's day-to-day activities. Fifteenth-century art manifested an even greater degree of naturalism and humanization. Through the use of perspective, human figures were firmly linked to their natural surroundings, and emotion and motion were even more convincingly depicted. This new mode of portrayal was effectually accompanied by an increased use of panel painting over the mosaic medium (Steer, 1970). In Venice, the art of Paolo Veneziano and Jacopo

Bellini exemplifies this narrative trend. Paolo Veneziano is the first Venetian artist known by name. He and his school were clearly influenced by Giottesque technique, yet their art still reflected Byzantine convention and a refined style. By Renaissance times, painting and sculpture became the primary media, a change that reflected the new aims of artists and their patrons. Painting and sculpture facilitate a much greater degree of realism than mosaic or enamel.

Prevalent themes throughout Venetian art always included biblical, liturgical, and hagiographical cycles. Historical events also became popular themes in the Renaissance, with preference shown for those events that portrayed the glory and power of Venice. The intention was fourfold: to decorate, to inspire, to teach, and to impress.

The state promoted the depiction of certain legends for political and economic reasons. For example, after Venice had obtained the relics of St. Mark in 829 and those of St. Isidore in 1125, the portrayal of the legends of these two saints became and remained particularly popular themes. Such subjects not only inspired veneration but also promulgated political and economic incentives. The veneration of saints' relics drew pilgrims, and therefore money, to Venice. But the illustration of scenes from the life of the apostle Mark and his transport to Venice also validated the city's possession of his relics and her claims to the Patriarchal seat. Another basis for the popularity of cycles of Saints Mark and Isidore was that St. Mark had become patron saint of Venice, while St. Isidore had been chosen as patron saint by the carpenters of the Venetian Arsenal.

By the thirteenth century, then, the function of art in Venice had become political as well as religious (Zampetti, 1969: 28), as is evident, for example, in the Cathedral of San Marco and the adjacent Ducal Palace. Previously considered the Doge's private chapel, San Marco, the church of the state and of the people, became the repository of politically important trophies garnered by the state in its military ventures (Demus, 1988: 2). The increasingly political motivation in Venetian art is also conspicuous in the decorative mural paintings of the Ducal Palace; numerous naval battles glorifying the city's impressive naval strength are seen in every room.[3]

The period of this study comes to an end just after the true beginnings of a "Venetian school." The new mode of representation was more realistic and emotional, a style that broke free from previous Gothic and Byzantine traditions and embraced many of the characteristics of Renaissance art. But Venetian art is uniquely Venetian in its flamboyant, exotic style, and, after the fifteenth century, its revolutionary use of light. One of the major fathers of the Venetian school is Jacopo Bellini, who had apprenticed under Gentile da Fabriano of Florence. Jacopo Bellini, in turn, greatly influenced Carpaccio, also considered one of the founders of the Venetian school. Numerous later Venetian artists also dramatically affected the history of art with their unique styles and interpretations of the Renaissance and subsequent Mannerist movements: Andrea Mantegna, Gentile Bellini and Giovanni Bellini, Giorgione, Tiziano (Titian), Bartolomeo Montagna, Tintoretto, Veronese, and Canaletto. Sansovino, originally from Florence, became an important architect in Venice. Palladio was another influential architect.

THE ARTISTIC MEDIA

The most common media in Venetian art are mosaic, enamel, manuscript illuminations (miniatures) and line-drawn illustrations for mercantile manuscripts or technical treatises, frescoes, painting, and forms of sculpture, including relief work in metal, wood and stone, and inscribing techniques used to create graffiti and engravings. Until the twelfth century, most Venetian art was executed in mosaic, with some in enamel and as manuscript illuminations. As artistic representation became more realistic, media that allowed greater detail and naturalism, such as fresco, oil painting, and sculpture, came into wider use. Painting and sculpture became more common beginning in the twelfth century and were key tools in creating a more convincing depiction of three-dimensional reality. This section discusses each medium and its major advantages and limitations.

Mosaics (figs. 2–28). Colored stone or highly reflective pieces of glass called tesserae are arranged to form a design in mosaic. Instead of blending pigments, mosaicists achieved contrast and the visual impression of blending by juxtaposing tesserae of different colors. Although the resulting images are not always realistic, it is an ideal technique for conveying the spiritual quality of themes popular in early medieval art.

In Roman and early Christian floor pavements, relatively small tesserae made of very durable natural stones formed geometric or naturalistic designs. Walls were later decorated with mosaics of less substantial materials such as terra-cotta, mother-of-pearl, porphyry, or glass (called smalto). Glass tesserae were often colored in brilliant shades or sandwiched around gold or silver leaf. The strong colors in the designs resulted in greater clarity at a distance. Medieval mosaics almost invariably appear on walls, usually far above the observer's head. Such demands of visibility forced the artist to utilize larger tesserae and to execute fairly simple designs. The resulting images were necessarily more geometrical, simplified, and one-dimensional. The lack of physicality or of any illusion of three-dimensionality resulted in a further spiritualization of a theme, and sometimes in errors of perspective, which apparently worried neither mosaicist nor viewer. By using large tesserae, spaced further apart, and setting each tesserae at its own angle of inclination, the medieval mosaicist produced varied scintillating effects of light and color (L'Orange, 1966: 3–12). Venetian mosaicists utilized unusual tesserae forms, such as round and teardrop shapes (Demus, 1988: 38).

When analyzing mosaics, it is critical to consider the restoration techniques employed. Within a century of their creation, mosaics had often begun to decay and crumble. By the mid-fourteenth century, the mosaics of San Marco had already started to deteriorate, a continuing problem to this day. Repairs, first initiated in the fifteenth century, have been carried out continually ever since, with varying degrees of accuracy and success. Often compositions in a contemporaneous style replaced earlier mosaics. The restoration of San Marco mosaics in the 1880s and 1890s involved complete removal and reapplication; it would seem that some differences from the original images resulted. A more accurate method was developed in 1937 and 1938: the mosaic crust remained *in situ* on a specially constructed support, and the masonry behind it was removed brick by brick and replaced to solidify the mosaic (Demus, 1984, vol. 1: 75). The method and exactness of restorations naturally affects the accuracy of any ship and boat representations.

Enamels (fig. 29). As with mosaic, enamel work juxtaposes pieces of colored material, and images are consequently stylized. With enamel, however, the artist creates color with small pieces of millefiore glass, cut cross strand and arranged on or in a metal background, or by mixing or adding various compounds such as oxides to other vitreous material, and firing the arrangement to fuse the colors. An enamel of the *Pala d'Oro* (fig. 29), for example, depicts a small round ship under sail in a very stylized manner, in part because of the enamel technique. Because enamels were designed to be viewed at close range, however, they are potentially more detailed than mosaics. They are also less subject to deterioration.

Wood Inlays (fig. 30). This artistic medium is similar to the techniques of enamel and mosaic, utilizing wood in place of glass or stone to form designs. Very few examples of Venetian wood inlay exist from the period under study.

Manuscript Illuminations (Miniatures), Illustrations from Mercantile Manuscripts, and Technical Illustrations (figs. 31–72). Manuscript illuminations illustrate medieval texts, both religious and secular in nature, but are small, thus the term "miniatures." Some are color while others are defined as line drawings, with little shading, and usually less detail portrayed than is possible with paint. Naturally, there is a broad range of quality, realism, and accuracy in the extant illustrations, depending on the skill of the artist (Farrel, 1979: 237), degree of natural perspective depicted, and intended function of the image. Nevertheless, the medium is potentially easy to interpret. A serious problem with manuscript illuminations, however, is how well the paint has remained bonded with the parchment, and the resulting condition of the image. A good example of this problem is evident in figure 49, where the image partly transferred to the other page, creating a mirror image.

Until the eleventh century, when illuminations became primarily religious in theme, the miniatures were characterized by naturalism, combined with an "intense spirituality and sumptuous colour" (Christe et al., 1982: 132). Thereafter the style of miniatures became more ascetic and abstract. Figures were schematically portrayed to appear dematerialized and otherworldly. Manuscripts of nonreligious themes also grew in popularity and were likewise decorated with miniatures. Because the medium developed further in Byzantine monasteries, where styles persisted in part due to the emphasis on precise copying of manuscripts, later miniatures were influenced by the stiff Byzantine style that had already developed, and they repeated earlier forms of iconography. For example, the Byzantine boat types exemplified in figures 35–36 closely resemble both earlier and later Byzantine representations of small boats. Other media, particularly the mosaic medium, were also strongly influenced by manuscript illumination style and perpetuated these static imagery forms. In fact, illuminated cycles illustrating Byzantine manuscripts were used as models for Venetian mosaic cycles (Demus, 1988: 14).

Technical illustrations (figs. 62–72) are by their very nature more precise than miniature illuminations. Because the intention of a technical treatise on ship construction is to define a ship, some manuscripts even include measurements for individual ship timbers and the whole ship.

Frescoes (figs. 73–91). The usual method of creating frescoes is to paint upon wet plaster. Because the artist must apply the image to the wall before the plaster dries, the image must be rapidly executed, and the results often appear spontaneous and impressionistic, although they can be quite naturalistic, depending on the style and talents of the artist. Fresco artists could adorn large spaces with just a bold, color-filled outline.

A few very poorly preserved examples of frescoes from the thirteenth and fourteenth centuries were located in this survey. Frescoes do not survive well in the damp lagoonal environment of Venice, and Venetian artists quickly turned to other media.

Faiences (fig. 92). Faience is a ceramic process in which glass glazes create colored designs on earthenware. The simplified design resulting from the melted colored glass does not allow great detail.

Paintings (figs. 93–110). No paintings have survived from the early medieval period; the earliest painted images found in this survey date from the first decades of the fourteenth century, when the gradual shift in emphasis from wall mosaics to painted polyptychs occurred. Besides the obvious technical improvements characteristic of painting for this time, this shift reflects an important psychological change toward humanization. Instead of remote and enormous mosaic figures placed in the upper reaches of the building, the holy figures, for example, appeared in more naturalistic paintings displayed at the viewer's level (Steer, 1970: 15). Figure 94 illustrates this trend well: the faces of St. Mark, the mariners, and details of the hull and rigging of the ship are realistically portrayed.

The paint medium allows far greater and more detailed accuracy than most other media, in fact, as much as the artist desires and is capable of, or as the style demands. Like the media above, painted representations have limitations for the purposes of scholastic interpretation, because they are two-dimensional media, inept at portraying three-dimensionality without the use of perspective. This is especially true of art prior to the fifteenth century, when perspective was poorly understood. The lack of perspective in medieval art often resulted in serious misrepresentation of form.

Sculptures (figs. 112–29). The category broadly defined as sculpture includes various techniques with different materials, related in that the artist carves into a material to form the design: work in relief, both high relief and bas-relief; the more complex techniques of repoussé and vermeil (silver gild); minting coins; incising techniques such as plate engravings and graffiti; and three-dimensional models. Three-dimensional sculpture has a distinct advantage for naturalism over other media; because carving techniques show a subject in relief, sculptural artists can more easily define a three-dimensional form realistically (Christe et al., 1982: 134). Graffiti and engravings share the limitations of two-dimensional media but depict a three-dimensional form most convincingly with the use of perspective. Fortunately, all known Venetian examples of engravings do have good perspective.

Despite its potential for realism, sculpture is still limited by the coarseness of the raw material. Many materials are used for sculpture, including wood, limestone, marble and metal. The characteristics of the material, whether hard or soft, grainy or smooth, affect the art created. Metal can be used as a special finish over another medium, such as gilding on a painting or wood sculpture, or alone, to mold coinage, to make plates for prints, to create objects in relief repoussé, or in three dimensions.

Either sculpture was relatively rare in Venice before the thirteenth century, or simply very little has survived. More prevalent in the thirteenth century is relief work, with the increased pursuit of realistic portrayal, both in terms of subject matter and a more convincing representation of physical form.

Maritime relief sculpture includes figures 112–21. Most examples are limestone or marble, though figure 120 is gilded wood, and figures 117–18 are repoussé. Repoussé designs are raised in relief by hammering on the reverse side of the metal plate. Coins (e.g., fig. 113), in another way, are a form of relief work. Vermeil is silver or bronze bas-relief work that has been gilded. Wooden sculptures were sometimes hollowed out and then painted and gilded. Initially, the gilding was simply applied in sheets. Later, two more effective techniques, water gilding and oil gilding, were used. Water gilding produced a very high luster. Bole (a red clay), mixed with a small amount of glue, was applied on top of the gesso layer. Then small squares of gold leaf were set, polished, and burnished. In oil gilding, the gold leaf was applied on a layer of oil, which was not burnished due to the weak adhesion, but effected an attractive matte surface. The application of a gilding finish to wood carvings or vermeil to metal relief work rendered them sumptuous and ostentatious, though perhaps less realistic (Christe et al., 1982: 255).

Incising techniques utilized in maritime artistry include graffiti (figs. 122–25), coins (fig. 113) and plate engravings (fig. 128). The schematic and sometimes haphazard nature of graffiti make them extremely difficult to interpret. Yet ship graffiti such as figures 122–25 can be valuable, especially when created by a knowledgeable layman such as a mariner. In most cases, however, it is difficult to date graffiti. Figure 126 is a metal plate engraving. Prints from woodcuts appear in Venice only in the last quarter of the fifteenth century, with the seascape of Venice being a common theme. Prints can be very detailed and realistic, and the late fifteenth-century views of Venice by Breydenbach (figs. 127–28) and Jacobo dei Barbari (Concina, 1988: fig. 68), for example, provide excellent details of ships executed with quite precise perspective.

Three-dimensional models of metal such as the silver votive, figure 129, are uncommon this early in Venice but lend themselves to a naturalistic portrayal of reality.

The unique advantages and limitations of each medium must be considered as one analyzes the maritime art of Venice. Generally stated, the earlier art, usually in mosaic and enamel, contains very stylized ship and boat depictions. Changes in techniques, especially within the paint and sculpture media, resulted in more accurate and detailed images of watercraft. Furthermore, one must be cognizant of the possibility of an archaizing tendency; artists may intentionally have portrayed the setting anachronistically to give the impression that the events depicted occurred in the past. Finally, the function of the art and the skill of portrayal should also be considered.

FACTORS AFFECTING AVAILABILITY AND TYPE OF SHIP OR BOAT DEPICTIONS

In medieval and early Renaissance art, maritime themes are relatively infrequent compared with other themes. Not surprisingly, however, they are far more common in Venice than in landlocked cities. The choice of themes primarily depended upon the preferences of the artist's patron. In Venice, maritime stories, particularly the Marcan cycle, are repeatedly depicted. In fact, certain episodes of the Marcan legends were more prominently displayed than others, depending on their perceived importance to the city; the *vita* of St. Mark is depicted only once in mosaics of San Marco, in the relatively inconspicuous position of the vestibule. In contrast, the more politically charged *translatio* is portrayed three times in the mosaics of the cathedral alone, and in positions of the greatest possible visibility: on the façade, in the antevestibule (which is now the enclosed Zen Chapel—it faces the sea and quay and originally served as one of the main entrances to the church), and adjacent to the altar, in San Clemente Chapel and near the entrance from the Doge's Palace (Demus, 1988: 179).

The dominant patron of medieval art was the church and maritime images that occur in early Venetian art are those necessary to relate certain hagiographical legends and biblical stories. These stories almost without exception incorporate merchant ships for the transporting of saints and small fishing boats for the various stories relating to fishing. These vessel types appear far more frequently in the earlier Venetian art than warship types. Warships were certainly well known by Venetian society, yet merchant ships and fishing boats monopolize most themes. This may be explained by the fact that the patrons of the church, thus the indirect patrons of the art, were citizens, most of whom were in some way involved in trade. Perhaps this self-absorbed interest in commerce explains the predominance of merchant ships in the art of Venice—in the public consciousness, "ship" meant "merchant ship." In later Venetian art, the state became a great patron to art, so politics became an increasingly significant factor in the choice of themes. Not surprisingly, the frequency and prominence of warship types increases dramatically in art of sixteenth-century Venice.

Other factors essential to consider are the skill of the specific artist, and the prevalent style and influences. Venetian artists were strongly affected by the Byzantine style. Byzantine themes were repeated stylistically, carefully reproducing earlier designs. As a result, the depiction of any particular ship or boat may be influenced less by contemporaneous ship design than by the iconographic convention for a "ship" or "boat." Also, the most common media in the early medieval period of Venice, the early forms of sculpture, mosaic and miniatures, permit little exact detail. Fortunately for this study, although Venetian art shows its Byzantine influence, it is often more realistic and incorporates a far greater range of designs than other medieval art (Demus, 1984, vol. 1: 70).

A final, but highly significant, factor is the effect of deterioration and restoration. Venice has been victim to numerous fires and wars throughout her history. Her churches have been continually rebuilt and restored. It is impossible to know how many and what type of ship depictions have been moved abroad, kept in private collections, or lost from the artistic record because of pillaging, destruction, or renovation. A good example of this is seen in San Marco's façade: of the five original thirteenth-century ship frescoes on the medieval façade, only one remains, but it has been reconstructed in a Baroque composition. The previous façade was fortuitously recorded in a fifteenth-century painting by the artist Bellini (fig. 23) and in the written records of the historian Stringa (Demus, 1984, vol. 1: 199). Had the records of Bellini and Stringa not been preserved, these segments of the important Marcan cycle frescoes decorating the façade of San Marco would not be known to us. There is no doubt that countless Venetian ship and boat representations have been lost or destroyed. Nevertheless, more than five hundred ship or boat images were located in this survey alone, and more certainly remain to be discovered in manuscript and museum collections around the globe.

A discussion of the most common maritime themes encountered in Venetian art completes the background for the catalog presented in chapter 2.

PREVALENT THEMES IN VENETIAN ART

The prevalent themes in Venetian art for the period covered by this study can be divided into five main categories: biblical themes (both Old and New Testament), liturgical themes, hagiographical cycles, historical and miscellaneous illustrations. Maritime themes are predominant in all categories except the liturgical; ships and boats were clearly an intrinsic part of the historical, legendary, and biblical stories most important to Venetians.

The biblical maritime themes most frequently depicted in Venetian art include "Noah and the Ark" (Genesis 6–8), "Jonah and the Whale" (Jonah 1:3–17; fig. 4), "The Calling of the Apostles" (Matthew 4:18–22; Mark 1:16–20; Luke 5:10–11; John 1:35–42; figs. 5, 74, 75, 79, 103, and 119), "The Miraculous Draught of Fishes" (Luke 5:1–11; John 21:1–11; figs. 16, 107, and 112), "Christ Dismissing the Multitudes" (fig. 36), "The Stilling of the Tempest" (Matthew 8:23–27; Mark 4:35–41; fig. 17), and "Peter Walking on Water" (Matthew 14:24–33; fig. 102).

A ship or boat image is often part of a system of symbols (iconography), but at times the image simply signifies "boat" or "ship." An example of the former is the mosaic of Noah's ark depicted in the atrium ceiling of San Marco (Demus, 1988: 135, fig. 69). The representation of the ark is hardly ship-like at all; it is a symbol that implies far more than just the biblical story of Noah and the ark. Iconographically, the Noah story signifies God's provision of salvation. The Noah's ark images located through this search exemplify a fascinating history of iconography. In the case of San Marco's medieval atrium mosaic, the box-like sarcophagus expresses the early Christian interpretation of the Noah legend: God's provision of salvation from eternal death is promised to the individual man (Newton and Neil, 1966: 9). Later Renaissance and baroque images portray a virtual cathedral atop a simplified hull, symbolizing that salvation for humanity is to be found in the Catholic Church. Devoid of information on contemporaneous Venetian watercraft, however, the Noah's ark images have not been included in the catalog.

Other biblical maritime themes seen in Venetian art are more realistically portrayed and consequently relevant to this study. Biblical themes were illustrated in all media, but they were particularly important themes in the mosaics covering the walls of medieval churches, functioning as a visual means to teach the Bible to the illiterate masses.

The thirteenth-century sculpted portrayals of craftsmen, including shipbuilders and fishermen with their respective boats located in the main portal of San Marco (e.g., figs. 115–16) are represented not as symbols but are intended to be portrayals of actual Venetian vessels.

Maritime episodes are integral parts of legends of four saints frequently depicted in Venetian art. By far the most important saint to Venice was St. Mark, followed by St. Isidore, and, of lesser significance, Saints Ursula and Clement. Hagiographical cycles were ostensibly depicted to inspire the viewer to emulate the lives of saintly men and women. Subtle though significant political motives, however, often accompanied the spiritual ones. In Venice, the regular depiction of legends of St. Mark, the Marcan cycles, illustrate such duality of purpose. At the most basic level, besides inspiring saintly living, the Marcan cycles affirmed in the minds of Venetian citizens that St. Mark, as patron saint of their city, could be appealed to for direction, protection, and health. At the political level, however, depictions of Marcan cycles represent an attempt to validate the claims of the State of Venice to the remains of St. Mark, and an effort to promote the pilgrim trade.

Venetians revered the disciple Mark, who became the missionary to Italy and the North Adriatic, founder of the Patriarchate of Venetia at Grado and the first bishop of Alexandria (died A.D. 74). Venetians considered themselves to be directly descended from this apostle, so, naturally, devotion to him was particularly strong and led her citizens to exonerate themselves from the sin of robbing Alexandria of St. Mark's relics. Maritime scenes from the *vita* of St. Mark include episodes from his various missions, including ship voyages to Aquileia, Rome, Pentapolis, and Alexandria. St. Mark *vita* scenes in Venetian art include figures 14, 24, 25, and 117. According to a Venetian version of his *vita* legend, during his voyage from Aquileia to Alexandria, his ship moored in the lagoons of Venice. While at Venice, the saint had a divine revelation in the form of a dream-vision, the *praedestinatio,* in which he learned that his bones would eventually find their final resting place among these lagoons (fig. 117). This legend originated in the first half of the thirteenth century and became a frequent cycle in Venetian art, i.e., it validated Venice's possession of the relics (Demus, 1984, vol. 2: 188).

The legend of the *translatio*, the posthumous transportation of the relics of St. Mark from Alexandria to Venice, goes further back in Venetian history (figs. 10–13, 23, 29, 93 and 94). According to legend, in 828, two Venetian merchants, Tribunus and Rusticus, just happened to have been driven off course to Alexandria, a predicament that perhaps justified their breaking the trade embargo Venice had declared against the infidels. While in Alexandria, these merchants learned that the caliph had plans to destroy the church that housed the relics of St. Mark. The merchants quickly persuaded the priest of the church, Theodorus, to relinquish the relics to Venice. Once hidden aboard the Venetian ship, the miraculously sweet smell emanating from the saintly remains aroused the suspicions of the custom officials in the harbor. The men sent to investigate were Muslims and sufficiently squeamish about examining the basket of pork that concealed the remains. The Muslim officials failed to locate the relics and allowed the Venetian ship to sail.

St. Mark's *translatio* legend, which originated in and for Venice, is a common theme in Venetian art, while elsewhere it was unknown, unaccepted, or unpopular. The narrative of the *translatio* of St. Mark contains numerous episodes worthy of illustration. Almost every scene that included ships was repeated frequently in Venetian art; the land-based episodes were often omitted in favor of the more popular maritime scenes. The *translatio* narrative is an essential aspect of Venetian iconography, "an integral part of the ideological foundation of the Venetian Church and State" (Demus, 1984, vol. 1: 71), for two reasons. First, because Mark came from Aquileia when he founded the patriarchate in Venice, Aquileia actually had prior claim to the patriarchal seat. With the *translatio* legend Venice underscored her claim to ecclesiastic primacy over Aquileia (Demus, 1984, vol. 2: 188). Once Venice and Aquileia had united, this was no longer necessary, but *translatio* cycles continued to be popular themes nonetheless, as they asserted the divine right of Venice to possession of the relics in the first place. In relating the full story of the acquisition, transportation, and reception of the relics of St. Mark, the iconographic program aimed "to remove any doubts as to the reality and the completeness of the *translatio*" (Demus, 1984, vol. 1: 71) and rationalized the appropriation of the saint's relics (Demus, 1984, vol. 2: 187), thus encouraging local and international veneration of the saint.

Another aspect of the *translatio* legend that also originated in the first half of the thirteenth century, the *passus* of the *translatio* (figs. 12 and 94), was considered further proof of Venice's rights to the saint. During the voyage bearing his relics to Venice, an incorporeal St. Mark awoke the sleeping sailors to warn them of dangerous shoals ahead; because St. Mark himself was a participant in the safe transportation of his relics, it was believed clearly God's will that St. Mark's relics should find their way to Venice. The merchants, though, still fearing governmental punishment for having broken the city's trade embargo, sent a messenger ahead with the news of their sacred cargo. When the herald received the Doge's promise of exoneration, the ship sailed into Venice, and the city celebrated its newly won possession of the relics (Demus, 1984, vol. 1: 65–66).

Another saint important in Venetian art is St. Isidore (A.D. 251), a Christian soldier of the third century from Alexandria, Egypt. Isidore traveled to Chios with his military fleet, including a companion named Ammianus. At Chios, Isidore was tortured and beheaded when he was discovered to be a Christian. According to legend, the *translatio* of his relics from Chios to the Church of San Marco in Venice occurred under the leadership of Doge Michiel and the priest Cerbanus on April 16, 1125. St. Isidore subsequently became the patron saint of the School of Carpenters of the Venetian Arsenal (Kaftal, 1978: 429). In the fourteenth century, the carpenters funded the renovation of St. Isidore Chapel, to the left of the main altar of San Marco, where the *vita* and *translatio* of St. Isidore were the predominant cycles depicted (figs. 26–28).

Ursula was a princess of Brittany living in the late fourth or fifth century. Before her impending arranged marriage to Aetherius, the son of the pagan king of England, she made a pilgrimage to Rome with 11,000 virgins. On her return trip, she was martyred at Cologne by the Huns (Kaftal, 1978: 1012–30). The story was included in *The Golden Legend,* a thirteenth-century compilation of legends, lore, verses from scripture, and Christian theology, which was an influential source book for Christian iconography. St. Ursula cycles became especially popular after the mid-fifteenth century when more than one hundred Latin copies had circulated in Europe, inspiring increased devotion to the saint in Venice and throughout Europe (figs. 97–101). Scenes from the *vita* of St. Ursula first appear in Venetian art beginning in the mid-fourteenth century in panel paintings and manuscript illuminations.

A final saint of some importance in Venetian art is St. Clement I (d. ca. A.D. 96). This disciple of St. Peter and St. Paul and companion to Cletus and Lunus, and bishop of Rome was martyred on the Chersonese. He was thrown from a small boat with an anchor tied to his neck and was drowned (Kaftal, 1978: 233). The figure of St. Clement I is portrayed in various mosaics and frescoes in Italy, including in San Marco; however, his martyrdom from the boat is not found in monumental Venetian art but only in a manuscript illumination of the fourteenth century (fig. 46).

Less prominently featured in Venetian maritime art are Alatiel (fig. 108), St. Andrew (fig. 83), St. Elpidinus, St. Eustace (fig. 78), St. Geminian (fig. 114), St. George (fig. 84), Helsinus (fig. 105), St. Jerome (figs. 89–91), St. John (fig. 53), the Virgin Mary (fig. 121), St. Martin (fig. 96), St. Nicholas (figs. 73 and 76), Blessed Odoric (fig. 85), St. Petronius (figs. 86–88), St. Simeone (fig. 118), and St. Thomas Becket (fig. 104).[4]

Historical events involving ships were also recurrent themes in Venetian art. For example, Aquileia Cathedral's floor mosaics of peaceful fishing and hunting scenes (figs. 2–4) symbolically allude to the triumph and peace achieved by the Edict of Milan (Muraro and Grabar, 1963: 12). Commemorations and reports of various wars and handbooks for crusaders also illustrate naval scenes (figs. 18–21, 31, 38–40, 54, 58, and 60). Various naval battles, particularly those glorifying the power of Venice, became common themes especially in paintings and manuscript illuminations from the fifteenth century onward.

A few miscellaneous themes with no particular historical or symbolic significance also incorporate ship images. These include simple fishing and boating scenes (figs. 32–34, 109, and 116), illustrations of ports and harbors (figs. 8, 30, 43, 77, 82, 127–28), ship or boat-building craftsmen (figs. 44–45, 98, and 115), illustrated maps (figs. 51, 56–57, 60–61) and initial letters in manuscripts (figs. 37, 50, and 52).

Chapter Two

CATALOG

Venetian Maritime Images

This chapter systematically describes recognizable nautical features in examples of the collected sample and provides a brief analysis of the ship or boat represented. The catalog is limited to material primarily gathered from Venice, with some images from other cities around the Venetia region, particularly Aquileia and Ravenna, as well as Belluno, Bolzano, Bologna, Faenze, Lucignano, Modena, Padua, Parma, Pomposa, Rimini, Udine, Verona, and Vittorio Veneto. The resultant catalog indicates a wide range in the ship and boat types used by Venetians and provides invaluable pictorial details of those watercraft.

An artist portrays ships in a certain way depending upon his chosen medium and its limitations, and also upon the period in which he is working. The catalog has therefore been arranged according to media (mosaics; enamels; wood inlays; manuscript illuminations and technical treatises; paint media including frescoes, faiences, and oils; and forms of sculpture, including relief work, coins, incision-made graffiti, three-dimensional sculptures and prints from engravings), then chronologically within each medium. Illustrated images from the same cycle are grouped and discussed together.

Different criteria can be used to define a typology. One classification system for ship types might describe their forms: long ships or round ships. These are useful, general terms we use here to describe the hull's basic shape. Long ships were elongated, low-sided, oared vessels, which usually had only one mast, if any. Their large crew, speed, and maneuverability made them ideal as warships. Round ships were beamy, high-sided ships that relied completely on sail power. Often they carried two or more masts, and usually traveled relatively unarmed. Their great carrying capacity, slow speed, and more economical crew sizes suited them for mercantile use. But sometimes these forms were altered, adding, for example, fortified castle structures to the long ships, horse ports to the round ship hull, or oars to elongated round ships (e.g., the merchant galley at the end of the thirteenth century). To make clear-cut distinctions among them is impossible when their uses became interchangeable in this way. To do so is also irrelevant, especially for the early periods; some ships were truly hybrids, becoming mercantile or martial to meet current needs.

The typology, discussed more completely in chapter 3, is based on function, not form. Subcategories are based on specialized use, number of masts (which roughly indicates the size), and rig.

Type I Small craft, lagoonal or river boats
- Ia Lighters
- Ib Fishing boats and lagoonal craft
- Ic Riverine (and coastal) war craft
- Id Riverine (and coastal) cargo vessels

Type II Seagoing warships
- IIa Oared galley warships (long ships) designed primarily for war
- IIb War transports

Type III Seagoing merchantmen (Most are the generically termed round ships, but this category also includes merchant galleys, which were in fact long ships in form).
- IIIa Single-masted, lateen-rigged merchant ships
- IIIb Two-masted, lateen-rigged merchant ships
- IIIc Three-masted, lateen-rigged merchant ships
- IIId Single-masted, square-rigged merchant ships
- IIIe Two-masted, mixed-rigged merchant ships
- IIIf Three-masted, mixed-rigged merchant ships

The relevant data and nautical features will be presented in the following sequence.

General information:

• Title, *titulus,* translation, theme, artist, author, location, date, general ship or boat type.

• Remarks on composition and any pertinent effects of restoration.

Description of nautical features:

• Rig: masts (number, position, inclination or rake, relative heights), spars, sail (square or lateen, furled or set position), mast lashings (wooldings), crow's nest ("fighting top"), rigging (shrouds/stays, parrels, robands, halyard, vang, tack, sheet, brace, tackle, etc.). Due to the nature of this artwork, it is at times quite difficult to distinguish between the various rigging, especially shrouds, stays, and halyards. Often the artist defined the standing rigging too generally to be able to make distinctions among them. Without the use of perspective, which was not well understood by medieval artists, it is impossible to indicate the side-to-side position of shroud lines when a ship is drawn in profile. In order to give the illusion that the lines run to the port and starboard sides, shrouds might have been drawn fore and aft of the masts, which would make them look like stays.

• Hull construction: basic shape, rockered or straight keel, stem and stern (relative height, termination, existence of castles), strakes (run of hull planking, any indication of bends, scarfs, joins, or nails), any visible tops of frames, sheer line, wales, protruding beams.

• Steering apparatus: placement of rudders or steering oars, type of mount, loom, and blade shape (balanced or unbalanced).

• Anchors (location, orientation, shape, fixed or unfixed stock).

• Armament.

Technical terminology is based primarily on the illustrated glossary found in *Wooden Ship Building and the Interpretation of Shipwrecks* (Steffy, 1994) and, for the medieval Italian vocabulary, as discussed by Pryor (1984, 1990) and

Bellabarba (1988). The concluding chapter 3 discusses the lateen and square rig, ship construction, stern variations, the *bellatorium,* steering devices and their mounts, anchors, and a typology of Venetian ships and boats. An English and Latin/Venetian nautical glossary is located near the end of the book.

A plan of the Cathedral of San Marco, figure 1, indicates locations within San Marco where thirteen ship or boat mosaics are set (figs. 10–14, 16–17, 23–28), the position of the enamel screen, the *Pala d'Oro* (fig. 29) at the altar, wood inlays in the Sacristy (fig. 30) and where ship graffiti exist (figs. 122–24). The dates given for the art of San Marco are the dates accepted by the *Procuratoria di San Marco,* the administration of the Cathedral Church of San Marco. Dates for the remainder of the art in the catalog are those generally accepted by art historians.

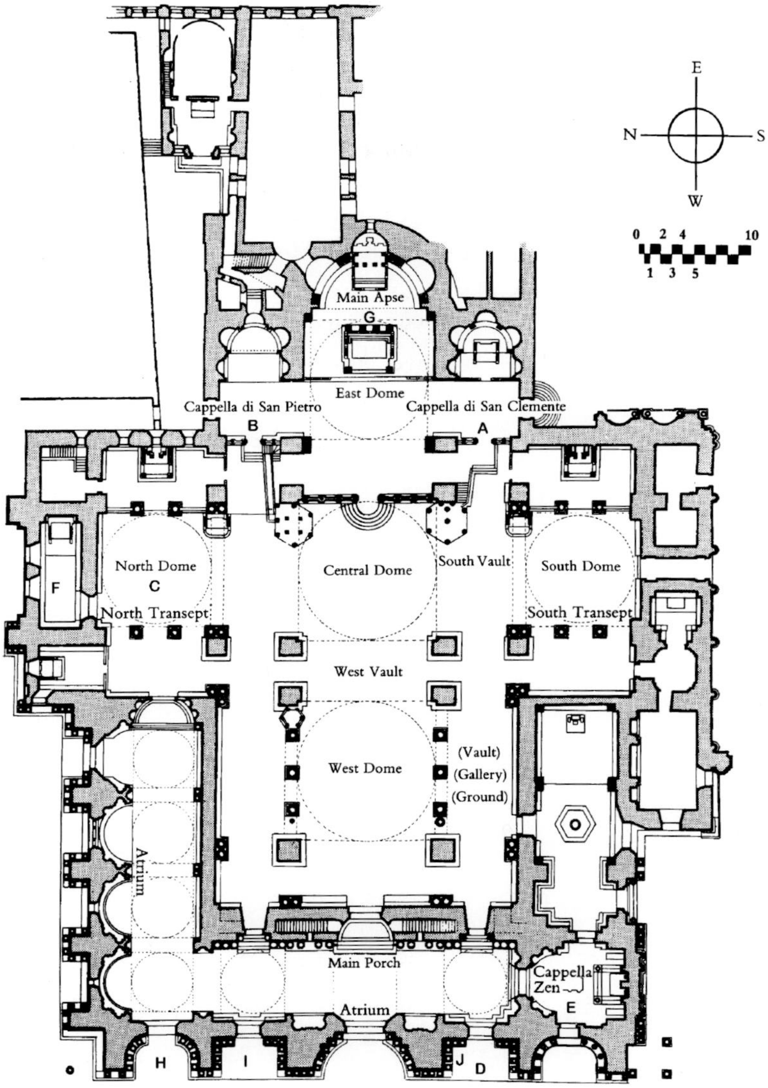

FIG. 1. Plan of San Marco. Mosaics including maritime scenes are located in (A) San Clemente Chapel (figs. 10–13), (B) San Pietro Chapel (fig. 14), (C) the north transept (figs. 16 and 17), (D) the fourth portal (fig. 23), (E) Zen Chapel (figs. 24 and 25), and (F) San Isidore Chapel (figs. 26–28). (G) The enamel *Pala d'Oro* is located at the altar (fig. 29). Letters H, I, and J mark the locations of façade columns with ship graffiti (figs. 122–24). Wood inlays (including fig. 30) are located in the Sacristy. *After Demus, 1984, vol. 1: 389; courtesy University of Chicago Press*

Mosaics

Figures 2–4

Theme: Figure 2: Line fishing scene.
Figure 3: Net fishing scene (left) and duck hunting scene (right).
Figure 4: "Jonah and the Whale."
Location: Floor mosaic, near epigraph of Bishop Theodore, Basilica di Poppo, Aquileia.
Date: Early fourth century (Göttlicher, 1985: 127).
Types: Four fishing boats (Type Ib).

Scenes of line fishing, net fishing, and duck hunting, and the episode of "Jonah and the Whale" illustrate four small fishing boats upon an ocean teeming with sea life on the floor of Aquileia's main cathedral. A contemporaneous mosaic of a seaside Roman villa complex likewise depicts relatively small craft for lagoonal and coastal travel. These craft at times utilized sailpower (Archaeological Museum, Venice [Correr inv. 53]).

The vessel in figure 2 is a *horeia,* a Roman

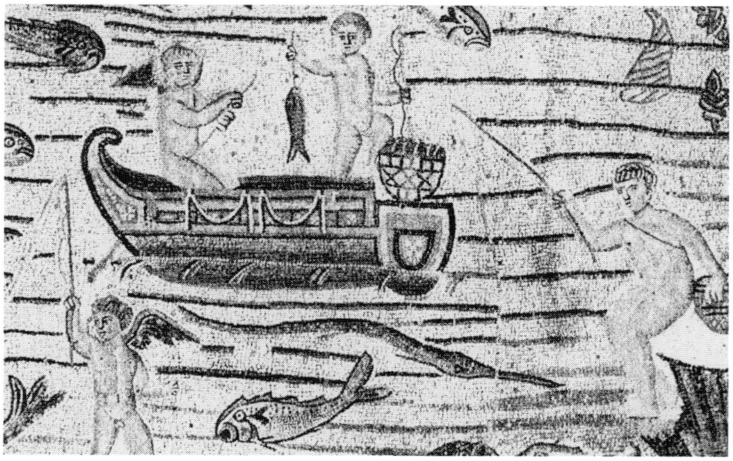

FIG. 2. Line fishing scene, floor mosaic in Aquileia Cathedral dating from the early fourth century.

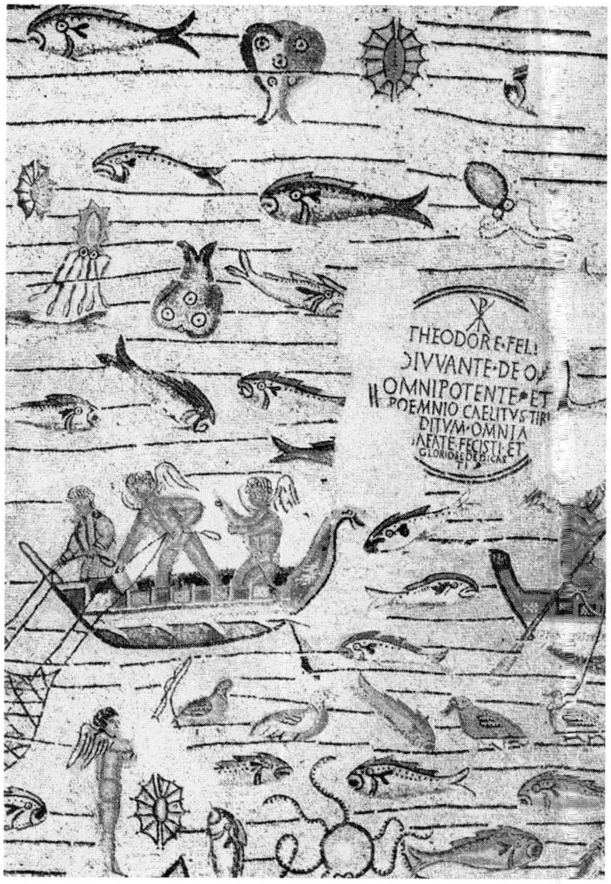

FIG. 3. Net fishing (left) and duck hunting (right) from floor mosaic of small boats in Aquileia Cathedral dating from the early fourth century

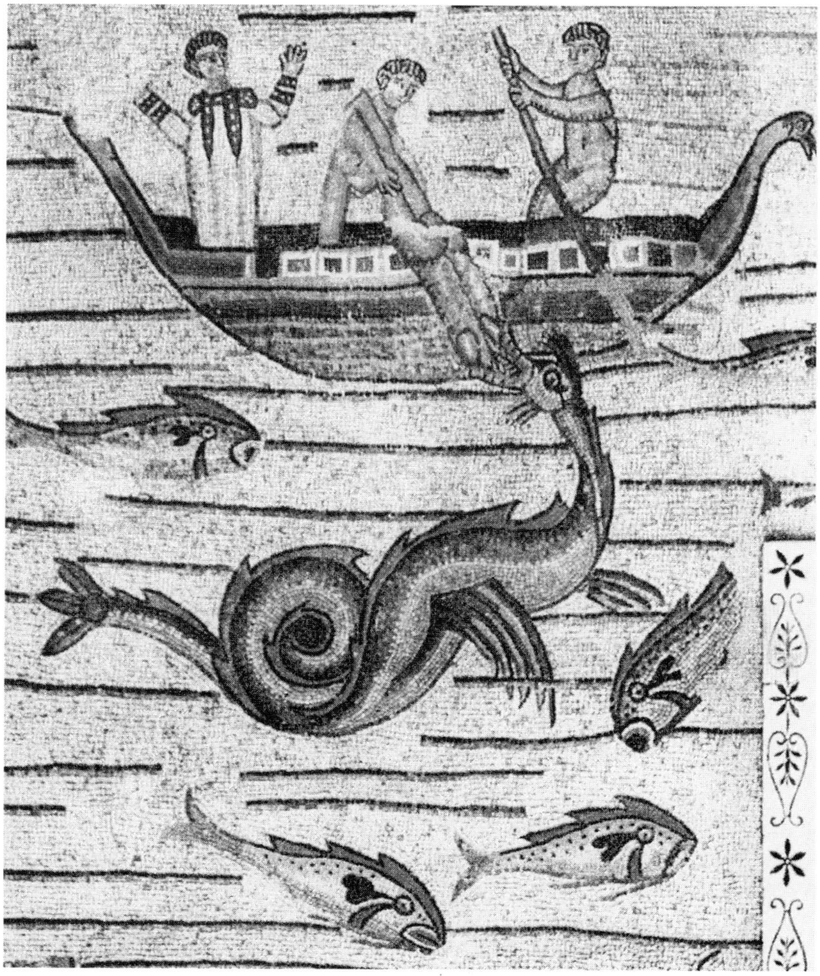

FIG. 4. "Jonah and the Whale," floor mosaic in Aquileia Cathedral dating from the early fourth century

boat type with an inward-curving stern, marked by the steering oar, a relatively flat bottom and a transom bow that would have permitted the vessel to moor head on to a dock, but which looks like the transom stern of a modern rowboat (Casson, 1971: 331 and fig. 137, no. 20). In figure 2, a basket in the bow and the height of the two figures on board suggest that the boat is decked.

The boats in figure 3 (left) and figure 4 differ somewhat from that in figure 2 in configuration. They have a more rockered keel, and their sternpost curves outwardly at the top and ends in a bird's head finial, similar in shape to other Roman boats, (e.g., a sculptural detail on a fourth-century sarcophagus in the Civic Mu-

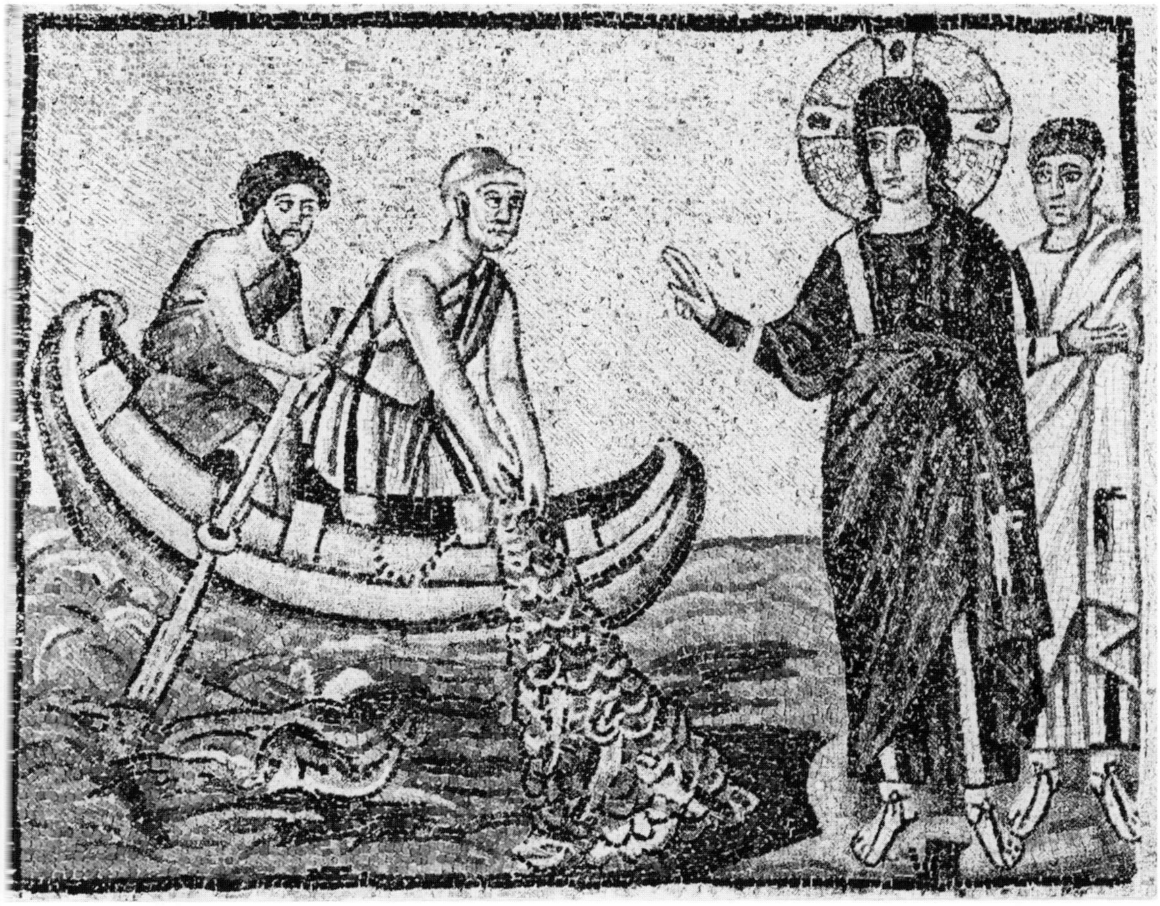

FIG. 5. "The Calling of the Apostles Peter and Andrew," panel mosaic in north clerestory (504–26), Sant'Apollinare Nuovo, Ravenna

seum, Pisa; also Throckmorton, 1972: fig. 2). The straightness in profile of the raking bow of either vessel, especially of the one in figure 3, could indicate that these boats also may have had transom bows. In figure 4, a nude man casts Jonah into the mouth of the whale, while far forward in the bow a clothed figure stands in an orant pose in supplication to God. On all three boats, a helmsman crouched in the stern holds an unattached, symmetrical-bladed steering oar.

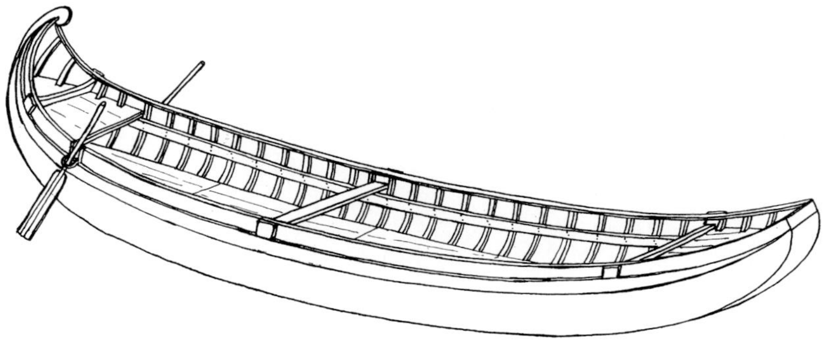

FIG. 6. Reconstruction of a sixth-century fishing boat, from the mosaic at Sant'Apollinare Nuovo, Ravenna (fig. 5). *Courtesy M. Bonino, 1991: fig. 2*

Figure 5

Theme: "The Calling of the Apostles Peter and Andrew."

Location: North clerestory panel, by entrance door, Sant'Apollinare Nuovo, Ravenna.

Date: ca. 504–26 (Bovini, 1971: 77).

Type: Fishing boat (Type Ib).

This well-preserved mosaic set in the clerestory of Sant'Apollinare Nuovo depicts a small, double-ended fishing vessel. Although the profile appears to show a rockered keel, the steep rise of the bow made Bonino conclude that it may in fact be flat bottomed, as he reconstructed it in figure 6 (1978a: 48). The stern ends in an inward-curving volute similar in shape to the stern of figure 2. Continuous rows of strakes, delineated in the mosaic with rows of white, yellow, green, and black tesserae, are roughly parallel amidships but converge into the posts at each end. An orange band of tesserae just above the waterline amidships may indicate a wale.

Three hefty beams extending above and through the uppermost strakes function as thwarts, but more importantly, provide lateral structural support. According to Bonino, these through-beams indicate the use of the shell-first hull construction technique and reveal its Roman heritage. Bonino's reconstruction of the mosaic, figure 6, shows two through-beams supporting half-decks at bow and stern, with a third thwart amidships (Bonino, 1978a: 35 and 48). Figure 7, Bonino's reconstruction of a first-century Roman boat, includes similar beams at bow and stern. In shell-first construction, planking is edge joined and fixed with mortises and tenons As the sides of the vessel are built up, the shipbuilder controlled the shape and regularity of the shell by inserting through-beams. Framing was inserted only after the basic shell had been completed.

Only one steering device is clearly depicted in the mosaic on the visible starboard side, attached slightly aft of midships through a thole bight hung on a thole pin. The steering oar consists of a rectangular, symmetrical blade attached to a loom. Bonino reconstructed the craft with two steering oars mounted at the stern, and two smaller paddles freely employed amidships.

Figure 8 (A: upper vessel B: middle vessel C: lower vessel)
Theme: "Port of Classis."
Location: North wall, upper left, near entrance to nave, Sant'Apollinare Nuovo, Ravenna.

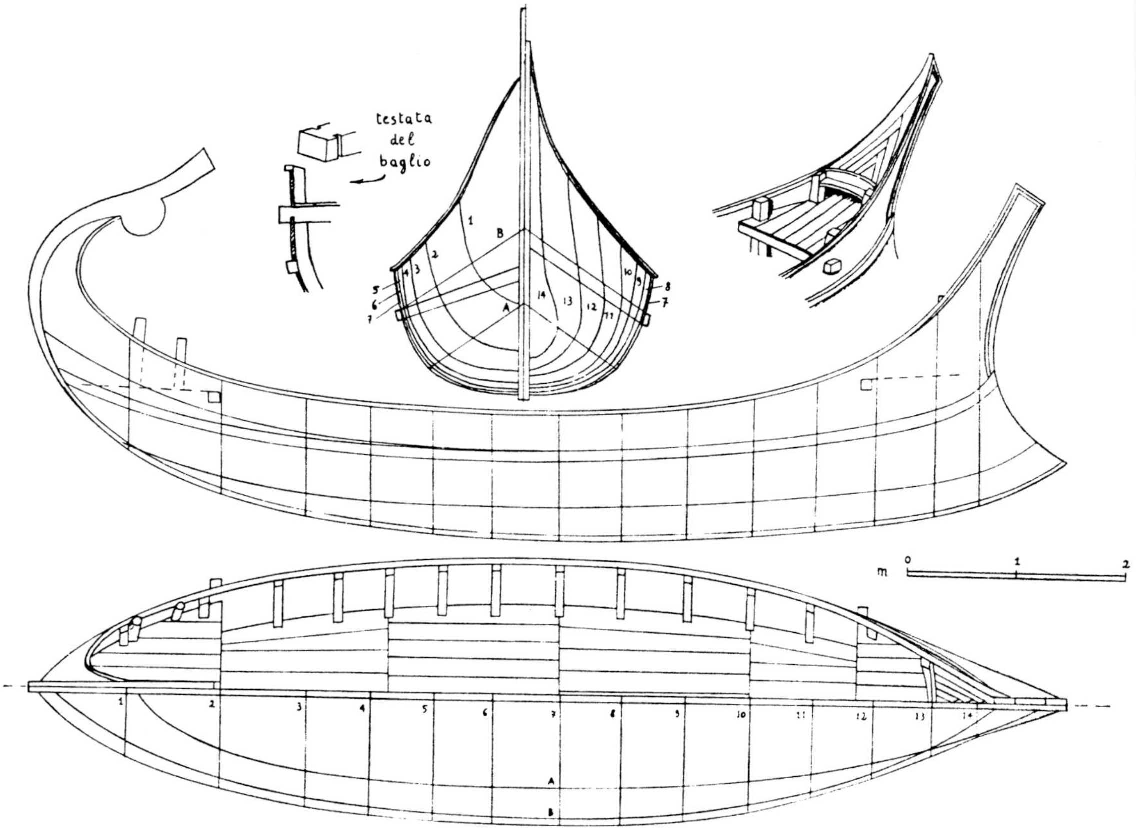

FIG. 7. Reconstruction of the Roman boat represented in the first-century stele relief of P. Longidienus, now in the Museo Nazionale, Ravenna. *Courtesy M. Bonino, 1978a: fig. 5*

Date: ca. 504–26 (Bovini, 1971: 77).
Types: Three riverine cargo vessels (Type Id).

This mosaic illustrating Classis, the port city for Ravenna—which sits at the mouth of the Montone River, less than forty miles south of direct access to the Po riverine system at Porto Garibaldi—offers a rare early illustration of small coastal or riverine vessels. The mosaic was somewhat altered after 561 and poorly restored in 1855 by Kibel. The renovated area at the top of the mast of A, the uppermost vessel, is known to be in error (Bonino, 1978a: 48), and the hulls of the bottom two vessels have been remade (Bovini, 1966: 93 ff.). Because of the uncertainties of the restoration work done, the nautical features of this enigmatic depiction must be considered with due caution.

Considering the mosaic's subject (an important port accessing the Po riverine system), its early date, as well as the depiction on each vessel of only one mast, it can be concluded that these are relatively small boats intended primarily for the local riverine and coastal trade. In all but vessel A, where a fourth line is probably hidden from view by the sail, a single, vertical mast set amidships is supported with two lines attached fairly far forward and two aft that probably indicate forestays and backstays. The sails of the middle and lower vessels, B and C, are not shown, but the sail of A is set, with its lower ends tied off fore and aft. The rig is ambiguously depicted with some characteristics of both the square sail and the lateen-rigged type.

Rather than the usual series of vertical lines—which apparently indicate the seam lines of the cloth sections making up the sail—recognizable on the sails in most depictions of lateeners (e.g., figs. 11, 18, and 26), here the sail is represented as a series of rectangles, abbreviated along the edges of the sail view depicted, indicating, apparently, where the sail is curled around, filled by the billowing wind. By depicting these rectangles, the artist probably intended to imply an overall square rather than triangular shape for the sail, although no corroborating evidence, such as brailing lines, is apparent. The sail is neither clearly square nor triangular in shape, and it is impossible to tell from the sail alone whether these vessels are meant to be square or lateen-rigged. Two details are indicative of a lateen rig, while two others imply a square sail. Before this mosaic was inaccurately restored by Kibel, the cross at the top of the mast inclined forward. A forward inclination of any projections at the top of the mast is common for lateen-rigged ships, as a completely vertical projection would impede

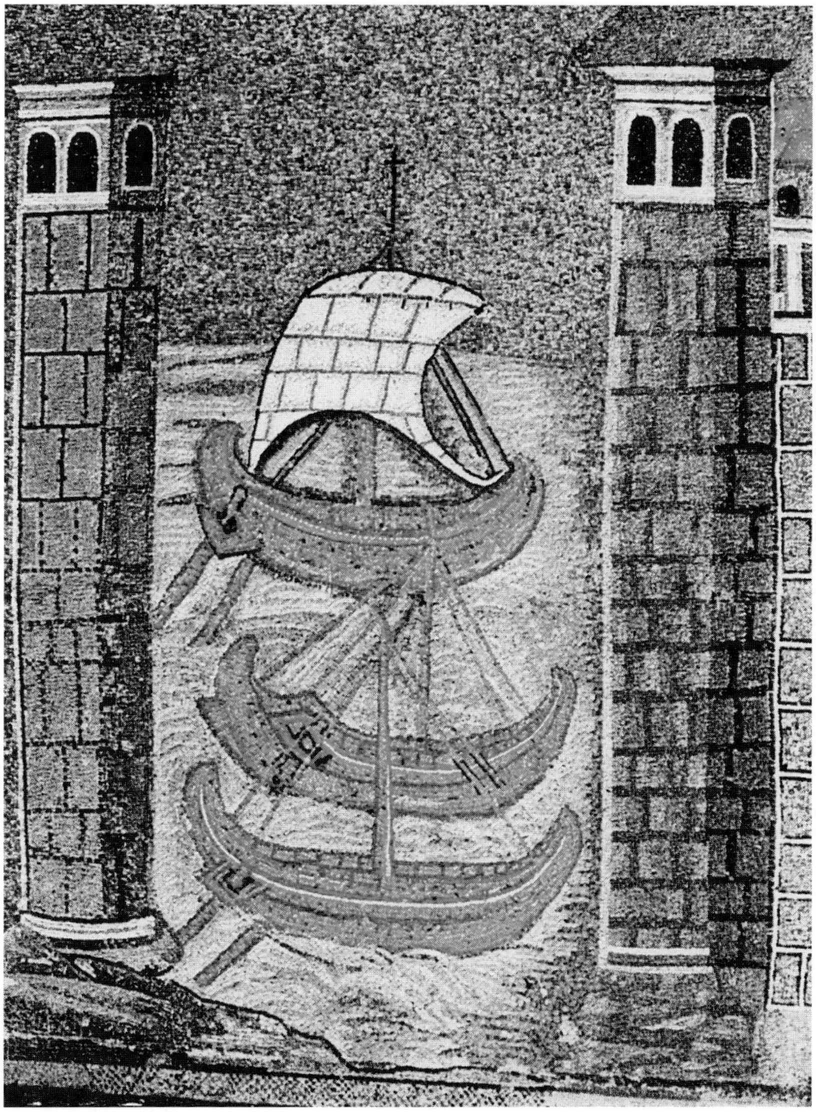

FIG. 8. "Port of Classis," with three river or coastal cargo boats. (A) upper vessel; (B) middle vessel; (C) lower vessel. Nave wall mosaic (ca. 504–26), Sant'Apollinare Nuovo, Ravenna

a tacking maneuver of a lateen-rigged vessel. Another feature more characteristic of a lateener than a square-rigged vessel is that the sail appears to be set abaft the mast and external to the stays, a position only feasible on a lateener. However, the central placement and vertical orientation of the single masts amidships, and the presence of forestays are evidence for square sails, which is reasonable, also considering the date of the mosaic. Bonino interprets the vessel as square-rigged for his reconstruction in figure 9, and estimates a waterline length of 27 meters (1991: 35).

In all three vessels, the sternposts are slightly higher than the stems. Strakes are shown roughly parallel amidships and converging at the posts. A slightly rockered keel running parallel to the sheer strake is delineated by a line approximately equal in thickness to the other strakes. In boat A, four black lines athwartships (paired aft and slightly forward of the mast) indicate two beams just beneath the level of the sheer strake.

Attachments for the visible starboard quarter rudders are clear in A and C; they are secured through a Roman box mount. Two closely spaced through-beams discovered on the seventh-century Byzantine ship wrecked at Yassi Ada are thought to have supported similar box-like mounts for the steering apparatus (Bass and van Doorninck, 1982: 52). The thin and symmetrical quarter rudders are greatly simplified in the mosaic and provide nothing but the most rudimentary information as to the shape and size of the rudders.

The stern shape and sheer of boat B differs from the other two vessels, though this is possibly a result of the renovations. A series of squares set parallel and below the sheer strake in B look like a balustrade or outrigger structure. No quarter rudders are depicted, but vessels with outriggers could set a removable rudder through the outrigger rather than building a separate mount system. As depicted, this vessel shows an important transition in the form of the side rud-

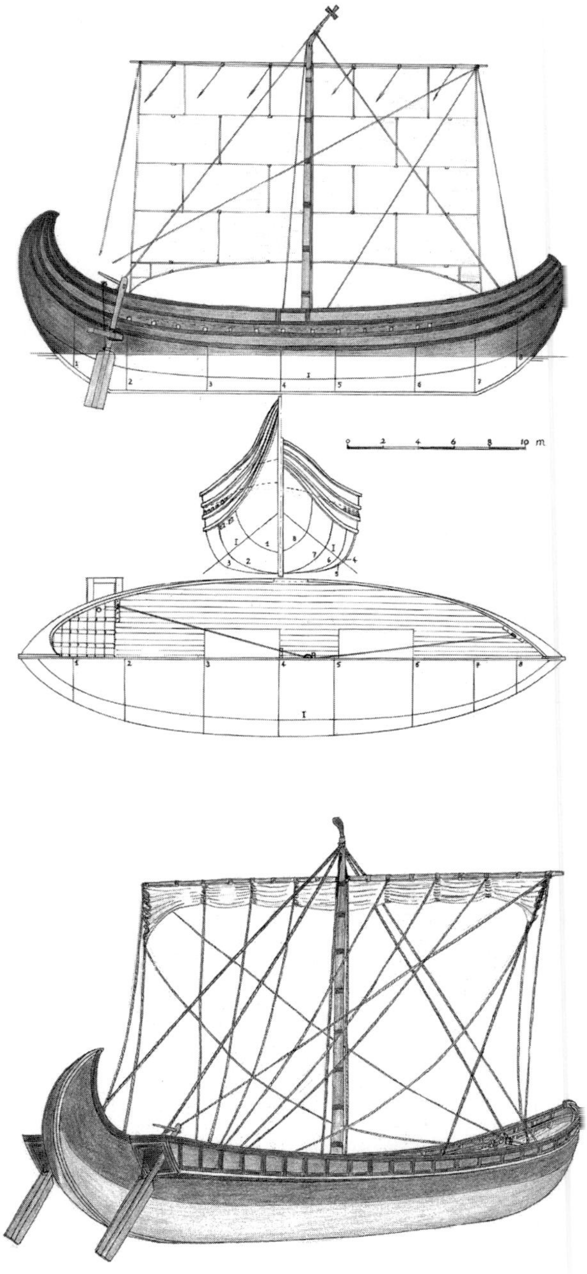

FIG. 9. Reconstruction of sixth-century river or coastal cargo vessels in the "Port of Classis" mosaic, Sant'Apollinare Nuovo, Ravenna. *Courtesy M. Bonino, 1991: figs. 6 and 7*

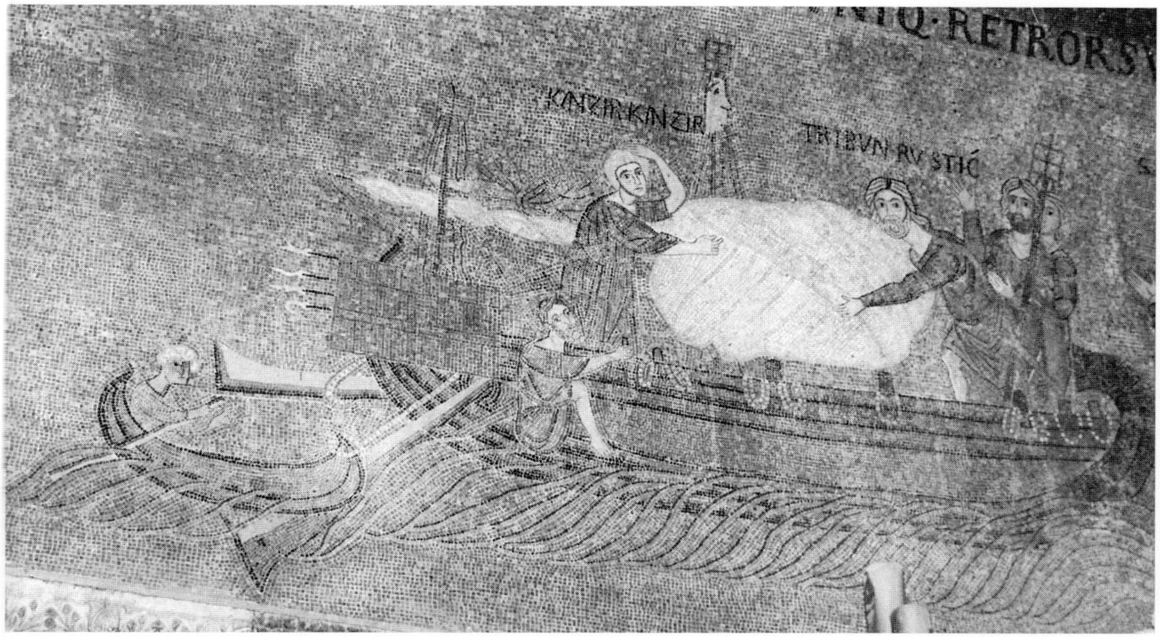

FIG. 10. *Translatio* of St. Mark: "Loading of St. Mark's Relics in Alexandria," east vault mosaic dating to the first half of the twelfth century, San Clemente Chapel, San Marco. *Permission to photograph courtesy the Procuratóre di San Marco*

der support to a robust outrigger structure where rudders were mounted, which is how Bonino reconstructs it (1978a: 48; fig. 9, bottom). This mount system was improved with the simpler type of box mounts on boats A and C.

Figures 10–13
Theme: *Translatio* of St. Mark.
Location: East, south, and west sides of vault, San Clemente Chapel (A), San Marco, Venice.
Date: First half of twelfth century.
Types: Four versions of three-masted, lateen-rigged, merchant ship (Type IIIc) and one lighter (Type Ia).

San Clemente and San Pietro are symmetrically oriented chapels flanking the altar of San Marco (fig. 1A and B). The mosaics of San Pietro depict scenes from the *vitae* of St. Mark and St. Peter pertaining to the prehistory of the Venetian Church and her ecclesiastical domain. Those in San Clemente, the Doge's chapel directly across the altar and originally with direct access from the Doge's Palace, illustrate the Doge's influence on Venetian church life, such as his involvement in the *translatio*, the posthumous transportation of the relics of St. Mark to Venice (Demus, 1988: 28 and 96).

The Marcan *translatio* cycle decorating San Clemente begins on the east half of the chapel's vault with the "Loading of St. Mark's Relics in Alexandria" onto a merchant vessel (fig. 10). The narration proceeds to the right, on the south wall and left of a circular window, with the "Departure from Alexandria" (fig. 11). The narration continues, not immediately to the right on the other side of the circular window, but on the west half of the vault, with the "Saving of the Ship by St. Mark" (fig. 12). The final episode, the "Arrival at Venice" (fig. 13), is back on the south wall, to the right of the circular window.[1]

Except for minor details, all four ship depictions in the cycle show the starboard side of an armed, three-masted round ship, with a small quarterdeck, two quarter rudders, and a relatively flat bottom. The vertical orientation of the central and aftermost masts in figures 10, 12, and 13 present a problem in interpreting the sail types as lateen. Sails shown in figures 11 and 12, however, are clearly triangular in shape, and have vertical running lines that probably indicate the seams in the sail cloth, and may signify the use

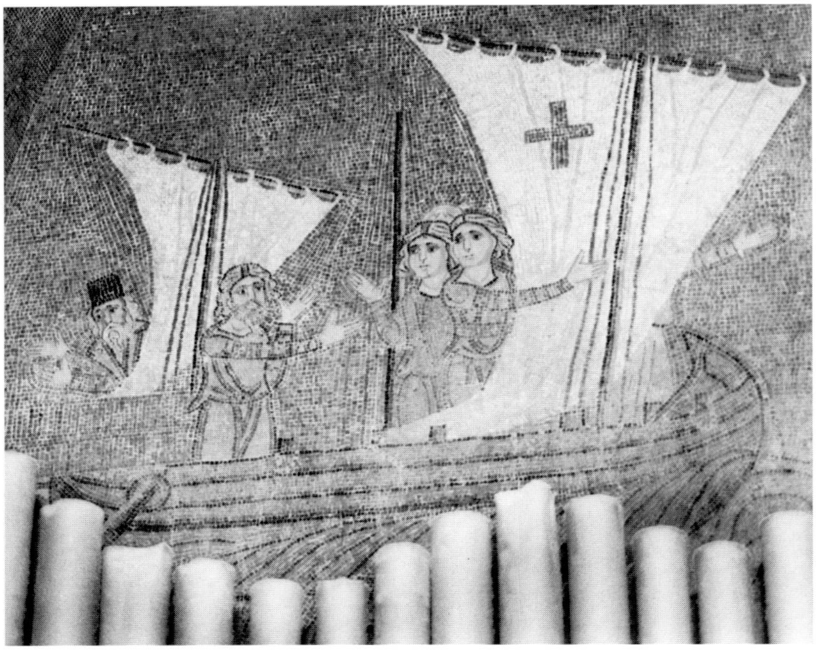

FIG. 11. *Translatio* of St. Mark: "Departure from Alexandria," south wall mosaic dating to the first half of the twelfth century, San Clemente Chapel, San Marco. *Permission to photograph courtesy the Procuratóre di San Marco*

of long, rectangular strips of fabric to form a lateen sail. Depictions of lateen sails commonly emphasize vertical lines (as in figs. 25–26, 65, 94, 97, and 117). Furthermore, the yard arm shown in figure 13 is longer, in fact, than the length of the ship, and, in figure 11, where it projects further aft than forward. This would only be possible on a lateener. These four, early twelfth-century ship mosaics, along with a similar one in nearby San Pietro (fig. 14), provide a rare early example of a third mast aft. Mediterranean textual sources first mention three-masted ships at the end of the eleventh century (Pryor, 1992: 31).

Here we encounter a difficulty of terminology. On two-masted lateen ships, Venetians called the principal mast *di proda* and the mast placed aft *di mezzo,* because it was in the middle of the ship, or amidships; from this, the forward sail came to be called the foresail, while the second, the mizzen. On two-masted lateen ships, the latter could be called the aftermast, as it is

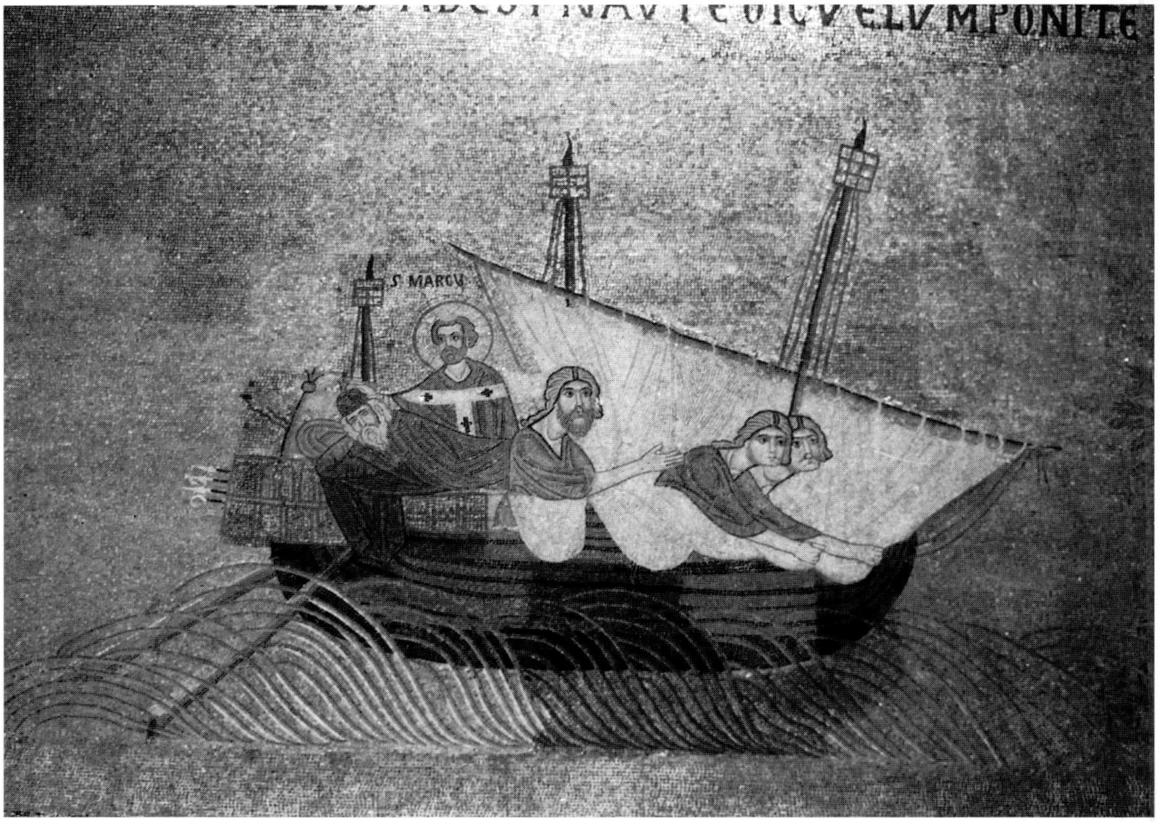

FIG. 12. The *passus* of the *translatio* of St. Mark: "Saving of the Ship by St. Mark," south vault mosaic dating to the first half of the twelfth century, San Clemente Chapel, San Marco. *Permission to photograph courtesy the Procuratóre di San Marco*

aft of the mainsail, and it is the aftermost mast. But on a three-masted ship, the aftermost mast is still called the mizzen. So what to call the central mast on a medieval three-masted lateener, or the later three-masted mixed-rig? For lack of a better term, it shall be referred to as the central mast (Bellabarba, 1988: 237).

Much more common in medieval depictions, though, are two-masted lateeners. In fact, a large, three-masted lateener is not often portrayed anywhere in the Mediterranean over the entire period of this study (Pryor, 1984, no. 3: 284), and it does not occur again in Venetian iconography until the fifteenth century, becoming common only in the second half of that century (see graph, fig. 155).

The central and mizzen masts appear vertical in the depictions, while the foremasts rake slightly forward, except for figure 13, where the completely vertical portrayal of the foremast may be the result of a poor restoration. Usually on multimasted ships, the foremast is taller than the other masts: This is so for all depictions but the ship in figure 10, where the central mast is tallest. Again, restoration may be the cause of this inconsistency. According to Demus (1984, vol. 1: 67), the strange face toward the top of this mast is of doubtful authenticity, and the mast's height is likely in error as well. The aftermost mast, the mizzen, is in all cases the shortest mast.

Lines for shrouds or stays and halyards are depicted, but it is difficult to distinguish them here, as in many medieval ship images. Adding to the confusion are simple errors in perspective the artist made. For example, the yards in figures 10, 12, and 13 are shown in front of all four standing rigging lines, which would imply that all four lines are secured to the port side, with none to starboard. Only in the case of figure 11, where two sails are completely unfurled and four standing rigging lines are visible in front of them, can any sense possibly be inferred: if the wind is coming from the stern, it would be possible to see part or all of the port shroud lines as well as the starboard shrouds in "front" of the sails. The three to four lines depicted fore and aft of the masts on all the ships, run up to the tops of the masts and down again, are probably all meant to indicate the shrouds, both to port and starboard. If the halyard is meant to be one of them, it should be the one closest to and aft of the mast.

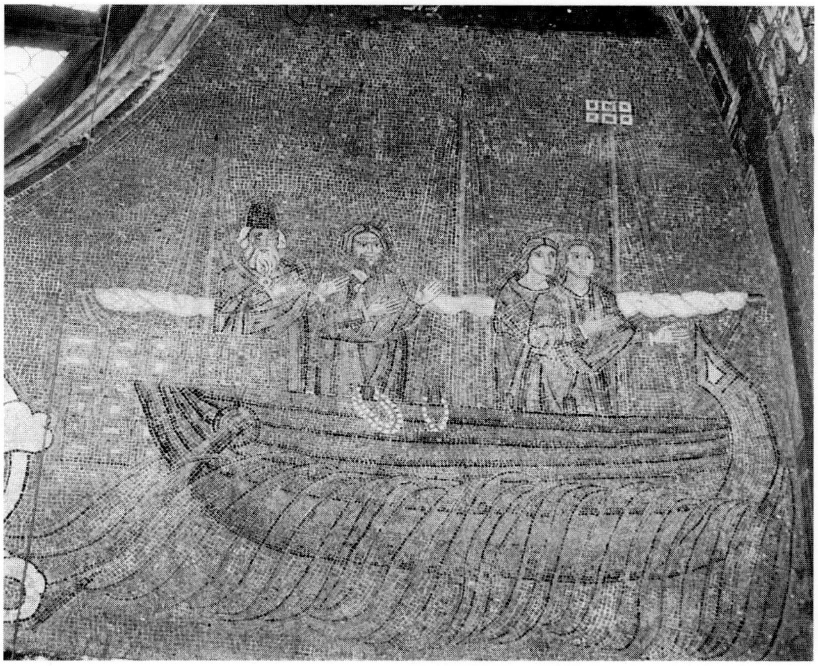

FIG. 13. *Translatio* of St. Mark: "Arrival at Venice," west wall mosaic dating to the first half of the twelfth century, San Clemente Chapel, San Marco. *Permission to photograph courtesy the Procuratóre di San Marco*

In figures 10 and 13, sails are furled on their yards, and stored partway up the mast. Vang or tack lines have been used to secure each yard. Where the ship is shown under way, with sails set (figs. 11–12), vang and tack lines are usually indicated by one or two lines each. The omission or inconsistency seen in the foremast sail of figure 11, where the vang and tack are completely lacking, is probably the result of deterioration or restoration work. Robands binding the sails to the yards are clearly represented in both ships with their sails set.

At the top of each mast, as in the adjacent chapel's ship mosaic (fig. 14), a rectangular feature has been depicted as a series of small red or white squares. Their large size relative to the mast makes them seem likely to be crow's nests. If

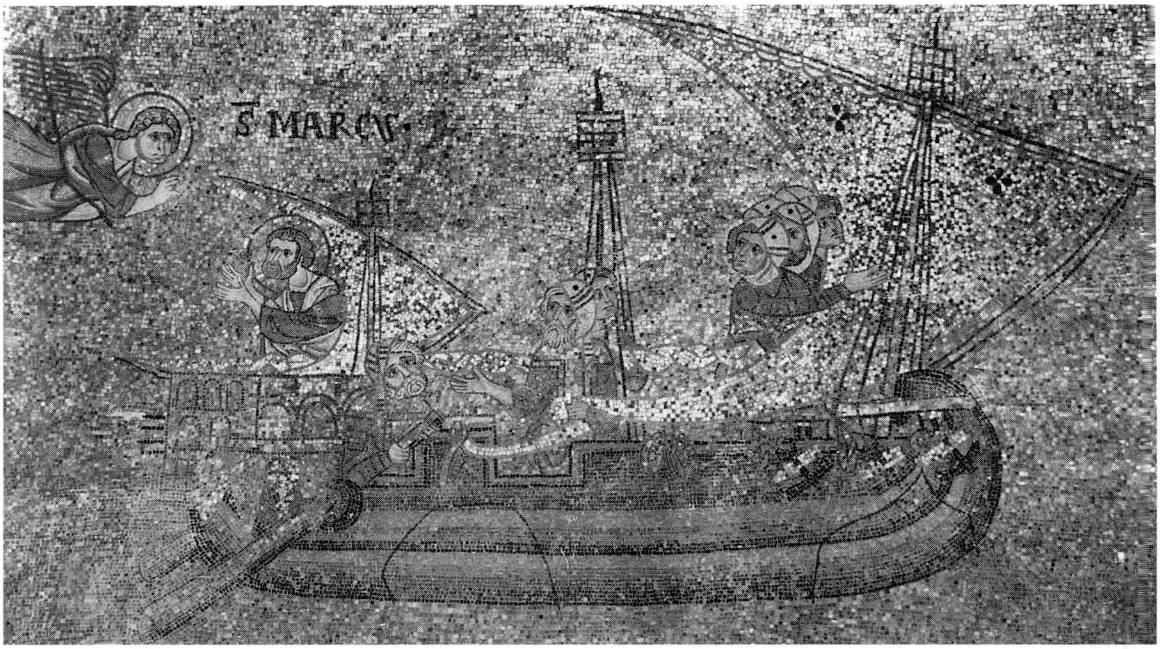

Fig. 14. *Vita* of St. Mark: "In the Pentapolis, St. Mark Receives Divine Guidance to Leave for Alexandria, Egypt," twelfth-century east vault mosaic, San Pietro Chapel, San Marco. *Permission to photograph courtesy the Procuratóre di San Marco*

crow's nests, their central placement at the top of the mast as portrayed in the ships of these mosaics and that of figure 14 poses a logistical problem. In each case, the mast appears to pass up through the center of the floor of the crow's nest and to continue above the top of the basket. Or perhaps the vertical projection is a pennant pole, set in the basket. A centrally placed crow's nest and any upper extensions at the head of the mast would hamper the tacking maneuver, because in tacking a lateener, the yard must be brought completely around the mast's forward side. Another interpretation of the vertical features above the baskets of the crow's nests might resolve this apparent difficulty. Best seen on the mizzen of figure 10, all masts of figure 12, and the central and mizzen masts of figure 13, the projection at the top of the crow's nests is actually a curving line, thick at its base, but tapering to a point, as one might depict a flame. It is possible that removable lanterns were placed in the crow's nests, and what appears to be upright projections are in fact lantern flames.[2] The central position of the baskets, however, would still seem to be an impractical arrangement for a lateener. Perhaps the baskets were movable, and could rotate around the mast as shown in a galley in figure 58, or a mariner was posted there when tacking to help the yard over the basket. A lateener's crow's nest is most commonly depicted positioned aft of the mast, as in figures 26 and 93, a position where the basket certainly could have been secured permanently while allowing the necessary maneuvers. In light of the fact that almost all the lateeners in the catalog portray their crow's nests aft of the mast, it seems reasonable to conclude that these baskets must have been either movable or removable, or their central placement as a crow's nest was an error of the mosaicist or an inaccuracy introduced during early restorations. A permanent, centrally positioned crow's nest is appropriate for a square-rigged ship, which would have been the type with which restorers of subsequent centuries were familiar.

Wherever not obstructed by sails or clothing (figs. 10–11, 13), the stem is shown as being slightly taller than the quarterdeck at the stern. All show top-timbers projecting above the sheer strake, except figure 12, where this area is concealed by the billowing sail of the foremast. In figures 10–11, the upper lengths of three or four top-timbers, some employed as bitts, are shown evenly spaced along the waist of the ship, and two to three more are visible in the bow, spaced slightly closer together. In figure 13 four are shown at the waist of the ship, but none are evident in the bow. This suggests a fairly regular room-and-space along the midsection of the ship, with more closely spaced frames toward the bow. Various lines can be seen tied off to most of the visible bitts.

The rudders in figure 10 alone have the blade aft of the shaft, the unbalanced foil design, while those represented in figures 11–13 are the balanced type of quarter rudder with an elliptical shape.

Four poles projecting horizontally from the quarterdeck of three of the ships in this cycle (figs. 10, 12, and 14; with details of all three sterns as fig. 15A, B, and C) illustrate the *bellatorium,* a fighting deck described in texts. Each pole has a uniquely shaped tip including a curved C-shaped and a sharp hook, a triangular arrow point, and a V-shaped prong-like form. The curved shapes might have been boat hooks or pole arms, but the others seem specialized for distinctly military purposes, and a sharp hook (fig. 12, second from top), C-shaped hooks (the bottom implement in figures 10 and 12) and V-shaped prong (fig. 10, top implement) could have been used to cut the lines of enemies' rigging, while the pointed implements appear to be iron-tipped weapons, such as hand-thrown javelins, pikes, or the bolts or quarrels launched with a crossbow. Figure 15D, a detail of a ship from a fifteenth-century French miniature, has three similar poles stowed vertically at the stern: a flaming pike mid-air shows this vessel is under attack. The central one with a projecting point may be a javelin, while the outer two poles with a small curved hook and a projecting point look like bills, other hand-thrown weapons, or are possibly implements for cutting the lines of enemy rigging.

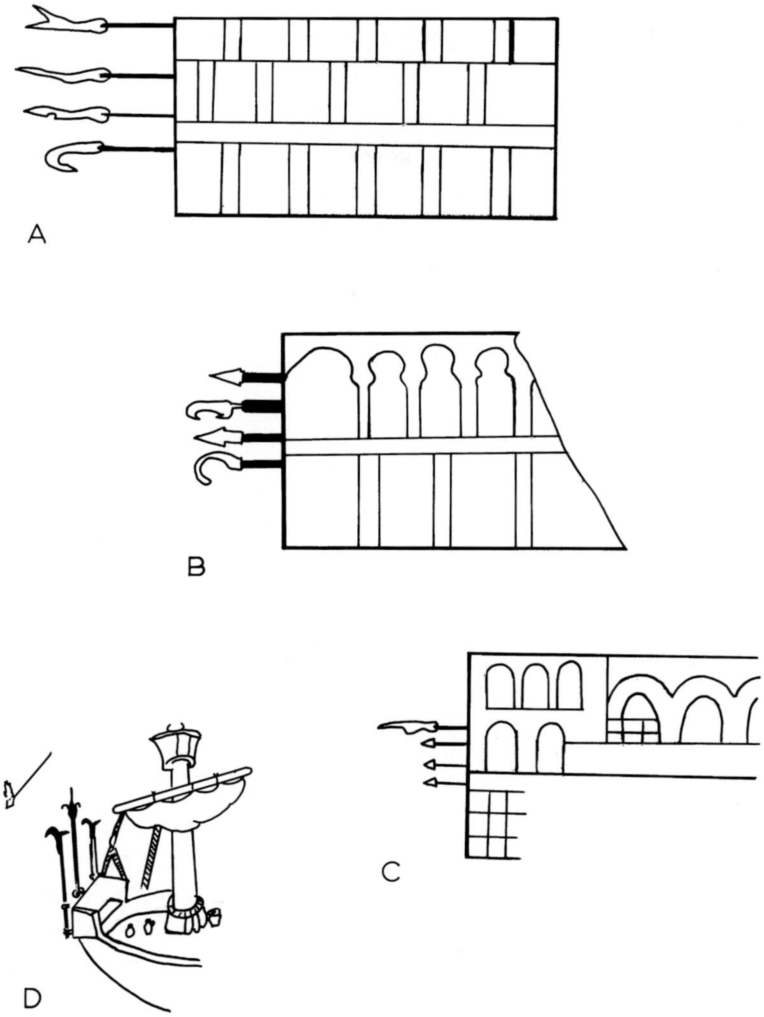

FIG. 15. Details of the quarterdecks' *bellatorium,* showing storage of weaponry. (A) from fig. 10, (B) from fig. 12, (C) from fig. 14, and (D) from ship in a fifteenth-century French manuscript *Tractatus de re militari et de machinis bellicis* (Bibliothèque Nationale, Paris, ms. lat. 7239, f° 61vo). *After Villain-Gandossi, 1979: fig. 12.9*

Figure 10

Theme: *Translatio* of St. Mark: "Loading of St. Mark's Relics in Alexandria." (The ship is examined by Muslims.)

Titulus: *CARNIBVS ABSCONSVM V VERVNT FVGIVNTQ VE RETRORSVM KANZIR KANZIR TRIBVN RVSTIC.*

Translation: They seek that which is hidden in the flesh and they flee backward. Pork, Pork. Tribunus and Rusticus.[3]

Location: East half of vault, lower register, San Clemente Chapel (A), San Marco, Venice.

Types: Three-masted, lateen-rigged merchant ship (Type IIIc) and lighter (Type Ia).

The first mosaic of the San Clement cycle has been badly restored. Although its composition is believed to be fairly accurate, almost no part of the mosaic, including most of the ship, is original; the gold background was completely replaced in the 1880s (Demus, 1984, vol. 1: 67 and note 73). Features of the ship represented must therefore be considered cautiously. Figure 10 shows a vessel from starboard, moored in port at Alexandria with two sails furled. Another sail serves to wrap the pork that hides the relics of St. Mark. Tribunus and Rusticus are identified in the bow. *"Kanzir, kanzir,"* written just aft of the central mast head, refers to the pork.

The vertical central mast is set aft of midships, while the other two masts rake forward. The rectangular crow's nests on each mast vary slightly: the foremast and mizzen examples consist of four squares while that of the central mast has six. The face of a man discernible at the head of the central mast is probably not original (Demus, 1984, vol. 1: 67).

Four parallel lines extending from the underside of the quarterdeck forward to the bow seem to represent in profile a slightly rockered keel, the garboard and the lowermost strakes, which all sweep upward at the bow parallel to the stem. The three uppermost strakes are also indicated, but the intermediate hull planking has been left plain and undefined. Stem and sternpost are symmetrical and curve dramatically inward. Small fishing boats depicted in "The Miraculous Draught of Fishes" and larger ships in the depiction of Noah's ark (late twelfth-century mosaics in the Cathedral of Monreale, Sicily; Moll, 1929: figs. 123, 124, and 125) have similar stem and stern posts.

The rectangular quarterdeck, which begins just above the top of the aperture for the starboard quarter rudder *(temon),* extends aft beyond the hull. This small sterncastle is defined by three levels of rectangles. The placement of the aperture for the starboard rudder and the rudder's orientation relative to the ship's side give an idea of the shape of the hull at this point. In order for the rudder to enter the water from this aperture, the hull must have narrowed considerably beneath and aft of the aperture. The blade of the port rudder is also visible, with a black and white rope rudder hoist of the type that simply looped around the lower end of the blade (cf. Mott, 1997: fig. 6.30 A). The rudders are of the asymmetrical, unbalanced type. This efficient rudder type is depicted in the atrium of San Marco, in the twelfth- to thirteenth-century mosaic of St. Phocas, bishop of Sinope (fig. 149), and numerous other ships in the catalog (e.g., figs. 26, 54, and 94). The design, with the placement of the rudder's blade aft of its shaft, exhibits the great improvement made on rudder design during the medieval period. The starboard rudder appears to be hung in the wrong direction; if the ship were under way, the side of the blade that flares out should be aft of the straight side of the blade, as seen in the port rudder. This ship, however, is in port, and not under sail: the rudder blade may be secured in this position in a normal procedure for mooring. Rudder blades were able to rotate freely. In fact, they were even movable from outboard the ship: "Geoffrey of Vinsauf tells us that when Richard the Lion Heart's galleys encountered a large Saracen ship off the coast of Palestine, one of the tactics used to overcome its resistance was for men to dive overboard and lash the steering oars in a turning position with ropes so that it could not escape" (Pryor, 1984, no. 3: 280).

The mosaic includes a very schematic representation of a small, double-ended service boat tied with a painter to the stern of St. Mark's ship. A steering oar or quarter rudder held by the mariner at its stern is indistinctly depicted.

Figure 11

Theme: *Translatio* of St. Mark: "Departure from Alexandria."

Titulus: Lost.

Location: South wall, lower register, left of window, San Clemente Chapel (Figure 1A), San Marco, Venice.

Type: Three-masted, lateen-rigged, merchant ship (Type IIIc).

Figure 11, the second of the San Clemente *translatio* cycle, shows the ship preparing to sail. Most of this mosaic was reset during the Renaissance; according to Demus, in most areas the restoration seems to be fairly accurate, although the *titulus* was lost. As they are not included in any of the other ship depictions in this cycle, the red cross on the foresail and the unusual decorative arcades under the *bellatorium* (obstructed from view by organ pipes in figure 11 but visible in Levi, 1892: table 42, fig. 2) may be due to this restoration (Demus, 1984, vol. 1: 65–67). Several centuries later, some round ships do exhibit similar decorative arches around the quarterdeck (cf. fig. 54 and Kaftal, 1978: fig. 613).

Two of the three lateen sails are hoisted. Vang and tack lines to control the peak and heel of the sails are evident on the mizzen sail only. Rigging details on the foresail were probably lost during the course of restoration. The crow's nests of this ship are consistently depicted with lines forming four simple squares.

The hull bottom profile is represented with one bold line. Of the side planking, only the uppermost three strakes have been defined: four lines run parallel from the stem but converge at the stern beneath the quarterdeck. The lowermost of these lines is thicker than the other three, perhaps indicating a wale.

The rendering of the stem is confusing, likely another result of the restoration work, as the bow area is known to be of questionable authenticity (Demus, 1984, vol. 1: 67). What appears to be a stem curves aft at about forty-five degrees. A line runs from its tip and disappears behind the top strakes. This may be an anchor line tied to a bower anchor ready for use.

The quarterdeck is depicted as a series of squares, possibly defining either one or two levels of upper internal cabin space, or a fenced open deck. If in fact this is part of the original mosaic, the arcaded area under the quarterdeck, shown as a series of arches in a seemingly unrealistic position well beyond the hull (cf. fig. 92), may be interpreted as fancy windows of internal cabins such as the *paradisi* or *vanna,* which were the best cabins of a Crusader ship (Pryor, 1984, no. 3: 278).

A circular aperture for the loom of the starboard quarter rudder is located toward the aft end of the sheer strake and the strake below it, placed beneath the forward half of the quarterdeck from where the rudders would have been worked. The small size of the visible oar is not realistic for a ship of this size, maybe yet another result of poor restoration.

Pole arms and/or weaponry project from the quarterdeck of this vessel as in the others of this cycle, but the features of their tips have been lost.

Figure 12

Theme: The *passus* of the *translatio* of St. Mark: "Saving of the Ship by St. Mark."

Titulus: *TELLUS ADEST NAVTE DIC VELUM PONITE CAVTE.*[4]

Translation: The earth is present to the sailor [They are nearing shore]. He said, "Put [away] the sails cautiously."

Location: West half of vault, lower register, San Clemente Chapel (fig. 1A), San Marco, Venice.

Type: Three-masted, lateen-rigged, merchant ship (Type IIIc).

The narrative continues on the west side of the vault, with a representation of the vessel in danger of shipwreck (fig. 12). This mosaic is fairly well preserved; St. Mark and Stauracius on the quarterdeck are the only areas to have been reset (Demus, 1984, vol. 1: 67). More of the original ship remains in this mosaic than any other in the *translatio* cycle.

Two of the masts stand almost vertically, one slightly aft of midships, and the other far aft, while the foremast rakes forward. Mariners in the bow are in the process of lowering the foresail in order to avoid the dangerous rock cliffs to the right. Shown roughly equal to the length of the hull, the length of this yard is not exaggerated; on some lateeners, it was even longer. In this image, the tack, two lines attached to the lower end of the yard, are clearly visible. A vang, attached to the upper end of the yard, is also shown. The sails of the mizzen and central masts have already been lowered. One of them has been furled on its yard and stowed along the central axis of the ship; this can be seen projecting aft, behind the head of St. Mark.

A wide, heavy line represents the keel and perhaps some of the lowermost strakes. Above it, strakes are shown continuously up the side of the ship; they converge at the stem. As discussed for figure 10, the aperture for the rudder shaft and its orientation to the hull imply a narrowing of the hull below the quarterdeck of the vessel. Distinguishable in this version of the ship are decorative finials on two inward-curving members at the stern (the port tip can be seen just above Stauracius's hat, while the starboard tip is left of it). Two inboard-curving timbers such as these are a common feature on medieval ship representations (e.g., figs. 18, 31, 46, 62, 87 and Landström, 1961: figs. 221–23). They appear to be the upper ends of structural timbers that originate lower in the hull and form the port and starboard frames of a transom stern. However, interpretation of the feature is a topic of debate. In Bonino's opinion such timbers would have supported a transverse bar, forming a crutch for the yard when not hung on its mast (1978b: 9), as, in fact, seems to be depicted here. The furled yard projects beyond the posts and may well rest on a crutch. At the after end of this visible furled yard, two lines, probably the vang, lead to the starboard inward curving post, apparently securing the yard there.

The quarterdeck consists of two levels: the uppermost is decorated with arches, the lower with simple squares. A section of this deck structure continues almost to midships, much farther forward than in the other depictions where it terminates close to the rudder aperture. How the quarter rudders were mounted is not clear from this mosaic, as that area has been obscured by Stauracius's cloak. But as the other examples in this cycle show (figs. 10, 11, and 13), it probably passed through a circular aperture beneath the quarterdeck. The quarter rudders portrayed in this mosaic are symmetrical and small, like those in figure 11.

Projecting horizontally from the quarterdeck are four poles, similar to those found in figures 10 and 14. One ends in a hook, the others, in diverse spear forms (detail, fig. 15B).

Figure 13

Theme: *Translatio* of St. Mark: "Arrival at Venice."

Titulus: Lost.

Location: South wall, lower register, right of window, San Clemente Chapel (fig. 1A), San Marco, Venice.

Type: Three-masted, lateen-rigged, merchant ship (Type IIIc).

Figure 13, the final mosaic in this cycle, was very badly restored between 1870 and 1890, and the current image is considered to be a poor copy only (Demus, 1984, vol. 1: 68).

The vessel is represented in port with sails furled. From the after end of the furled yard, two lines lead to the quarterdeck near its after end; these lines are probably the vang used to secure the furled sail. Forward are two lines, presumably the tack, securing the furled sail and yard in the bow.

The completely vertical orientation of the foremast is unrealistic for a lateen-rigged ship. Because the vertical foremast occurs only in this scene of the cycle, it seems likely to be the result of the poor restoration work. The crow's nest on this mast is also distinct from the other representations in this series: it has been delineated with six small squares set within six larger squares. Other crow's nests are similarly defined as a series of squares, two or three in each row, but in no other case do the squares contain smaller squares within. Two superimposed rows of eight squares each, beginning just forward of the rudder aperture and extending aft beyond the sternpost, represent the quarterdeck. Below the quarterdeck and beyond the stern, another four superimposed rows of squares are harder to interpret. This area beyond the hull proper is depicted in one other scene of this cycle (fig. 11). Both cases might be additions made during renovations, or perhaps the extension is original, and meant to represent inner cabins of a sterncastle (cf. fig. 92).

The five uppermost strakes, defined by six lines, converge at the stern; at the bow, they end where the lowest of these lines swoops upward to form one side of the stem. The stem appears the continuation of the line defining the keel. A circular aperture for the elliptically shaped rudder is set aft and high, between the second and fourth strake.

Figure 14

Theme: *Vita* of St. Mark: "In the Pentapolis, St. Mark Receives Divine Guidance to Leave for Alexandria, Egypt."

Titulus: *NVNCIAT HIC PERGIT SVTORIS VVLNERA TERGIT.*

Translation: He announces, "This one goes. He wipes away the wounds of odor."

Location: East half of vault, lower register, San Pietro Chapel (fig. 1B), San Marco, Venice.

Date: Second quarter of the twelfth century.

Type: Three-masted, lateen-rigged, merchant ship (Type IIIc).

In the vault immediately to the northwest of the main altar, mosaics portray scenes from the *vitae* of Saints Mark and Peter that emphasize the prehistory and ecclesiastical dominion of the Venetian church (Demus, 1988: 28 and 96). In the one maritime scene, figure 14, St. Mark, called to evangelize, is directed by an angel and sails for Alexandria. In many respects, his vessel resembles the three-masted, lateen-rigged vessel in the Marcan *translatio* cycle located across the altar in San Clemente (figs. 10–13).

The preservation of this mosaic is generally quite good. The golden teardrop shapes along the side of the quarterdeck at the stern are the only areas missing the original tesserae; these have been replaced with gold ones, which stand out clearly, and the remainder of the mosaic is believed to be authentic (Demus, 1984, vol. 1: 63).

Set far forward in the bow, the foremast is tallest and rakes slightly, while the central and mizzen masts stand vertically. The mizzen is shortest. The sails of the foremast and mizzen are raised, while the central mast's sail has been furled on its yard and stored along the centerline of the ship. The foresail is decorated with two florets or crosses. On both open sails, two lines at the forward end of the yard represent the tack. No vang are evident. Robands securing each sail to its yard are visible. Standing rigging is schematically depicted as two to four lines for each mast.

A quarterdeck is depicted with arches. A series of squares below (again, outside the hull proper; cf. figs. 11, 13, and 92) may indicate the windows of internal cabin space. The helmsman working the starboard quarter rudder is shown in an unrealistic and awkward position leaning outside the sheer; in reality, on a ship as large as this one, the loom would have passed inboard through the aperture in the side of the hull for steerage from the quarterdeck.

The sheer strake is irregular: two large openings near midships and aft of it are cut into the adjacent strakes. This well illustrates movable side panels such as those found on one of the Contarina ships (Contarina I, ca. 1300; Relazione, 1901: 30), where a section of the side planking could slide aside in a groove to provide an opening for loading cargo. Similar pictorial examples can be seen in figures 41 and 44 and a fifteenth-century fresco painting of the conversion of St. Ranieri by Andrea da Firenze (in the Camposanto of Pisa), modeled after the thirteenth-century original by Giotto (Casson, 1964b: fig. 96 and Nebbia, 1932: fig. 17).

The visible top-timbers are utilized as bitts; various lines are shown tied off to them.

Three anchors with fixed anchor stocks are hung from their rings off the starboard bow, with their crowns slightly forward; this is the only example found of anchors in such a position. Usually the shank is hung horizontally, with the crown almost always aft (as in figs. 26, 41, 42, 77, and 94). No hawse holes are shown; apparently, during this early medieval period, the anchors' cables were just passed over the sheer strake and made fast inboard.

Pole arms or boat hooks project from the aft end of the quarterdeck (fig. 15C), like those discussed for figures 10 and 12.

Figure 16
Theme: "The Miraculous Draught of Fishes."
Titulus: *IVSSIT PISCANTVR CAPIVNTVR VEL NVMERANTVR.*
Translation: He orders. They fish, [fish] are caught, are counted.
Location: East half of vault, east bay of the north transept, San Marco, Venice.
Date: Second quarter of the twelfth century.
Type: Fishing boat (Type Ib).

The prototype for this cycle (figs. 16 and 17) was an eleventh-century Byzantine Gospel book (Demus, 1988: 50). Both boat mosaics have been badly restored, although the theme is accurately recorded (Demus, 1984, vol. 1: 121), so the vessels in figures 16 and 17 must be considered with caution.

In the east half of the vault, Christ is shown in the stern of a small boat along with seven of his disciples (fig. 16). The enlarged figures make

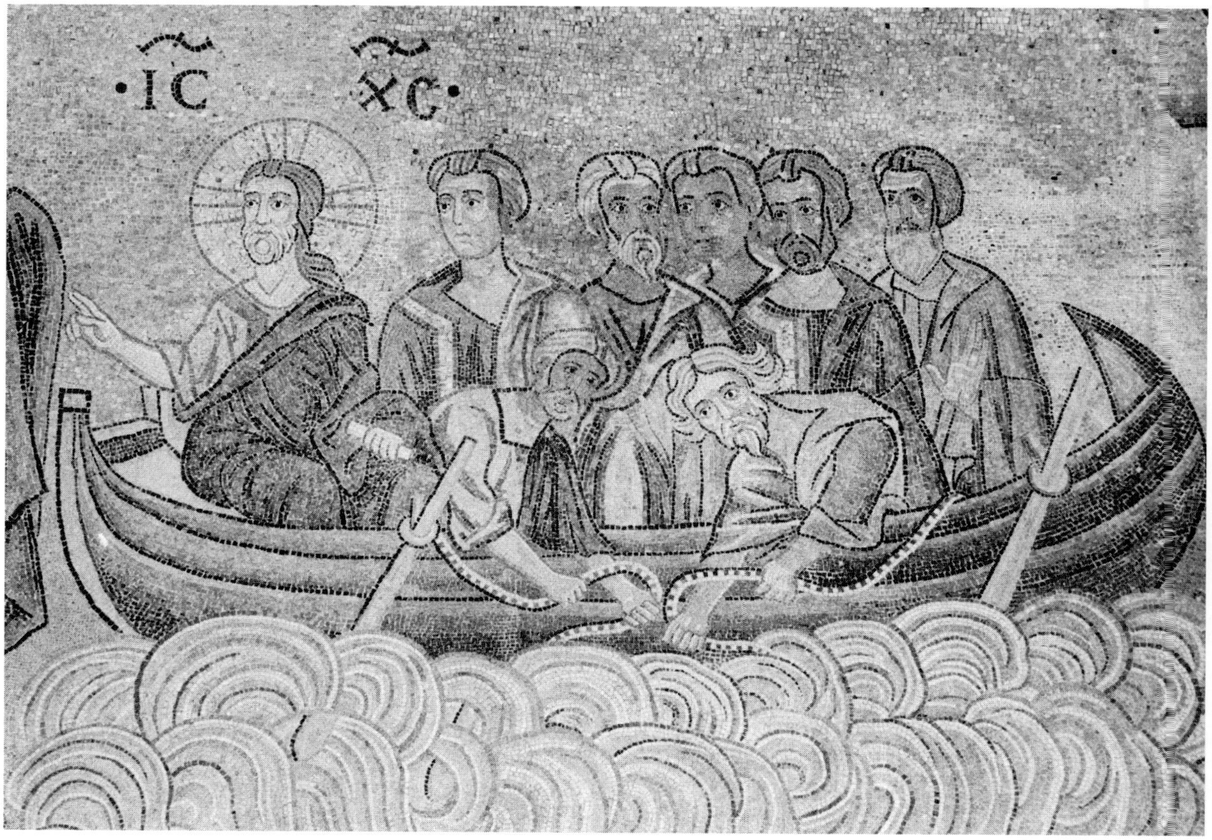

FIG. 16. "The Miraculous Draught of Fishes," second half of the twelfth-century vault mosaic, north transept, east bay, San Marco. *Permission to photograph courtesy the Procuratóre di San Marco*

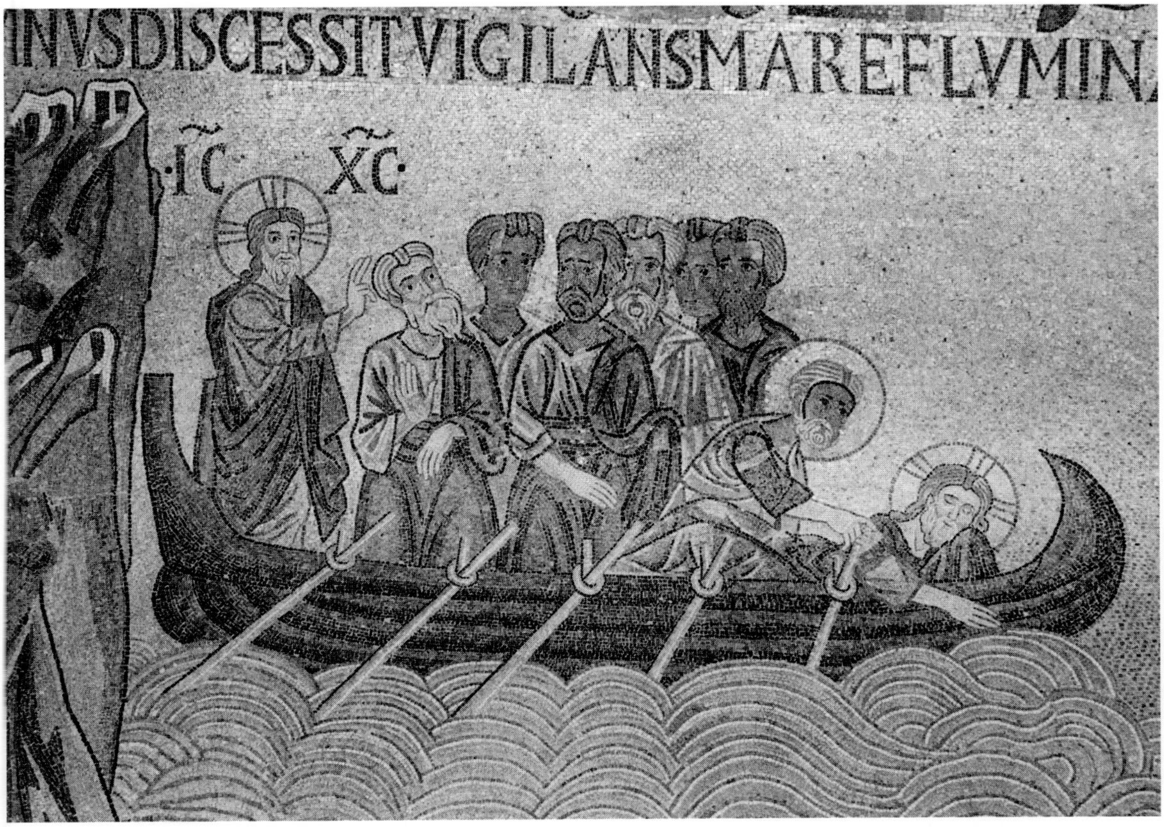

FIG. 17. "The Stilling of the Tempest," second half of the twelfth-century vault mosaic, north transept, west bay, San Marco. *Permission to photograph courtesy the Procuratóre di San Marco*

the small boat appear dangerously overloaded. Peter (depicted with a short beard and hair) and Andrew (depicted with a long beard) lean overboard to draw in fishing nets, while Christ turns to address the Pharisees on shore.

The stem, slightly higher than the stern, curves inward, and the ends of the few strakes depicted seem to be butted against it. At the stern, two sturdy timbers, originating low in the hull, sweep upward to form a transom stern. The area between these two posts is probably filled in with horizontal planking; only the uppermost of these is visible. The three uppermost strakes are generically defined with four parallel dark lines that converge slightly at the stern but continue parallel to finish at the stem. Between the stem and the lower-most visible strake at the bow, a scarf, and possibly two nails, can be seen.

On the visible starboard side, two oars are depicted, one at the bow and one slightly aft of midships. Their looms pass through grommets hung on thole pins. The shapes of the aft starboard oar and part of the aft port oar can be seen amidst the waves; the oars have slender, symmetrical blades.

Figure 17

Theme: "The Stilling of the Tempest."

Titulus: *SOMNVS DISCESSIT VIGILANS MARE FLVMINA PRESSIT.*

Translation: Sleep departs. The wakeful sea presses its streams [or, the watchful sea calms its waters].

Date: Second quarter of the twelfth century.

Location: West half of vault, east bay of the north transept (fig. 1C), San Marco, Venice.

Type: Fishing boat (Type Ib).

Like the boat mosaic across the vault (fig. 16), this mosaic has been poorly restored (Demus, 1984, vol. 1: 120) and should be critically considered.

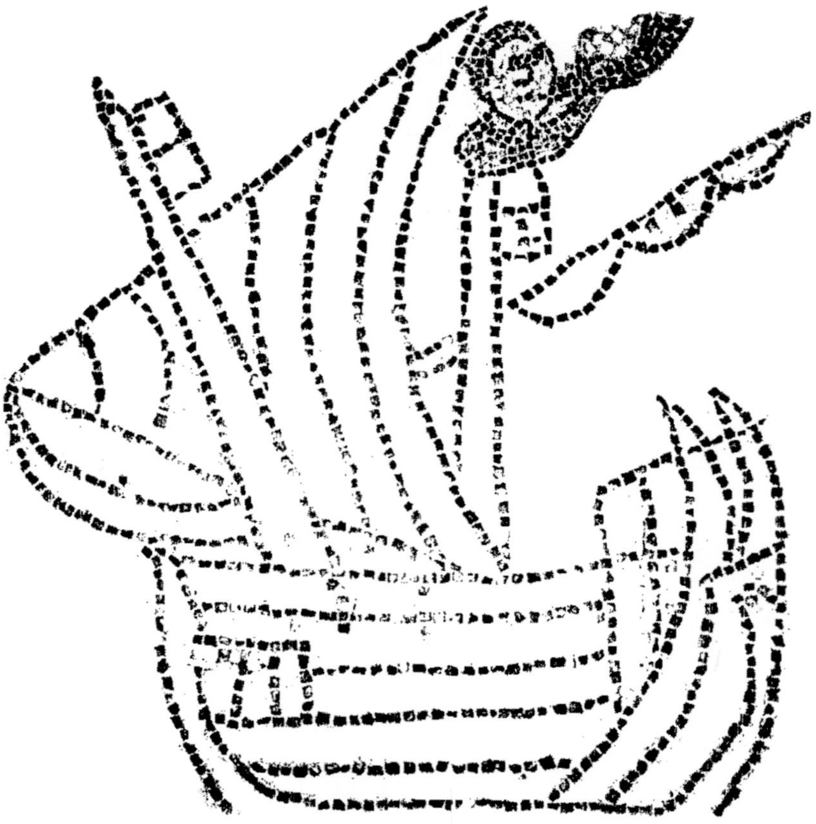

FIG. 18. Ship of the Fourth Crusade, with a trumpeter in the crow's nest. Originally part of floor mosaic (ca. 1213–35), San Giovanni Evangelista, Ravenna

To show progression in the narration depicted, Christ is portrayed twice; He is shown sleeping in the bow of the small boat, and then, awakened, at the stern, from whence He calms the stormy seas.

The vessel depicted in figure 17 is similar to the boat of figure 16 both in size and function. Certain features, however, are quite different: the two posts of the transom project much higher, and are depicted as extensions of the uppermost timbers. Rows of tesserae of three shades seem to define four or more of the strakes. These strakes converge at the stern to finish beneath the uppermost timbers but continue parallel to the stem. The shape of the stern is unusual and probably unrealistic: the hull itself appears to bulge outward below the transom. At the bow, a straight scarf with two nails is visible between the uppermost strake and the inward-curving stem.

On the starboard side, five oars in grommets hung on thole pins are equally spaced amidships.

Figures 18–21

Theme: Episodes from the Fourth Crusade: the taking of Zara and Constantinople.

Figure 18: Ship with trumpeter in crow's nest.

Figure 19: Ship during a siege, bow only.

Figure 20: Ship during a siege.

Figure 21: Ship, stern only.

Location: Originally floor mosaics, fragments now framed, hung along south wall, San Giovanni Evangelista, Ravenna.

Date: 1213–35 (Carile, 1976: 112 and Bovini, 1971: 42).

Type: Four war transports (Type IIb).

These four ship mosaics, originally from the floor pavement of San Giovanni Evangelista, illustrate episodes from the Fourth Crusade. The ship type represented is probably a *usiache (usciere),* the Crusader horse transport mentioned in the chroniclers' reports of the Crusades (e.g., Robert Geoffrey de Clari and G. de Villehardouin). The ships lack oars, and their full shape reveals that, although clearly associated with war here, such bulky transports relied on sail power and could also have been used for commerce.

Three of these medieval ship mosaics are fragmentary; only figure 18 is complete. All four share common features defining the ship almost to the last detail.

In each representation, the masts, lateen sails, keel, and several rows of strakes have been delineated as a relatively realistic line drawing. The hull's almost box-like shape is emphasized. The ship has two masts, lateen-rigged. Wherever preserved, the crow's nest is shown aft of the masts, a practical position that would have allowed a lateen-rigged ship to tack easily. The mizzen is set vertically amidships while the taller foremast rakes forward in the bow.

A trumpeter in the mizzen mast crow's nest calls the other ships to commence their journey to the Holy Land in figure 18 (Carile, 1976: 120).[5] The mizzen sail is still furled on its yard. The

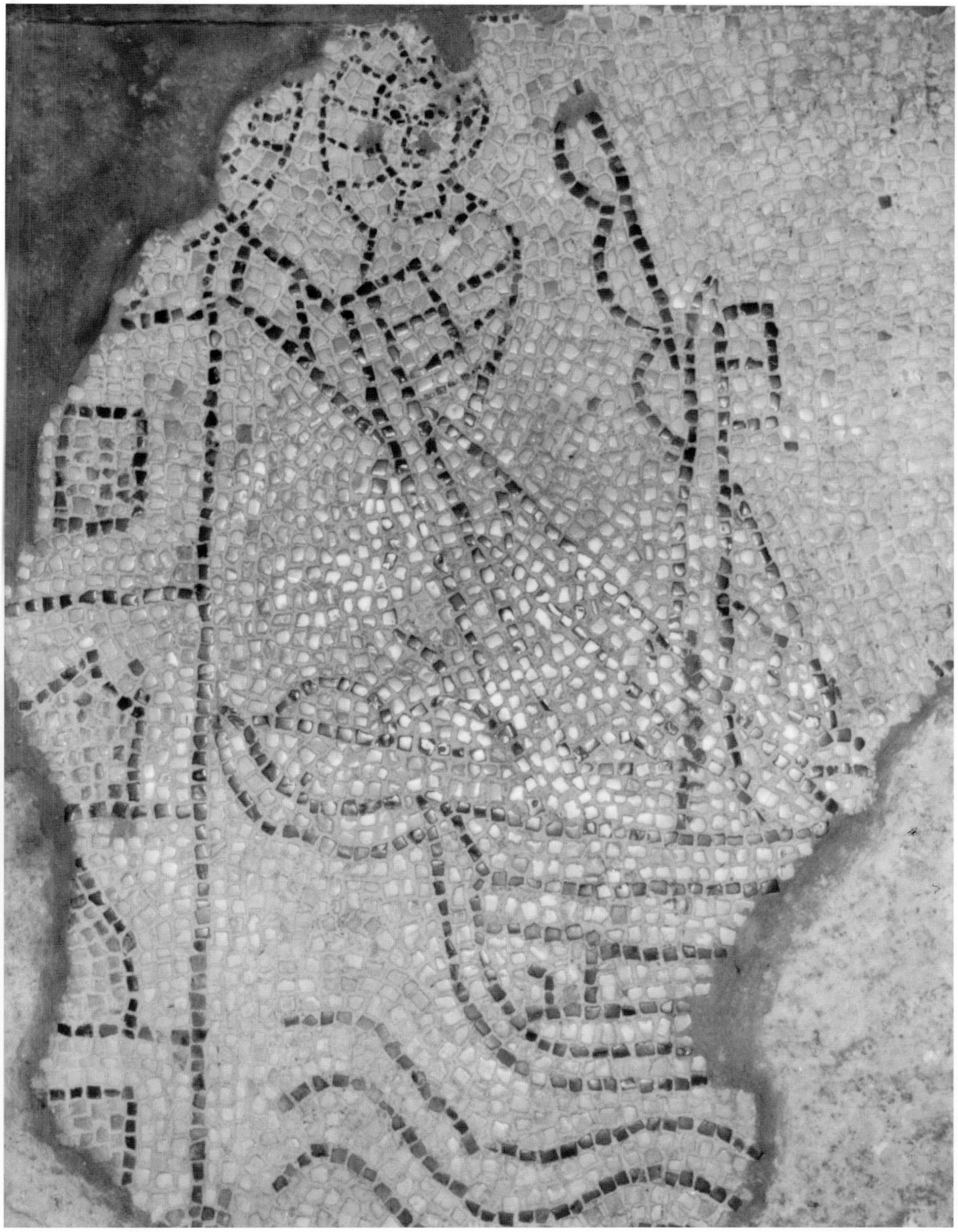

FIG. 19. Fragmentary floor mosaic (1213–35), detail of the bow of a ship of the Fourth Crusade during siege, from San Giovanni Evangelista, Ravenna

foresail is unfurled; its taller mast rakes forward while the mizzen amidships is vertical. The two tack of the foresail lead from the *cares,* the lower end of the yard, and are tied near the base of the mast. Slightly curving vertical lines accurately indicate the rectangular sections of cloth that were sewn together to form lateen sails. Medieval lateen sails were bellied (Pryor, 1984, no. 4: 365), thus the slight curvature of the seam lines.

Of the four ship mosaics of San Giovanni Evangelista, it is figure 18 that most clearly depicts the bulky and box-like shape of the hull. A lack of accurate perspective is apparent; a full profile of the port side as well as a partial view of the stern are shown. Obviously, both would not have been visible in a profile view of a ship; those features must have been considered significant characteristics distinguishing the ship's type.

The mosaicist seems to have depicted a straight keel and both stem and stern posts as one continuous timber with no scarfs defined; likewise each strake is shown as a single unscarfed timber. He did attempt to define a complex-shaped stern: two large, curving timbers flank and parallel the inward-curving sternpost but rise above it. These are clearly structural; perhaps they form the outer jambs of a horse port. As depicted in figure 18, their lower ends appear butted against the aft end of the keel from where they sweep tine-like upward and inboard (Bonino's reconstruction, figure 22, shows them beginning at deck level instead, as they appear in figures 20 and 21). Two lines drawn in perspective roughly perpendicular to these timbers define the width of the transom stern. The lower horizontal element, just above the top of the sternpost, may represent the *trigànte* (tragent) specified for two-decked round ships of crusader contracts, like that more clearly depicted in the round ship of figure 26.

The bow area is more simply terminated: horizontal lines defining strakes of consistent width finish into the stem. Three vertical lines at the bow could be interpreted as a window, a loading port, or for stowage of long spars or planks.

Only the bow area of the two-masted, lateen-rigged ship in figure 19 has survived. The mizzen is vertically set, while the slightly taller foremast rakes forward. Sails are furled: the yard of the mizzen is stored semi-vertically along the mast, while the foremast's yard is stored, roughly horizontally, above deck level. A crusader besieges the city from siege machinery supported by the foremast, leaning onto the city walls. The details of the ship's hull are identical to that of figure 18, with the exception of the short vertical lines representing a window or loading port at the bow: here there are only two lines, placed lower in the hull and slightly further aft.

A second fragmentary image, figure 20, shows another two-masted lateener with siege apparatus supported by the foremast. The bow and top of the mast areas have been obliterated, but the rest is well preserved and similar in details to the others, though the stern most closely resembles that of figure 21. Part of the starboard quarter rudder is visible, but it is on the far side of the vessel, and neither the mounting nor any details

FIG. 20. Fragmentary floor mosaic (ca. 1213–35) depicting a ship of the Fourth Crusade during siege, from San Giovanni Evangelista, Ravenna

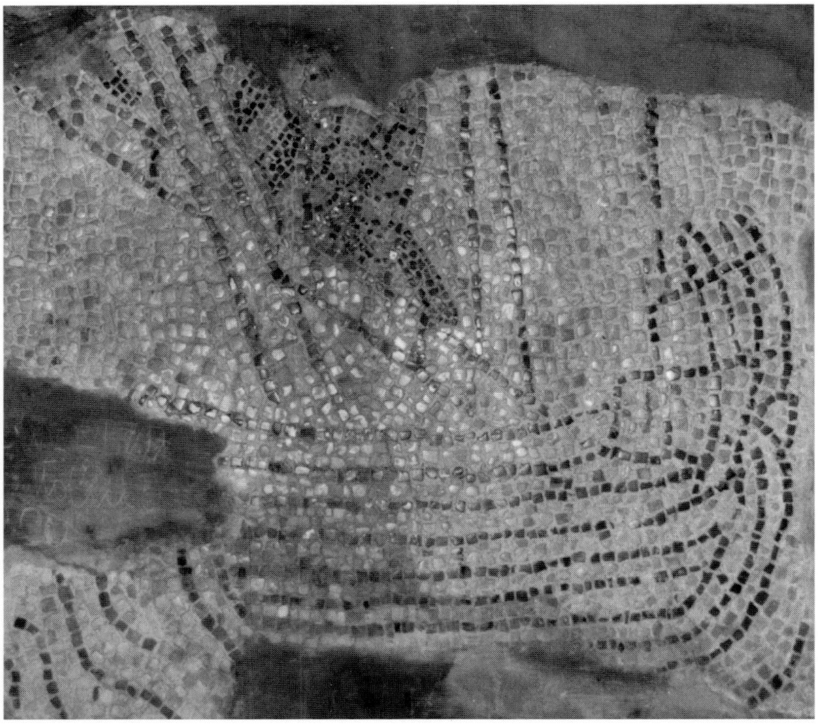

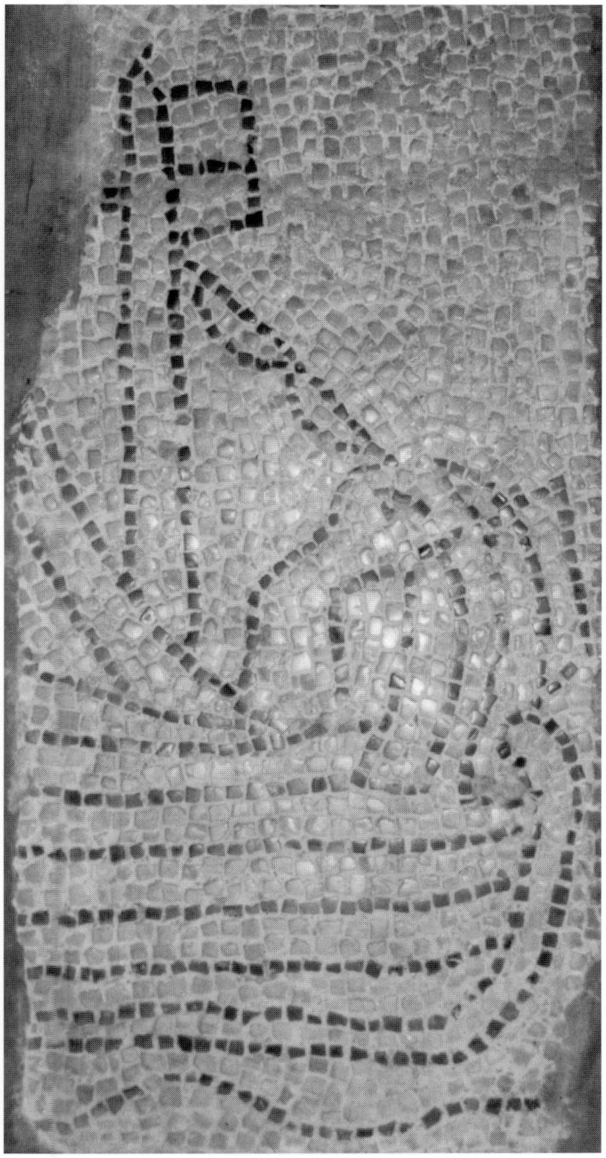

FIG. 21. Fragmentary floor mosaic (ca. 1213–35) detail of the stern of a ship of the Fourth Crusade, from San Giovanni Evangelista, Ravenna

can be seen. The depiction of only one quarter rudder is unusual; the ship would have had a pair. The port rudder may have been raised for mooring.

Figure 21, the last fragmentary mosaic, shows a ship's stern and the mizzen. The sail of this mast is furled, but the remaining bottom corner of the foresail indicates that the sail is open and lateen like figure 18. From either side of the inward curving sternpost, two large posts project upward and curve inboard. In this version and in figure 20, the two posts begin above deck level, and not at the keel. This may be the quarterdeck or sterncastle. Bonino's reconstruction is based on these versions, rather than the rendering in figure 18, where the posts originate at the keel and the artist has emphasized a larger, square structure perpendicular to the posts.

In his accomplished reconstruction of the ship type represented in these mosaics (fig. 22), Bonino calculates their dimensions to have been approximately 33.2 meters long, with a beam of 9.6 meters, and their rate of travel to have been approximately 5 knots. These proportions are inferred from "... the distance between the two decks, the height of the ports, the position of the foremast *(arbor di prora)* with respect to the structure of the prow, probably protruding cross beams . . . the shape of the raised quarter-deck

FIG. 22. Reconstruction of ships of the Fourth Crusade in 1202, based on the mosaics (figs. 18–21) of San Giovanni Evangelista, Ravenna. *Courtesy M. Bonino, 1978a: fig. 13*

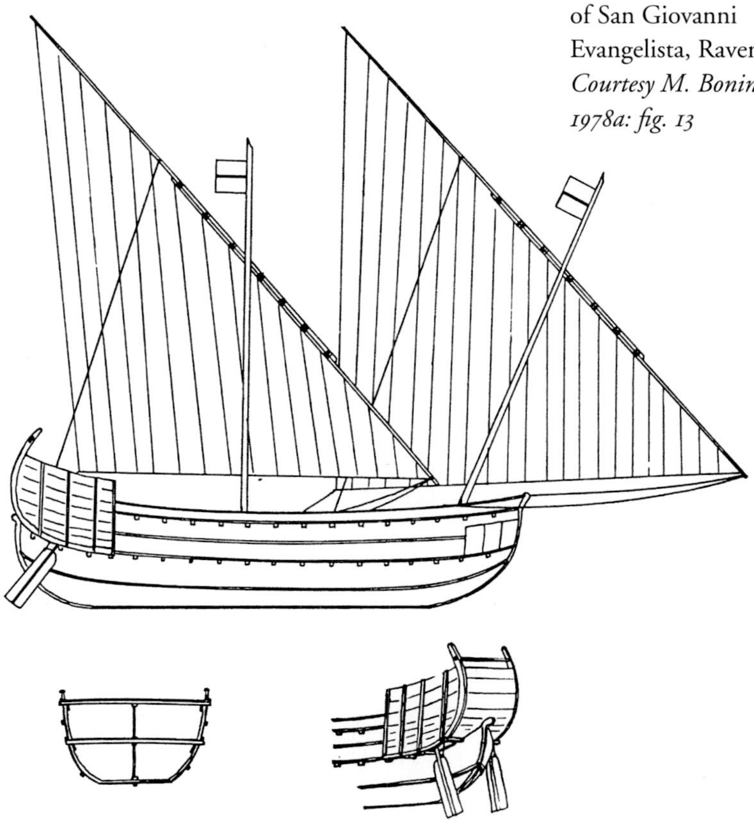

(paradisus) and of its ends, which rise above the railing-like wings *(ali),* in order to build a stand on which the yards could rest, and the yards (1978b: 9).

Although not visible in figure 18, this mosaic offers the only evidence for the rudders in these mosaics; only part of the quarter rudder was depicted on the far starboard side, thus concealing the mount. Bonino's reconstruction has the quarter rudders passing through the floor of the sterncastle; this is only corroborated by later images such as those in the Zibaldone manuscript (fig. 63), where quarter rudders passed through the floor of the sterncastle. The roughly contemporaneous San Marco ship mosaics (figs. 10–14) clearly depict two quarter rudders passing through circular ports in the hull.

Bonino has interpreted the vertical lines at the bows of figures 18 and 19 as a horse port (1978b: 12). Pryor has suggested that these vertical lines may portray an open deck area beneath the level of the *corridoria* and bulwarks, where vertical uprights seem to be bitts for anchor cables or posts for windlasses in other representations, such as a miniature from *Annales januenses,* and a bas relief on the leaning tower of Pisa (1984, no. 3: 277; fig. 1L and K). These lines at the bow may represent a small port, or a window, and the upright, inward-curving timbers aft are in fact structural timbers framing a horse port at the stern. On some ships, horse ports were nailed closed, sealed, and caulked on large round ship transports; the lower part of the door sat below the water line while under way.

Figure 23

Theme: *Translatio* of St. Mark: "Loading of the Relics in Alexandria, and Departure."

Location: Original thirteenth-century façade mosaic in *sopraporta* (the arched area above the door), above fourth portal, immediately to the right of the main entrance, San Marco, which has been completely replaced. Now known only through a painting by Gentile Bellini, *Procession in Piazza San Marco,* ca. 1496, in the Galleria dell'Accademia, Venice (cat. 567).

Date: ca. 1260–1270 (Demus, 1988: 187).

Type: Two-masted, lateen-rigged merchant ship (Type IIIb) [Part of same cycle, to right: Two-masted, lateen-rigged merchant ship (Type IIIb) and one lighter (Type Ia)].

A thirteenth-century *translatio* cycle that decorated four of the five portal niches of San Marco's façade has been completely obliterated by newer baroque compositions. The original cycle may have incorporated as many as eleven scenes of St. Mark's *translatio* story; seven are visible in the late fifteenth-century painting by Gentile Bellini, *Procession in Piazza San Marco* (Demus, 1984, vol. 1: 66 and vol. 2: pl. 348). Two of these seven niche illustrations contain maritime images that are included in the typology.

From Bellini's painting and a contemporaneous literary description of it by Stringa, we know which segments of the *translatio* story were represented in the original façade. The *titulus* of the first sopraporta as recorded by Stringa, read:

Tollitur ex archa furtim Marcus Patriarcha
Quem sporta ponunt carnes, caulesque reponunt;
Canzir dicentes Marcum vitant referentes:
In barcam corpus mittunt ex rupe deorsum
(Demus, 1984, vol. 1: 199),

meaning that the relics were put in a boat to be taken to the ship of the Venetian merchants. The second sopraporta's inscription continued:

De scapha sportam tollunt velisque reponunt;
Presbyter has turbas verens non vadit ad urnas.
Clam Monachus Marcum sequitur, quem thure recondunt.
Tellus adest, Nautae dic, velum ponite caute.
(Demus, 1984, vol. 1: 200),

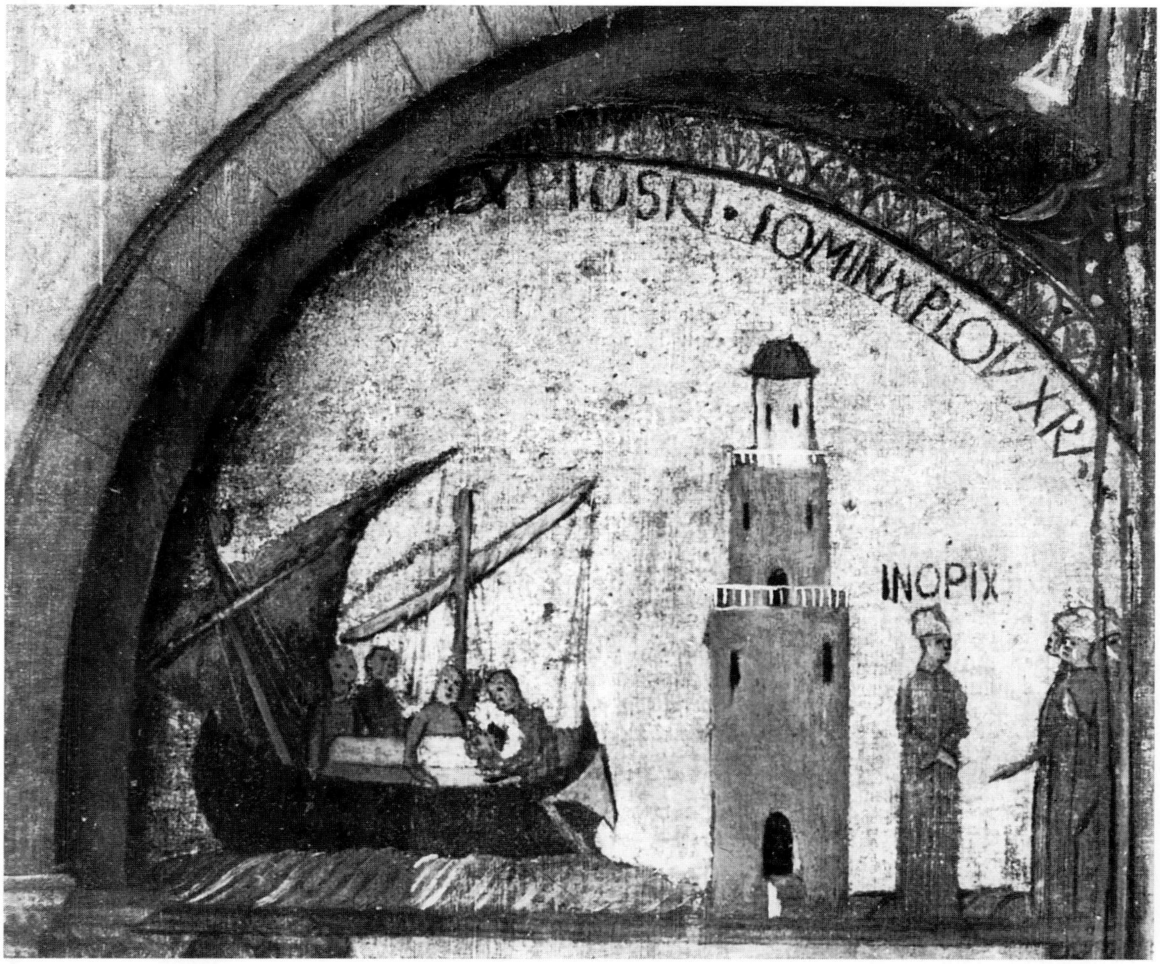

FIG. 23. *Translatio* of St. Mark: "Loading of the Relics in Alexandria, and Departure," detail of previous façade mosaic of San Marco (ca. 1260–70), now known through a painting by Gentile Bellini in the Galleria dell'Accademia. *Courtesy Böhm*

describing the subsequent scenes of the cycle, including the hiding of the relics in the sail.

Bellini's detail of the fourth portal (Demus, 1984, vol. 2: fig. 348) includes the two maritime scenes concerning the loading of the relics and the departure from Alexandria. In a foreshortened rendition on the right side of the barrel vault, a basket with the relics is being transferred from a lighter to the ship. Decorating the lunette (the flat area of the sopraporta) the ship, setting sail, is clearly represented (fig. 23). On shore, to the right of the *Pharos,* the lighthouse of Alexandria, stands the priest Theodorus, easily identified by his white hat. The subsequent scenes in the left side of the barrel vault are not visible in Bellini's painting, but Stringa's literary record indicates that these positions originally depicted the *praedestinatio,* the Saving of the Vessel from Shipwreck *(Tellus adest, naut[a]e dic, velum ponite caute),* and the final scene, the Arrival of the Ship in Venice (Demus, 1984, vol. 1: 199–201), as well.

The ship illustrated by figure 23 is a medium-sized, two-masted, lateen-rigged round ship. Because the portal is such a tiny part of Bellini's composition, the details of the ship are gross. Yet one can see the mizzen's sail still furled on its yard, while the foresail has been set, and the ship is departing from port with the saintly treasure. The foremast rakes forward, while the mizzen just aft of midships is nearly vertical. Lines defining the shrouds on each mast are just discernible. The tack and vang of the foresail are defined, as is the vang of the mizzen, passing through its block twice to gain advantage. The quarter rudder is obscure.

The general hull shape and the triangular-shaped feature at the stern are characteristic of a small round ship type nearly identical to that seen in figure 25, with a single mast.

Figure 24

Theme: *Vita* of St. Mark: "Dream Vision" *(praedestinatio).*

Titulus: CUM TRANSITUM FACERET PER MARE UBI NVNC POSITA EST ECCLESIA SCI MARCI ANGELVS EI NUNCIATUIT QVOD POST ALIQVANTUM TEMPVS A MORTE IPSIVS CORPVS EIVS HIC HONORIFICE LOCARETVR.

Translation: When they had made a crossing through the sea where now the church of St. Mark has been founded, an angel announced to him that a little time after his death, his body would be placed here honorifically.

Location: East half of vault, lower tier, Zen Chapel (fig. 1E), San Marco, Venice.

Date: ca. 1275 (Demus, 1988: 182).

Type: Lagoonal craft (Type Ib).

Zen Chapel contains the *praedestinatio* and "Voyage to Alexandria" from the *vita* of St. Mark

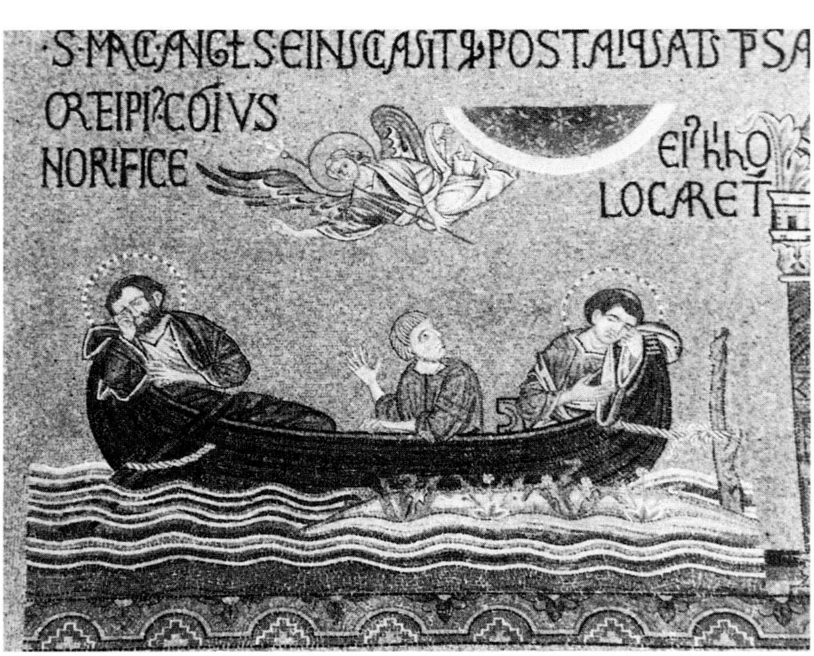

FIG. 24. *Vita* of St. Mark: "Dream Vision," east vault mosaic (ca. 1275), Zen Chapel, San Marco. *Permission to photograph courtesy the Procuratóre di San Marco*

(figs. 24 and 25). In figure 24, St. Mark and two companions rest in a small boat that is tied to a piling. This method of mooring is still practiced today in the Venetian lagoons and elsewhere. The figures, especially the central one and the angel above, are badly disfigured due to an early nineteenth-century restoration (Demus, 1984, vol. 1: 186), but the boat itself is believed to be original.

The small craft depicted is a simple boat with steering oars. The view illustrates the starboard oar affixed through a box mount, with the flared side of the blade aft. Just aft of the figure in the bow, an oarlock shows that a steering oar could also be mounted forward for facility in river and lagoonal navigation. The shape of this oarlock, called *forcole* in Italian, is characteristic of Venetian watercraft to this day. Here it is set with the oar slot aft. Strakes converge simply into the hull ends. They appear to be lashed securely together at the uppermost end of the bow.

Figure 25

Theme: *Vita* of St. Mark: "The Voyage to Alexandria."

Titulus: PERGIT NAVIGIO ALEXANDRIAM

Translation: The vessel sails to Alexandria.

Location: West half of vault, upper tier, Zen Chapel (fig. 1E), San Marco, Venice.

Date: ca. 1275 (Demus, 1988: 182).

Type: Single-masted, lateen-rigged merchant ship (Type IIIa).

St. Mark's head is much affected by an early nineteenth-century restoration, but otherwise the mosaic is believed to be authentic (Demus, 1984 vol. 1: 186).

Two mariners release the sail of the single mast as they approach the harbor of Alexandria with St. Mark. The middle figure mans the vang, while a mariner amidships works what appears to be the halyard. Robands join the sail at each seam to the yard. A third line, tied from the lower end of the yard, the *cares*, to the base of the mast, represents the tack. The tack disappears behind

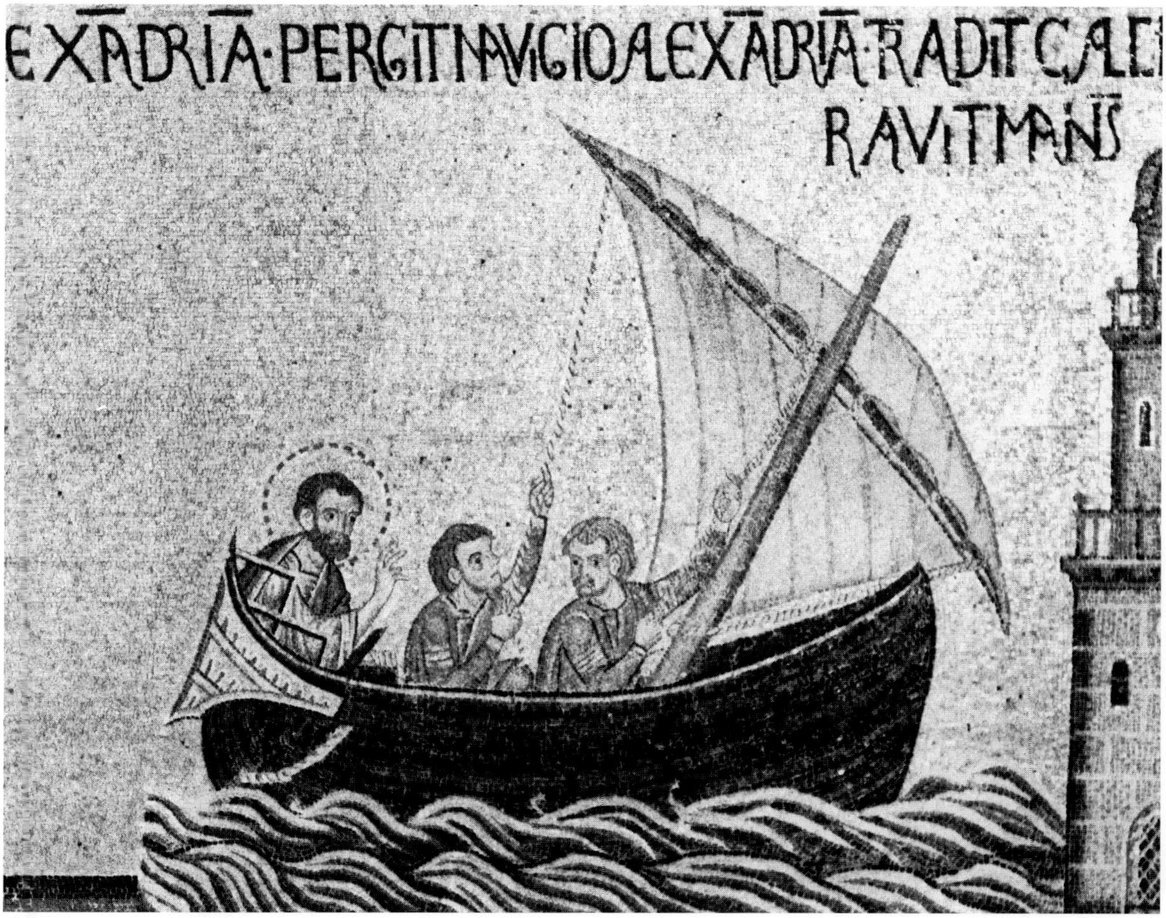

FIG. 25. *Vita* of St. Mark: "The Voyage to Alexandria," west vault mosaic (ca. 1275), Zen Chapel, San Marco. *Permission to photograph courtesy the Procuratóre di San Marco*

the point of the bow, as if it runs on the port side of the hull at the bow. This is possible, as the billowing of the sail shows the wind to be coming from astern. A questionable feature is the rake of the mast; thirty-two degrees off vertical is too extreme for any lateen rig. No shrouds or stays have been indicated.

Although details of the quarter rudder are difficult to make out, the loom is secured in a modified box mount and passes inboard to a decked area with railing at the stern. A rudder hoist is also evident, attached to the upper aft part of the rudder blade. All rigging and rudder lines are red and white ropes.

The hull's full, rounded shape and a feature defined at the stern are repeated in other medieval illustrations (e.g., figs. 23 and 40). The stern of the small vessel type when depicted in profile shows an almost triangular-shaped feature that seems to indicate something structural behind it, perhaps the rudder mount to secure the rudders through to the open, decked area astern, from whence a helmsman steered the vessel.

Figure 26

Theme: *Vita* of St. Isidore: "St. Isidore and Amenion Depart from Alexandria" (Kaftal, 1978: 434).

Titulus: HIC S YSIDORV RECE OIT DE ALEXA_DRIA.

Translation: Here St. Isidore departs from Alexandria.

Cartoon artist: Paolo Veneziano (Muraro, 1970: 27).

Location: South wall of San Isidore Chapel (fig. 1F), lower register, San Marco, Venice.

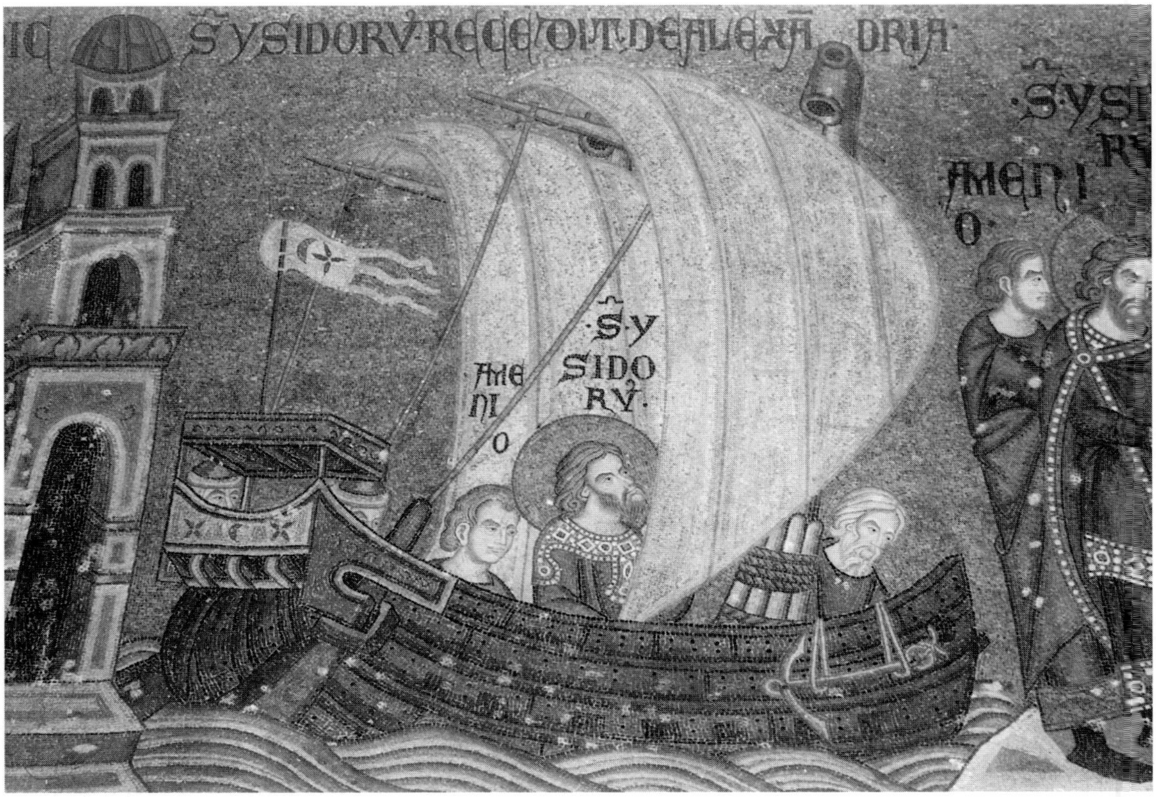

FIG. 26. *Vita* of St. Isidore: "St. Isidore and Amenion Depart from Alexandria," south wall mosaic (ca. 1348–55), San Isidore Chapel, San Marco. *Permission to photograph courtesy the Procuratóre di San Marco*

Date: ca. 1348–55 (Muraro, 1970: 26).
Type: Two-masted, lateen-rigged merchant ship (Type IIIb).

St. Isidore Chapel is decorated with scenes from the *vita* (fig. 26) and *translatio* (figs. 27 and 28) of St. Isidore. In figure 26, a remarkably detailed and realistic mosaic designed by Paolo Veneziano and executed by mosaic craftsmen, St. Isidore, Amenion, and several mariners set sail from port. Their vessel is a large, two-masted, round ship fitted with lateen sails. As usual, the foremast is the taller mast and rakes forward. Vertical lines on the sails delineate the vertical strips of cloth that made up the sail. Two barrel-like crow's nests are secured atop the masts, aft. A backstay and the starboard vang are apparent on the foremast; on the mizzen, the port vang is visible. No tackle is evident. Wedges, lashed tightly in place, gird the base of the mast at deck level. These wooden chocks were placed around the mast where it passed into the partner, to immobilize the mast and help set it to the desired inclination (as in figs. 28, 63, and 99). Robands are clearly depicted at the uppermost ends of both yards, wherever not obstructed by the billowing sails.

Details of the hull planking are exceptionally distinct for mosaic work, though not completely realistic. Strakes alternate between thicker and thinner planks; possibly some indicate wales, as seems to be the case of the one that projects forward at the bow. Planks are depicted as abutting each other squarely, rather than being diagonally scarfed together, with a regular paired nailing pattern evident on all the wide strakes. This suggests that the planking was fastened to pre-erected frames. On the sixth strake depicted from above, seven through-beams project through the hull. These through-beams support the main deck, on which the figures are standing. Strakes at the ample, rounded stern finish under a horizontal beam designating the tragent. Described in St. Louis's contracts for crusader transports, the *trigànte*, "a lateral beam set into the top of the sternpost to provide the base for the aftercastle" (Pryor, 1984, no. 3: 278), is well defined in this view of the ship's stern.

Parts of both asymmetrical quarter rudders can be seen at the stern. The loom of the more visible starboard rudder is shown passing through a square box mount and then inboard through the floor of the quarterdeck. A stock-less anchor, slung through two ropes attached inboard, hangs at the bow.

Figure 27

Theme: *Translatio* of St. Isidore: "Doge Michiel and the Priest Cerbanus Arrive in Chios" (Kaftal, 1978: 434).

Titulus: CHIO. ONIC MICHAEL DUX MCXIII–MCXXX.

Translation: Chios . . . Doge Michiel 1118–30.

Date: ca. 1348–55 (Muraro, 1970: 26).

Cartoon artist: Paolo Veneziano (Muraro, 1970: 27).

Location: North wall of San Isidore Chapel (fig. 1F), left of window, San Marco, Venice.

Types: Two oared galley warships (Type IIa).

In this scene of the arrival of Doge Michiel's fleet in Chios in 1125, two dromons (long, oared warships), are shown in the process of unloading. Gangplanks have been set from the stern to shore. Both warships have a small, raised quarterdeck. Two forked stanchions support a horizontal bar, which in turn provides the frame for a tented area over the quarterdeck, similar to the one pitched in galleys of two French manuscript

FIG. 27. *Translatio* of St. Isidore: "Doge Michiel and the Priest Cerbanus Arrive in Chios," north wall mosaic, left of window (ca. 1348–55), San Isidore Chapel, San Marco. *Permission to photograph courtesy the Procuratóre di San Marco*

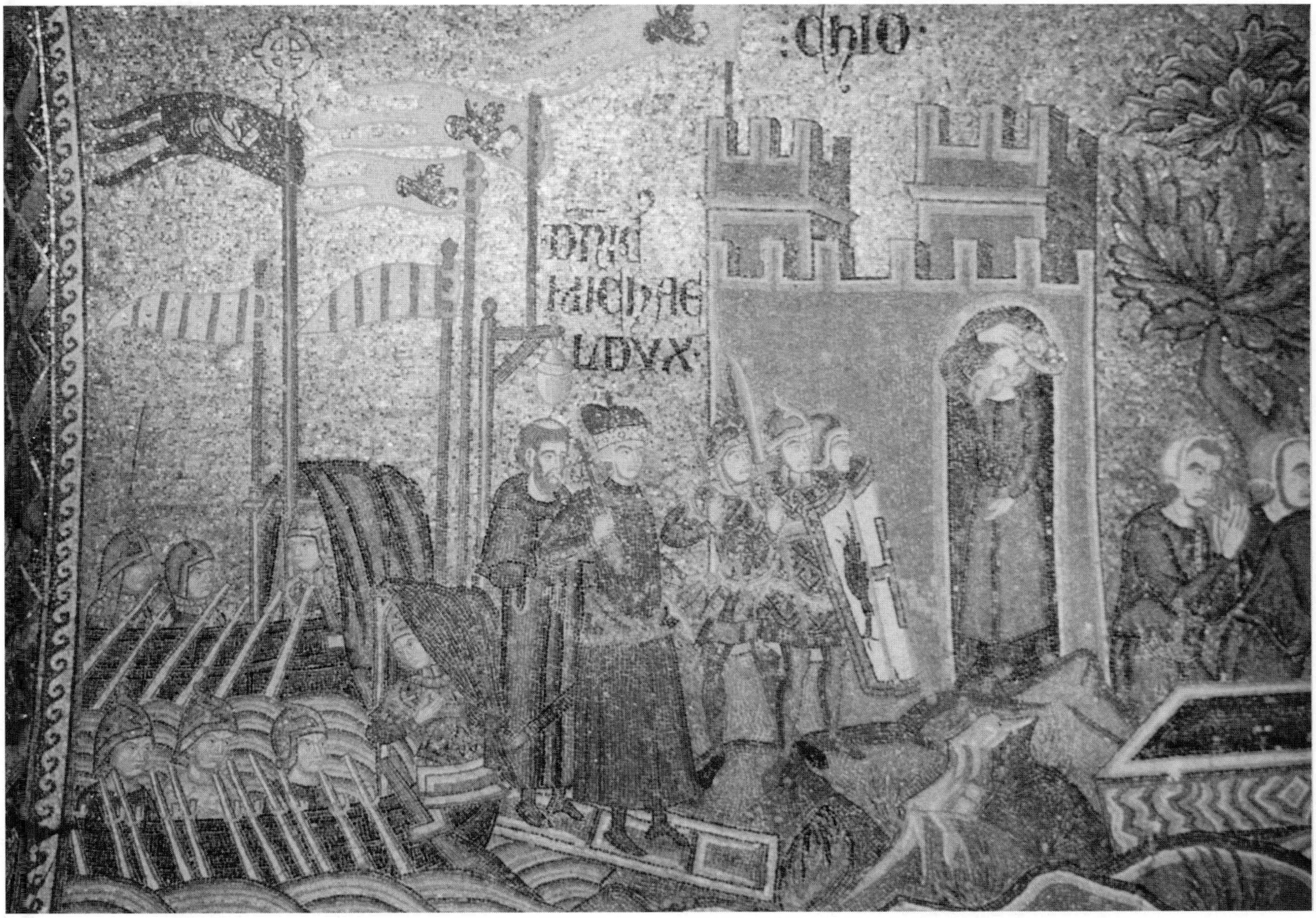

illuminations (Zorzi, 1988, fig. 64 and fig. 45), and comparable to ones seen on later Venetian galleys (figs. 65 and 69).

The grouping of oars on the foreground ship reveals that the oarsmen sat two to a bench, all on the same level, in an arrangement called *a zenzile* in Italian.

As seen in figure 26, a mosaic from the same cycle located across the chapel, strakes, along with their nailing pattern, are carefully delineated and finish at a tragent below the quarterdeck.

The asymmetrical port steering rudders on both ships are partly visible, mounted through a simple box mount like that seen in two of the sixth-century vessels in the Port of Classis mosaic, figure 8A and C.

FIG. 28. *Translatio* of St. Isidore: "The Saint's Body Is Embarked," north wall mosaic, right of window (ca. 1348–55), San Isidore Chapel, San Marco. *Permission to photograph courtesy the Procuratóre di San Marco*

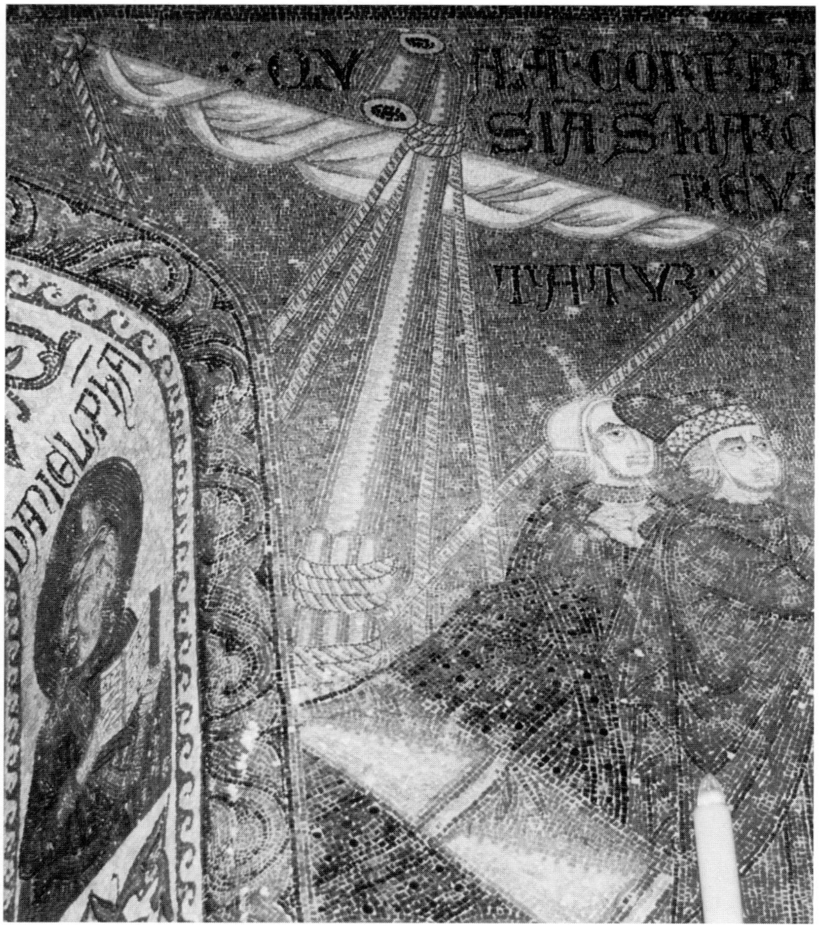

Figure 28

Theme: *Translatio* of St. Isidore: "The Saint's Body Is Embarked."

Titulus: QVALT COPRBMI ISIDORI DEI CVI SIA SMARCICVMASIMH BEVERENCIA APORTATVR (Kaftal, 1978: 437; Bettini, 1974: 27, pls. 94–97; Pallucchini, 1964: 78; Demus, 1984: 64).

Translation: Here the body of St. Isidore . . . in which St. Mark . . . carried.

Cartoon Artist: Paolo Veneziano (Muraro, 1970: 27).

Location: North wall of San Isidore Chapel (fig. 1F), right of window, San Marco, Venice.

Date: ca. 1348–55 (Muraro, 1970: 26).

Type: Two-masted, lateen-rigged merchant ship (Type IIIb).

This mosaic represents the retrieval of St. Isidore's relics from a church of Chios and implies the subsequent loading onto the Venetian merchant ship depicted. The vessel in figure 28 is very similar to the round ship in the St. Isidore *vita* sequence located across the chapel depicting the saint's departure from Alexandria (fig. 26), but only the bow area is depicted in this image. The foremast is so far forward, the vessel must have had a second mast close to midships like the vessel depicted for the same story in figure 26.

At the starboard bow, a gangplank has been set to shore. The sail is shown furled, and the yard securely stored high upon the foremast with vang and tack lashed somewhere near the base of the mast. Four shrouds, two to port and two to starboard, are evident. Three turns of rope at the head of the mast represent a rope parrel. Wedges around the foot of the mast, a crow's nest aft at its top, and a hawse hole in the visible starboard bow are clearly featured.

As in figure 26, every other strake is extra wide and affixed to the frames within by pairs of regularly spaced nails. The hull strakes run parallel into the stem, except for the uppermost two strakes. The sheer strake rises gradually toward the bow but then turns abruptly with a horizontal run to finish into the stem. The lower adjacent strake finishes into the sheer where it runs horizontally. This bow design appears repeatedly in round ships of all sizes in this sample (e.g., figs. 44, 48, 63, 93, 96, 97, 99, 116, 118, and 127), probably to enlarge the area available for a foredeck. A hawser is visible on the starboard bow.

Enamels

Figure 29
Title: Enamel panel from the *Pala d'Oro.*
Theme: *Translatio* of St. Mark.
Titulus: HIC DEFERTVR CORPVS SCI MARCI.
Translation: Here the body of St. Mark is transported.
Location: Altar (fig. 1G), San Marco, Venice.
Date: ca. 1105 (Kaftal, 1978: 670; Gauthier, 1972: 65).
Type: Single-masted, lateen-rigged merchant ship (Type IIIa).

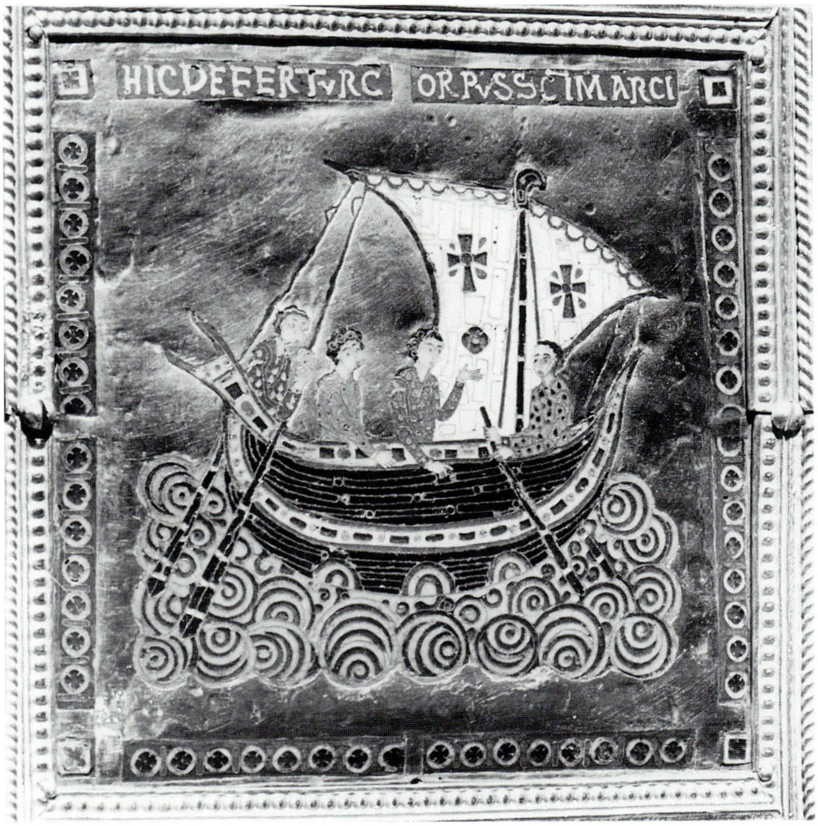

FIG. 29. *Translatio* of St. Mark, enamel panel of the altar screen *Pala d'Oro,* San Marco, ca. 1105. *Courtesy the Procuratóre di San Marco*

The *Pala d'Oro,* the famous gold, enamel, and bejeweled altar of San Marco, was commissioned shortly before 1105. The altarpiece was initially executed by Byzantine artists with Venetian collaboration. The present altar is believed to have been redesigned by Gianpaolo Boninsegna in about 1345 to display the many enamels later acquired as booty from the Church of Pantocrater monastery in Constantinople (Lorenzetti, 1982: 189).

The lower right *cloisonné* enamel on the screen is one of the original enamels (fig. 29). It depicts the Marcan *translatio,* with a scene of the ship at sail. Four flamboyantly dressed figures aboard include mariners at bow and stern and two men amidships, the Venetian merchants of the legend. The representation is stylized and not rendered in true perspective, partially due to artistic conventions and in part due to the limitations of the medium. The hull is unrealistically walnut shaped, and the three figures to the left have been placed in an implausible position: they appear to be located as being outboard of the ship's port side.

Details do reveal a degree of nautical realism. The single lateen-rigged mast is set far forward, just slightly off vertical. The sail, decorated with two green crosses, is attached to its yard with stylized robands. Other rigging details have also been generalized. The mariner to the far left works the starboard vang. Both port and starboard vang are rigged through tackles that have been indicated simply as a curved line near the point of attachment to the yard. Tack lines and at least one tackle are evident as well. Two shrouds run beneath the yard and masthead. For sailors to tack a lateen-rigged ship, however, the shrouds needed to be fixed above the parrel. The halyard has not been represented but would have passed through the clearly depicted hook-like *calcet* at the masthead, identical to *calcets* depicted in two different Byzantine manuscript illuminations (fig. 35, and a tenth-century one by a Syrian artist illustrating the oldest known version of Homer's Iliad [Zorzi, 1988: Plate 10]). The hook shape would have kept the halyard as far forward of the mast as possible, to allow the unfettered movement of the yard necessary for tacking. This perfection of the mast head had occurred by the ninth century, but it continued to evolve. By the fourteenth century, there was only a simple "groove at the top of the mast where the rope for the halyard ran" (Bonino, 1978a: 49).

Only three small waves are indicated against the hull itself, so the overall shape of a rockered keel is revealed. The broken band shown running along the middle of the side of the hull from stem to stern might be a purely decorative element, but it may represent a main wale or possibly through-beams, which would indicate a lower deck level. Strakes are shown running parallel to the keel partway up the hull. Above the main wale, the after ends of the planking strakes curve upward into the uppermost strake, while at the bow they seem to run into the main wale. It is difficult to make out the orientation of the strakes near the bow and stern below the main wale, but they probably converge into the posts. A few overly large nails are represented, but are so sparsely and sporadically placed that they are obviously intended to indicate only the joining technique and not an actual nailing pattern.

The after ends of the uppermost strakes to port and to starboard sweep upward and beyond the stern. These two tine-like timbers that flare out at their after ends may seem merely decorative and of no significance. This is unlikely, however, in view of numerous other ship representations, where similar upright features appear to be the continuations and terminus of significant structural timbers projecting beyond the stern both on the port and starboard sides. In this case, they continue either the uppermost wale or the sheer strake, while in other illustrations they originate lower in the hull, either continuing a main wale or flanking the keel and extending upward from it. The slight twisted perspective at the stern allows part of the inside of the stern to be seen. Parallel lines perpendicular to the two projecting timbers seem to represent planking filling in the area between them. The configurations of the sterns in figures 12, 18, 20, 21, and 45 corroborate what is seen here: two upright posts far aft seem to indicate a wide and flat-ended transom stern, and the two projections are filled in with cross-planking.

This ship employs two elliptically shaped steering oars at the stern, plus two slender sweeps toward the bow to help it tack (Mott, 1997: 51). It is not clear how these oars are mounted.

Wood Inlays

Figure 30
Theme: Venetian Molo.
Artists: Antonio and Paolo Mola di Màntova.
Location: Sacristy, San Marco (fig. 1K), Venice.
Date: 1498–1502.
Types: Mixed-rigged merchant ship (Type IIIf).
[Nearby: lagoonal craft (Type Ib) and riverine cargo vessel (Type Id).]

Two wood inlays in the sacristy of San Marco illustrate Venetian maritime scenes; one contains two small lagoonal boats (Type Ib and Id) in the background without much detail. Figure 30, a large, mixed-rigged vessel moored along the Molo is defined more clearly.

Sails are furled, leaving open to view all masts, including a massive one amidships with a crow's nest at its top, a smaller one aft, a medium-sized one toward the bow. The main yard carried a square sail as revealed by the central placement of the crow's nest and the lifts supporting the

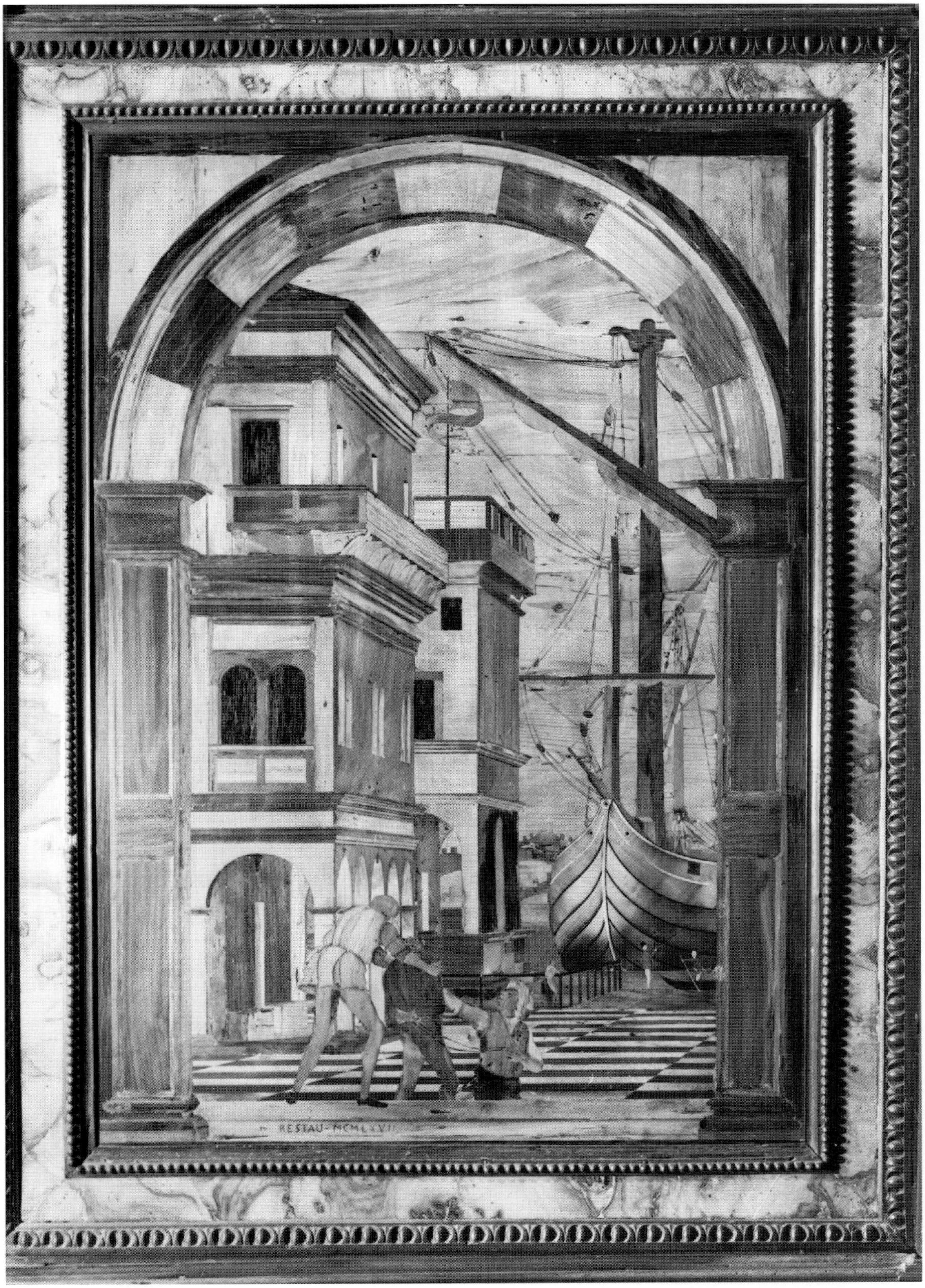

FIG. 30. Wood inlay by Antonio and Paolo Mola di Màntova depicting a ship at the Molo, Venice (ca. 1500), Sacristy of San Marco. *Courtesy the Procuratóre di San Marco*

main yard. The foremast has its yard fixed perpendicular to itself and braces run to the head of the mast; it appears to be square-rigged, while the mizzen is lateen. A bowsprit projects off the bow.

Strakes converge in the stem to form a pronounced bow similar to the large merchant ships in figure 58.

Manuscript Illuminations

Figure 31
Theme: Siege techniques.
Artists: Venetian school.
Location: Biblioteca Apostolica Vaticana, Rome.
Date: eleventh century (Thubrin, 1980: 33).
Type: Four war transports (Type IIb).

This illumination, from an eleventh-century Venetian manuscript in the Vatican Library, shows four warships besieging city walls (fig. 31). A fifteenth-century Marciana Library codex, *Miscellanea Varia* [Biblioteca Marciana Cod. Lat. Z. 339 (=1550) cc. 43^{v}–44^{r} (Zorzi, 1988: 132)], contains three works concerning warfare, war machinery, and siege techniques translated in Venice from Greek into Latin. The first of these, *De re militari et instrumentis bellicis,* discusses and illustrates techniques of siege and includes an illumination from slightly above six warships that are virtually identical to the four illustrated in figure 31. These two Byzantine illuminations differ only in minor details, such as the placement of the human figures. The Marciana manuscript illumination appears to be a copy of the earlier Vatican one.

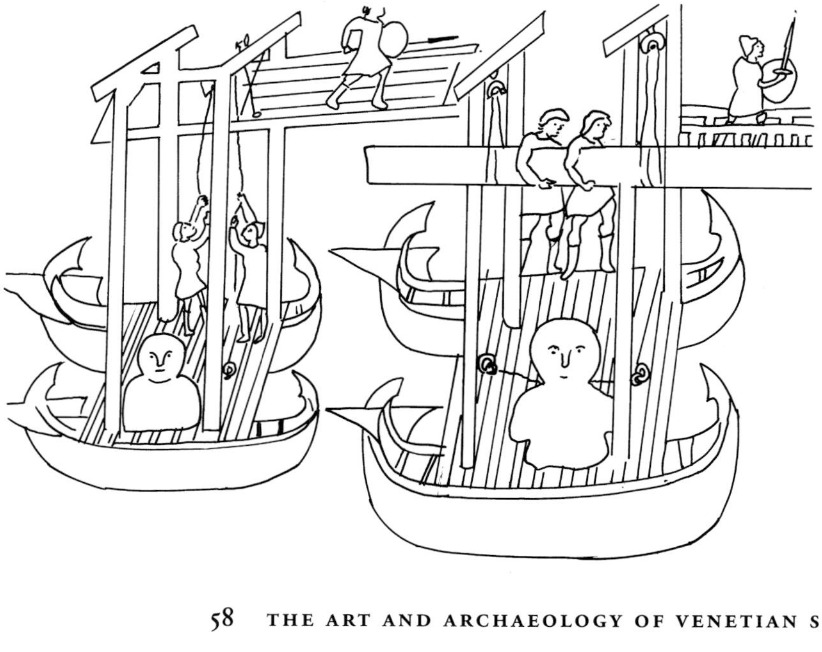

FIG. 31. Siege scene, from an eleventh-century Venetian manuscript in the Biblioteca Apostolica Vaticana, Rome. *After Thubrin, 1980: 33*

In figure 31, two pairs of warships are temporarily joined by planking laid down over the bulwarks so that the two vessels together might support makeshift siege platforms, or flying bridges, as Villehardouin described was done during the Fourth Crusade in the siege against Constantinople (Villehardouin, book 52: sec. 240, translated by Marzials, 1965: 60–61): ". . . the ships that carried the scaling ladders should be bound together, two and two, so that two ships should be in case to attack one tower; for they had perceived that day how only one ship had attacked each tower, and that this had been too heavy a task for the ship, seeing that those in the tower were more in number than those on the ladder." The Venetians' flying bridges were "maneuvered onto the tops of the walls, forming a passage by which as many as three soldiers abreast could advance from the ship to the ramparts" (Queller, 1977: 101). The siege platforms had to be completely reconstructed for each engagement (Dolley, 1949: 52), because they utilized parts of the ship necessary for its navigation: the yards and masts.

In this illumination, the two uprights on each ship represent its two masts, the four masts on each pair of joined vessels now supporting a siege platform or battering ram. Both masts are shown as being set completely vertically, although, if lateen-rigged, the foremast at least would have inclined forward. The vessels were most likely two-masted lateeners; the vertical orientation of the foremast may be the artist's error or simplification in depicting the flat platform.

Each vessel is simply depicted as a double-ended hull with a minimal amount of detail. The keel seems to be slightly rockered. Both posts curve inward, flaring like the stem of figure 10 and the stem and stern of vessels in twelfth-century mosaics of Monreale Cathedral in Sicily (Moll, 1929: figs. 123–25).

No steering device has been illustrated, but a three-quarter view of the stern conspicuously illustrates a pair of unique wing-shaped features at the stern of each of the four ships. The after edge of the pair of triangular wings is set perpendicular to the sternpost where the latter begins to curve back toward the bow, and either wing has its lower juncture with the side of the vessel at the level of the sheer strake. In depictions of similar triangular features elsewhere in this catalog, they appear to be in other positions. If the triangular wings were able to fold up, they would appear as in figure 39, while if they folded down against the outside of the hull, they would then resemble those of various other depictions (e.g., figs. 23, 25, 26, and 40). In fact, the Marciana codex (Zorzi, 1988: pl. 72) illustrates both positions; so the wings must be a mobile fixture, perhaps related in some way to a "triangular" rudder mount system.

The function of this stern configuration, however, remains uncertain. Perhaps the enigmatic feature illustrates the puzzling term *ali,* which has been translated as "wings;" it is certainly wing-like here. The stern of these double-ended vessels, however, is distinctly different in shape from transom sterns framed with two upright timbers, which offer another interpretation for the term *ali.*

Figure 32

Manuscript title: *Oppianus (pseudo) Cynegetica.*
Artist/author: Oppianus, from Apamea, Syria.
Theme: Fishing scene.
Location: Biblioteca Nazionale Marciana, Venice, Cod. Marc. Gr. Z. 479 (=881), folio 3r.

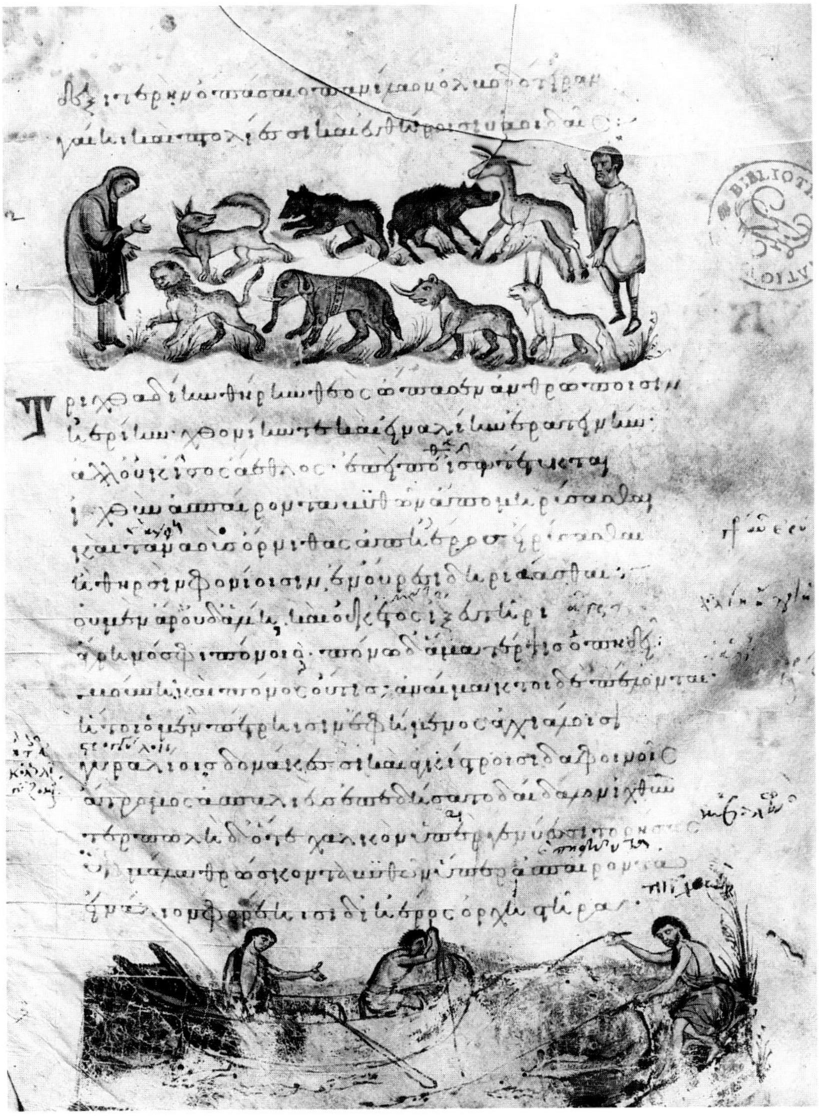

FIG. 32. An eleventh-century Syrian manuscript illumination of a fishing scene, from *Cynegetica. Courtesy the Biblioteca Nazionale Marciana*

Date: Mid-eleventh century (Zorzi, 1988: 64).
Type: Figure 32: Fishing boat (Type Ib).
Figure 33: Riverine cargo vessel (Type Id).
Figure 34: Two oared galley warships (Type IIa).
[Other folios: Two fishing boats (Type Ib).]

This Byzantine treatise, manufactured by Oppianus in Apamea, Syria, concerns fishing, mythological, hunting, and naval sea battles. The manuscript is a product of the school of Renaissance Macedonian bookmaking and copies earlier poems on hunting, fishing, mythological

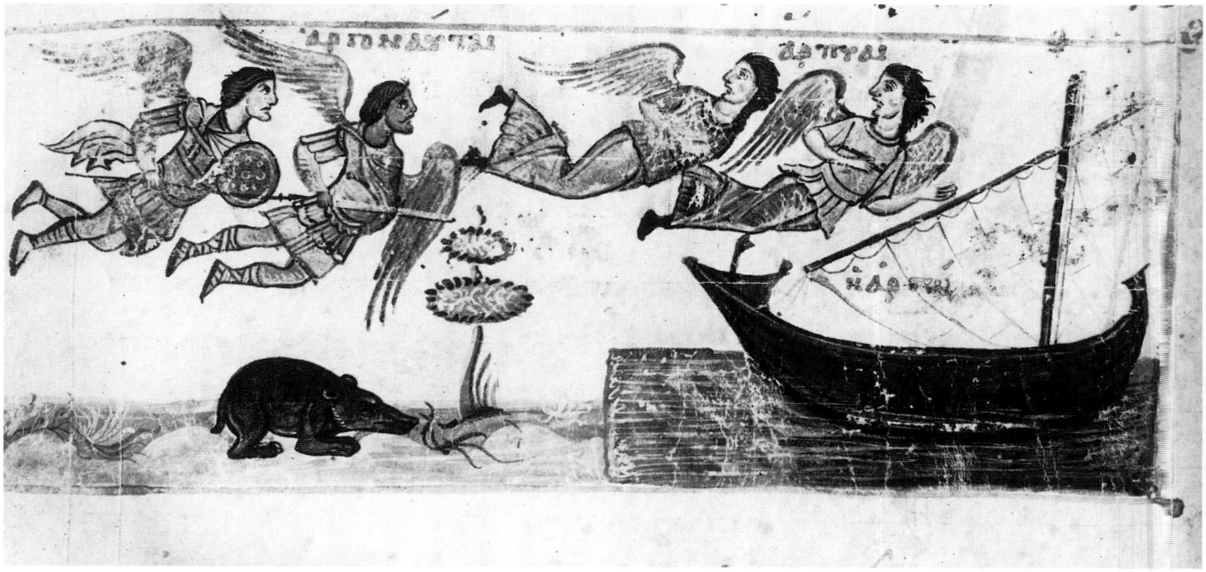

Fig. 33. An eleventh-century Syrian manuscript illumination of Zetes and Calais pursuing the harpies, from *Cynegetica. Courtesy the Biblioteca Nazionale Marciana*

scenes, and naval sea battles (Bettini, 1974: 39); Byzantine artists worked in Venice as well, keeping to their stylistic traditions, which are reflected in the early Venetian mosaics. Because the manuscript originates from Syria, these vessels are excluded from the typology developed in chapter 3.

Five manuscript illuminations are of watercraft. Figures 32–34 are illustrated here to exemplify the mid-Byzantine style. The other maritime folios of this manuscript not reproduced here depict two simple small double-ended fishing boats (Type Ib) in a typical Byzantine style (Bettini, 1974: 39 and Weitzmann, 1951: 164). Folio 59^{r}, shows three fishermen night fishing. A bulbous light (labeled in Greek, φανόc) affixed to the bow of the vessel was used to attract fish. Another represents the child Dionysus brought to Euboea.

Figure 32 depicts two men aboard a small boat near a man ashore, who is line fishing. The boat's details are minimal. It appears to be relatively flat bottomed, with an inward-curving, pointed bow like figure 16. The most significant feature is the depiction from the inside of the timbers that form a flat transom stern. The visible paddle for rowing is elliptical in shape. The man at the bow seems to be punting.

Figure 33

Theme: Mythological scene: "Zetes and Calais Pursue the Harpies" (Weitzmann, 1951: pl. 41).

Titulus: αργοναυται αρπναι.

Translation: Argonauts and the Harpies.

Location: Biblioteca Nazionale Marciana, Venice, Cod. Marc. Gr. Z. 479 (=881), folio 39^{v}.

Type: Riverine cargo vessel (Type Id).

Another illustration in *Oppianus Cynegetica* depicts the mythological scene of Zetes and Calais pursuing the harpies (fig. 33). The boat is a typical Byzantine-style portrayal of a small lateen-rigged vessel, but because it was not actually produced in Venice, it is not included in the typology. The stern area is viewed slightly from above. The single vertical mast is set far forward in the bow, but too close to vertical for a lateen rig, although the sail shape is clearly triangular. Lines defining the sail seem to indicate the seams joining the rectangular sections of the sail cloth. The yard is tilted downward in the wrong direction. Three lines from the *cares* represent bowlines and the *mulgaranus,* which should have been secured in the bow and not the stern. These errors may be due to artistic license: perhaps the

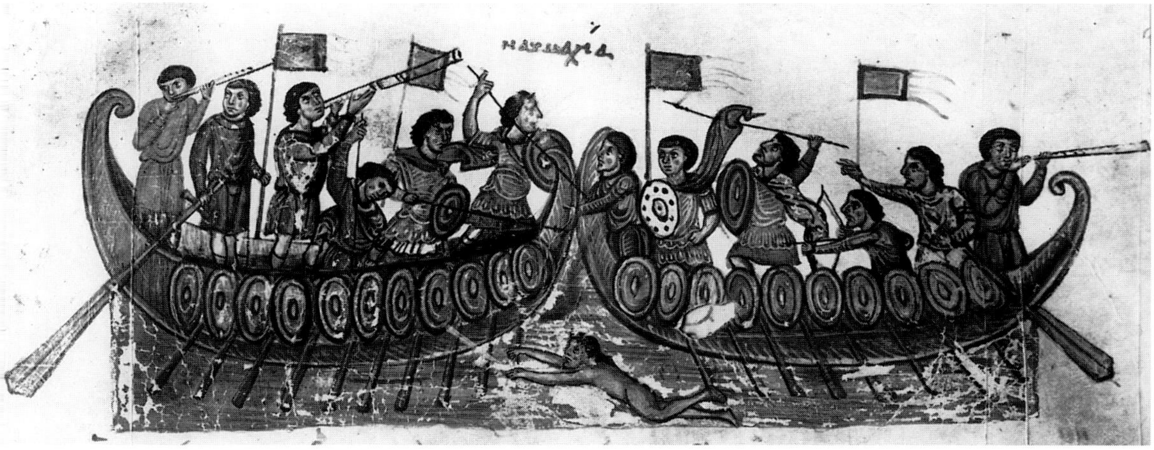

FIG. 34. A mock naval battle from the eleventh-century Syrian manuscript, *Cynegetica. Courtesy the Biblioteca Nazionale Marciana*

artist was creating a central space in the image for the harpies. No shrouds or stays have been represented. A halyard is visible on the forward side of the mast.

The keel seems slightly rockered. The flaring stem curves inboard to finish, similar to that in figures 10 and 31. The sternpost rises gradually, flanked by two continuations of longitudinal timbers to port and starboard, forming perhaps the most interesting feature of the image: a transom stern in which each framing timber is finished off with a decorative finial similar to figure 42. Lines defining straking are only vaguely discernible.

Figure 34
Theme: Mock naval battle.
Titulus: Ναυμαχια.
Translation: Naval battle.
Location: Biblioteca Nazionale Marciana, Venice, Cod. Marc. Gr. Z. 479 (=881), folio 23^r.
Type: Two oared galley warships (Type IIa).

Maritime images of the *Oppianus Cynegetica* manuscript are not included in the typology. Byzantine stylization has resulted in few worthwhile details, though this illumination does exemplify Byzantine warship iconography, a simple hull with voluted ends, identical to those seen in the background vessels in a siege scene (Zorzi, 1988: pl. 72).

In figure 34, the two galleys engaged in battle have eight and ten oars per side. Shields hung along the side of the hull offered some protection to the rowers. A large, symmetrical steering oar is present on the visible sides of both vessels. The bow and sterns are inward curving at their ends, with the stern slightly higher than the bow.

Figure 35
Title: Lectionary.
Theme: "The Calling of James and John."
Location: Church of Giorgio dei Greci, Venice, lectionary, folio 63ro.
Date: eleventh century.
Types: Figure 35: Riverine cargo vessel (Type Id).
Figure 36: Fishing boat (Type Ib).

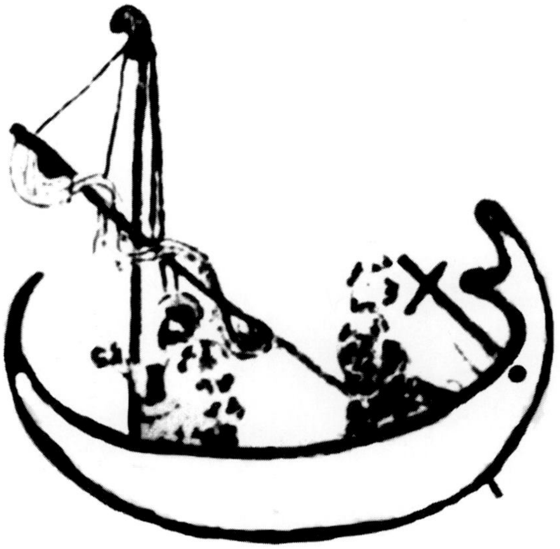

FIG. 35. "The Calling of James and John," from an eleventh-century lectionary of the Church of Giorgio dei Greci.

A lectionary made in Venice by Byzantine artists illustrates two small boats, figures 35 and 36. The lateen-rigged boat in figure 35, particularly its tine-like or prong-shaped stern, is the typically stylized small boat of Byzantine art, and details are predictably minimal. The hull is essentially double ended, with a rounded hull and inward-curving timbers. Its most interesting feature is the accurately depicted hook-shaped calcet at the mast head, complete with running rigging, identical to that seen in figure 29.

Figure 36
Theme: "Christ Dismissing the Multitudes."
Location: Church of Giorgio dei Greci, Venice, lectionary, folio 98ro.
Type: Fishing boat (Type Ib).

Like figures 33 and 35, this illumination exemplifies the formalized Byzantine conventional rendition of a small craft. The hull appears rounded, and the stem and sternposts both curve inboard sharply. Here the stem and stern both finish in simplified tine-like prongs. The sheer strake is extra wide and projects beyond the sternpost. The keel is also emphasized as an extra thick timber running along the hull bottom and continuing into the posts.

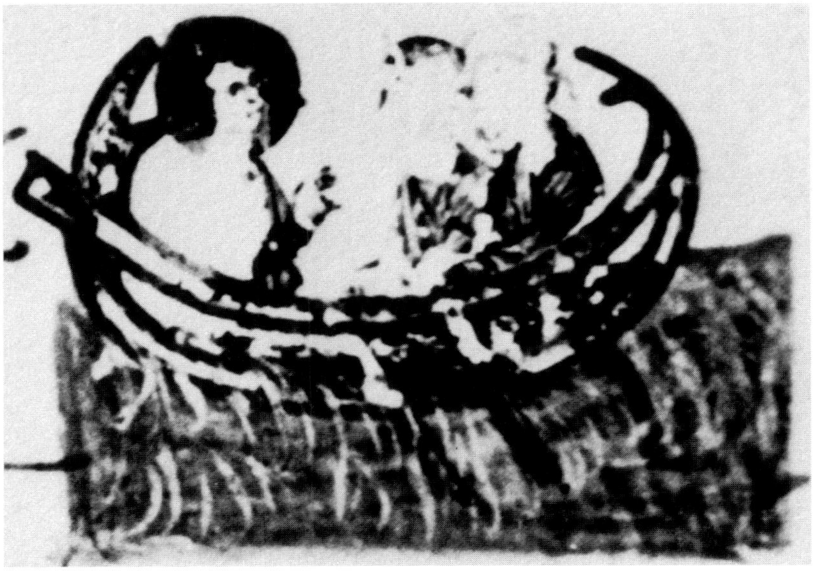

FIG. 36. "Christ Dismissing the Multitudes," from an eleventh-century lectionary of the Church of Giorgio dei Greci.

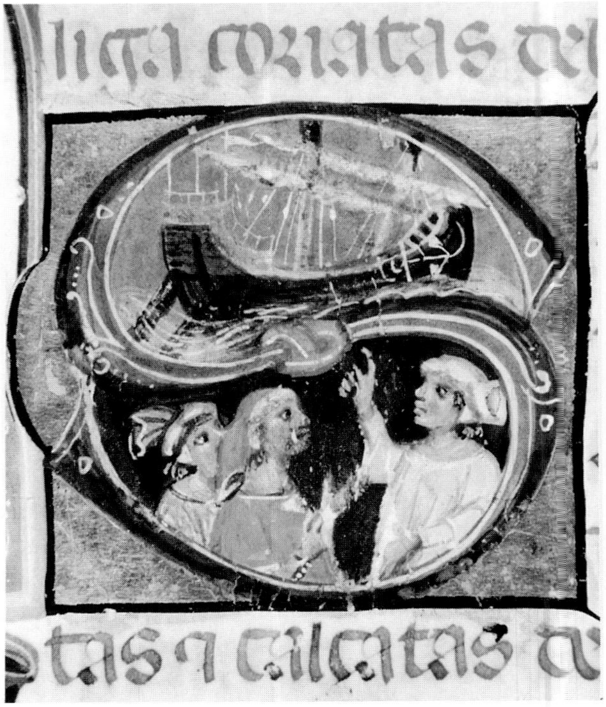

FIG. 37. Round ship decorating an illuminated initial "S," from a copy of the Venetian Maritime Code of 1255 in the Biblioteca Querini Stampalia. *Courtesy Fondazione Querini Stampalia, Venice*

Figure 37
Manuscript title: *Capitolarium nauticum pro navis.*
Theme: Venetian maritime codes.
Location: Biblioteca Querini-Stampalia, Venice, Cl. IV, Cod. I (Mss=147), folio 84^{r}.
Date: 1255.
Type: Two-masted, lateen-rigged merchant ship (Type IIIb).

This merchant ship illustration decorates the top half of an illuminated initial "S" in a copy of Zeno's *Statuta navium* of 1255, maritime codes that applied to two-decked round ships ranging in carrying capacity from 200 to 1000 *milliariis* (between 94 and 470 dead weight tons).[6] The round ship in figure 37 is viewed from the starboard side, slightly from the stern, while the bow area is seen slightly from above in twisted perspective. The mizzen is set slightly aft of midships, while a foremast inclines forward in the bow. Both lateen sails are furled on their yards and remain hung upon their respective masts. Each mast supports a large crow's nest aft at its top, as seen in the twelfth-century mosaics, figures 10–14. Shrouds, stays, vang, and some pulleys for the running rigging are realistically placed.

The ship's bow area is shown to be full and rounded. The twisted perspective at the bow reveals regularly spaced inner framing. The stern is slightly higher and clearly flat ended, a transom stern, with two substantial timbers. These structural timbers, perhaps continuations of water line wales, form the outer sides of the transom stern. They originate low in the hull and pass perpendicularly to a heavy horizontal beam—the tragent *(trigànte)*—approximately at the poop's deck level. Below the tragent, hull planking runs vertically and parallel to the two timbers, while above, horizontal fill planking is delimited.

A rope parapet runs along the perimeter of the quarterdeck area. Three vertical poles of differing heights (perhaps to fit within the initial?) project from the poop. The one to starboard displays a pennant.

The looms of the two unbalanced quarter rudders project through holes to the quarterdeck near the after ends of the sides of the vessel. A large-fluked anchor is catted up at the bow, crown forward, in reverse from the usual position depicted.

Figure 38

Manuscript title: *Secreta fidelium crucis.*
Theme: Handbook for crusaders.
Artist/Author: Marino Sanudo (Torsellus), of Venice.
Location: Bodleian Library, Oxford University, MS.Tanner 190, folio 22^{r}.
Date: 1321–24 (Pächt and Alexander, 1970: 118).
Types: Figure 38: Oared galley warship (Type IIa).
Figure 39: Oared galley warship (Type IIa).
Figure 40: War transport (Type IIb).

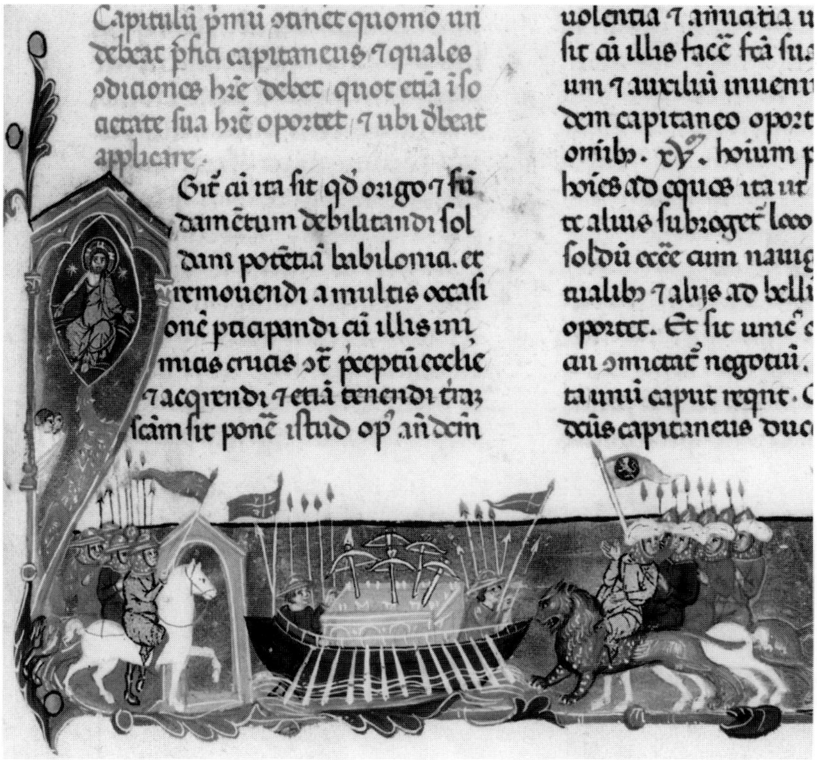

FIG. 38. Departure of an oared warship, from the Venetian manuscript *Secreta fidelium crucis,* ca. 1321–24. *Courtesy the Bodleian Library*

Secreta fidelium crucis, a handbook for aspiring crusaders, has several interesting ships illustrated, figures 38–40. Figure 38, a small galley, is propelled with thirteen oars per side, all arranged on the same level. Its flat-ended transom stern differs dramatically in shape from the pointed bow. Above the sheer strake, an outrigger runs the length of the vessel. Five crossbows are stored, ready for use, pointed upward from a large yellow structure amidships, possibly representing a fighting deck, while pikes or bolts are stowed, also pointed upward, in the bow and stern areas, as seen in figures 39 and 153. Pennants fly at both bow and stern. A helmsman controls the loom of the visible starboard rudder, which passes through a *luctatorium* in the side of the hull.

Figure 39

Location: Bodleian Library, Oxford University, MS.Tanner 190, folio 20^{v}.
Type: Oared galley warship (Type IIa).

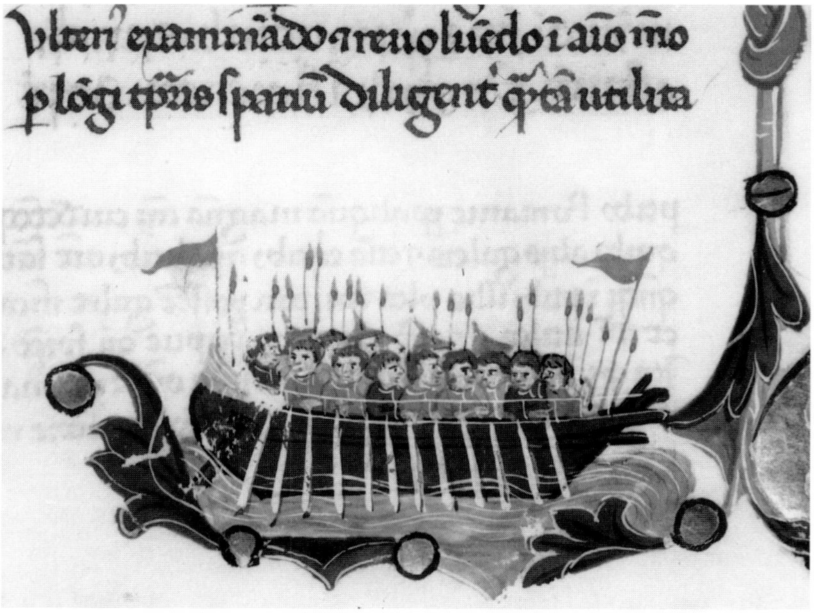

FIG. 39. Oared warship, from the Venetian manuscript *Secreta fidelium crucis,* ca. 1321–24. *Courtesy the Bodleian Library*

Figure 39, a small galley depicted in *Secreta fidelium crucis,* is rowed with 12 oars per side in one level. It is similar to that of figure 38 in terms of function, although the two vessels differ in shape. The stern of this vessel is more rounded and slightly fuller than that of figure 38, while the stem rises more steeply at the bow and the main wale and an uppermost wale or the sheer strake continue horizontally beyond the stem to form a *sperone* projecting from the bow. Above the stem and apron are visible.

The helmsman controls the visible starboard quarter rudder from the small quarterdeck. The gilded triangular area at the stern is reminiscent of figures 23 and 25, as well as figure 31, except that here it is a slightly different shape, more triangular by excluding two tip extensions at the bottom two corners. This may be part of a rudder mount system. Pikes or bolts are stored vertically along the whole length of the vessel and pennants fly at both bow and stern.

Figure 40
Location: Bodleian Library, Oxford University, MS.Tanner 190, folio 17v.
Type: War transport (Type IIb).

In figure 40, also from *Secreta fidelium crucis,* Sanudo emphasizes the imminence of departure by illustrating the two-masted, lateen-rigged transport ship impractically being loaded with both her sails unfurled. Both masts incline forward and have a crow's nest set aft at their tops. Vang and tack are visible only on the foremast; the vang is being used to maneuver a barrel of provisions on board. The vessel is comparable in shape to the ships of mosaics in Zen Chapel and on the original façade mosaic of San Marco (figs. 23 and 25). Note the general shape of the hull and the gilded triangular-shaped area at the stern, which may be part of the rudder mount system.

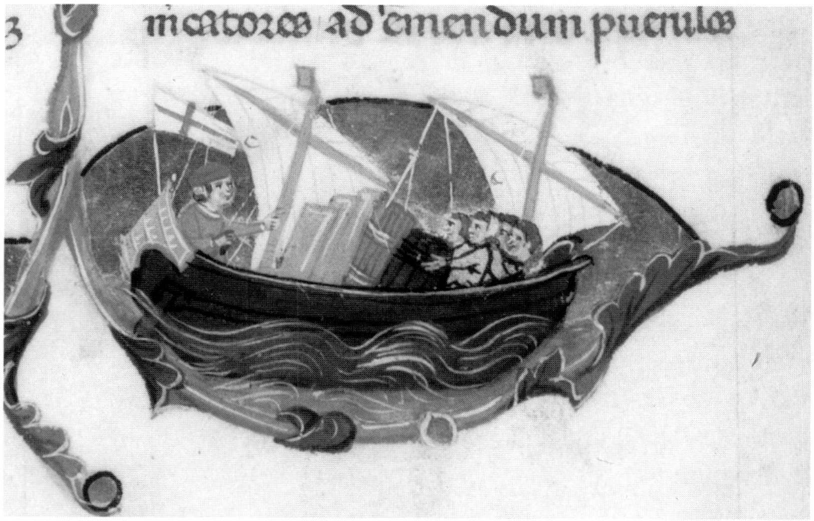

FIG. 40. Transport ship loading, with sails raised, from the Venetian manuscript *Secreta fidelium crucis,* ca. 1321–24. *Courtesy the Bodleian Library*

Figure 41
Manuscript title: *Romans de Troie.*
Theme: Story of the Trojan War: ship entering port.
Artist: Napoletan.
Author: Benoit de Saint-More (French).
Location: Biblioteca Nazionale Marciana, Venice, Cod. Marc. Fr. Z. 17 (=230), folio 21v.
Date: 1330–40.

Types: Figure 41: Single-masted, lateen-rigged merchant ship (Type IIIa).
Figure 42: Two-masted, lateen-rigged merchant ship (Type IIIb).
Figure 43: Eight single-masted, lateen-rigged merchant ships (Type IIIa).
Figure 44: Two single-masted, lateen-rigged merchant ships (Type IIIa).
Figure 45: War transport (Type IIb).

The French manuscript, *Roman de Troie,* bequeathed to the Marciana Library in the seventeenth century, contains five interesting ship illuminations, figures 41–45, illustrated by Italian artists from Naples. These cannot contribute then, to the Venetian typology, although they are included here because they are informative for Mediterranean shipbuilding in general. Figure 41, a small, single-masted, lateen-rigged round ship carries five disproportionately large men, at least three of whom are working mariners. One works the quarter rudder at the helm, while others handle the tack rigging at the bow. The single mast is set unrealistically far forward, but appropriately inclined for the lateen rig. It is supported by six visible shrouds and stays. A cylindrical crow's nest sets aft of the mast head. Robands are simple ties of rope. Running rigging and their respective block tackle are nicely represented. The vang is secured behind the helmsman at the stern. The sheet is visible near the base of the mast.

As for the hull, its shape is full at both bow and stern, although the stern is probably flat ended, with a small rectangular decked area, while the bow is pointed. Several ends of beams supporting the main deck are indicated in the visible starboard side. The depiction of the uppermost planking provides an excellent illustration of a removable sheer strake on merchant round ships, as was noticed in figure 14 and on the Contarina ship (ca. 1300), where a section of the sheer strake slid aside in a specially cut groove. One function of this must have been to lower the side of the vessel to facilitate disembarkation or loading.

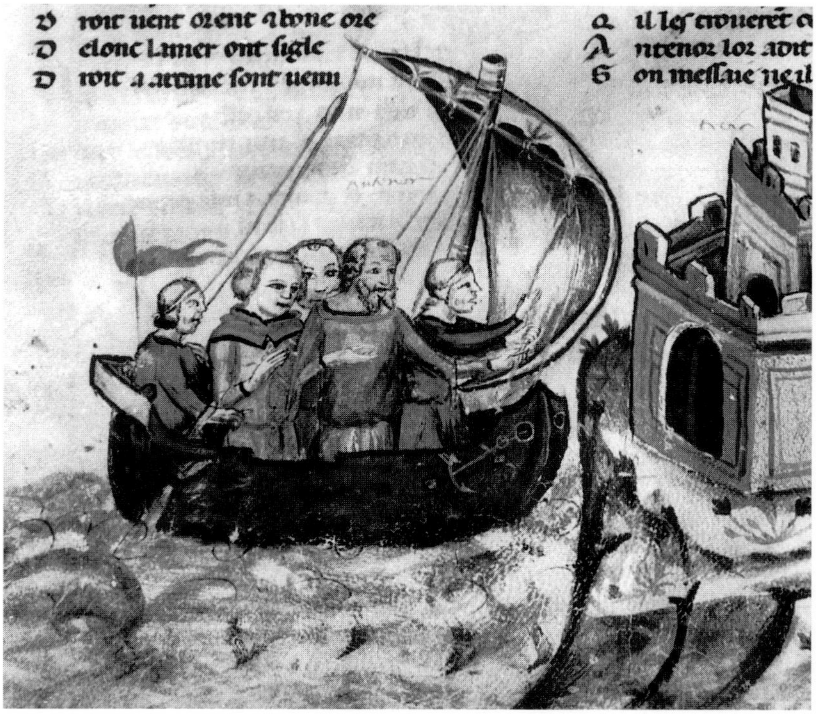

FIG. 41. Round ship entering port, from the French manuscript *Roman de Troie,* ca. 1330–40. *Courtesy the Biblioteca Nazionale Marciana*

Although it is difficult to make out the details clearly, the quarter rudder seems to be mounted through a yoke, with the aft type mount similar to that seen in figure 42. A crescent-shaped anchor is catted up at the starboard bow, crown toward the stern.

Figure 42
Theme: Story of the Trojan War: ship at storm.
Location: Biblioteca Nazionale Marciana, Venice, Cod. Marc. Fr. Z. 17 (=230), folio 22v.
Type: Two-masted, lateen-rigged merchant ship (Type IIIb).

The lateen-rigged vessel in figure 42 from the French manuscript, *Roman de Troie,* has been caught by storm. The foremast, set far forward in the bow, has snapped in half, and a mariner desperately tries to control its lateen sail. A second mariner deals with the lateen sail of the mizzen set aft of midships. Robands on both yards are represented. On the mizzen, several lines of rigging, including shrouds or stays, halyard and vang, and some tackle, are depicted;

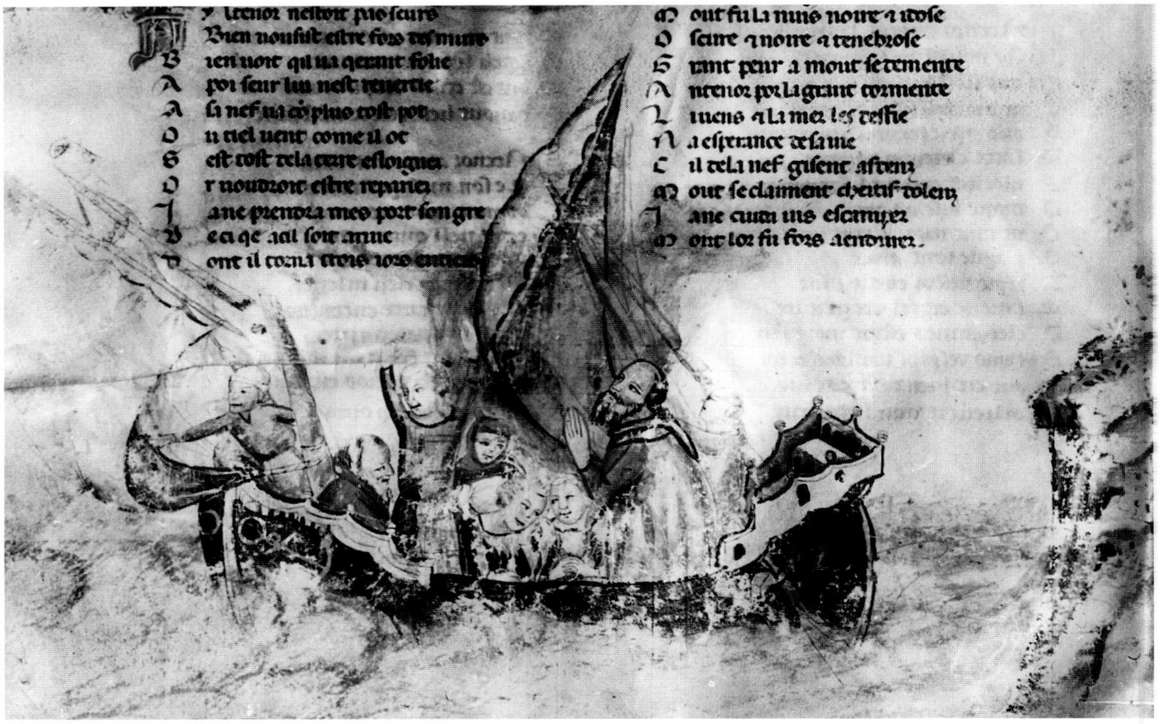

FIG. 42. A round ship caught in a dangerous storm breaks its foremast. From the French manuscript *Roman de Troie,* ca. 1330–40. *Courtesy the Biblioteca Nazionale Marciana*

on the foremast, only the upper section of the halyard and a sheet are visible. A detail depicted on the foremast constitutes, significantly, a rare medieval representation of the parrel, attaching the yard to the mast. It consists of a strand of wooden beads, used to reduce friction between the yard and the mast, and thus facilitating the yard being hauled up and down the mast. Its tackle allowed the yard to be tightened to or loosened from the mast.

The general shape of this vessel and the gilded finials decorating the bow and quarterdeck are similar to figure 108, where decorative finial balls run all along the sheer strake. The stern is made spacious with two outer timbers that end at a tragent beam perpendicular to the central sternpost. The angle depicted shows part of the inside of the small quarterdeck and reveals a small raised deck area as well as the inboard side of the transom stern.

The loom of an asymmetrical quarter rudder has been attached aft of a through-beam and mounted through a wooden or metal ring called the *luctatorium*. The *luctatorium* was "fixed to the hull and kept the oar from hitting the hull but still permitted the blade to move freely" (Pryor, 1984, no. 3: 282). The rudder has an asymmetrical foil-design blade, similar to one depicted in the fourteenth-century manuscript illumination, figure 51 (details, fig. 150I and K), although there it is mounted differently, with the swing mount. A crescent-shaped anchor is catted up at the port bow, crown slung aft, with its hawser passing through a hawse hole very close to the stem.

This French illumination is not included in the typology.

Figure 43

Theme: Story of the Trojan War: arrival scene; ships anchored in harbor.
Location: Biblioteca Nazionale Marciana, Venice, Cod. Marc. Fr. Z. 17 (=230), folio 38ʳ.
Types: Eight single-masted, lateen-rigged merchant ships (Type IIIa).

Eight single-masted ships, in the moments just after arriving in port, are the subject of figure 43, an interesting French illumination of a me-

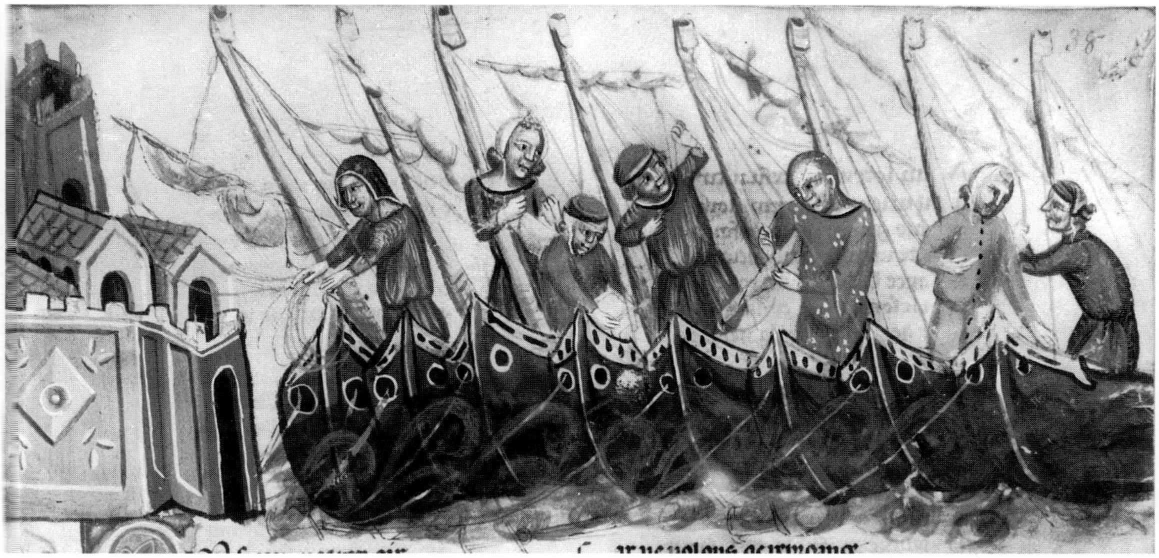

FIG. 43. Eight round ships anchored in port. From the French manuscript *Roman de Troie,* ca. 1330–40. *Courtesy the Biblioteca Nazionale Marciana*

dieval city's ramparts from the manuscript *Romans de Troie.* The eight lateeners, viewed from their bows, have already been anchored, tied side to side, and they share anchors. Seven mariners are shown in various activities related to their arrival in port. The first from the right is in the process of lowering the lateen sail and coiling down; he actually holds a vang line from the yard of the ship to his left, not of the ship on which he stands. The port hawse hole was apparently inadvertently forgotten on the sixth vessel from the left. These errant particulars, coupled with the inaccurate placements of the masts themselves, show that the representation is not accurate to the finest detail but was a hastily made sketch. Other details, however, prove the artist's nautical competence.

The fifth mariner from the left is in the process of furling his sail and tying it to its yard; the third and sixth are stowing gear; and the seventh mariner is lowering his yard. The artist of the illumination is apparently quite familiar with these procedures to be able to illustrate such mundane activities. Seven of the eight vessels have a hawser tied from the starboard hawse hole; the first from the left has a line running from the port hawse hole as well. All anchors are crescent shaped and set toward the shore on the seabed. The anchors are naturalistically depicted, with each anchor's stock lying flat, and one fluke imbedded in the sea floor.

These ships are not included in the typology because the manuscript is French.

Figure 44

Theme: Story of the Trojan War: shipbuilding scene.

Location: Biblioteca Nazionale Marciana, Venice, Cod. Marc. Fr. Z. 17 (=230), folio 26^{v}.

Types: Two single-masted, lateen-rigged merchant ships (Type IIIa).

Frame-first construction is illustrated in figure 44, from the French manuscript *Romans de Troie.* An earlier stage of frame-first ship construction is shown in figure 98. Men work on two round ships from below and from within. Many of the shipwrights' tools are shown. At the bow of the closer, more complete vessel, a ship carpenter bores holes with an auger, while to his far left, another hammers nails, attaching the strakes to the frames. Between them, a caulker works, filling the seams of the attached strakes. From above, to the far left, another shipwright drills with an auger, and the second figure employs a T-shaped ax to finish off the apron. Two

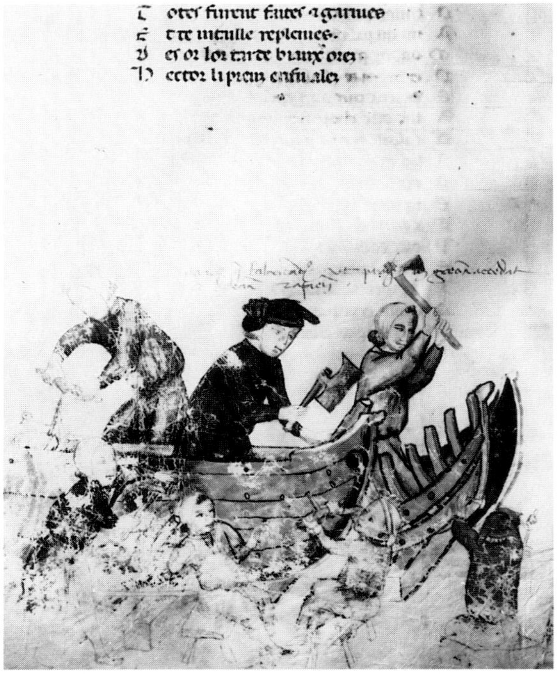

FIG. 44. Ship construction scene from the French manuscript *Roman de Troie,* ca. 1330–40. *Courtesy the Biblioteca Nazionale Marciana*

rows of evenly spaced nails secure the flush-laid strakes at the edges. A section of the uppermost strake of the starboard side is cut away (where the man with the T-shaped ax stands). This may be in preparation for a removable sheer strake as seen in figures 14, 41, and on the Contarina ship of ca. 1300 (see fig. 142G).

On the far ship, a carpenter nails strakes to the framing at the bow, while from above, another utilizes a bearded ax to work edges off the timbers within. The ax was the most important tool to the medieval shipwright, used to shape and size timbers (Goodman, 1964: 28 and Singer, 1956: 389). Strakes have been set only about halfway up the side of this hull: a consistent room-and-space is apparent. The lower strakes of this ship are shown as fixed with one centered row of evenly spaced nails.

This French illustration is not included in the typology.

Figure 45

Theme: Story of the Trojan War: shipbuilding scene.

Location: Biblioteca Nazionale Marciana, Venice, Cod. Marc. Fr. Z. 17 (=230), folio 37^{r}

Type: War transport (Type IIb).

Figure 45, another ship construction scene illustrated in the French manuscript, *Roman de*

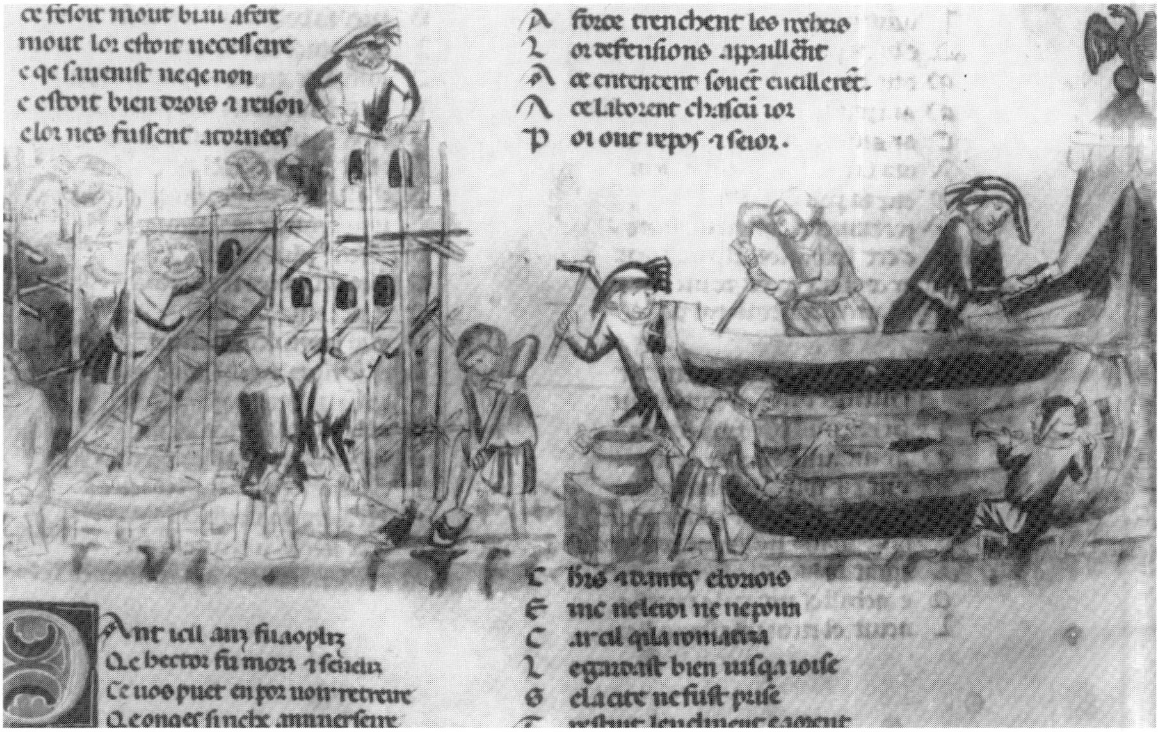

FIG. 45. Transport ship under construction. From the French manuscript *Roman de Troie,* ca. 1330–40. *Courtesy the Biblioteca Nazionale Marciana*

Troie, shows a ship that by its shape could be interpreted as a either a merchantman or a transport, although the tent and regal eagle at the stern both imply a military use for the ship. The vessel is nearing completion: all planking is attached, and a final layer of pitch is being applied to seal the hull. The sweep of the lower hull strakes can barely be distinguished, but they do finish at the tragent forming a full stern (detail, fig. 146E), resembling those of figures 20 and 21. Above, stanchions support a tent structure (a continuation of the visible port sheer strake forms the port stanchion). This clearly illustrates at least one of the functions of the upright posts common to medieval ships' sterns: they support a tented area above the quarterdeck, for the nobility in command (cf. the galleys in figs. 27 and 153).

The depiction is not detailed enough to indicate much beyond the basic shape of the hull and the horizontal keel, although the wide range of tools employed is again informative. A worker at the bow hefts an ax. To his right, from inside the hull, another carpenter bores with an auger, while a third trims a timber at the stern. From below, a caulker spreads pitch, taken from a heated cauldron, onto the exterior of the ship's hull. Another man works hemp into the seams with his caulking iron.

Because the artist is French, this ship is not included in the typology.

Figure 46
Theme: "The Martyrdom of St. Clement I."
Date: First half of the fourteenth century.
Artist: Venetian school.
Location: Biblioteca Nazionale Marciana, Venice, Cod. Marc. Lat. III, 111, folio 173^{v}.
Type: Lagoonal craft (Type Ib).

The Venetian manuscript illumination figure 46 depicts St. Clement's martyrdom from a small lagoonal craft. The undecked vessel is double ended, with no evidence for a mast or sail. The sheer strake, or caprail, is defined by two parallel lines, curving in a sweet sheer until nearing the stem and sternposts, where it turns almost ninety degrees to finish into the posts. This effect indicates a slight broadening of the bow and stern, probably to form a small deck area fore and aft, similar to the full bow design to the larger vessel of figure 28, though the foreground ship in figure 128 defines it even more clearly. The stem and sternposts in figure 46 rise fairly steeply from a slightly rockered keel and finish at an approximately equal height. One steering oar or paddle is visible toward the stern, near—but not actually engaged in—the typically Venetian oarlock on the starboard side, with its oar slot facing aft. Two figures in the boat lower the anchor line, tied around the neck of the sinking saint. The round stone anchor is of the millstone type.

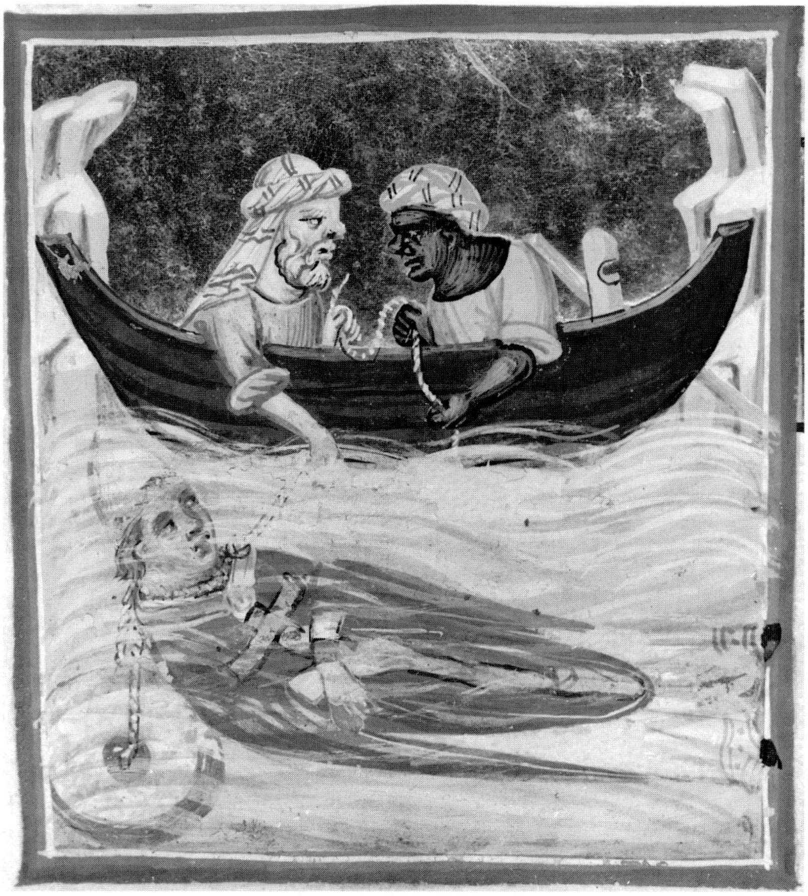

FIG. 46. "The Martyrdom of St. Clement I," illumination from a Venetian manuscript of the Biblioteca Nazionale Marciana dating to the first half of the fourteenth century. *Courtesy the Biblioteca Nazionale Marciana*

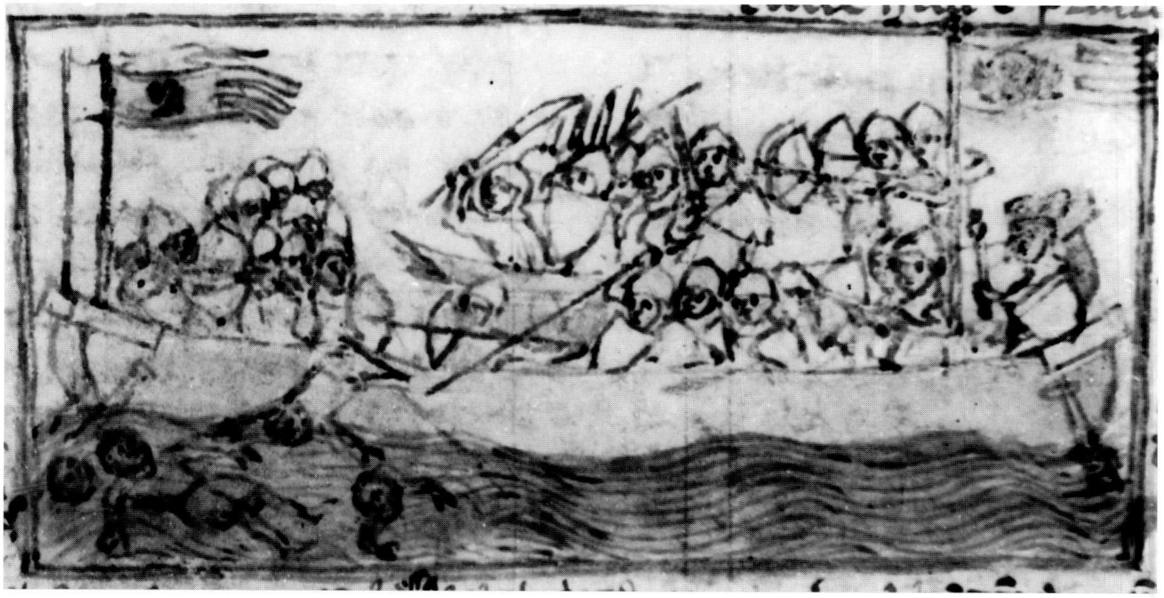

Fig. 47. Naval battle, from the Venetian manuscript *Chronologia magna* (first half of the fourteenth century). *Courtesy the Biblioteca Nazionale Marciana*

Figure 47
Manuscript title: *Chronologia magna.*
Theme: World Chronicle: naval battle.
Artist: Possibly Avignese.
Author: Paulinus Venetus.
Location: Biblioteca Nazionale Marciana, Venice, Cod. Marc. Lat. Z. 399 (=1610), folio 77ᵛ.
Date: First half of fourteenth century (Pallucchini, 1964: 216–23).
Types: Figure 47: Four oared galley warships (Type IIa).
Figure 48: Two war transports (Type IIb).

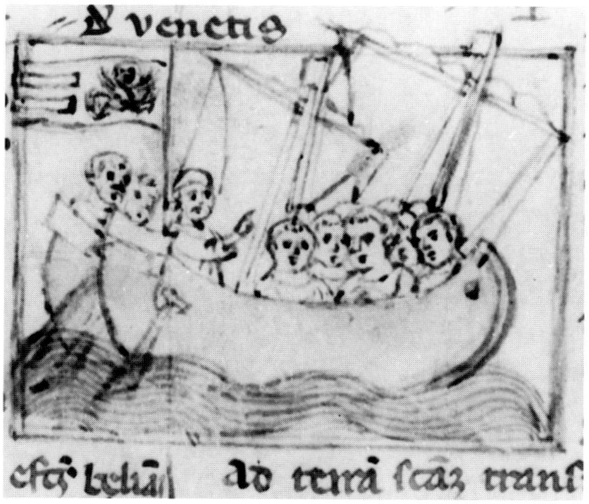

FIG. 48. Two transport ships under sail, from the Venetian manuscript *Chronologia magna* (first half of the fourteenth century). *Courtesy the Biblioteca Nazionale Marciana*

Figure 49: Two war transports (Type IIb) and two lighters (Type Ia).
[Other folios: One lighter (Type Ia), seven lagoonal craft (Type Ib), seven oared galley warships (Type IIa), and twenty-six war transports (Type IIb)].

The Venetian friar Paulino or Paulinus, who eventually became a papal diplomat and vescovo of the Pozzuoli, wrote numerous historical works and attempted to correct the geographical maps of his day, with the goal of effecting a new crusade. His world chronicle, *Chronologia magna,* including a section on the Crusades, contains fifteen folios with ship illustrations. All the folios represent a total of three lighters (Type Ia), seven small fishing boats (Type Ib), eleven oared galleys (Type IIa), here with a small mast and sail for supplemental power, and thirty transports (Type IIb); three representative folios are illustrated (figs. 47–49).

A naval battle is depicted in figure 47. Two long ships face two of their opponent's galleys. The ships are simplified to the bare essentials: the emphasis of the image is on the warriors and their battle. There is no evidence for either oars or sails.

The vessels have a relatively horizontal sheer. The visible quarter rudders are mounted with a *luctatorium* and pass through the side of the hull to the small quarterdeck, represented in profile as an elongated rectangle. The warships have a pointed beak at the bow, called the *sperone*, which served as a boarding bridge (Casson, 1964b: 74).

Figure 48
Location: Biblioteca Nazionale Marciana, Venice, Cod. Marc. Lat. Z. 399 (=1610), folio 78[v].
Type: Two war transports (Type IIb).

Figure 48, also from the world chronicle, *Chronologia magna,* shows two transport ships sailing abreast. The transport ships are shorter and much higher sided than the long ships in figure 47, but their sterns and rudder mounts are similar. Each of their single masts supports a lateen sail and a cylindrical crow's nest aft of the mast head. Two or three shrouds or stays and the tack and vang lines are generically delineated. From the slightly rockered keel, stem and sternposts rise and curve inward. The line of the hull generated by these timbers is almost oval. Each asymmetrical rudder is attached through a *luctatorium*. They are similar in shape to some illustrated in the *Fabrica di galere* manuscript, where a rudder detail is depicted on folio 13[r], and on the Flanders galley (fig. 66; detail of its rudder, fig. 150L) on folio 14[v]. A hawse hole is indicated at the bow of the front ship.

This manuscript contains numerous other illustrations of ships, from small fishing vessels to many similar warships at oar, sail, or fighting, but by far the most interesting illustration is the next figure, one of a transport ship in the process of loading.

Figure 49
Theme: World Chronicle: loading a round ship.
Location: Biblioteca Nazionale Marciana, Venice, Cod. Marc. Lat. Z. 399 (=1610), folio 12[r].

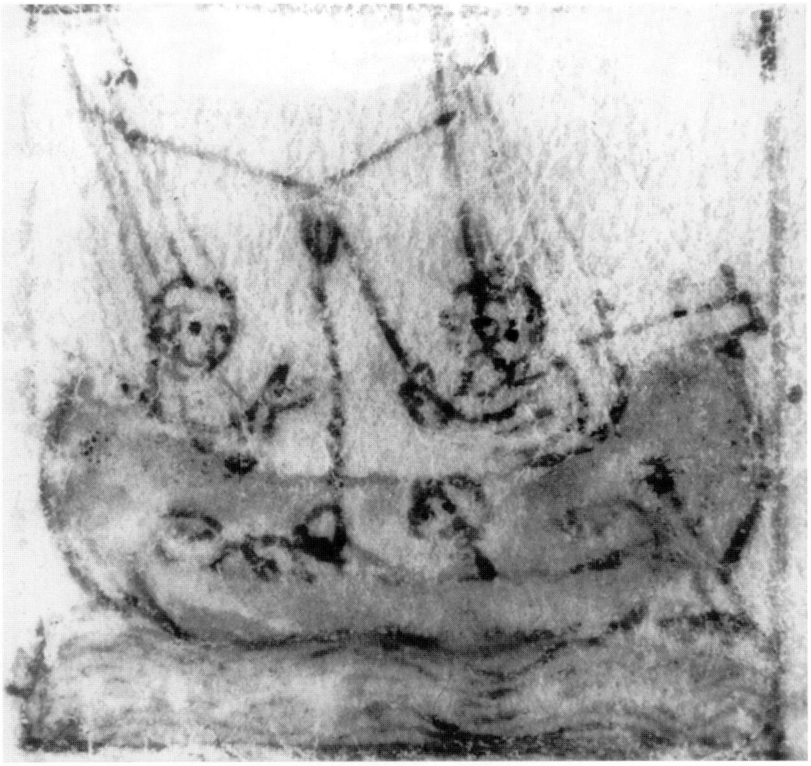

FIG. 49. Transport ship in the process of loading, from the Venetian manuscript *Chronologia magna* (first half of the fourteenth century). *Courtesy the Biblioteca Nazionale Marciana*

Types: War transport (Type IIb), and, in foreground, a lighter (Type Ia).

The state of preservation of this manuscript, *Chronologia magna,* is poor, which is especially unfortunate as this folio contains maritime images of great interest. One is nearly a mirror image of the other; the original image seems to have transferred to the verso page. The more complete one, showing the starboard profile of a ship and lighter, is illustrated as figure 49.

One can barely discern a lighter in the foreground, from which cargo is being loaded onto a transport ship very similar to those seen in figure 48. The two masts, both forward raking at about twenty degrees, have been employed to fashion a lifting device. A line runs from the head of one mast to the other's. Near the center of that line hangs a whip tackle. Through it runs another line, being hoisted by a man near the stern, to lift cargo aboard. The tackle depicted in this illumination may be a rare representation of what texts have referred to as *ternarius,* which

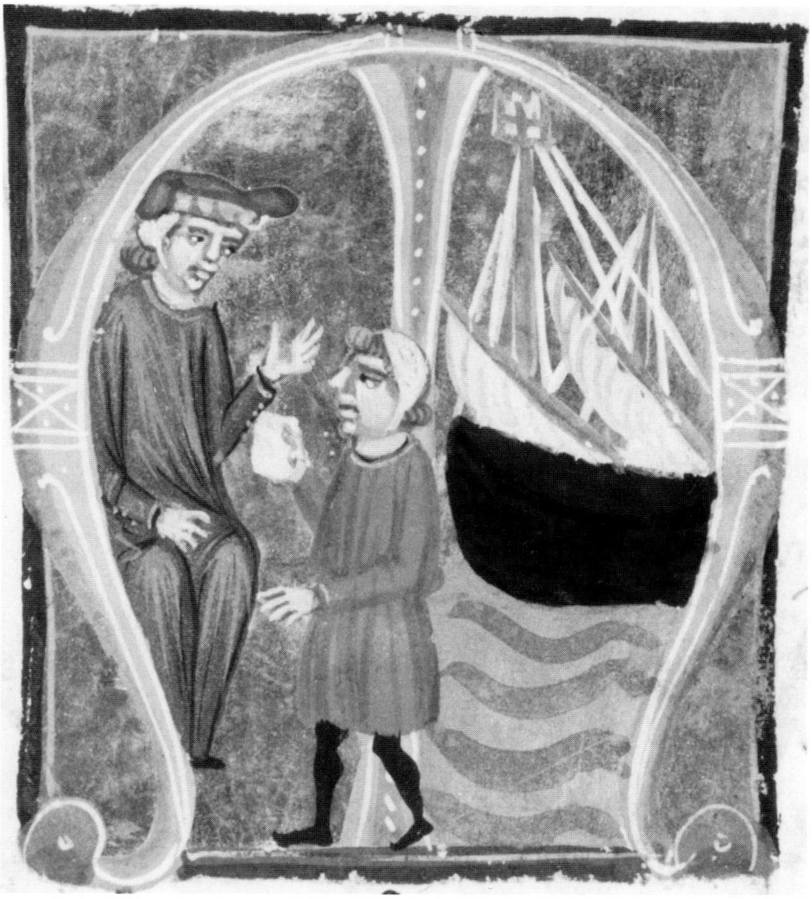

FIG. 50. Round ship decorating an initial from a copy of Venetian Statutes, ca. 1350. *Courtesy the Department of Printing & Graphic Arts, The Houghton Library, Harvard University*

Pryor has translated as "large tackle [used] for stowing gear" (1984, no. 2: 215). The cargo would have scraped along the sides of the ship if loaded in such a manner, but this is clearly the way it was done. Backstays and shrouds provide their masts support.

Figure 50
Title: *Liber statuor[um] et Legu[m] Veneto[rum].*
Theme: Venetian Statutes.
Location: Houghton Library, Harvard University, Typ. 140H, fol. 66ᵛ.
Date: ca. 1350.
Type: Two-masted, lateen-rigged merchant ship (Type IIIb).

Details are minimal in this tiny initial decoration from a Latin manuscript in the Houghton Library, but a small ship with two lateen-rigged masts is recognizable. Only the front half of the ship is included, and the hull is too darkly painted to reveal any hull details beyond the basic round shape. Seven lines running to the mast heads indicate stays; the mizzen mast is slightly shorter than the mainmast. The two yards are lowered as if the ship was just arriving in port.

Figure 51
Title: The Pizzigani Portolan.
Theme: Venetian marine chart.
Artists: Francesco and Marco Pizzigani.
Location: Present location unknown; published in Zanetti (1841: 38, fig. 1) and Lane (1973: 121, fig. 8).
Date: 1367 (Lane, 1973: 121 and fig. 8).
Types: Two three-masted, mixed-rigged merchant ships (Type IIIf).

The published section of this portolan contains two large ships (fig. 51). The flags identify the one to the right as a Genoese ship, while the one to the left is Venetian. Both exemplify the transitional mixed-rigged ship where the square mainsail provided the maximum driving force, and the lateen sail aft improved its ability to sail into the wind. The ships may illustrate the Mediterranean-style *cocha* (round ship) described in *Fabrica di galere,* where the type is also called *nave quadre* in reference to the square mainsail (Bellabarba, 1988: 113).

The Venetian ship's mainmast employs a square sail; the shorter mizzen aft, a lateen one. The square sail consists of a series of squares, with a bonnet added to the bottom; the lateen sail features parallel vertical lines. These lines indicate the shape of the sections of sail cloth sewn together for each sail type. The ship's bow is difficult to interpret. What seem to be the forestay of the mainsail and the foremast have been similarly represented as a pair of lines with evenly spaced cross marks. Rigging lines with blocks are visible on the foremast, as are the port

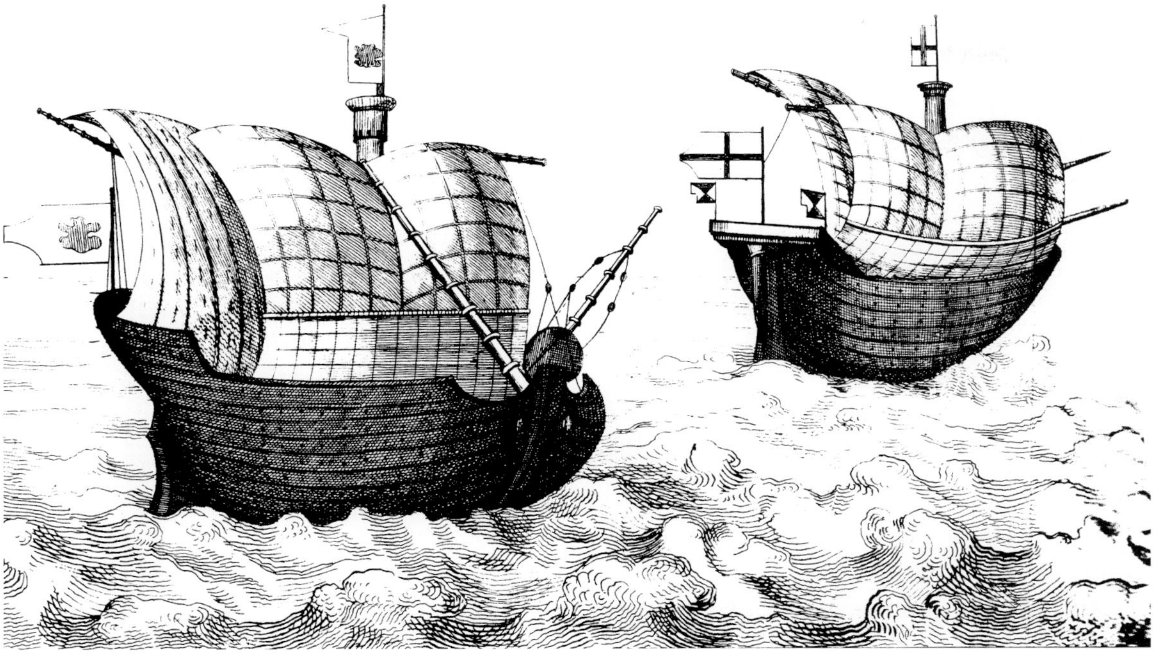

FIG. 51. Venetian (left) and Genoese (right) round ships, from the Pizzigani portolan, 1367. *After Zanetti, 1841; courtesy the Museo Storico Navale*

brace of the mainsail and the starboard vang of the mizzen's sail. The sterncastle is clearly an integral part of the hull. From amidships, the sheer runs horizontally until it nears the bow, where it dips down just before finishing at the stem. Parallel strakes are visible, secured with a single line of evenly spaced nails.

Like the Venetian ship, the Genoese ship has a similar sail arrangement, with a square sail on the main, a bonnet below, and a lateen on the mizzen. This depiction is unique in illustrating square sections instead of vertical strips on the lateen sail. This ship is viewed slightly from the stern, revealing a single stern rudder.

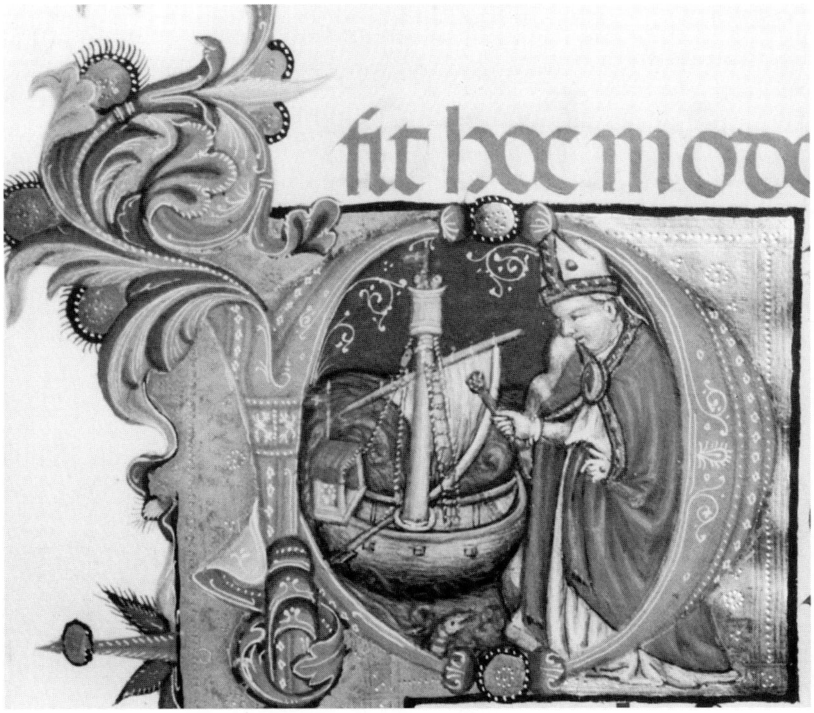

FIG. 52. Round ship decorating the initial "P," from a manuscript dated ca. 1380. *Courtesy the Department of Printing & Graphic Arts, The Houghton Library, Harvard University*

Figure 52

Artist: From Vittorio Veneto.
Location: The Houghton Library, Harvard University, Typ. 1, fol. 39r.
Date: ca. 1380.
Type: Single-masted, lateen-rigged merchant ship (Type IIIa).

A Latin manuscript from Vittorio Veneto

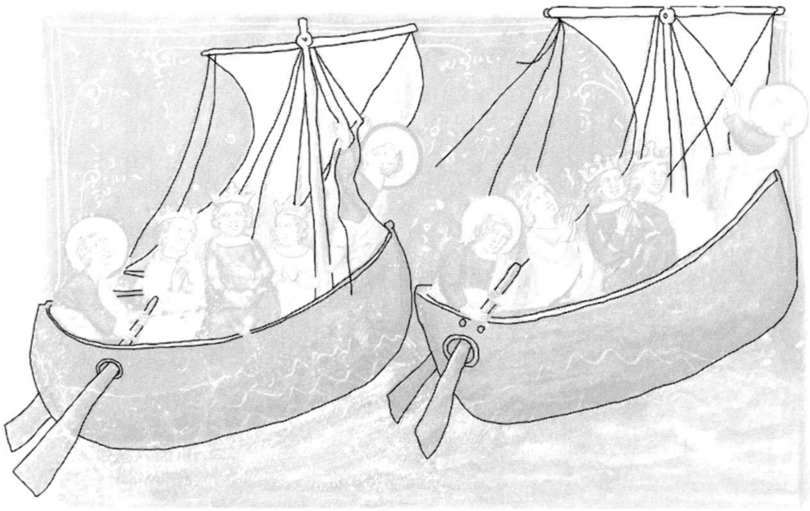

FIG. 53. Galla Placidia and her children, while in a square-rigged round ship, are saved by St. John the Divine. From a fourteenth-century manuscript of Biblioteca Classense, Ravenna. *Helen C. Dewolf, after Kaftal, 1978: fig. 690*

illustrates a lateen-rigged round ship (fig. 52) in an initial "P." A rope ladder in front of the mast leads to the crow's nest, and a halyard with tackle is visible just aft of the mast. Three through-beams amidships probably indicate deck level. Just below and aft is the visible quarter rudder. A square structure represents the castle at the stern.

Figure 53
Artist: School of Giotto, from Romagna.
Location: Biblioteca Classense, codex 406, Ravenna.
Theme: St. John the Divine Saves Galla Placidia and Her Children.
Date: fourteenth century.
Types: Two single-masted, square-rigged merchant ships (Type IIId).

Galla Placidia's family sailed in a simply portrayed round ship in figure 53. Two vessels are depicted to relay the passage of time but represent just the ship the family used for their journey. The Apostle John is illustrated in four different positions, as the saint steers and adjusts rigging to ensure the royal family's safety. Braces, shrouds, and the halyard are illustrated on both ships. The luctatorium for the quarter rudders is clearly depicted on the starboard sides.

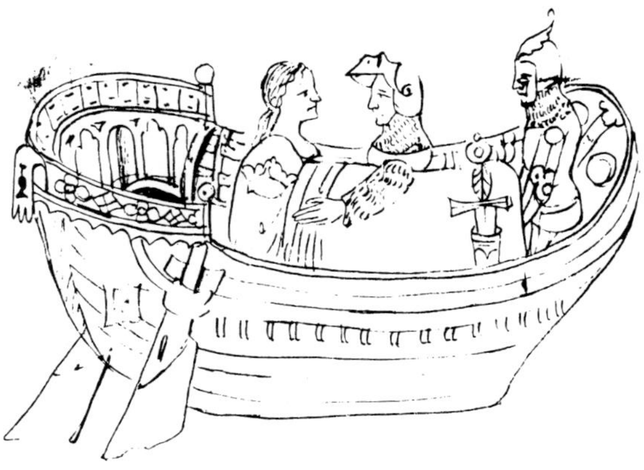

FIG. 54. Crusaders' departure, from an untitled fourteenth-century manuscript. *Courtesy the Biblioteca Nazionale Marciana*

Figure 54
Manuscript title: *Miscellanea.*
Theme: Departure for Crusades.
Location: Biblioteca Nazionale Marciana, Venice, Cod. Marc. Gr. II, 17 (=1295), folio 20ʳ.
Date: fourteenth century (Concina, 1988: fig. 31).
Type: War transport (Type IIb).

Figure 54, an illustration from a Byzantine manuscript manufactured in Venice, portrays a crusader bidding farewell to his lady aboard a transport, or possibly a merchant ship in use as a transport.

The vessel has been sketched with a flat bottom, a steeply rising stem and an elaborately decorated full stern similar to the shape of that in figure 102. Fifteen pairs of vertical lines roughly halfway up the hull define the through-beams supporting the main deck, like those more clearly depicted in figure 26. Due to the bird's eye view portrayed, both hawse holes are seen from the inside of the bow as well as the inside of the quarterdeck. The unbalanced rudders, mounted with a swing mount, are set in reverse, which would have made the ship totally unnavigable if under way. However, the ship is not under way; the rudders may have been stored in this position while in port (see the starboard rudder in fig. 10).

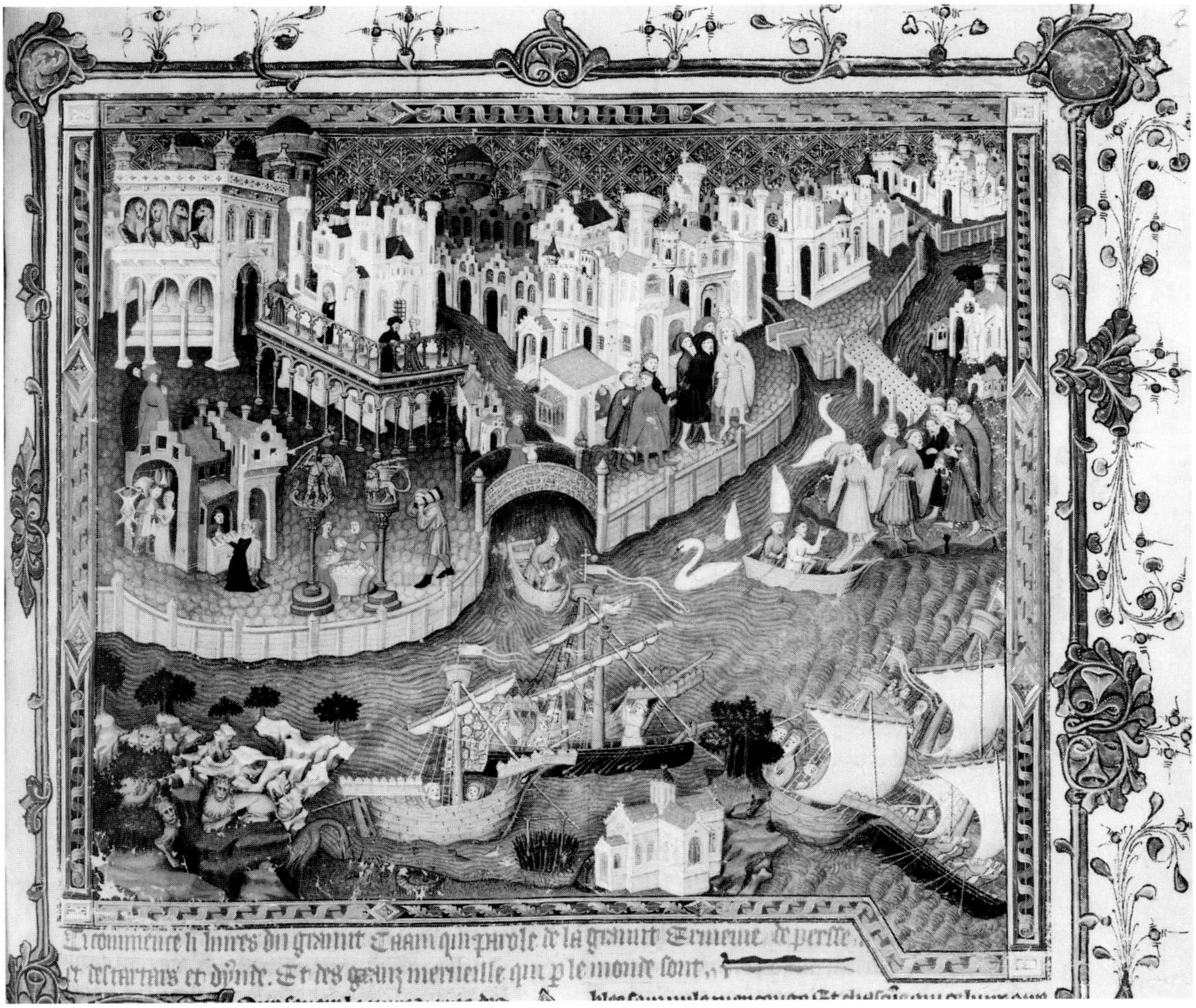

FIG. 55. Marco Polo's departure from Venice. From the manuscript *Li livres du Graunt Caam* (1400). *Courtesy the Bodleian Library*

Figure 55

Manuscript title: *Li livres du Graunt Caam.*

Theme: Marco Polo's own account of his travels: setting sail from Venice in the year 1271.

Authors: Marco Polo; Graunt Camm.

Artist: Johannes.

Location: Bodleian Library, Oxford University. Frontispiece of a copy illuminated in England. MS.Bodl. 264, folio 218^{r}.

Date: ca. 1400.

Types: Four single-masted, square-rigged merchant ships (Type IIId); two oared galley warships (Type IIa); two lagoonal craft (Type Ib).

The Molo of Venice bustles with activity as several ships to the right make their way out of harbor. The scene, figure 55, includes four medium-sized ships fitted with a square sail amidships and a single rudder astern. Two (to the right) have sails set, while those of the other two (left and center) are still furled. All four have prominent, centrally placed crow's nests, accessed via ratlines. Rigging, including shrouds, stays, braces, and robands, is accurately defined throughout. The hull construction can best be seen in the one to the left. Parallel strakes are delineated and shown to be fixed with evenly spaced, vertical pairs of nails. Castles at bow and stern are braced from below, and a single stern rudder is affixed with pintles and gudgeons.

Both of the oared galley warships are triremes with oars clustered in groups of three, but they also have two lateen-rigged masts. The stern of the galley to the right is blocked visually by another ship, but a tented area is visible on the stern of the second galley. The galley's dark color obscures details of hull construction, beyond the basic elongated shape and lines indicating the outrigger.

Two lagoonal craft have flat sterns like many rowboats of today. Strakes and the nailing pattern are delineated, and the stems are well defined, though different in form: one curves inward while the other protrudes. A small bench seat is visible on the boat under the bridge; two men on the other craft appear to sit on similar benches.

Although the subject is certainly Venice, this image is not technically Venetian and so is excluded from the typology in chapter 3.

FIG. 56. A single-masted, square-rigged ship, from the 1436 *Mappamondo* of *Andrea del Bianco. Permission to photograph courtesy Seminario Patriarchale*

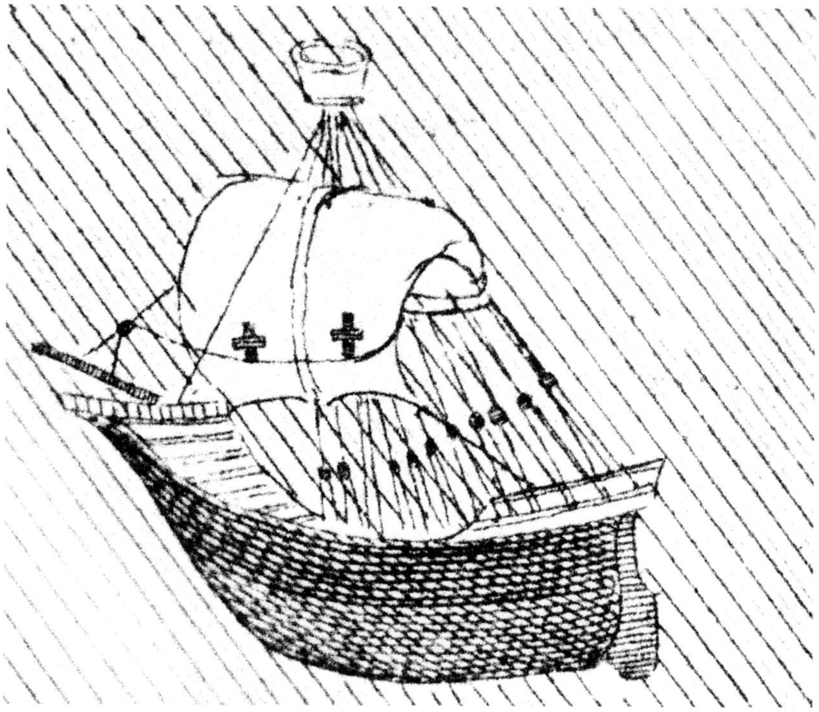

Figure 56

Manuscript title: *Atlante nautico* of *Andrea del Bianco.*
Theme: World map.
Artist: Andrea del Bianco.
Location: Biblioteca Nazionale Marciana, Cod. Marc. It. Z 76 (=4783). Lat. 81, folio 70r.
Date: 1436.
Type: Single-masted, mixed-rigged merchant ship (IIIa).

In the fifteenth century, Venetians were making the most accurate maps of newly discovered coasts (Lane, 1973: 277), called *Mappamondi,* World Maps. Unfortunately, it has not been possible to survey this source of evidence adequately, as no Venetian maps were seen in the original. The few ship depictions found in reproductions or published material have been included in the catalog as figures 56, 57, 60, and 61.

One famous Venetian cartographer, Andrea del Bianco, illustrated a merchant ship (fig. 56) and two galleys (fig. 57) sailing the seas of his map of 1436. He is believed to have been the first to record America cartographically. Following the early Christian tradition, Andrea placed the east at the top of his map, representing terrestrial Paradise, with the origins of the four great rivers, the Tigris, Euphrates, Nile, and Ganges. Also traditional is his central placement of Jerusalem. Certain areas, such as the Mediterranean, are fairly accurate; Africa is distorted and pointed east, though clearly circumnavigable.

Figure 56, the merchant ship, has a single rudder affixed to the stern. The mainmast set slightly forward of midships is fitted with a square sail and a large crow's nest centrally placed at its head. Bowlines from the mainsail run to the bowsprit. The forestay, shrouds, and backstays are defined.

The keel is slightly rockered, and the stem rises rather steeply at the bow. The sternpost is nearly straight, with a single stern rudder attached. The foredeck is much higher than the sterncastle or quarterdeck; both are integrated into the lines of the hull and have parapets. No tumble home is indicated. Strakes run parallel to the keel and the sheer, with no apparent convergence to fit into the post. Cross-planking, like that illustrated in figure 110, represents the after side of the forecastle.

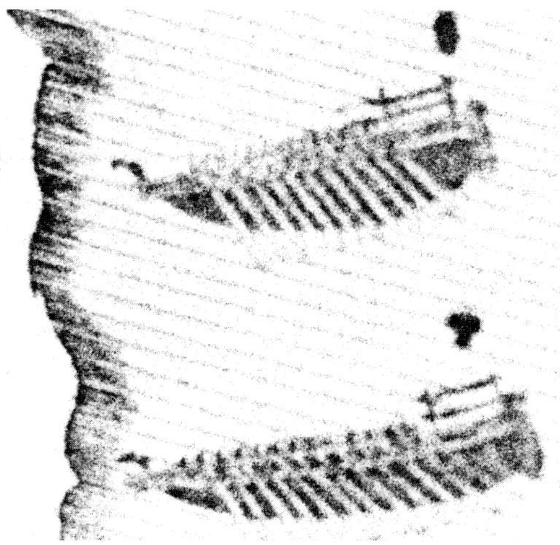

FIG. 57. Two oared galleys, from the 1436 *Mappamondo* of *Andrea del Bianco. Permission to photograph courtesy Seminario Patriarchale*

Figure 57

Location: Biblioteca Nazionale Marciana, Cod. Marc. It. Z 76 (=4783). Lat. 81, folio 70^{r}.

Types: Two oared galley warships (Type IIa).

Although neither galley in figure 57 illustrates masts, they probably had removable ones. The frames visible at the quarterdeck appear in other illustrations to function as tent stanchions (e.g., fig. 58). The upper vessel has eleven oars arranged along one level, while the lower vessel has thirteen. These galleys have a gradually rising stem and a straight stern, where a single stern rudder is attached. A *sperone*, possibly a continuation of the main wale, projects beyond the bow of each vessel.

Figure 58

Manuscript title: *Hesperis.*

Theme: Epic poem written in praise of Sigismondo Malatesta.

Author: Basinio de'Basini of Parma.

Artist: Either Matteo de' Pasti or Giovanni di Bartolo Bettini da Fano.

Location: From Rimini; now kept in Oxford University, Bodleian Library, MS.Canon.Class.Lat.81, folio 16^{v}.

Date: ca. 1457–68.

Types: Figure 58: Three coastal cargo craft (Type Id), four oared galley warships (Type IIa), two two-masted, mixed-rigged merchant ships (Type IIIe).

Figure 59: Two two-masted, mixed-rigged merchant ships (Type IIIe).

[Other folios: One lagoonal (Type Id), thirteen warships (Type IIa), five two-masted, mixed-rigged merchant ships (Type IIIe)].

The manuscript *Hesperis* has six maritime illustrations. The first folio reproduced here (fig. 58) is characteristic and the most informative, as it represents all ship types portrayed, under various means of motivation: three coastal craft (Type Id), four oared galleys (Type IIa), and two mixed-rigged ships (Type IIIe). Figure 59 is a detail of the stern area of a mixed-rigged ship, with another in the background (Type IIIe). Total vessels in the manuscript include four small craft (Type Id), seventeen warships (Type IIa), and nine round ships (Type IIIe).

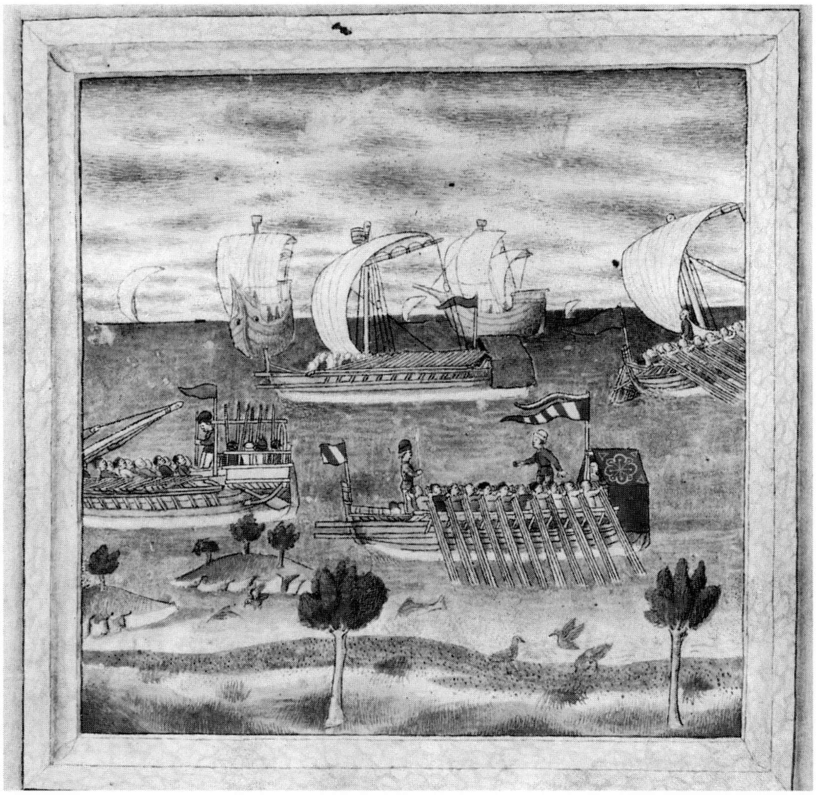

FIG. 58. *Coche* (carracks) and oared galleys, from *Hesperis,* a manuscript from Rimini dating to ca. 1462. *Courtesy the Bodleian Library*

Four galleys are shown under way in figure 58: the two in the middleground, at center and right, are powered by oars and sail while the two in the foreground travel solely under oar power. The galley to the left is in the process of lowering its mast. The two with their masts stepped show a single mast set forward of midships. The central galley has the more visible crow's nest, but it is oddly positioned forward of the mast; perhaps the crow's nests could rotate around the masts for tacking maneuvers. Five lines are indicated on the central galley, representing the vang, with its tackle, the tack lines, the shrouds or stays, and possibly a halyard. Robands are also defined on the galley to the right, the tack with its tackle are visible, but due to the position of the sail, no vang, and only two of the robands and two (shroud?) lines from the head of the mast are shown.

The galleys are triremes: their oars are grouped in threes, *a terzaurolo,* supported by an outrigger. Each has a *sperone* beak or boarding platform at the bow and a tented area at the stern. No tent has been raised on the stern of the foreground galley to the left, revealing weaponry and several seated soldiers, as well as the swing mount rudder system and its unbalanced rudder.

In the far background are three generic small coastal or lagoonal craft with one lateen sail each, and two vaguely defined, two-masted, mixed-rigged carracks, similar to the more detailed figures 59, 70, and 107.

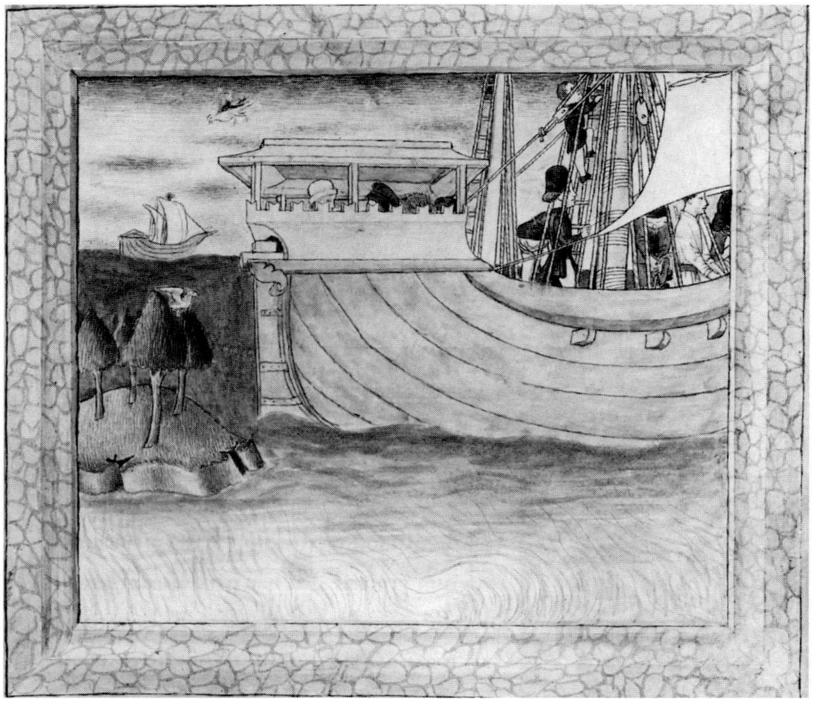

FIG. 59. Stern detail from *Hesperis,* a Riminese manuscript dating to ca. 1462. Note the figure climbing the rope ladder. *Courtesy the Bodleian Library*

Figure 59

Location: From Rimini; now kept in Oxford University, Bodleian Library, MS.Canon.Class.Lat.81, folio 70^r.

Type: Two two-masted, mixed-rigged merchant ships (Type IIIe).

The other illustrations in *Hesperis* are undetailed background images; in figure 59, the artist pictures the stern half of a large ship, close up, with another in the distance. The two masts show rope ladders as well as their stays and some pulleys. Probably the mizzen held a lateen sail while the main held a large square sail. A man climbs the rope ladder behind the mainmast, where bands of lines are also detailed to indicate the wooldings. The mainsail has been hoisted, though only a small corner of it is in the picture—the sheet is secured toward the sterncastle.

Three through-beams near the mainmast give support to the deck. Lines indicate strakes, with the lower ones finishing into the sternpost and the upper ones under the sterncastle. A single, curved stern rudder is affixed at the sternpost with pintles and gudgeons.

Figure 60

Manuscript title: *Mappamondo* of *Fra Mauro.*

Theme: World map.

Artist: Fra Mauro.

Location: Biblioteca Marciana, Venice; facsimile in Boston Public Library, G 1026 M35 1956 folio (Zorzi, 1988: table 71).

Date: 1459.

Types: Figure 60: Single-masted, square-rigged

merchant ship (Type IIId), three-masted, lateen-rigged merchant ship (Type IIIc).

Figure 61: Lighter (Type Ia), three-masted, mixed-rigged merchant ship (Type IIIg).

[Forty-three other vessels on the *Mappamondo* include seven Type Ia, five Type Ib, seven Type Id, two oared galley warships (Type IIa), two? Type IIIa, thirteen Type IIId, seven Type IIIf].

Fra Mauro, a Camaldolite friar who lived in the San Michele monastery on Murano, collaborated with Andrea del Bianco. Fra Mauro corrected some of Ptolemy's geography and compiled contemporaneous travelers' accounts to form his world maps. He was especially knowledgeable of interior and southern Africa, and the original map he made for Alfonso V of Portugal in 1457–59 inspired the Portuguese exploration of the African coast.

This *Mappamondo,* a copy of the one for the Portuguese king, is executed on parchment skin on wood, painted in bright colors and gold. The ship to the left in figure 60 has a mainmast with a crow's nest and a square sail. The ship image is too small to show details of rigging, but the basic hull shape is shown with a relatively flat bottom and resembles figure 56. Integral castle structures are evident at bow and stern, though no tumble home has been indicated. A single stern rudder and a small *di proda* bowsprit are detailed.

The sailed merchant galley to its right is larger and similar in shape to figure 69, with tent stanchions on the quarterdeck and three lateen-rigged masts. The elongated hull is relatively flat bottomed and is steered with a single stern rudder. The galley is shown sailing, but galleys also could travel under oars.

Figure 61

Types: Lighter (Type Ia), multimasted, mixed-rigged merchant ship (Type IIIf).

This large, mixed-rigged merchant ship from the *Mappamondo* of *Fra Mauro* appears to be quite a massive ship. It enters port under its main square sail, trailing a simple lighter. Remarkably, four vertical masts are illustrated (large, multimasted, mixed-rigged ships do occur later). On the mast farthest forward, a horizontal spar and lifts seem to indicate that the mast held a square sail. The mast amidships has an open square sail, with sheets and tack illustrated; two yards angled in front and behind this mast seem to be for lateen sails. Perhaps the front one was intended to represent a bowsprit; if so, it should incline forward from the forecastle. The hull is

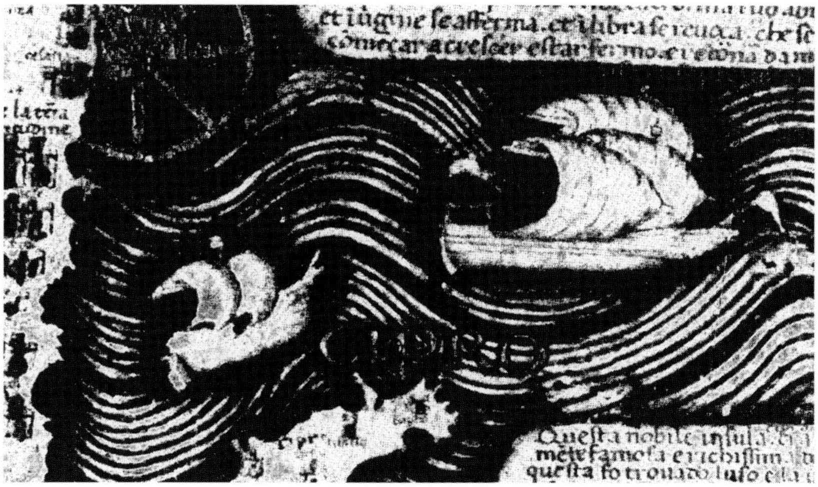

FIG. 60. A square-rigged ship and a merchant galley, merchant ships of differing shapes, on the 1459 *Mappamondo* of Fra Mauro. *After Nebbia, 1932: fig. 109*

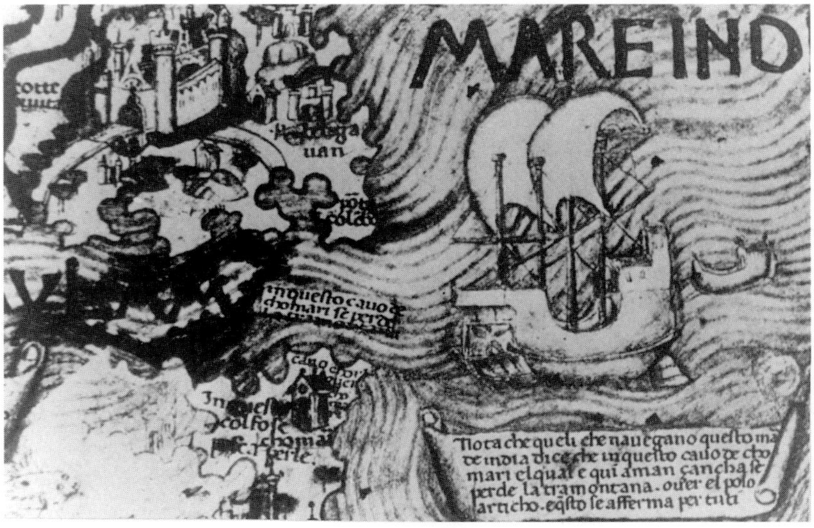

FIG. 61. A massive mixed-rig merchant ship with its lighter, from the 1459 *Mappamondo* of Fra Mauro. *After Nebbia, 1932: fig. 109*

carrack-like, but the sterncastle appears substantially higher than the forecastle. A pronounced tumble home is indicated.

Illustrations from Mercantile Manuscripts and Technical Treatises

Delving into the texts of manuscripts concerning ship construction, seamanship, or trade is beyond the scope of this study. To consider the texts of these sources could be useful, but the calligraphy alone presents formidable problems, and the majority of the manuscripts are of a later period anyway. Because illustrations from the few early manuscripts are informative as a form of artistic representation of ships, these have been included in the catalog and typology.

Figures 62–63
Treatise title: *Zibaldone da Canale.*
Artist/author: Zibaldone da Canale.
Theme: Venetian mercantile manuscript.
Location: Copy in Yale Beinecke Rare Book and Manuscript Library, Yale University.
Date: ca. 1312.

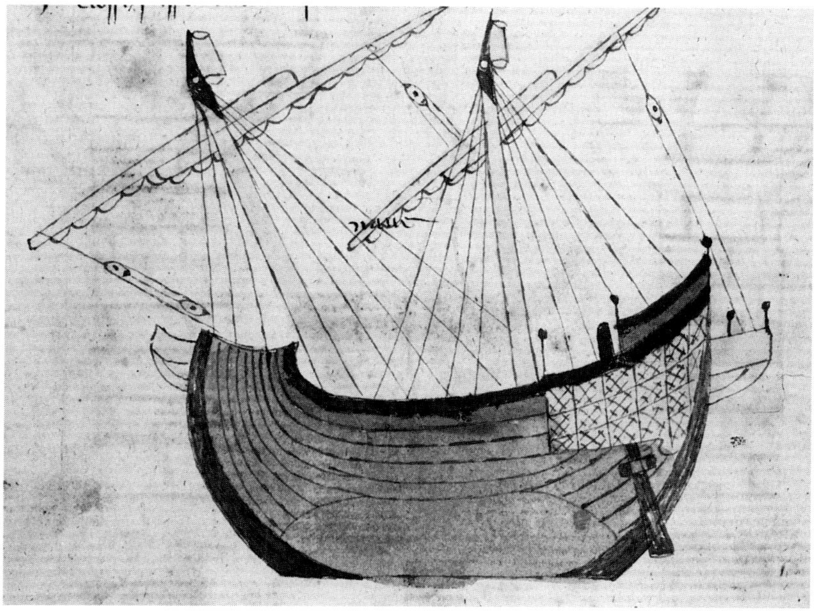

FIG. 62. Merchant ship from the Venetian manuscript *Zibaldone da Canale* dating to ca. 1312. *Courtesy the Beinecke Rare Book and Manuscript Library, Yale University*

Types: Figure 62: Two-masted, lateen-rigged merchant ship (Type IIIb).
Figure 63: Two two-masted, lateen-rigged merchant ship (Type IIIb).
[Other folios: Four two-masted, lateen-rigged merchant ship (Type IIIb)].

Five folios with a total of seven round ships (Type IIIb) are illustrated in *Zibaldone da Canale* [In print, *Zibaldone da Canale, Manoscritto mercantile del sec. XIV* (Stussi, 1967)]. The manuscript primarily concerns practical aspects of seamanship, such as setting up rigging, sails, etc., with one section devoted to ship construction. The ships represented are two-masted, lateen-rigged merchantmen with their sails furled, fitted with brace-mounted quarter rudders. Two representative folios are reproduced in this catalog (figs. 62 and 63). All seven folios represent the same basic ship type and differ only in a few details or careless omissions on the part of the artist. For example, wedges are defined around the mast at deck level in all of the examples, except in figure 62. One consistent nautical error in all the folios is found in the portrayal of the shrouds: usually three per side are sketched as passing from the top of the mast to deck, but only on the "front" side of each yard, regardless of whether that vessel is shown from port or starboard. In actuality, half of the lines—those on the far side of the yard—would have passed behind, to secure the mast to the other side of the ship. Another problem occurs with the vang and tack; often one or both are omitted or incomplete.

All the representations share certain features, however, best illustrated by figure 63, which depicts two vessels in profile, bow to bow. Each has two masts: the mizzen stands nearly vertical, slightly aft of midships, while the foremast is set roughly halfway between midships and the stem. Each mast is supported with six shrouds. On the ship to the right, a fourth line aft of both masts may be the halyards, secured aft and doubling as

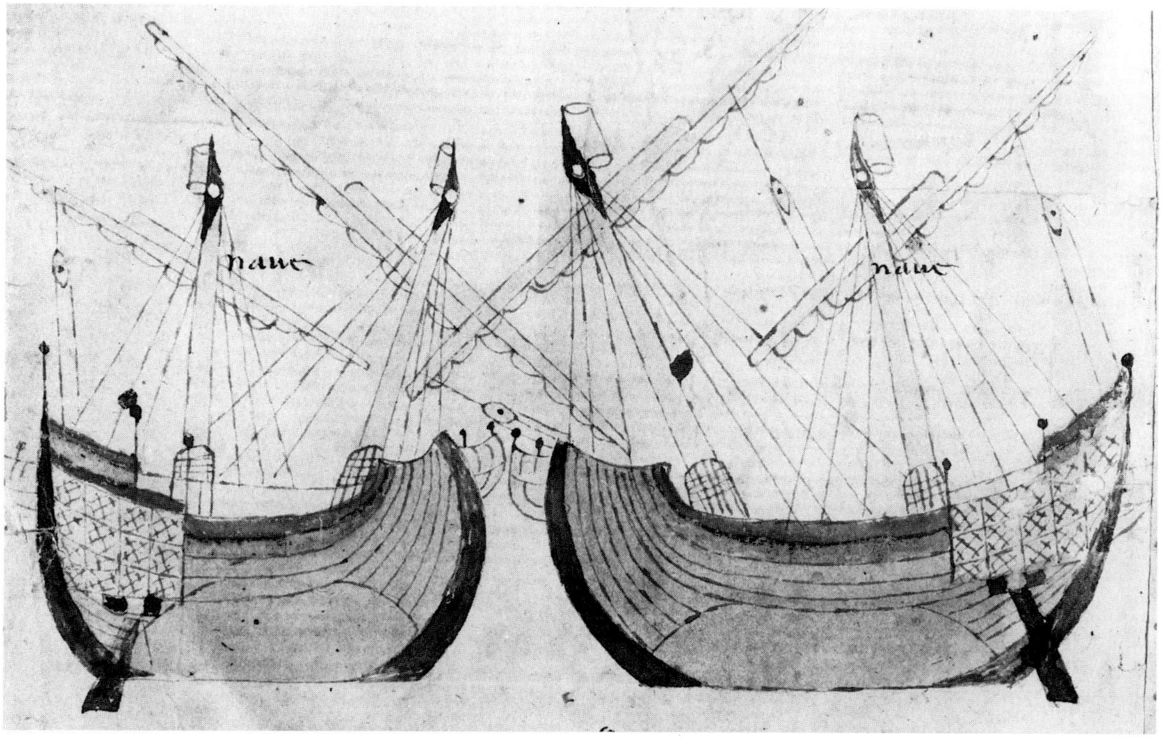

FIG. 63. Two merchant ships illustrated in *Zibaldone da Canale,* a Venetian manuscript dating to ca. 1312. *Courtesy the Beinecke Rare Book and Manuscript Library, Yale University*

a backstay. A fifth line is aft of the mizzen. These three lines are not defined on the ship to the left. The furled yards, hung high on their masts, are composed of two distinctly represented spars, the cares and the *pennae.* A cylindrical crow's nest is attached to the aft side at the top of each mast, where a well-defined sheave block, the *cholzexe* is evident (also well detailed in fig. 93).

Only four of the eight vang and tack required for two, two-masted lateeners have actually been drawn in figure 63. On the left ship, only the mizzen vang is sketched, while on the right ship, the mizzen vang is evident, as are both vang and tack on the foremast. When sketched, vang and tack can be seen with their respective pulleys, generally tied off to bow or stern, though in some versions (such as fig. 62), the mizzen vang is secured to the small platform projecting aft of the sterncastle. In other cases, the foremast vang is omitted entirely (e.g., fig. 63, left ship), or, the foremast vang appears to end at the yard of the mizzen sail (e.g., fig. 63, right ship). Perhaps the artist made such errors in order to simplify the rigging, so as not to confuse with other lines.

Like the Contarina ship, the bottoms of these vessels are flat. The stem and sternposts curve gently upward, inward at the bow. The stem is slightly more curved than the stern, implying a fuller, rounded bow. Planking runs parallel to the sheer and the stem and converges at the forecastle. Details of the upper planking at the stern are covered by the quarterdeck structure.

Though the ships differ slightly in shape at bow and stern, both ends have platforms projecting beyond the main lines of the ship. These platforms are supported by braces below and have thin uprights decorated with finials at each corner. The small platform at the bow was probably used for working the foresail and possibly as a riding bitt for catting up the anchor. The sketches show that the aft platform was used to secure the vang, but it may have also been the *bellatorium* or *ballador,* a fighting platform. A quarter rudder is shown attached with a brace-mount visible just below the quarterdeck; the

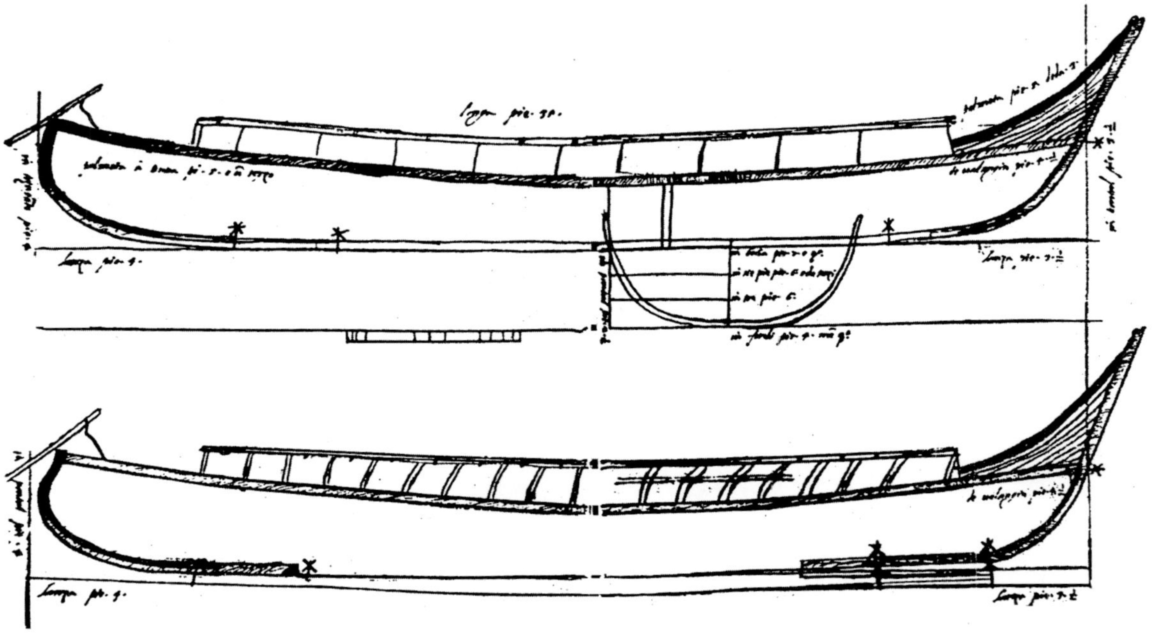

FIG. 64. Flanders galley profiles, from *Arte de far vasselli,* sixteenth-century copy of original material dating to ca. 1410

rudder shaft passed through the floor of the quarterdeck to inboard.

Figure 64

Treatise title: *Arte de far vasselli.*

Theme: Venetian technical treatise on galley construction.

Location: Vienna Osterreichische Nationalbibliothek, *Cod.* 6391 (nearly identical copy of *Fabrica di galere* manuscript in the National Library of Florence, Cl. XIX, n. 7), Vienna.

Date: Late fifteenth-century or sixteenth-century copy of original material, ca. 1410.

Types: Figure 64: Three-masted, lateen-rigged merchant ship (Type IIIc).
Figure 66: Three-masted, lateen-rigged merchant ship (Type IIIc).
Figure 67: Single-masted, square-rigged merchant ship (Type IIId).

[Other folios: Four construction plans of single-masted, lateen-rigged merchant ships (Type IIIa); framing details; single-masted, square-rigged merchant ship (Type IIIe). From the related, original manuscript: three-masted, lateen-rigged merchant ship (Type IIIc) (Lane, 1934: fig. III)].

This version of the manuscript dates from the sixteenth century, but it is a copy of an earlier Venetian manuscript from ca. 1410 called *Fabrica di galere* (Lane, 1934: fig. III). The manuscript includes cross sections, profiles, and sketches of various framing timbers for several ship types, labeled in the manuscript as the galleys "of Flanders," "of Romania," or, *"nave latina,"* (lateen-rigged ship, fig. 66) and *"nave quadre,"* (square-rigged ship, fig. 67). The square-rigged ship was sometimes called *"cocha,"* a Mediterranean-style "cog." It also contains information about rigging and sailmaking (Anderson, 1945: 160–61; Bellabarba, 1988: 225–39). Three informative folios have been selected for discussion, two illustrating the Flanders merchant galley, first, in plan form (fig. 64), then, lateen-rigged, under sail (fig. 66), and the *nave quadre*, the one-masted, square-rigged round ship under sail (fig. 67).

Figures 64 and 66 offer an idea as to the shape and construction of the early fifteenth-century Flanders merchant galley, a compromise between a round ship and an oared galley, which would have traveled under oar and sail (resembling figs 57 and 58). The profiles sketched in figure 64 indicate a 4.5:1 length-to-beam ratio. The keel line is nearly straight. Two asterisks marked at either end of the keel indicate the position of the scarf for the stem and sternposts. The stern is slightly fuller than the bow, where the rake is pronounced. An outrigger, seen also in figure 66, runs along most of the length of the ship. Bellabarba found the hull proportions, whether lateen- or square-rigged, very similar, with differences in profile above the waterline (1988: 116). The square-rigged ship was rigged, as far as is technically possible, according to criteria and proportions typical of lateen-rigged ships (1988: 235). Chiggiato's reconstruction (1991: figs. 9 and 10) is illustrated as figure 65.

Figure 66

Theme: Venetian technical treatise on galley construction: Flanders merchant galley under sail.

Location: Vienna Osterreichische Nationalbibliothek, Cl. XIX, no. 7; Cod. 6391, folio 14^{V}. (nearly identical copy of *Fabrica di galere* in the National Library of Florence), Vienna.

Type: Single-masted, lateen-rigged merchant ship (Type IIIa).

Figure 66 from *Arte de far vasselli* is of particular interest because this single-masted, lateen-rigged merchant galley illustrates a Flanders merchant galley with the transitional steering system, having both side and stern rudders. In the similar illustration of the original manuscript, even the lifting tackle used to raise the starboard side rudder is depicted (Lane, 1932, fig. 3). A ship like that made from the sections in figure 64, but smaller, is under sail.

Any ship with a curved rudder on the sternpost (elsewhere in the manuscript called *temon bavonescho*) still needed the supplementary quarter rudders, called *zanche,* to be manageable. Later, a straight stern rudder was securely attached with tempered iron pintles and gudgeons to a straight sternpost, and side rudders became superfluous.[7]

The nearly vertical orientation of the single mast is in error for a lateener. Its yard is shown as four spar sections spliced together instead of the normal two; extra sections were added whenever a larger sail was required. Seams along rectangular bands of sailcloth were sewn together at their ends and sides to form the sail, bellied to the wind. Lashings for the shrouds and a pennant are visible at the head of the mast. Four sets of lines with tackle aft of the mast probably indicate the shrouds or backstays, and the halyard. The vang is tied off aft, to both port and starboard. No tack is indicated, but three more pairs of lines with tackle secured forward of the mast represent more shrouds.

Two crutches brace a horizontal bar, stanchions to support a tent on the quarterdeck surrounded by a parapet (as in figs. 27, 69, and 153). The manuscript specifies the ship had seventy-three or seventy-four frames (Lane, 1934: 8). An outrigger, with nine supports defined below and a balustrade above, runs forward from the quarterdeck to the bow, just aft of where a grapnel is hung with its crown slung forward. Note the capstan on deck.

Figure 67

Theme: Venetian technical treatise on galley construction. "Nave" under sail.

Location: Vienna Osterreichische Nationalbibliothek, *Cod.* 6391, folio 52 (nearly identical copy of *Fabrica di galere* manuscript in the National Library of Florence, Cl. XIX, n. 7), Vienna.

Type: Single-masted, square-rigged merchant ship (Type IIId).

Figure 67, shown under sail, is labeled a *"nave"* in the manuscript *Arte de far vasselli,* though similar vessels are identified *"nave quadre"* and *"cocha"* elsewhere in the manuscript (Bellabarba, 1988: 113). It has one square-rigged mast stepped vertically amidships. A large, centrally placed crow's nest crowns the mast. Seven lines secured to the base of the crow's nest represent the lifts of the square sail. One brace is shown, secured to the

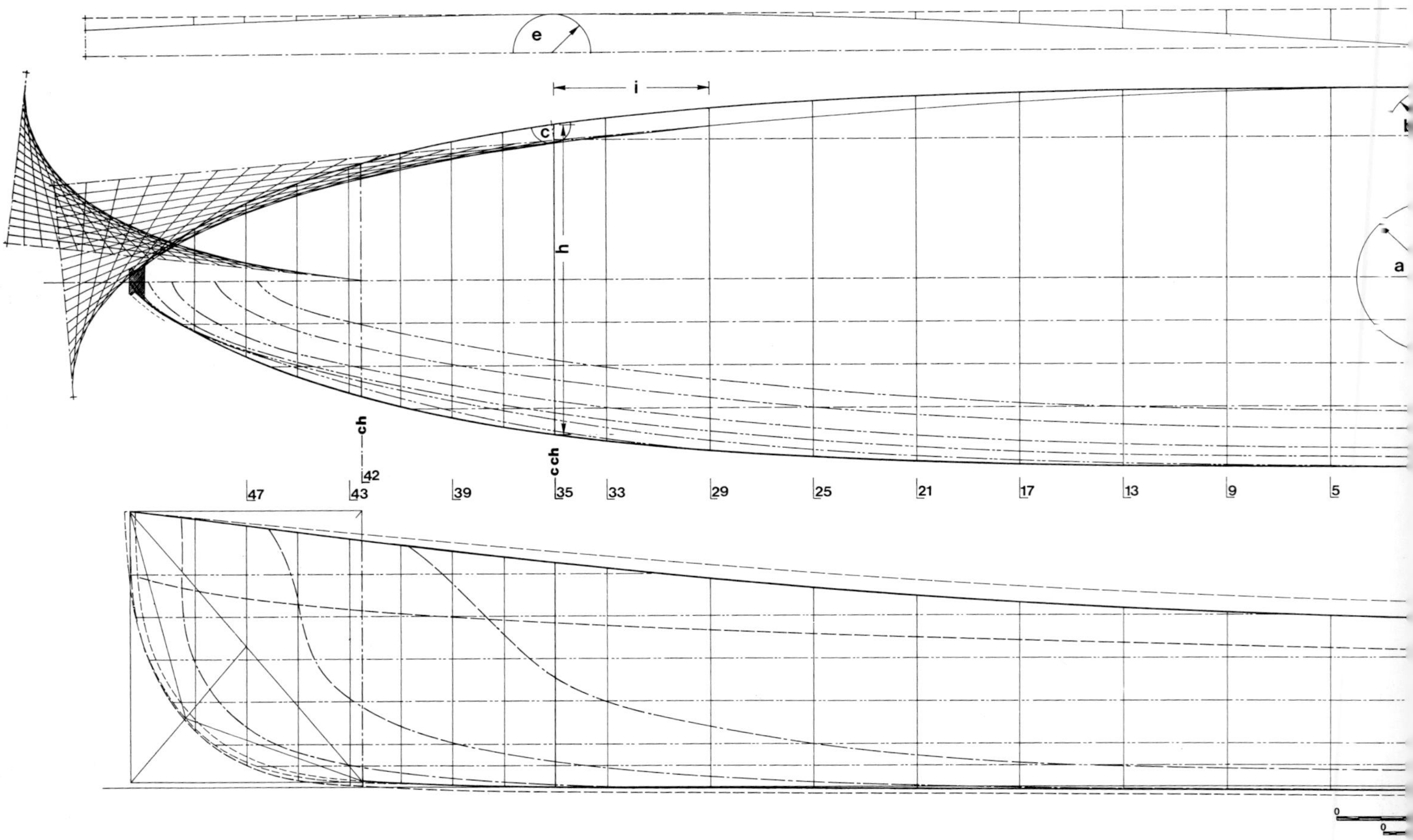

Fig. 65. Reconstruction of the fifteenth-century merchant galley in *Fabrica di galere.* Alvise Chiggiato's translation of his original captions: Longitudinal sections [above]. Plan for a Flanders *galea del sexto,* Venice, c. 1410. Double scale: upper scale in *pie* (Venetian *piede*), lower scale in meters. Evaluation of reliability: 95%, due to some unexplained copyist errors. The numbers diverging from midships show the progressive numbers of frames. The geometric construction of the deck plan, allowing the widths g and h, requires the application of the [parabolic] mold originating not at the *chodera chorba,* but 6 *moduli* back, toward midships.[8] Normally, instead, the sinusoid curve *[partixon del mader de bocha]* and parabolic mold are consecutive.[9] It is a variation of the standard system permitting a more regular rounding, found, until now, only in the Fabrica. (a) *partixon de fondi*[10] (b) *partixon del mader de bocha*[11] (c) *partixon del ramo*[12] (e) *schorer del sexto*[13] (f) *lata* [the main beam] and 4 *chorbe de mezzo*[14] (g) beam at deck level at the *chodera chorba* of the bow (h) beam at deck level at the *chodera choba* of the stern (i) moving backwards the origin placement of the parabolic mold (ch) *poselexe del choltro* (c ch) *chodera chorba.* Transverse section [right]. Sequence for a Flanders *galea del sexto,* Venice, c. 1410. Double scale in *pie:* upper scale in *pie* (Venetian *piede*), lower scale in meters. Evaluation of reliability: 100%. *Courtesy A. Chiggiato, 1991: figs. 9 and 10*

foredeck, where there is a bowsprit; three lines, tack and sheets, tied aft, manage the foot of the large sail. Three lines with tackle aft of the mast represent shrouds and a backstay.

The ship reflects some characteristics of a *coche* (cf. figs. 110 and 122). The hull appears to have a relatively straight keel, a sharp rise to the stern, and a transom stern, integrated castle structures but no tumble home. Side planking and wales are generically represented with pairs of parallel

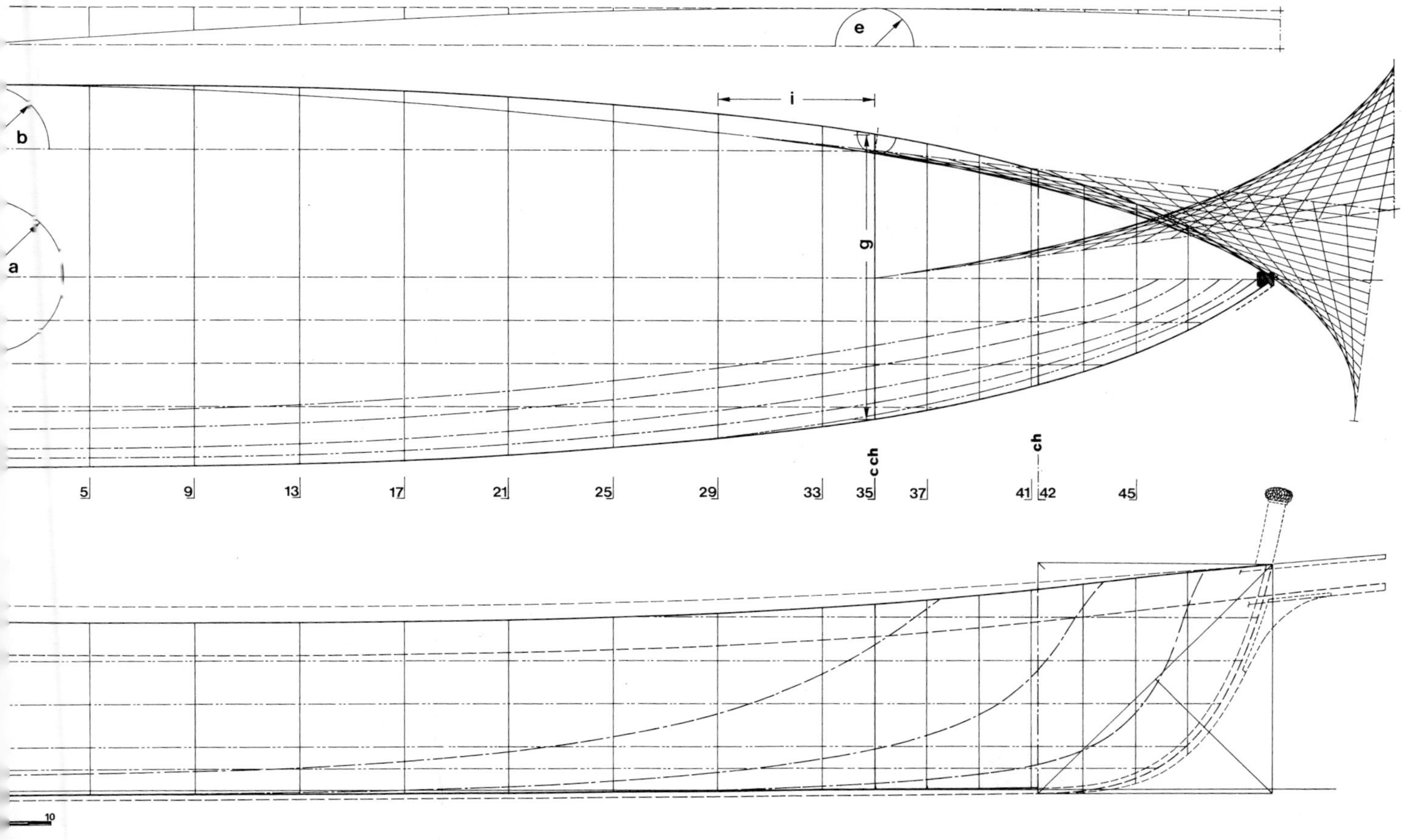

running lines from the end of the stern but bending upward in the bow to finish at the foredeck; Bellabarba pointed out that this is not a typical run of skeleton-first construction (1988: 239). This may indicate lapstrake siding better defined on the foredeck exteriors of the carracks in figures 70 and 71.

One straight rudder is mounted at the stern; no supplemental side rudder is shown. In the manuscript, the straight rudder is described as two feet longer than the stern post, and its width is a quarter of its length *"alla pala,"* which Bellabarba has interpreted to mean "at its widest point" (1988: 117).

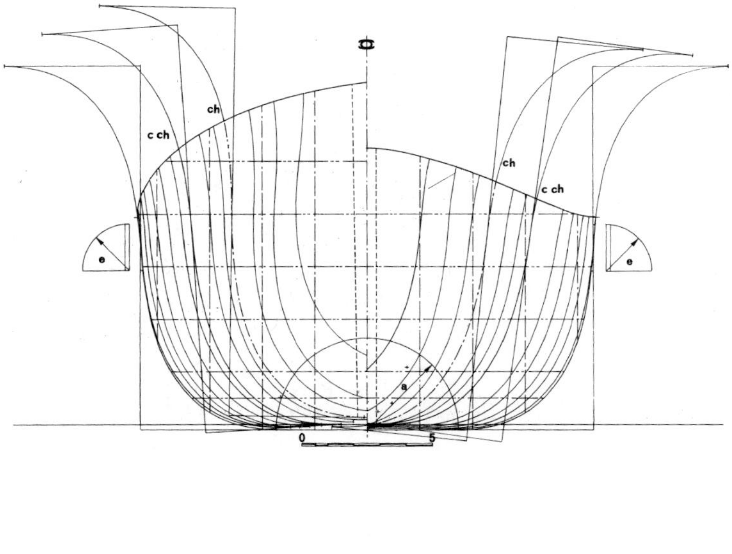

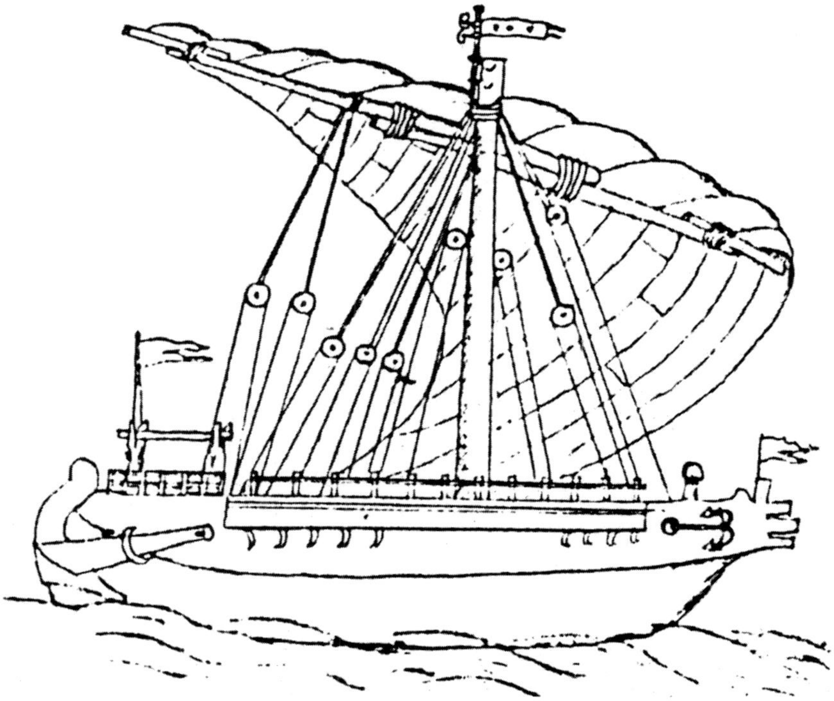

FIG. 66. Flanders galley under sail, from *Arte de far vasselli,* sixteenth-century copy of material dating to ca. 1410. Note the redundant steering systems and the grapnel anchor and capstan at the bow.

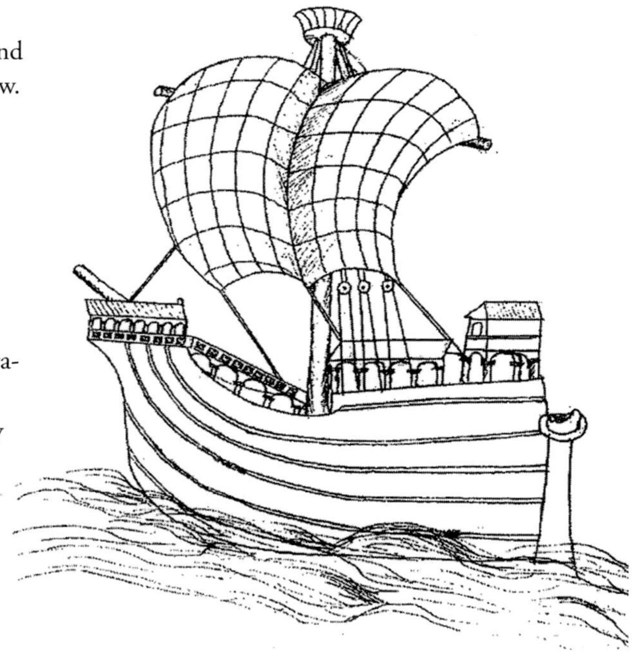

FIG. 67. Mediterranean-style *coche* under sail, simply identified as *"nave"* in *Arte de far vasselli,* the sixteenth-century copy of material ca. 1410

Figure 68
Title: *Book of Zorzi.*
Artist/author: Zorzi Trombetta (trumpeter) of Modon, mistakenly referred to as "Timbotta."
Theme: Venetian technical treatise on seamanship, music, and other subjects: Fig. 68 shows a profile construction plan of merchant galley.
Location: British Museum Library, London, MS.Cotton Titus A, XXVI, folio 57^r.
Date: 1444.
Types: Figure 68: Three-masted, lateen-rigged merchant ship (Type IIIa).
Figure 69: Three-masted, lateen-rigged merchant ship (Type IIIa).
Figure 70: Two-masted, mixed-rigged merchant ship (Type IIIe).
Figure 71: Single-masted, square-rigged merchant ship (Type IIId).
[Other folios: Six lateen-rigged merchant ships (Type IIIc), two two-masted, mixed-rigged merchant ships (Type IIIe)].

Zorzi's notebook contains information on construction, yards, rigging, and sailmaking for both long ships and round ships, as well as designs of siege machinery and other implements of war. Including figure 68, there are seven similar sketches of merchant galley profiles, with details for joining different framing timbers (e.g., a keel scarf, fig. 134). Five sketches of completed vessels include an oared merchant galley with three lateen-rigged masts (Type IIIa; fig. 69), three large *nave*, carracks on folios 37^v and 42^r, two Type IIIe of 700 *botti,*[15] roughly 420 dead weight tons; and one, Type IIIe, of 1000 *botti*, or about 600 tons (fig. 70), and one single-masted, square-rigged merchant ship (Type IIId; fig. 71).

Figure 68, a construction plan, shows profiles and dimensions for a merchant galley, propelled by three large lateen sails and supplemented by rowers as illustrated in the completed vessel, figure 69. The beam at midships is specified on the profile sketch as 5.5 *pie* (1.9[illegible] meters)[16]; the width in *fondo* (across the bottom

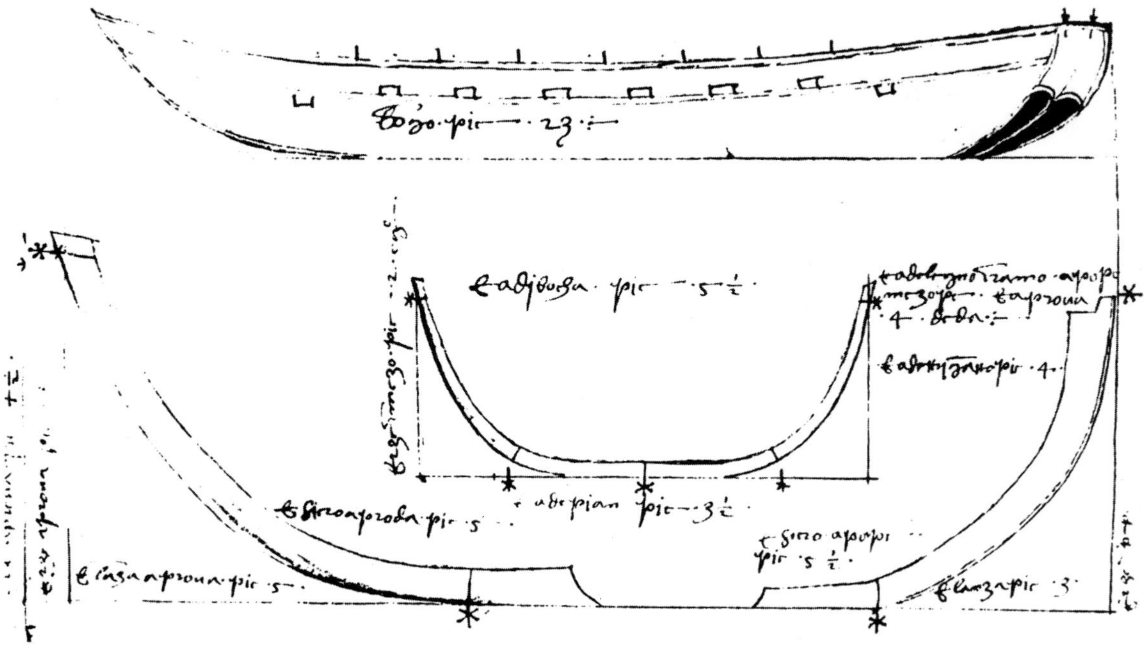

FIG. 68. Profile sections of a galley from the mid-fifteenth-century book of Zorzi of Modon. Note the shape of the stern.

of the hull) is 3.5 *pie* (1.22 meters); and the overall length is 23 *pie* (8 meters). Other merchant galleys (folios 57^{v}, 58^{r}, 58^{v}, 59^{r}, 59^{v}, and 60^{r}) range in length from 15 to 35 1/2 *pie* (5.22 to 12.35 meters).

The representative galley, figure 68, is flat bottomed, with a straight keel and shallow draft. Strakes, although not defined, would have paralleled the main wale to finish at two outer stern timbers and not into the central sternpost. This brings us to the illustration's most noteworthy characteristic. The stern is a wing transom, not evident in the profile view of the completed vessel, figure 69, where it might be interpreted as having just a single post. The construction view of the stern in perspective clearly reveals a slightly curved transom shape. It is formed by two curving outer posts flanking the central sternpost, where a rudder would be fitted to the post's curve (visible in fig. 69). The stern's shape permitted the necessary movement of a single, curved, stern rudder, yet this design would be improved with a flat transom stern, to which a stronger and more efficient, straight stern rudder could be mounted as in figure 70.

Figure 69

Theme: Venetian technical treatise on seamanship: merchant galley under sail.
Location: British Museum Library, London, MS.Cotton Titus A, XXVI, folio 48^{v}.
Type: Three-masted, lateen-rigged merchant ship (Type IIIa).

The grouping of the fifty-seven oars (and their thole pins) in threes, *a terzaruolo*, identifies figure 69 from the Book of Zorzi as a trireme merchant galley. The long ship has three lateen-rigged masts that diminish in height. Their sails correspondingly are reduced in size, from the largest, foremast, to the smallest, mizzen. All masts are shown as nearly vertical except strangely enough, the central mast, which inclines slightly forward. The foremast especially should incline further forward for a lateener. A pair of spars form each yard; these are lashed together at two places on

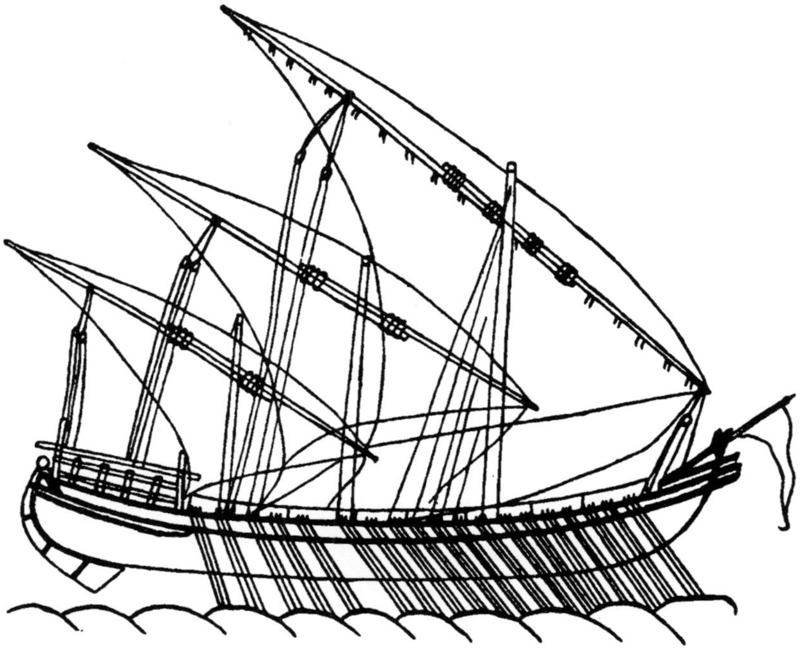

FIG. 69. Galley under navigation, from the mid-fifteenth-century book by Zorzi of Modon

the smaller mizzen and central masts' yards, but at four places on the foremast's large yard. All these yards were quite heavy and would have necessitated a large crew. No crow's nests have been depicted.

Certain rigging lines have been accurately placed while others are omitted. On the foremast, there are five shrouds to starboard alone, with none shown to port, and a pair of vang lines, which are both secured to starboard. Here is the first example of the *mulgaranus*, a heavy rope attached to the base of the cares, secured amidships. With the help of its tackle, the mariners could control the yard's fore and aft movement. This was necessary to peak the yard while tacking and to obtain maximum efficiency of the sail while under way. Just forward of the *mulgaranus*, tack are also tied to the lower end of the *cares*, one set to haul to port and the other to starboard. Sheet, tack, and vang are defined for the sails of the central and mizzen masts, along with the vang tackle.

Although much larger and sleeker in shape, this galley is similar to figure 66. In both cases, the keel is almost completely straight. A balustrade surrounds the quarterdeck, where two stanchions supporting a horizontal bar served to frame a tent (as in figs. 27, 45, 65, and 153).

This vessel, dating from the mid-fifteenth century, already appears to be completely dependent on the new system of a single rudder attached to the curved sternpost with pintles and gudgeons. It is shown to curve gently beneath the hull, which is a weak design, but there is no evidence for supplementary quarter rudders. This design would improve with a straight stern rudder attached to a flush transom-style stern (as in fig. 70), instead of this slightly curved stern shape.

Figure 70

Theme: Venetian technical treatise on seamanship: two-masted, mixed-rigged round ship.

Location: British Museum Library, London, MS.Cotton Titus A, XXVI, folio 41v.

Type: Two-masted, mixed-rigged merchant ship (Type IIIe).

Zorzi gives the base dimensions for eight different ships ranging in size from 200–1000 *botti*. The caption of this folio identifies figure 70 as Zorzi's fifteenth-century concept of a 1000 *botte nave* (Type IIIf), which corresponds roughly to 600 dead weight tons. It is a good representation of what we would call a carrack, built the Mediterranean way—frame first, with castles integrated into the hull at both ends. Dimensions given in the manuscript indicate a keel length of 85 *piede* (29.56 meters), a width at the level of the first deck of 11 piede (3.83 meters), and 34 *piede* (11.82 meters) at the level of the second deck (Lane, 1934: 237 and table C). It also had additional deck levels at the sterncastle and the forecastle.

Masts are not illustrated; only a bowsprit is in place. A ship of this size would have had at least one mainmast, rigged square, and probably a mizzen, rigged lateen, as does the very comparable figure 110.

Because of the clarity and simplification of

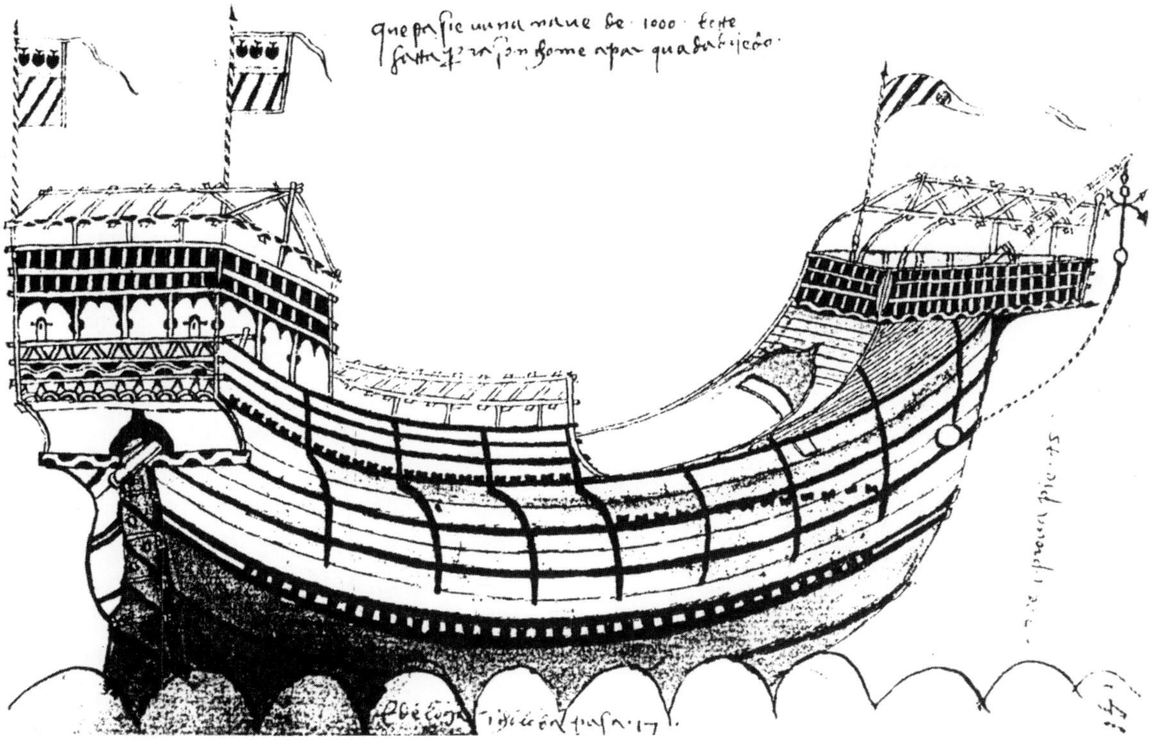

FIG. 70. Carrack labeled *"nave"* of "1000 *botte,"* from the mid-fifteenth-century book by Zorzi of Modon. Note a grapnel anchor hung from the bowsprit.

the lines representing the strakes and wales, this illustration is helpful in interpreting the ship type. The stern configuration is distinctive. A row of thirty-five through-beams defines the level of the first deck. The hull planking beneath and just above the first deck level finish into the sternpost, while higher strakes, along the line of the hull where it begins to bulge outward (below the tumble home) finish into the tragent. The strakes above these, forming the tumble home and bulwarks, end at the corners of the sterncastle. The result is a full, flush-ended stern, a characteristic type of transom seen in many late medieval representations. Along the upper side of the tumble home a row of twenty-three through-beams defines an upper deck level aft of midships, with vertical reinforcements on the upper sides of the hull. A portion of this sterncastle area is open, with just awning structures; however, a massive castle construction astern is more complex, with an arcaded framed structure above housing two capstans and the rudder's whipstaff for the helmsman. The single stern rudder is attached, *alla bavonescho,* to the straight sternpost with pintles and gudgeons. This straight rudder is distinctly different from one that curves along the curved sternpost and beneath the hull in figure 69.

A horizontal row of thirteen through-beams forward of midships defines the foredeck. The lapstrake siding, the after side of the forecastle with horizontally planked arched entrance, and the lattice-worked palisade are characteristic in form for carracks. Of particular interest is the way the sides and back of the forecastle are planked, like a wooden structure on land; house carpenters did the upper works of vessels at Venice. A grapnel anchor hangs from the bowsprit; its hawser passes through the starboard hawse hole.

Figure 71

Theme: Venetian technical treatise on seamanship: square-rigged round ship.

Location: British Museum Library, London, MS. Cotton Titus A, XXVI, folio 49^{r}, London.

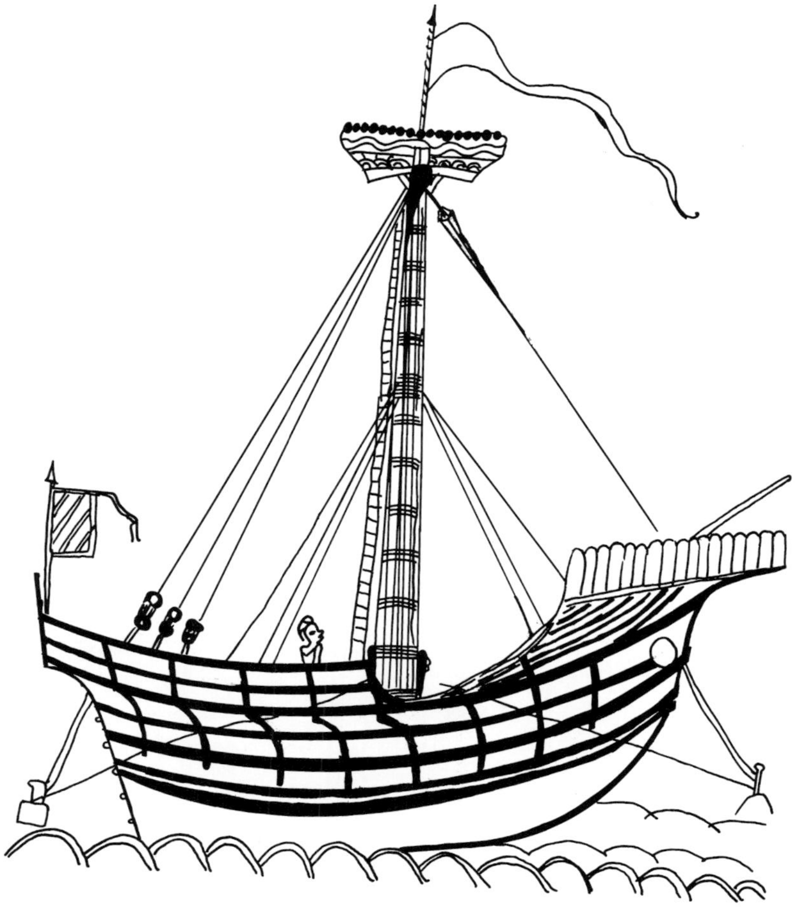

FIG. 71. *Cocha* (carrack) from the mid-fifteenth-century book by Zorzi of Modon

Type: Single-masted, square-rigged merchant ship (Type IIId).

Another folio from Zorzi's notebook illustrates a single-masted *cocha* or carrack (fig. 71). The mainmast stepped vertically amidships and the large, centrally placed crow's nest point to a square-rigged mast. The vessel is moored ashore, and the yard and sail, not depicted, are apparently stored. Wooldings—regularly spaced mast lashings—are evident all the way up the mast. These girdings and the vertical lines running the length of the mast indicate that it was made up of many pieces (cf. fig. 110). This either indicates that the ship was quite large or, at the time of its construction, there was a shortage of adequate lumber. A rope ladder aft of the mast provides access to the crow's nest, from where a pennant is displayed. A bowsprit inclines forward from the forecastle.

On the mainmast, three stays, attached to the top of the mast, are fixed toward the stern bulwarks through blocks; a forestay runs through blocks to the foredeck. Six lines attached at the mast's midpoint also appear to tie off forward and aft; these might be intended as shrouds secured to each side.

Like figure 70, the hull shape is typical of the carrack, with characteristic tumble home. The keel appears relatively straight, with a gradual rake to the stem, and ends presumably at the bottom of the transom stern. The bow is slightly higher than the stern and has a forecastle. Regularly spaced lines represent strakes, the main and upper wales. Vertical girding timbers strengthen the upper sides' tumble home. At the stern, the wales seem to end at the outer edge of a transom. The forecastle is defined by lapstrake side planking curving upward to an upper palisade. Barely visible is the arched opening on the after side of the forecastle.

The rudder is not indicated. It must have been the straight, stern-mounted type. No anchors are visible, but lines run from the base of the mast, starboard, and through the port hawse hole, and from the port quarterdeck, to moorings tied ashore forward and aft of the ship.

Figure 72
Title: *De architectura.*
Theme: Architectural drawing, Venetian palace.
Artist/Author: Antonio Averulino (the "Filarete").
Location: Biblioteca Marciana Nazionale, Cod. Marc. Lat. VIII, 2 (=2796) 157[r], Venice (Zorzi, 1988: table LXXXIIIV).
Date: second half of the fifteenth century.
Types: Lagoonal craft (Type Ib) and three-masted, mixed-rigged ship (Type IIIf).

Antonio Averulino's architectural sketches include a gondolier passing in front of a palace and a three-masted, mixed-rigged ship to the right in the background (fig. 72). Although both vessels are simply defined, their forms are nonetheless quite precise. As one sees today along the canals of Venice, the gondolier stands at the stern of the gondola, working his oar in a forcole. His boat, a simple open hull with upward curving ends, is black. Gondolas are designed in an asymmetric form, which makes them tend to starboard. This helps adjust for continual strokes from the starboard to maintain a straight path. Further correction can be obtained by repositioning the load.

The background ship is simplified to bare essentials, but its profile resembles the *coche*, with pronounced castles at bow and stern, perhaps also exemplified by figures 56, 60, and 67. Although no hawser is visible, the ship is apparently at anchor, with sails and yards stowed. The central yard for the square sail hangs inclined off its mast, while the smaller yards are not shown. All three masts stand vertically.

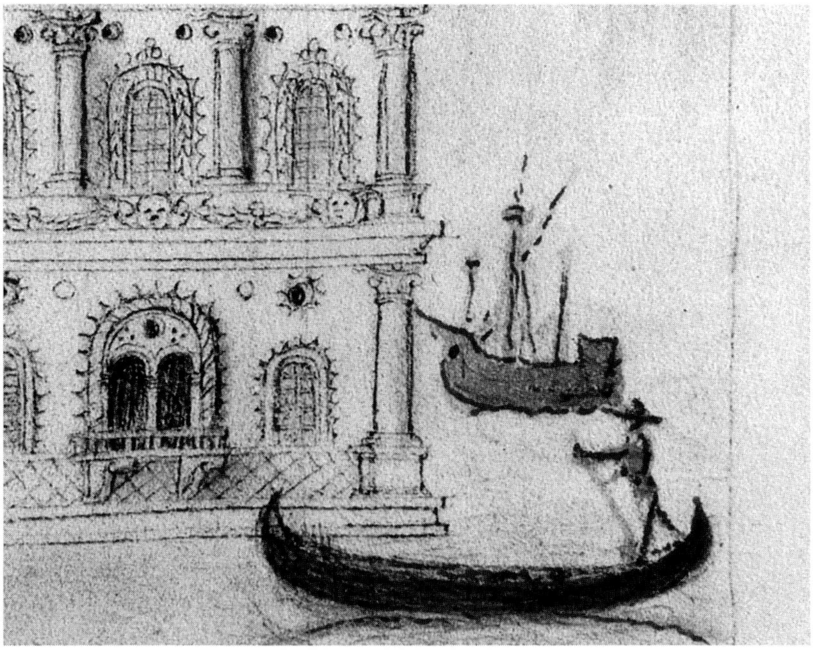

FIG. 72. A three-masted *coche* ship and a gondola, detail from a book on architecture by Antonio Averulino, second half of the fifteenth century. *Courtesy Biblioteca Nationale Marciana*

Frescoes

Figure 73
Theme: "St. Nicholas Saves a Ship in Storm."
Artists: Bolognese-Riminese school.
Location: San Giovanni Chapel, Church of San Domenico, Bolzano.
Date: 1330–40.
Type: Two-masted, lateen-rigged merchant ship (Type IIIb).

The ship's hull is dark and obscure in this fresco (fig. 73), but the superstructure features

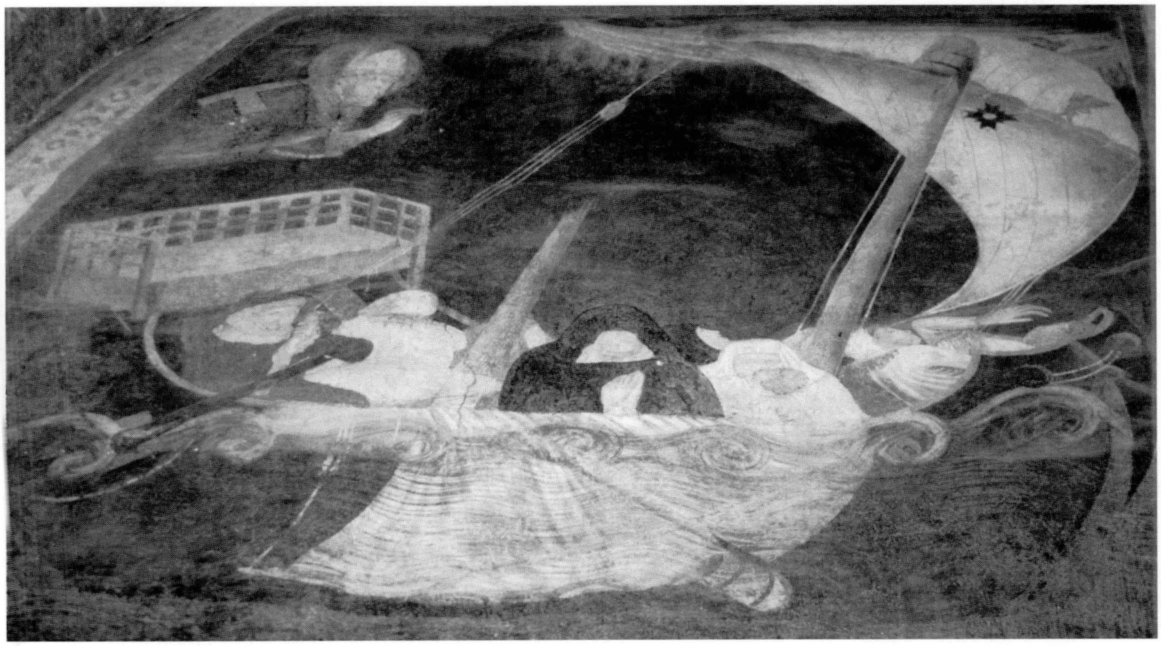

FIG. 73. "St. Nicholas Saves a Ship in Storm" (ca. 1330–40), fresco in the Chapel of San Giovanni, Church of San Domenico, Bolzano

of this two-masted, lateen-rigged round ship in storm are detailed. It has a high, large, rectangular quarterdeck with parapet. The forward limits of this deck were created by the continuation of the sheer strakes. Part of the mizzen has broken during the storm; its mast head, sail, and rig drag in the sea. The wooden parrel is just above the break in the mast. Strong winds buffet the foresail.

The bases of both masts rake strongly forward. The *calcet*, the sheave block at the head of the mast for the halyard (called *cholzexe* in Venetian), and the crow's nest are clear on both mast heads (one, broken free and underwater). Three lines defined fore and two aft of the standing foremast indicate the stays and the halyard. Robands secure the sail to its yard. A vang passing through its sheave block twice is apparent; its fall is being hauled by a sailor at the stern. At the bow, two mariners frantically work to control the sail. A short length of the sheet can also be seen.

The hull itself seems quite rounded and full, with a steep rake at bow and stern and a straight, level sheer strake. The stem and two hawse holes are visible at the bow. The full stern represented must be the transom type, beneath a large quarterdeck. Remaining details of a single quarter rudder and its external mount are too vague to interpret.

Figure 74
Theme: "The Calling of the Apostles James and John."
Artists: Bolognese-Riminese school.
Location: San Giovanni Chapel, Church of San Domenico, Bolzano.
Date: 1330–40.
Type: Fishing boat (Type Ib).

In figure 74, Jesus, standing ashore, calls the men, just returning from fishing, to follow Him. Their small fishing boat is typically lagoonal—with a *forcole* oarlock. The boat appears to be flat bottomed and has a gently rising, pointed stem and an inward-curving stern, roughly equal in height. Two symmetrical oars are worked free of the oarlock as paddles, aft and amidships.

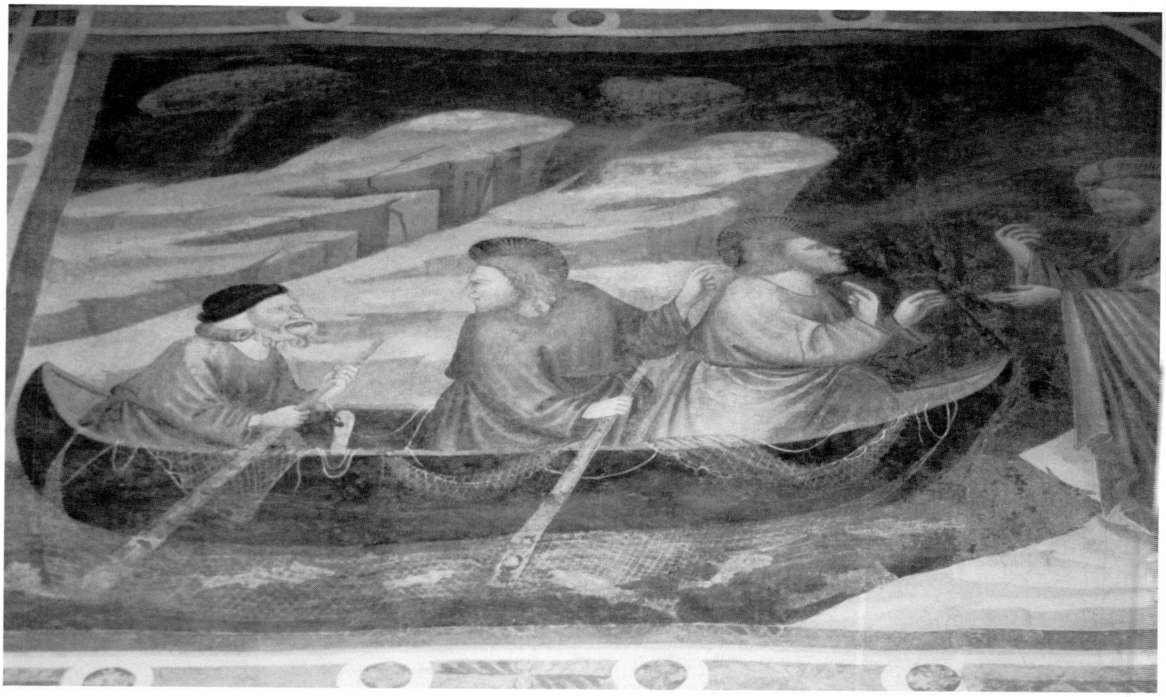

FIG. 74. "The Calling of the Apostles James and John," fresco in the Church of San Domenico, Bolzano (ca. 1330–40)

Figure 75
Theme: "The Calling of James and John."
Artist: Riminese School.
Location: S. Agostino, Rimini (Kaftal, 1978: fig. 674).
Date: First half of fourteenth century.
Type: Three fishing boats (Type Ib).

As is the case with many frescoes, the details of the fresco figure 75 are faded and difficult to make out. Three fishing boats amidst numerous human figures are very simplistically detailed. The basic rounded hull and a few strakes are visible on each craft, but no masts or rigging are defined. Two men on the closer boats each hold a paddle or oar.

Figure 76
Theme: "St. Nicholas of Bari."
Artist: Vitale da Bologna.
Location: Udine Cathedral (Kaftal, 1978: fig. 1002).
Date: 1349.
Type: Single-masted, lateen-rigged merchant ship (Type IIIa).

This poorly preserved fresco (fig. 76) relates a story about a man who made a vow to St. Nicholas because he desired a son. The long-awaited son drowned when the man broke the promise.

Only a few basic lines define a round ship: its wale and sheer strake, a side rudder, and a lateen sail.

Figure 77
Theme: Ship at sail.
Artist: School of Giotto, Pace da Faenze? (Bonino, 1978a: 65).

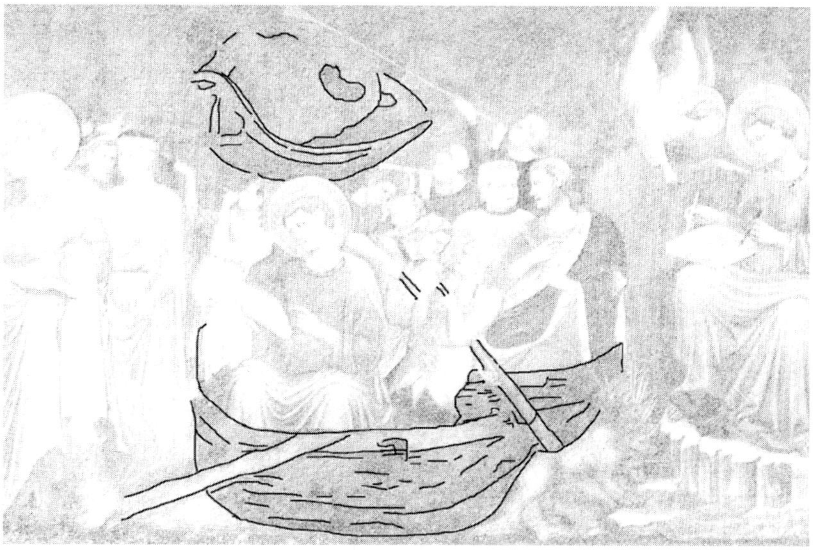

FIG. 75. Three fishing boats from "The Calling of James and John," a fourteenth-century fresco in S. Agostino, Rimini. *Helen C. Dewolf after Kaftal, 1978: fig. 674*

Location: Imola, now lost; recorded by Levi (1892: pl. 26, fig. 2).
Date: Mid-fourteenth century (Bonino, 1978a: 65).
Type: Two-masted, mixed-rigged (?) merchant ship (Type IIIe?).

Details of this representation of a decked and armed merchantman, figure 77, must be consid-

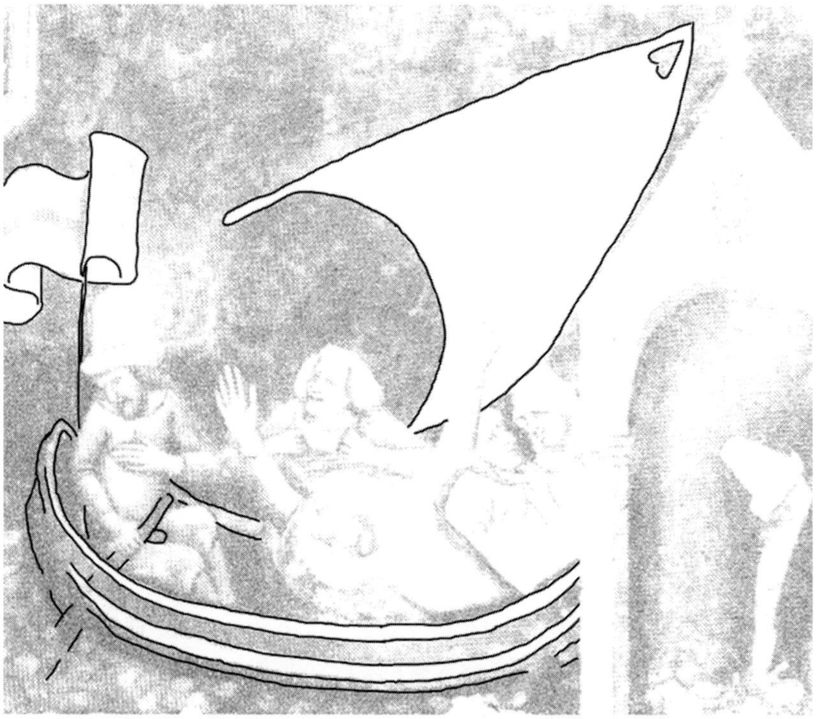

FIG. 76. Round ship from a fresco, "St. Nicholas of Bari," by Vitale da Bologna in Udine Cathedral dating to 1349. *Helen C. Dewolf after Kaftal, 1978: fig. 1002*

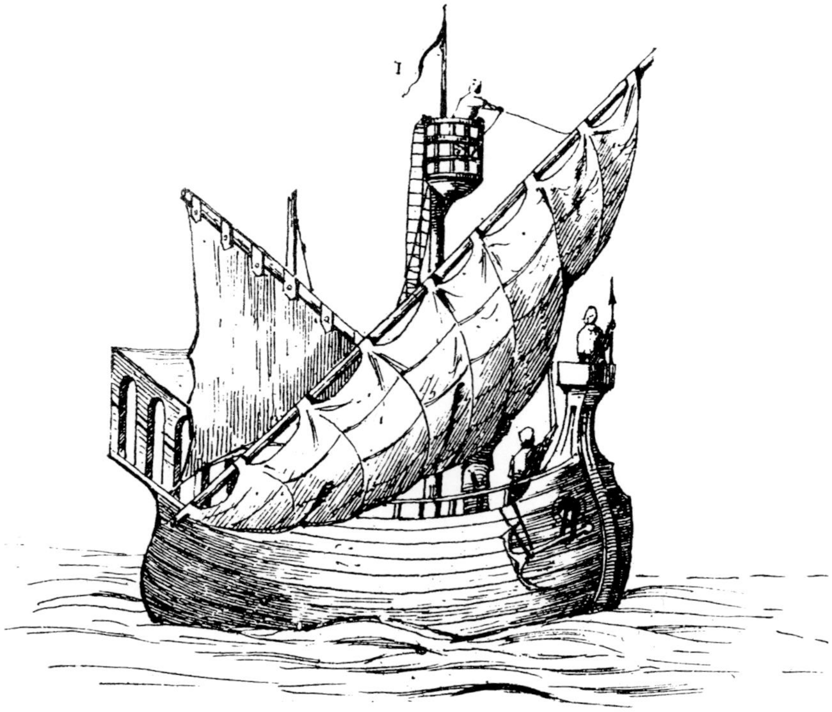

FIG. 77. Mid-fourteenth-century Imola of Faenze fresco by the school of Giotto. *Levi, 1892: pl. 26, fig. 2*

ered with due caution, as the fresco has not been preserved. The only evidence we have for it is a rather problematic rendering of it recorded by Levi in 1892, when the fresco was probably already in a very deteriorated state. Levi's ship is shown under sail, with two seemingly lateen sails. The yards of its two sails are arranged wing to wing, with one inclined to port and the other to starboard; the wind is coming directly from the stern.

Several aspects of Levi's sketch are questionable. The crow's nest is not centrally placed. It is on the forward side of a vertical mast. A lateen-shaped mainsail amidships is shown as being composed of square sections of cloth sewn together, similar to a much earlier ship, figure 8 (which is most likely a square-rigged vessel), and the contemporaneous mixed-rigged figure 51 with a large square sail amidships. Depictions of lateeners that detail sail seams almost without exception show elongated, rectangular sections (figs. 11, 12, 18, 25, 26, 73, 94, 102, 117, 118, and 126). This suggests that Levi erred in his interpretation of the then fading fresco. It seems more likely that the fresco represented the mixed-rigged vessel type that first appeared in the mid-fourteenth century, having its mainmast rigged with a square sail and the mizzen aft, lateen. The presence of the high forecastle is more common to square- or mixed-rigged ships (cf. Bonino, 1978b: fig. 10) than to lateen-rigged ships.

The sails in figure 77 are shown attached to the yards with thin sections of the sail cloth brought around the yard and grommeted closed. This also seems implausible. In other representations where a sail's robands are visible, they are apparently simple, strong rope loops or metal rings. Very little rigging has been detailed. The crow's nest is reached by rope ladders aft of the mast. From this high vantage point, a mariner, aided by another manning a sheet below, begins to swing the yard about, initiating a tack. Of the mizzen's rigging, only the top section of the halyard is shown.

The hull of this ship seems full at both bow and stern. It probably had a transom stern. The stem curves outward near the hawse holes; above, the stem curves inward, and then upward and forward to support the high forecastle like figure 90, where a soldier stands guard. No quarter rudders are evident; a single rudder may have been fixed to the stern. The sterncastle with arch-shaped windows may have had two decks, and it seems integral to the width of the hull. Strakes are shown running parallel to the keel all the way from the stem to the stern. No wales are indicated. Above the sheer strake, along the forward half of the ship not blocked by the sail, the balustrade is visible.

An anchor is shown hung at the bow; its cable passes through a hawse hole, and its shank is supported by a rope tied off inboard. This is the earliest known example of a grapnel anchor in the Romagna region (Bonino, 1978a: 65).

Figure 78

Theme: "St. Eustace Sails to Egypt on a Round Ship."

Artist: Vitale da Bologna, school.

Location: Pomposa Abbey.
Date: 1351.
Type: Single-masted, square-rigged (?) merchant ship (Type IIIa).

Another poorly preserved fresco relates the *vita* of St. Eustace (fig. 78). The sailboat he sails is lacking detail, but the rounded hull, the top of the mast, and what looks to be a square sail are vaguely recognizable.

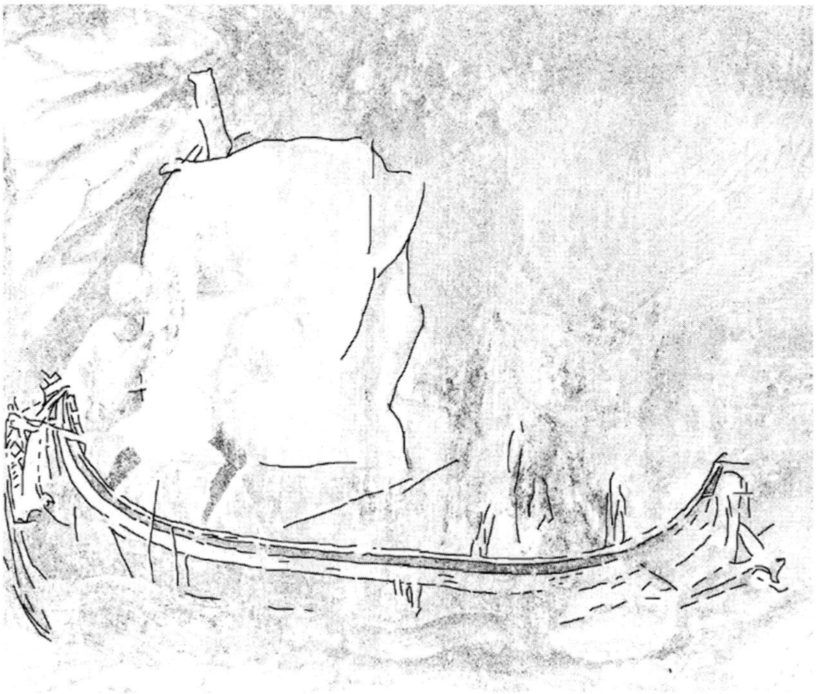

FIG. 78.(above) "St. Eustace Sails to Egypt on a Round Ship," from a fourteenth-century fresco by the school of Vitale da Bologna in Pomposa Abbey. *Helen C. Dewolf after Kaftal, 1978: fig. 364*

Figure 79 (A: foreground vessel; B: background vessel, detail)
Theme: "The Calling of Peter and Andrew."
Artist: Giusto de' Menabuoi.
Location: Baptistry of the Duomo, Padua.
Date: Second half of fourteenth century (Pallucchini, 1964: 124 and Vegas, 1966: Plate 15).
Types: Two fishing boats (Type Ib).

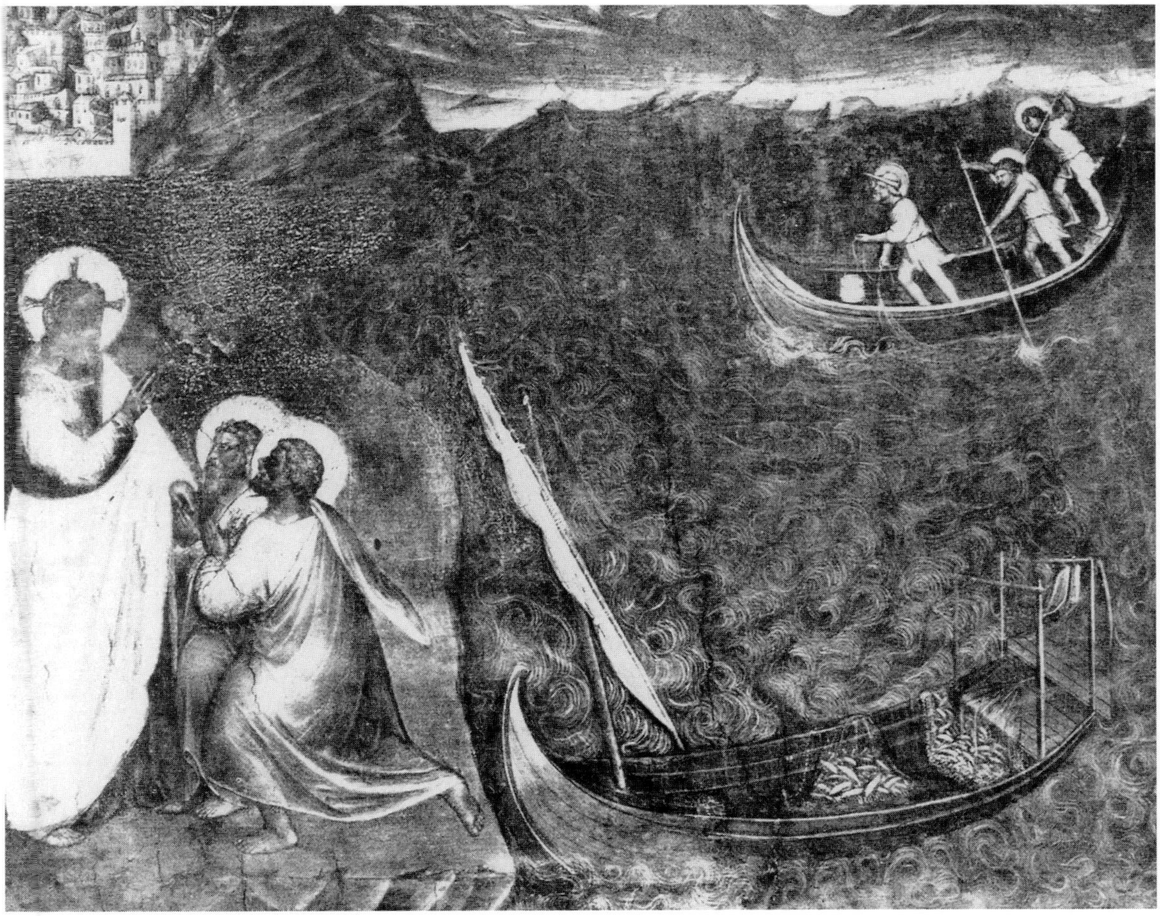

FIG. 79. "The Calling of Peter and Andrew," second half of the fourteenth-century fresco by Giusto de' Menabuoi, Baptistry of the Duomo, Padua. (A) Foreground vessel; (B) Background vessel. *After Pallucchini, 1964: 124*

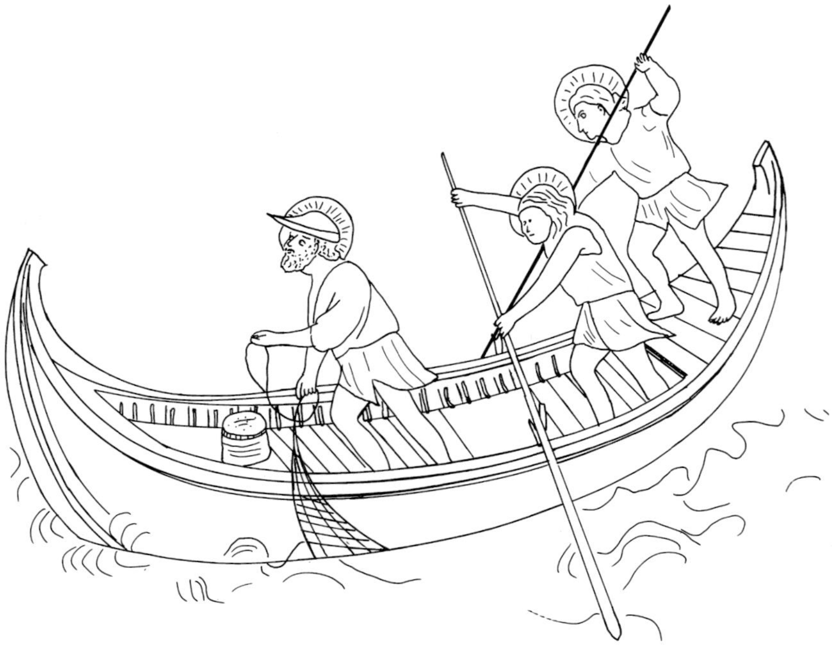

FIG. 80. Punting or paddling a small fishing craft, detail of fig. 79B. *After Vegas, 1966: pl. 15*

This fresco by Menabuoi portrays two medium-sized fishing craft (fig. 79). Peter and Andrew have just returned from a successful fishing trip in the foreground vessel, A. Inboard, two nets are full with a catch of small fish, perhaps mackerel and sardines like those still caught with drift and lampara nets in Italy to this day (Gunda, 1984: 217).

The foreground vessel A, shown just landed ashore, carries a single, forward-raking mast stepped far forward. A lateen sail is furled on its two-spar yard, still hung on the mast. Robands are indicated, although no rigging details are distinguishable.

Through the angle of view he depicted, Menabuoi has portrayed part of the interior of these hulls. Figure 79A has a small, bi-leveled deck platform at the stern, finished with transverse planking, that is, planking arranged perpendicularly to the keel. A square structure of poles framing the lower of the platforms may have supported an awning for shade, or perhaps it was useful in the casting of fishing nets.

A detail of the background vessel, B, is shown as figure 80. No mast has been depicted, but it is likely it also had one that could be simply unstepped. Two men, one balanced on the small deck at the stern, the other, standing on the floor, punt or paddle, while a third draws in their nets.

Menabuoi's fresco of these fishing vessels portrays a type of watercraft best suited for use in shallow, calm water: the minimal keel, high ends and low midships draught would make it rather unseaworthy. The detail in his depiction is remarkable and especially exceptional in showing details of the inside of a small lagoonal fishing craft (as in fig. 107). Framing, set with a consistent room and space, terminates at a rigid, strong sheer strake (see detail, fig. 80). Floor planking has been set perpendicularly to the keel. The craft represented is probably the common *burchio* or the *battèllo*—a lagoonal vessel that was sailed, rowed, or punted—approximately 10 meters long, 3 meters in beam, and with a height at midships of 1.6 meters. The *burchio* resembled the *rascòna* type of the Po, which continued to be used on the Piacenza-Ostiglia of the Po even up until the early twentieth century (Bonino 1978a: fig. 26).

Perhaps similar to (although smaller than) the roughly contemporaneous Logonovo boat, which had a completely flat bottom and no true keel (ca. 1400), these double-ended vessels seem ideal for lagoonal navigation. Stem and stern rise sharply from a flat bottom and finish in high and pointed ends roughly equal in height.

Figure 81

Theme: "St. Ursula and Pope Ciriaco Travel to Colonia."

Artist: Venetian.

Location: Church of St. Ursula, Vigo di Cadore, Belluno.

Date: Late fourteenth century.

Types: Ten single-masted (?) merchant ships (Type IIIa).

This fresco shows a fleet of round ships under sail (fig. 81). The composition and results of deterioration make it difficult to be sure which

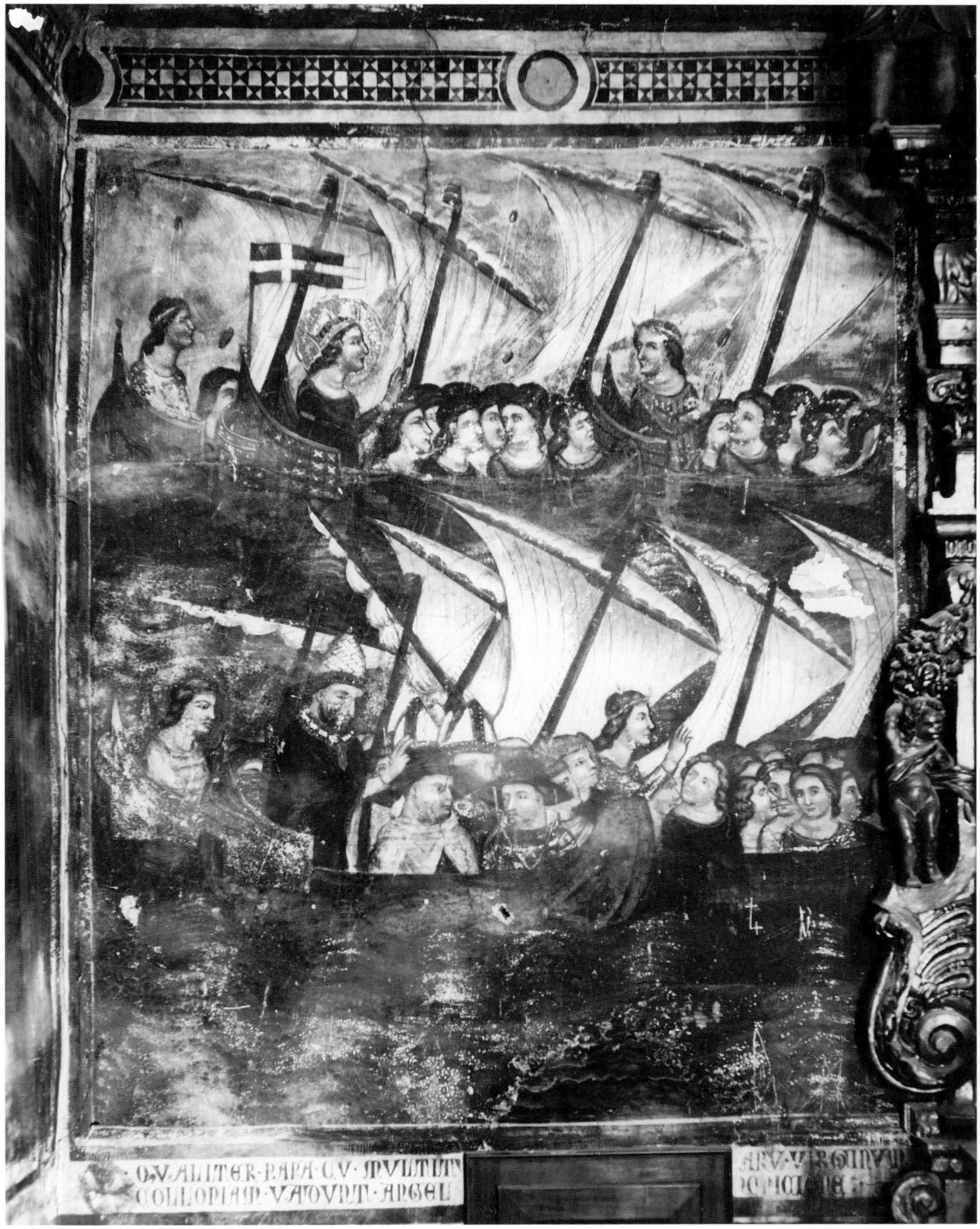

FIG. 81. "St. Ursula and Pope Ciriaco Travel to Colonia." A fleet of round ships from a late fourteenth-century fresco in the Church of St. Ursula, Belluno. *Courtesy Böhm*

of the ten masts go with how many vessels; the image represents between six and ten round ships of one or two masts each. The ships are lateen-rigged, masts inclined forward, with barrel-shaped crow's nests set aft of the mast head accessed by rope ladders. Eight sails are set, while two are furled. Some rigging is visible here and there; note particularly vang and stay tackle and lines on ships in the upper row.

The shape of the hulls resembles figure 87, among others, particularly in the shape of the quarter deck and the triangular, gilded feature at the stern, which may be part of the rudder mount. The second ship from the left, in the bottom row, reveals a blunted bow shape like that seen in figures 73 and 94, and its stempost is defined. Otherwise, few details of actual ship timbers are discernible.

Figure 82
Theme: Ship by *Molo* and Piazzetta of Venice.
Artists: Unknown.
Location: Church of Misericordia at Lucignano, Val di Chiana (Arezzo).
Date: fourteenth century.
Type: Single-masted, mixed-rigged merchant ship (Type IIId).

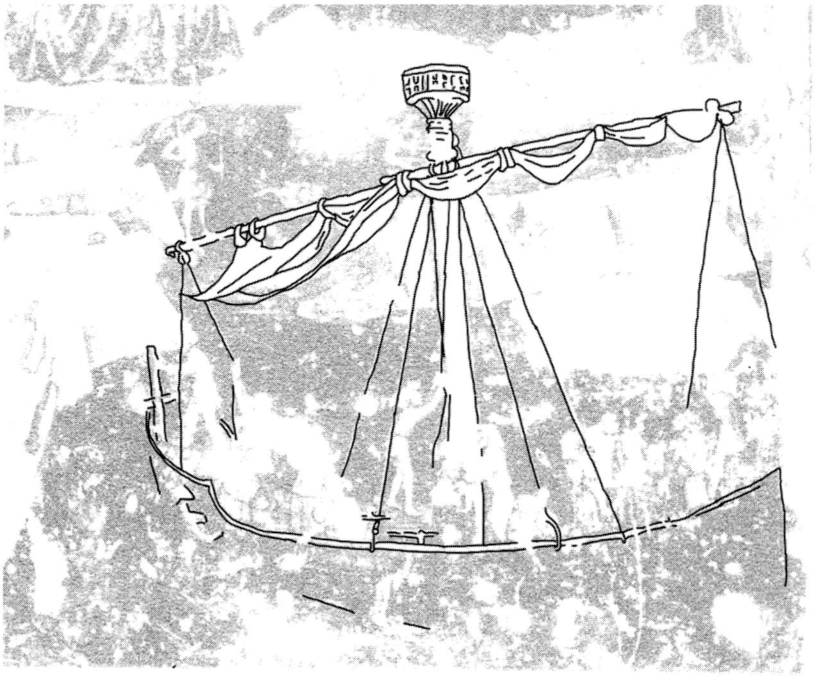

FIG. 82. A fourteenth-century fresco of the Venetian Molo in the Church of the Misericordia at Lucignano, Val di Chiana. *Helen C. Dewolf after Nebbia, 1931: fig. 23*

In figure 82, mariners are in the process of securing the ship's sails after arriving at the quay of Venice. Unfortunately, many details are obscured in this poorly preserved fresco, which Nebbia interpreted as representing a *tarida* (1932: 43). The placement of the single mast amidships in a nearly vertical orientation, the central position of the crow's nest, and the equidistant arms of the yard indicate that the ship is square rigged. Four shroud (or stay) lines are delineated, two fore and two aft of the mast, running to port and starboard, and brace lines forward and aft. The sail itself has been raised completely to stow it, and a man forward of the mast ties off the halyard, while a mariner on the forecastle secures a brace to the stem, or nearby it. Very little of the hull remains, but it is enough to determine the basic round shape with a broadened bow area better defined by figure 128.

Figure 83
Theme: *Vita* of St. Andrew.
Artist: Bertolino dei Grossi (?).
Location: Valeri Chapel, Parma Cathedral (Kaftal, 1978: fig. 55).
Date: ca. 1417–22.
Type: Two-masted, mixed-rigged (?) merchant ship (Type IIIb).
["Calling of Andrew": Two fishing boats (Type Ib) (Kaftal, 1978: figs. 50 and 52)].

Valeri Chapel in Parma Cathedral has some maritime frescoes relating scenes from the *vita* of St. Andrew. Demons have waylaid this ship (fig. 83) carrying forty men on their way to be evangelized by Andrew, drowning them all. The saint later finds their bodies and baptizes them.

Both masts have snapped as the men fight for survival. The tiller of the port rudder is held by the helmsman. It is difficult to be sure of the sail

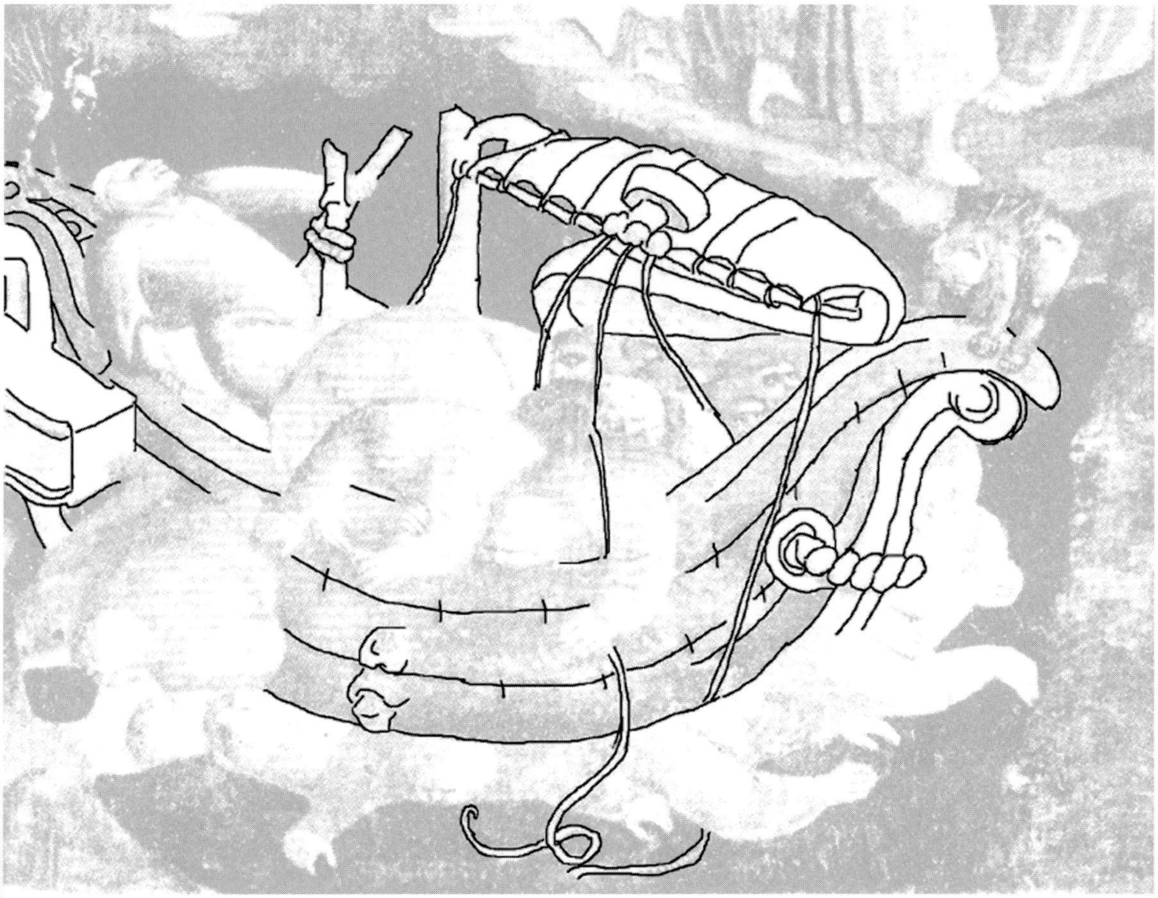

FIG. 83. Round ship in storm, from a fresco of the *vita* of St. Andrew by Bertolino dei Grossi (?) (ca. 1417–22) in Parma Cathedral. *Helen C. Dewolf after Kaftal, 1978: fig. 55*

type. The orientation of the mast and the centrally placed crow's nest seem to indicate a square rig for the mainmast, though that sail seems to show vertical seam lines typical of lateeners. Five rigging lines are loose. At the bow, a large hawser passes around the stem. The rounded stern resembles figures 83 and 96.

Figure 84
Theme: "St. George and the Princess."
Artist: A. Pisano.
Location: Museo di Castelvecchio; formerly in Pellegrini Chapel, Church of San Anastasia, Verona (Kaftal, 1978: 349 and fig. 411).
Date: ca. 1435–36
Type: Riverine cargo vessel (Type Id).

The single-masted, lateen-rigged craft depicted in this now-detached fresco (fig. 84) is a rare portrayal of a river or lagoonal cargo craft with a covered area from somewhere in the stern to about midships. Note the flat bottom that continues forward at the rake to form the blunted bow; there is no keel. Bonino has interpreted the vessel as being of the *burchio* type (1978a: 89). Four shrouds, three to starboard and one to port, are evident, as is the *calcet*. Vang with tackle are secured on the starboard side.

Figure 85
Theme: *Vita* of Blessed Odoric of Pordenone.
Artist: School of the Friuli under Bolognese influence.
Location: S. Francesco, Udine (Kaftal, 1978: fig. 1035).
Date: 1434.
Type: Two-masted, lateen-rigged merchant ship (Type IIIa).

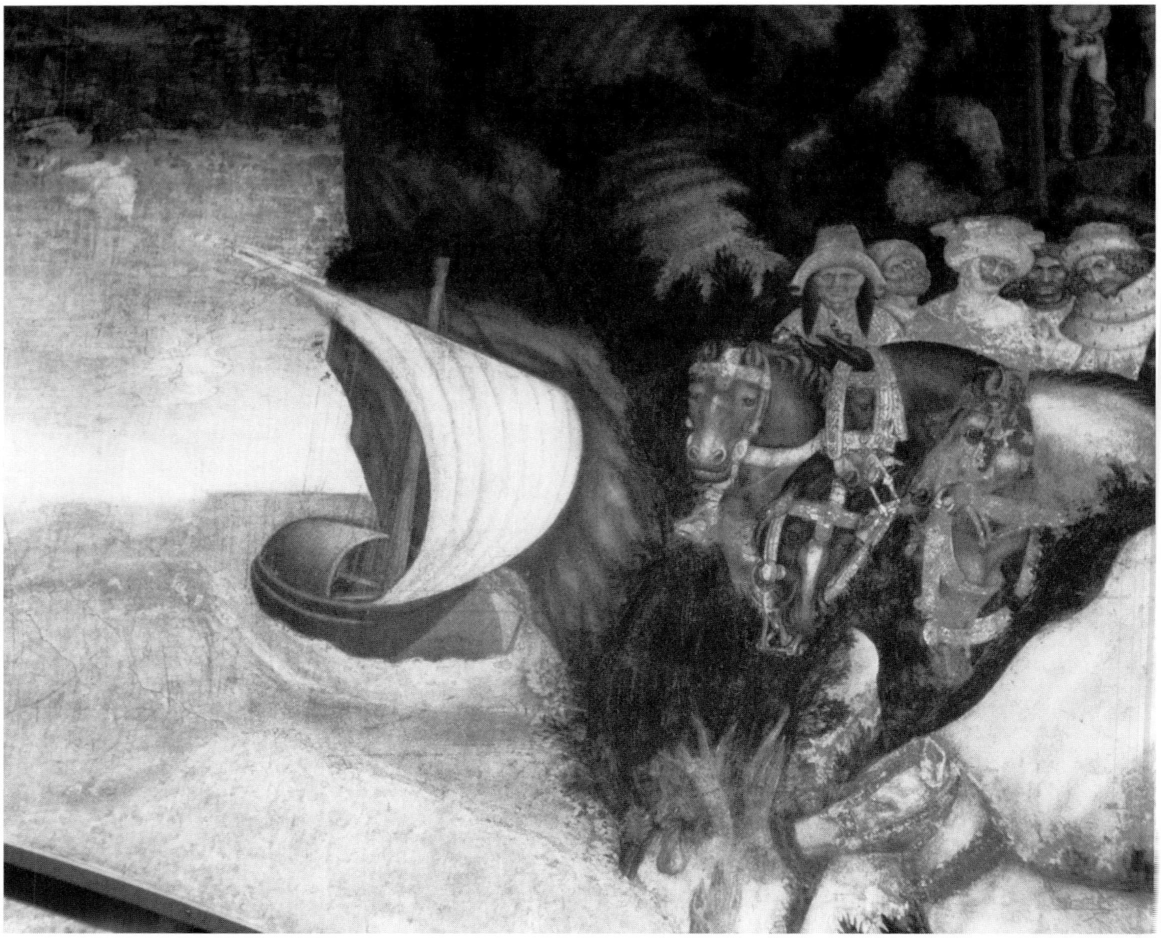

FIG. 84. Detail of a fresco by Pisano, "St. George and the Princess" (ca. 1430), from San Anastasia, Verona

[Others in cycle: Two single-masted (?), lateen-rigged merchant ships (Type IIIa) (Kaftal, 1978: figs. 1033, 1034)].

As a Franciscan missionary to Asia, Odoric went to India to retrieve bones of three martyrs and had various adventures at sea. Odoric died in Udine, and a fresco cycle in San Francesco dedicated to him includes three maritime scenes, though none are well preserved.

Figure 85 shows his ship in harbor. The fresco is very degraded with areas completely missing. A few lines of the mizzen sail are all that is left of that area. The mainsail is lateen, defined with vertical lines to indicate the sail sections. Two crosses decorate the sail, and a crow's nest is just partly visible. Most of the hull is lost, except the very front, which illustrates a broadened bow shape.

Figure 86

Theme: *Vita* of St. Petronius: "He Leaves Constantinople for Rome." (He is bearing a message to the pope from his brother-in-law, Emperor Theodosius.)

Artist: Giovanni da Modena.

Location: S. Petronio, Bolognini Chapel, Bologna (Kaftal, 1978: 861).

Date: Early fifteenth century (Chastel, 1963: 446).

Types: Figure 86: Single-masted (?), lateen-rigged merchant ship (Type IIIa?).

Figure 87: Single-masted (?), lateen-rigged merchant ship (Type IIIa?) and lighter (Type Ia).

Figure 88A foreground: Oared galley warship (Type IIa),

Figure 88B (right) and C (left): Two single-masted, lateen-rigged merchant ships (Type IIIa),

Figure 88D foreground and E background (left): Two lagoonal craft (Type Ib),

Figure 88F background (right): Riverine cargo vessel (Type Id).

Three frescoes in Bolognini Chapel include ship images (figs. 86–88) illustrating scenes from the *vita* of St. Petronius, bishop of Bologna. Only the bow area and one mast can be seen in Kaftal's reproduction of figure 86, but because St. Petronius's ship in the related scenes has only one lateen-rigged mast, this is likely the sole one. This tall mast stands vertically, although a lateen-rigged mast should actually incline forward. The lower part of the sail has been wrapped around the foot of the mast several times, minimizing the sail area (cf. Bonino, 1978a: fig. 12A). The halyard, vang, and two stays or shrouds are illustrated, as are robands. The hull has been defined with a few lines depicting a rounded hull, a few strakes, and a decorative parapet around the foredeck. A grapnel anchor is hung horizontally near a hawse hole, crown aft.

Figure 87

Theme: *Vita* of St. Petronius: "Buying Relics of St. Florian in Palestine" (Kaftal, 1978: 865).

Types: Single-masted (?), lateen-rigged merchant ship (Type IIIa?) and lighter (Type Ia).

Another fresco from St. Petronius's *vita* in Bolognini Chapel, figure 87, shows the stern of a round ship. Only one mast is visible, set aft of midships, with the lateen sail furled high on the yard. Vang, shrouds, and a rope ladder are depicted. Lashings connecting the two spars of the yard are detailed.

The hull is full and rounded, with a large quarterdeck at the stern. In the foreground, enough detail is given to see that wide planking is attached to frames by evenly spaced nails along both edges of each plank. The view of the stern, slightly from above, shows a curved support strut beneath the quarterdeck and perhaps illuminates the design of other high, rounded quarterdecks,

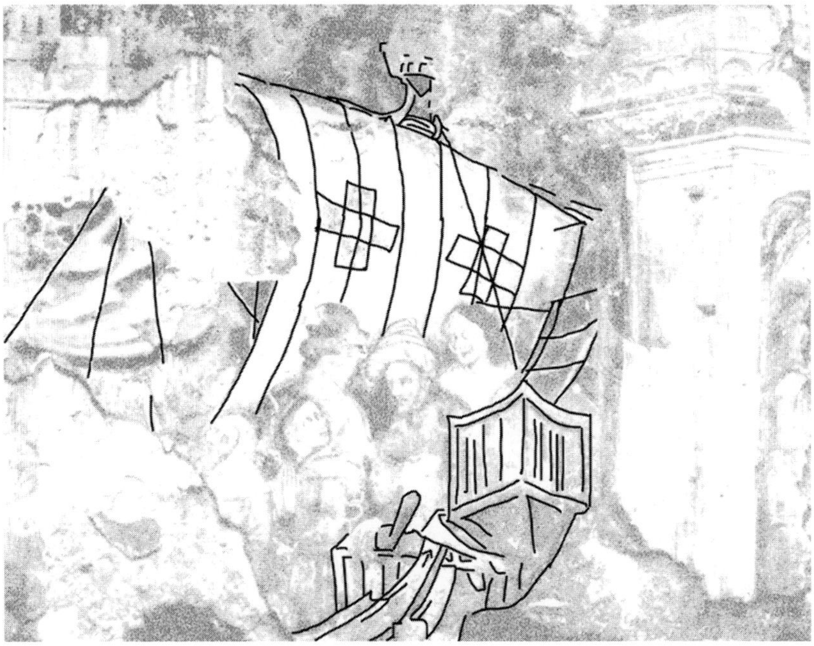

FIG. 85. Merchant ship from a degraded fresco; the *vita* of Blessed Odoric (1434), San Francesco, Udine. *Helen C. Dewolf after Kaftal, 1978: fig. 1035*

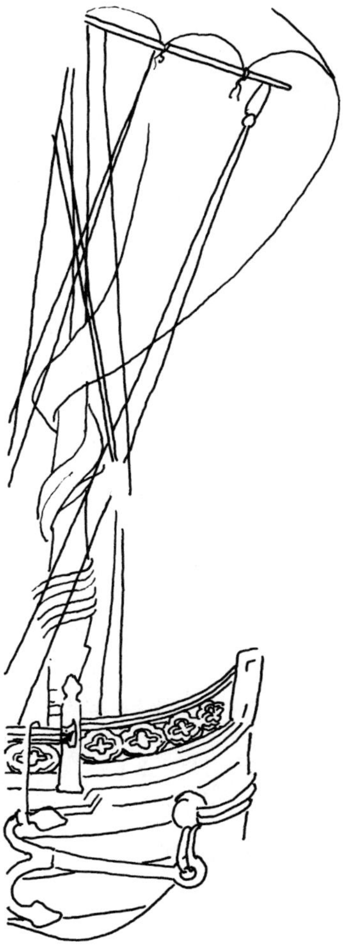

FIG. 86. *Vita* of St. Petronius: "He Leaves Constantinople for Rome." Early fifteenth-century fresco by Giovanni da Modena, San Petronio, Bolognini Chapel, Bologna. *Helen C. Dewolf after Kaftal, 1978: fig. 1135*

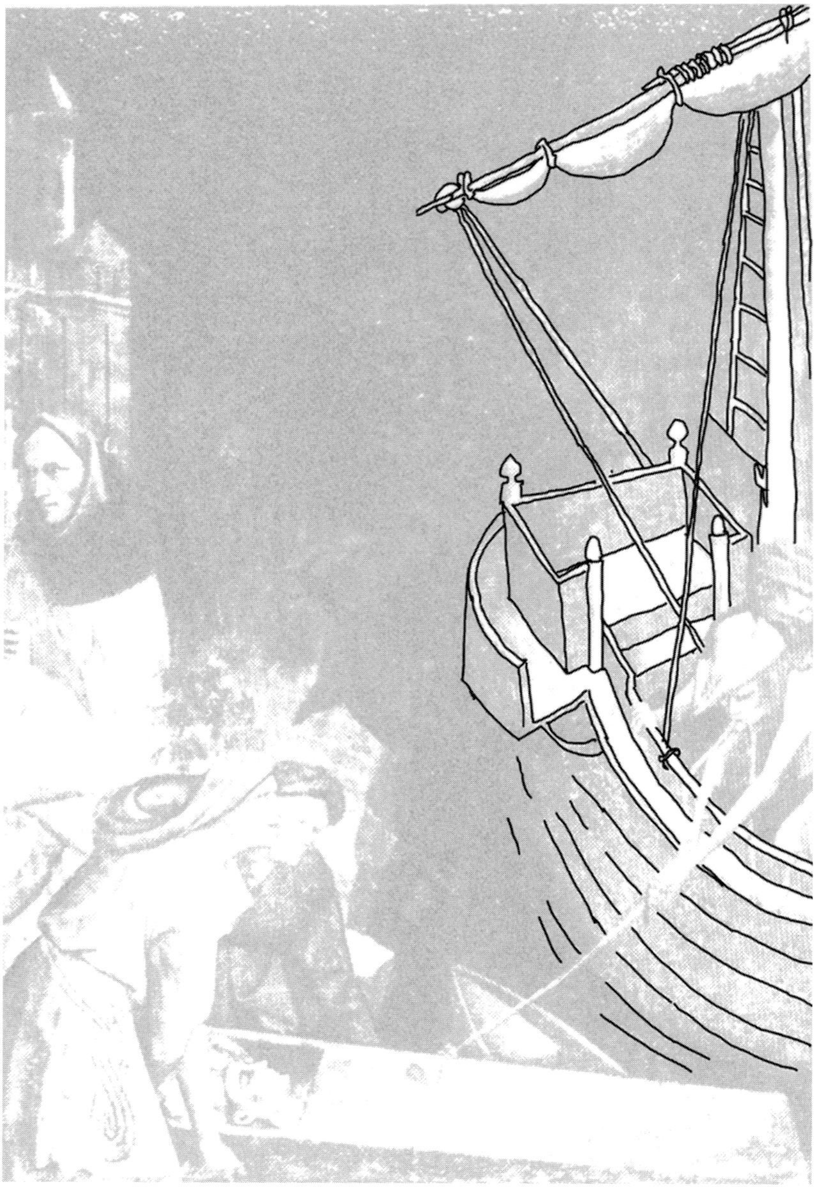

FIG. 87. *Vita* of St. Petronius: "Buying Relics of St. Florian in Palestine." Early fifteenth-century fresco by Giovanni da Modena in San Petronio, Bolognini Chapel, Bologna. *Helen C. Dewolf after Kaftal, 1978: fig. 1140*

such as those in figures 54, 84, 102, 104, and 118. A rectangular-shaped inner construction is surrounded by a semicircular parapet. A small double-ended lighter between the ship and shore is used in loading St. Florian's relics.

Figure 88

Theme: Vita of St. Petronius: "Loading Ships in Harbor."

Types: A (foreground): oared galley warship (Type IIa);
B (right) and C (left): Two single-masted, lateen-rigged merchant ships (Type IIIa);
D (foreground) and F (background, right): Two lagoonal craft (Type Ib);
E (background, left): riverine cargo vessel (Type Id).

This fresco from the *vita* of St. Petronius in Bolognini Chapel illustrates three types of vessels: one warship, two round ships, and three lagoonal or coastal craft. Figure 88A, the warship in the foreground, is a bireme in the process of loading; note the ramp to shore. On the quarterdeck, which is surrounded by a latticeworked parapet, a three-dimensional frame supports a tent and pennant.

Both lateen-rigged round ships have stays, halyard, robands, vang, and tack visible. Figure 88B, the round ship to the left, is just getting under way; a mariner near the top of the mast helps ready the sail. In both round ships, B and C, a mariner hauls on the halyard. The ample quarterdeck and parapet of both round ships resemble that seen in figure 87.

Figure 88E, the craft in the middle background with a small lateen sail rigged at the bow is probably the common *burchio* type. Note the cylindrical structure slightly aft of midships as seen in figure 84. Figure 88F is very obscure in the background, right, but it seems to be a small lagoonal fishing boat like figure 88D.

Figure 89

Theme: *Vita* of St. Jerome: "St. Jerome and St. Filippo Benizi Leave Aquileia for Rome."

Artist: Giovanni Badile.

Location: Guantieri chapel, left wall, first panel, second row, right, Santa Maria della Scala, Verona.

Date: 1443–44.

Types: Figure 89: Single-masted, lateen-rigged merchant ship (Type IIIa).
Figure 90: Single-masted, lateen-rigged merchant ship (Type IIIa).

Figure 91A: foreground: Two-masted, lateen-rigged merchant ship (Type IIIb).

Figure 91B: background: Single-masted (?), lateen-rigged (?) merchant ship (Type IIIa) and lighter (Type Ia).

The *vita* cycle of St. Jerome (cardinal in 420 and founder of the Hieronymites) decorating a chapel in San Maria della Scala in Verona includes ships in figures 89–91. Unfortunately, these frescos have suffered from deterioration. The ship in figure 89 has one mast set forward of midships but with too little rake for the lateen rig. Seven lines to the sides of the mast represent shrouds and the halyard, and part of the vang is visible. A figure has climbed the rope ladder to the mast head, where there is no crow's nest.

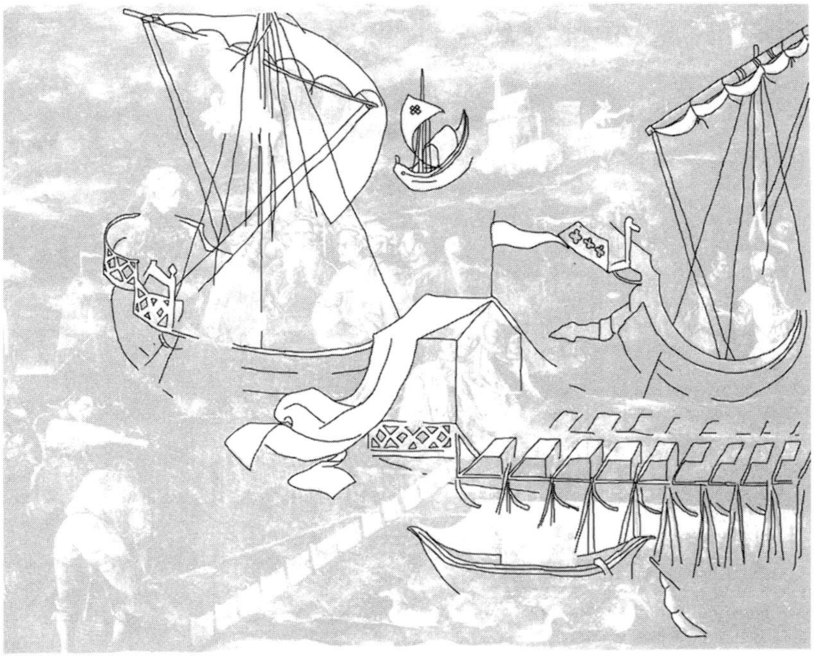

FIG. 88. *Vita* of St. Petronius: "Loading Ships in Harbor." Early fifteenth-century fresco by Giovanni da Modena, in San Petronio, Bolognini Chapel, Bologna. *Helen C. Dewolf after Nebbia, 1932: fig. 20*

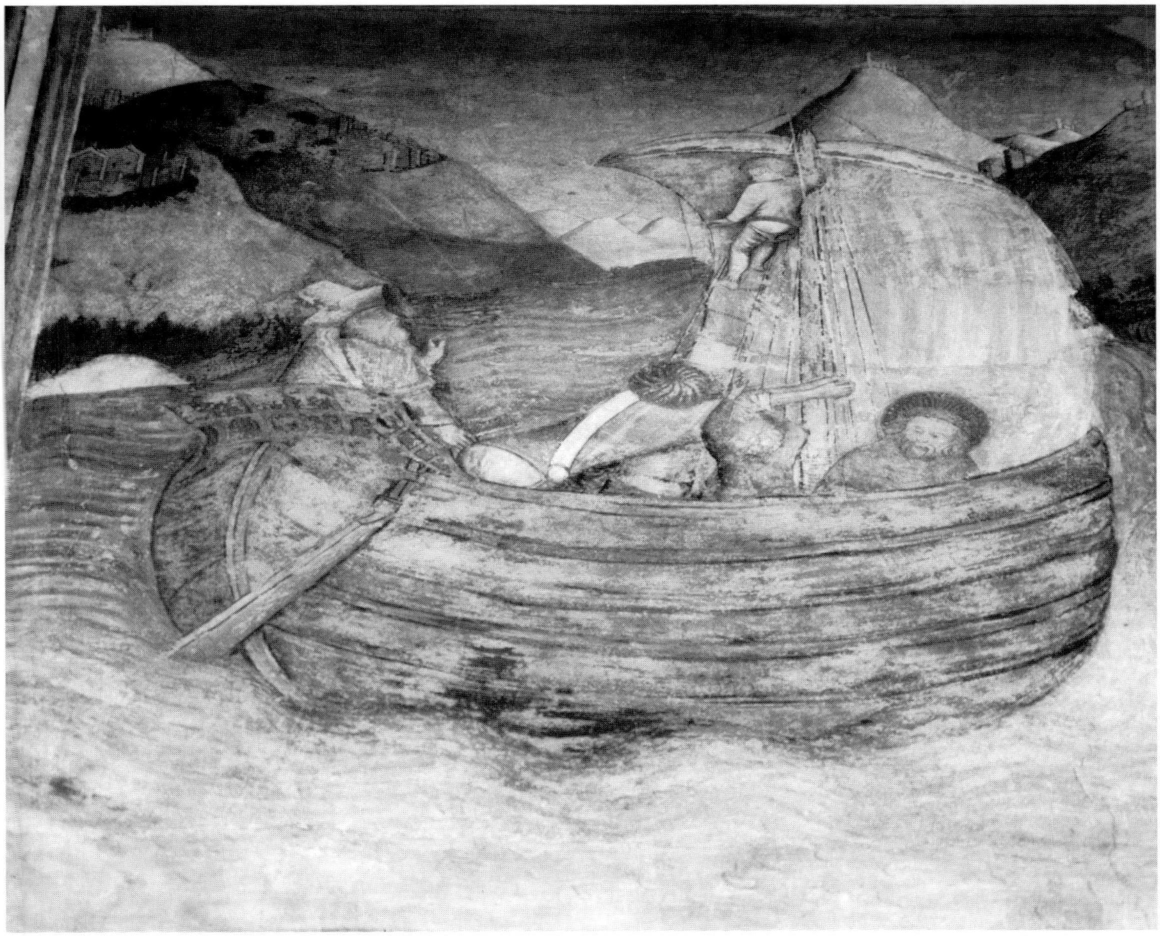

FIG. 89. *Vita* of St. Jerome: "St. Jerome and St. Filippo Benizi Leave Aquileia for Rome," fresco by Badile (ca. 1443–44) in Santa Maria della Scala, Verona

The hull is very full and rounded. Planking is indicated running from stem to sternpost, with just the uppermost planking finishing into the tragent. The tragent defines the width of a broad quarterdeck. Only one quarter rudder is depicted, although most of a port one would be visible if it were mounted; one must wonder if perhaps the ship could be controlled by a single quarter rudder. It is unbalanced and mounted on the starboard with two external braces where the tiller leads through to the quarterdeck.

Figure 90

Theme: *Vita* of St. Jerome: "St. Jerome and St. Filippo Benizi Leave Rome for Aquileia."

Location: Guantieri chapel, left wall, second panel, second row, right, Santa Maria della Scala, Verona.

Type: Single-masted, lateen-rigged merchant ship (Type IIIa).

This single-masted round ship from St. Jerome's *vita*, figure 90, is also lateen rigged. The poor preservation has left only a few rigging lines including the halyard and its tackle, one stay, and segments of the vang and tack lines. A mariner adjusts the peak; this area is better preserved, and the vang, secured to the port quarterdeck, runs through a block near the peak of the sail. Much of the hull has been lost, but enough of the fresco remains to show strakes and the stem—forming a rounded bow with a small raised foredeck like that seen on figure 77—and a full rounded stern similar to the shape seen in figure 118.

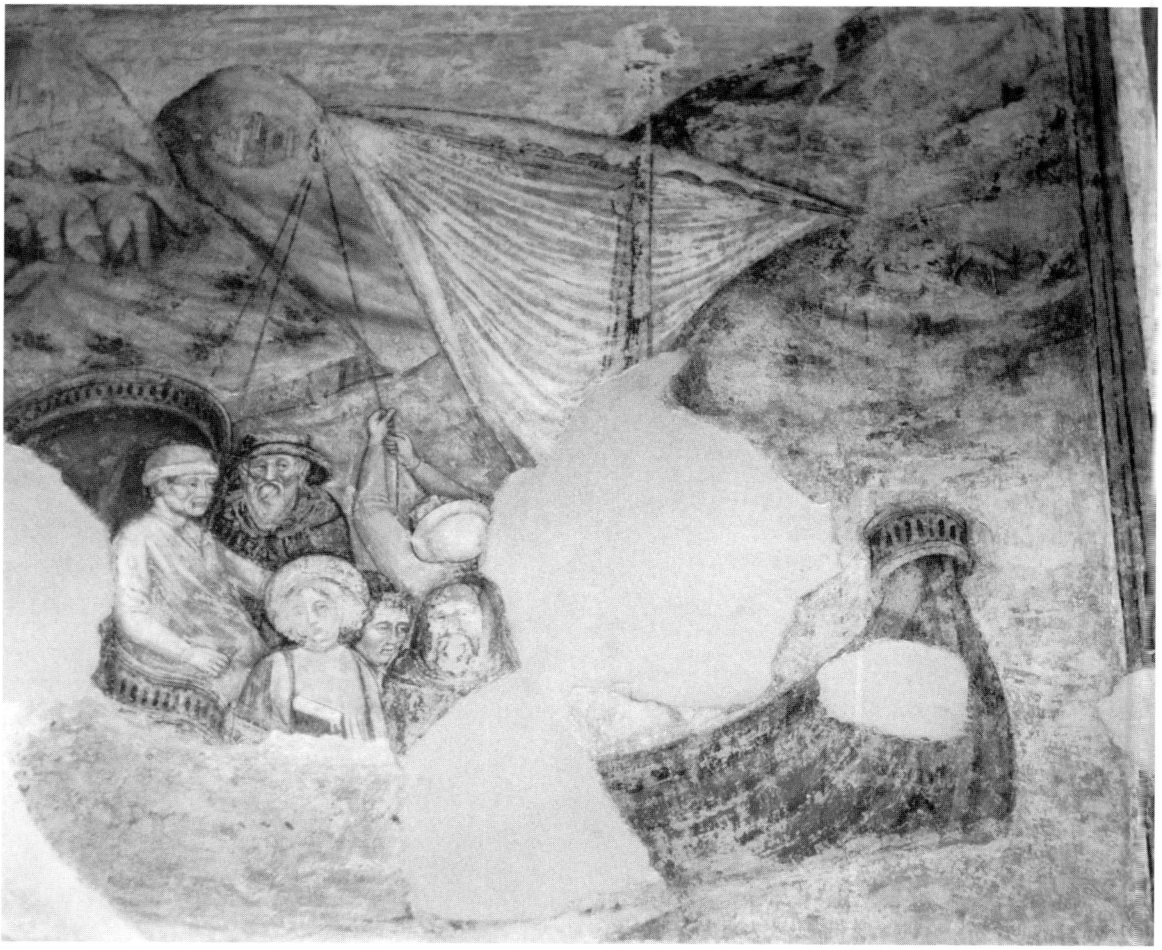

FIG. 90. *Vita* of St. Jerome: "St. Jerome and St. Filippo Benizi Leave Rome for Aquileia," fresco by Badile (ca. 1443–44) in Santa Maria della Scala, Verona

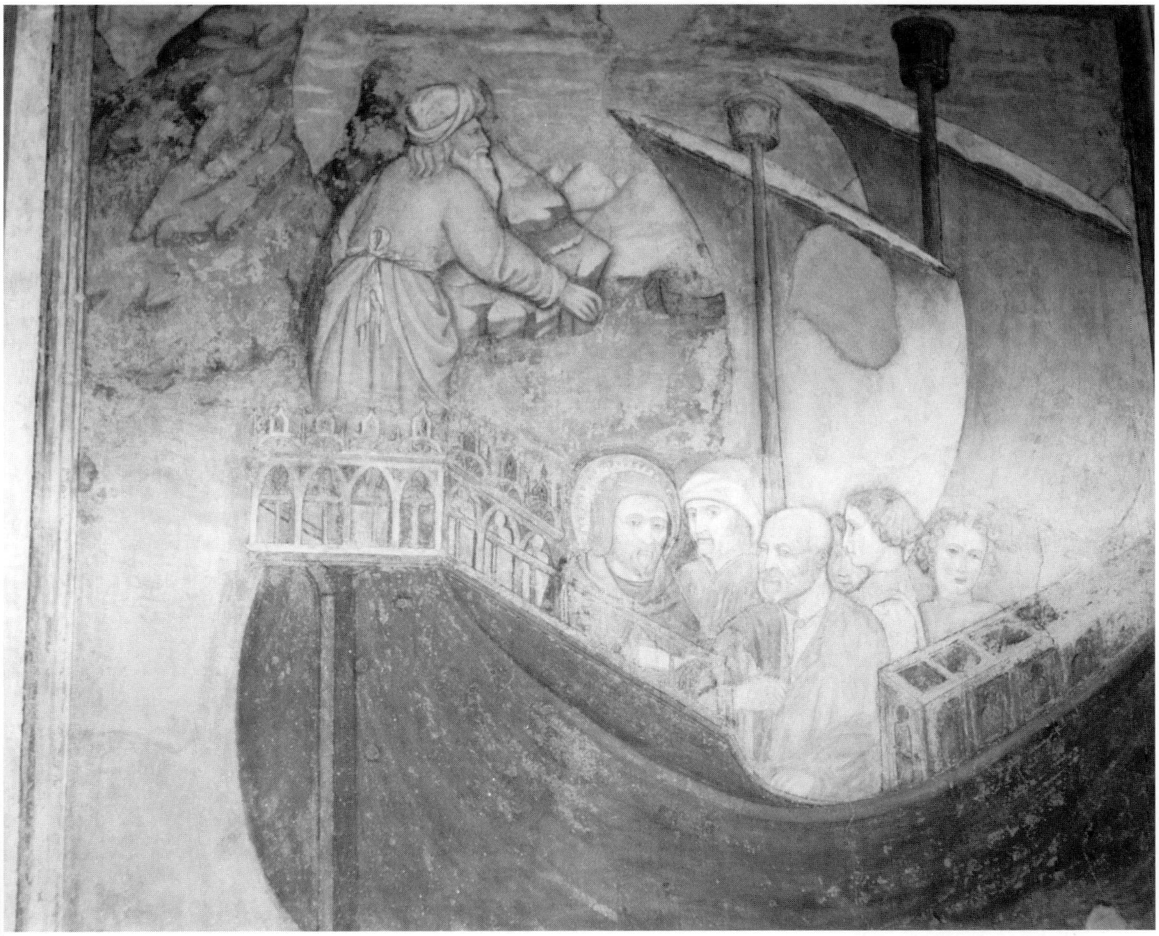

FIG. 91. *Vita* of St. Jerome: "St. Jerome and St. Filippo Benizi Leave Aquileia for Antioch," fresco by Badile (ca. 1443–44) in Santa Maria della Scala, Verona

Figure 91

Theme: *Vita* of St. Jerome: "St. Jerome and St. Filippo Benizi Leave Aquileia for Antioch."

Location: Guantieri chapel, left wall, second panel, fourth row, lower left, Santa Maria della Scala, Verona.

Types: A (foreground): Two-masted, lateen-rigged merchant ship (Type IIIb).

B (background): Single-masted (?), lateen-rigged (?) merchant ship (Type IIIa) and lighter (Type Ia).

The foreground vessel, figure 91A, from St. Jerome's *vita*, shows a two-masted, lateen-rigged round ship, with the foremast taller than the mizzen. It is unrealistic in two details: the masts appear to be set vertically (this may be explained by the view depicted: the starboard side, seen slightly from the stern), and the crow's nests are set centrally at the mastheads. But other details are more naturally depicted. The robands, securing the unfurled sails to their yards, are realistic.

The hull is also fairly well defined, with a sterncastle decorated with an arcaded parapet. Lower hull planking finishes into the sternpost; higher strakes, into the tragent. A heavy sheer strake runs from the bow to the corner of the sterncastle. A straight rudder is fixed to the stern.

In the background, just left of the mizzen sail are a lighter alongside a single-masted round ship, B. This area is unfortunately very deteriorated, though the full bow with a decorative parapet and a few lines of planking finishing into the stempost are still clearly visible on the ship.

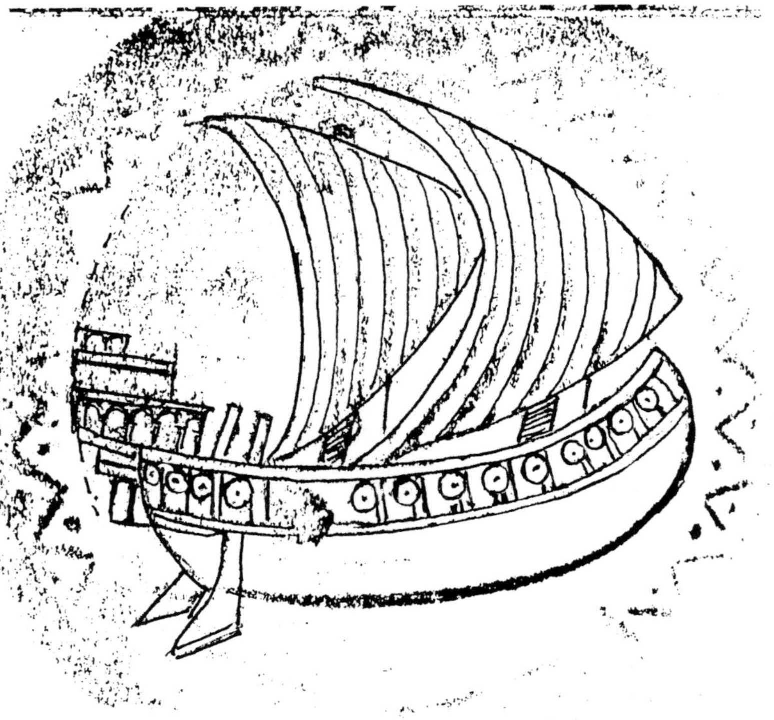

FIG. 92. Round ship on a faience basin, painted in the Islamic style (ca. 1254–66), San Francesco Church, Bologna. *Courtesy M. Bonino after Nepoti, 1973: Plate 10*

Paintings

Figure 92
Title: Painted faience basin.
Artists: Local Bolognese artists (imitating Islamic style).
Location: Front wall, San Francesco Church, Bologna (Nepoti, 1973: Plate 10).
Date: ca. 1254–66.
Type: Two-masted, lateen-rigged merchant ship (Type IIIb).

Figure 92, a faience basin painted in the Islamic style, decorates the façade of San Francesco. The basin was remounted upside down after restoration.

A two-masted lateener fills the round shape of the basin, perhaps explaining why the mizzen has been drawn slightly taller than the foremast. Both sails are set on forward-raking masts, and lines depicting their seams are indicated. Only a short section of rigging forward of the masts is defined—a stay, shroud, or halyard.

A flat hull bottom is simply defined, but the bulwarks and sterncastle include more detail. The sterncastle is depicted with as many as five deck levels, which resemble figures 11, 13, and 14 in having what looks like lower decks aft of the main line of the ships and not just above. The middle and uppermost decks are arcaded. Bulwarks are defined between the main and uppermost wale or sheer with thirteen perpendicular beams flanking thirteen circular features, which are probably shields. The unbalanced steering oars pass inboard through the bulwarks, and the upper ends of both looms are visible above.

Figure 93
Title: *Pala Feriale,* the weekday cover of the *Pala d'Oro.*
Theme: *Translatio* of St. Mark: "Ship at Anchor in Alexandria." (Tribunus and Rusticus obtain the saint's relics.)
Artists: Paolo Veneziano and sons Luca and Giovanni.
Location: Marciano Museum, San Marco, Venice.
Date: ca. 1343–45 (Pallucchini, 1964: 36).
Type: Figure 93: Two-masted, lateen-rigged merchant ship (Type IIIb).
Figure 94: Two-masted, lateen-rigged merchant ship (Type IIIb).

Merchant ships appear in two panels of the *Pala Feriale,* the magnificent painted altarpiece cover for the *Pala d'Oro* of San Marco by Paolo Veneziano and sons. In the first scene, figure 93 the ship is at anchor in Alexandria (note the famous lighthouse in the background); in the second, the *passus* of the *translatio* scene, the ship is under sail (fig. 94). The detail in these paintings is remarkable. Decorations on the sail, robands, rigging, pulley systems, shrouds, barrel-like crow's nests, anchor cables, and details of the ship timbers are meticulously depicted.

Figure 93 shows the anchored vessel from the bow, at an angle, revealing part of the port side and a small section of the starboard bow. The painting includes only enough of the bow to indicate one lateen foremast, but it is most likely

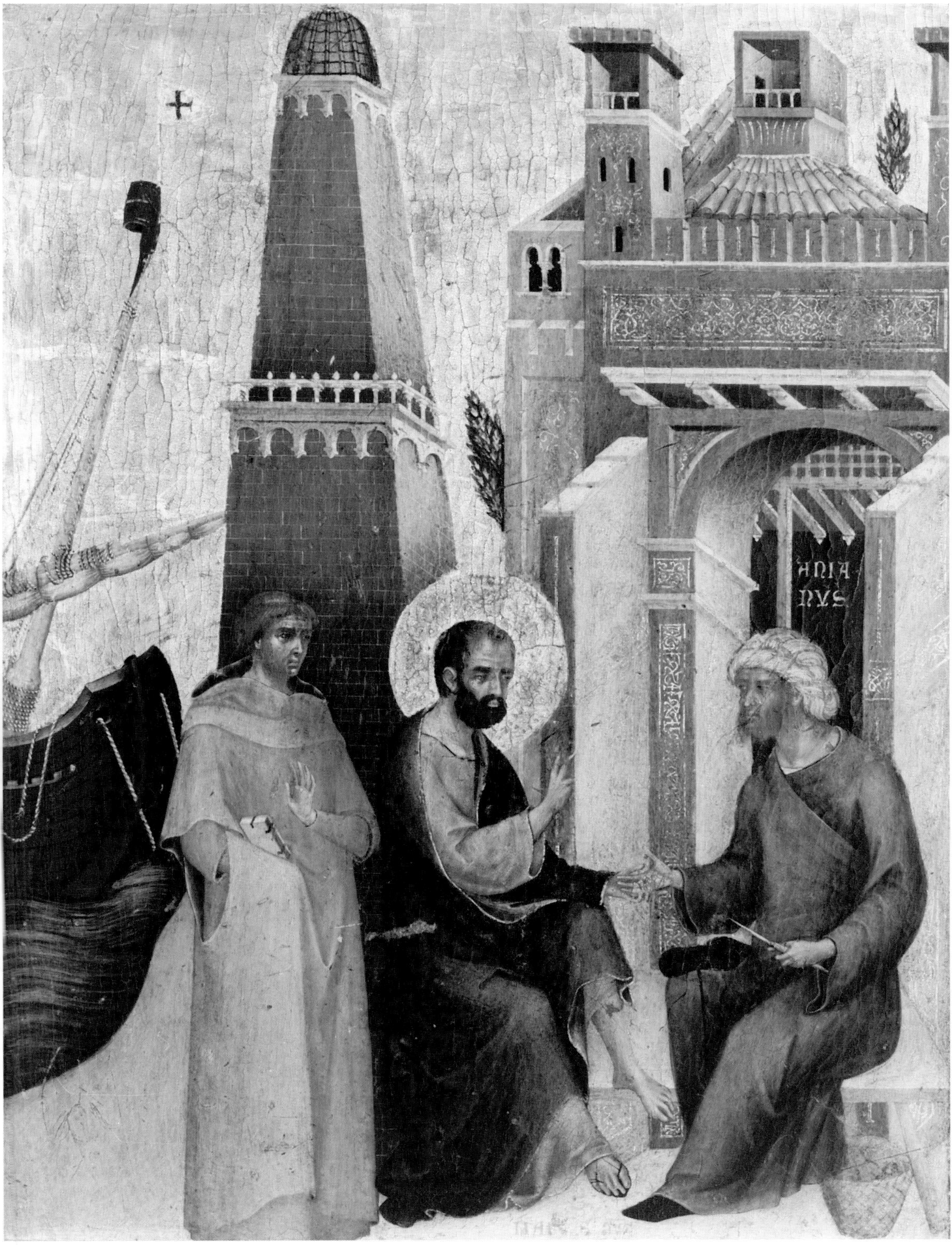

FIG. 93. *Translatio* of St. Mark: "Ship at Anchor in Alexandria," detail of the Veneziano painting *Pala Feriale* (ca. 1343–45), Marciana Museum, San Marco. *Courtesy Böhm*

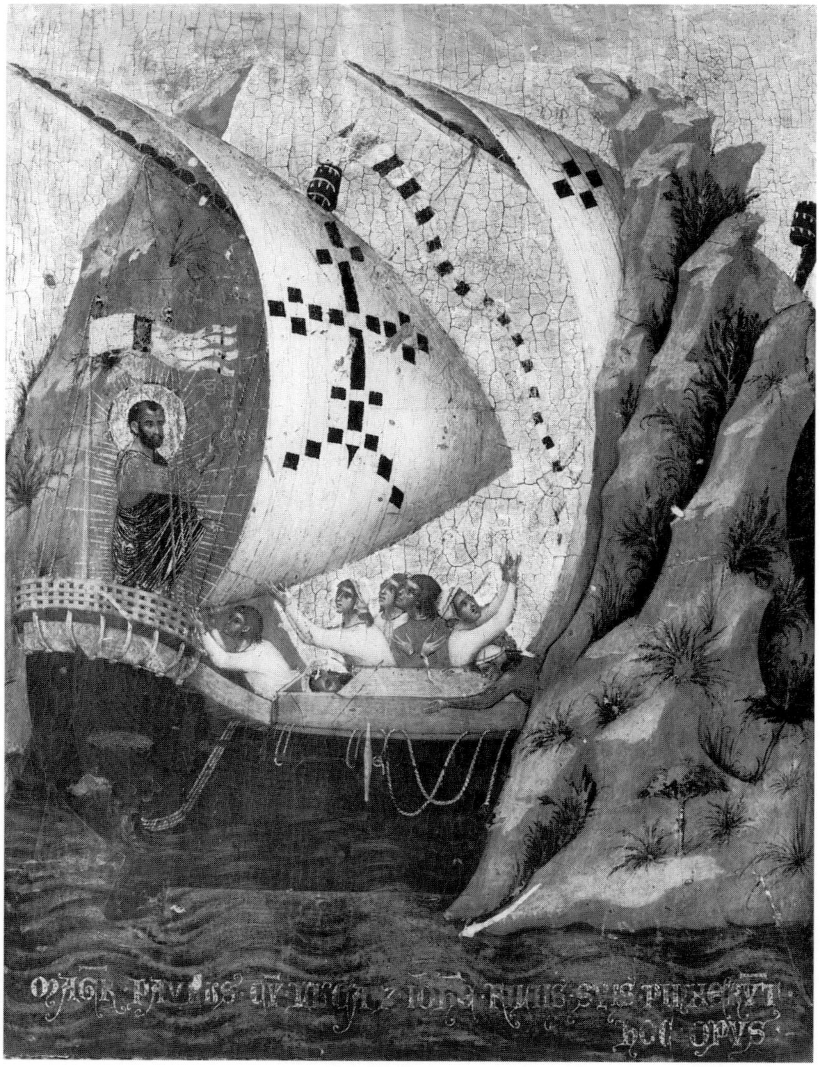

FIG. 94. *Passus* of the *translatio* of St. Mark, detail of the Veneziano painting, *Pala Feriale* (ca. 1343–45), Marciana Museum, San Marco. *Courtesy Böhm*

two masted as in figure 94. The foremast is set fairly far forward, with a strong rake. Its sail is furled on the yard, comprised of two spars lashed together. Ropes secure the cylindrical crow's nest aft, at the head of the mast. A slightly thickened section scarfed at the head of the mast represents the *cholzexe* or sheave block, also clearly depicted in the Zibaldone manuscript illustrations (figs. 62 and 63).

Of the rigging, at least three shrouds and the halyard are shown running aft of the mast. A band of chocks lashed together around the mast at deck level, wedging the mast firmly in place, is also carefully depicted.

Visible elements of hull structure include strakes, the stem and the false stem, and through-beams. Note the waterway at deck level: one strake has been left off the side of the vessel to allow water to run off the deck. Strakes are shown running parallel to the sheer strake. As first seen in figure 28, the run of the sheer strake seems to indicate a broader bow type, probably for a small foredeck, instead of finishing at a narrow, pointed stem. Anchor cables run through the hawse holes set high and far forward in the bow on both port and starboard.

Figure 94

Theme: *Translatio* of St. Mark: the *passus* of the *translatio*.

Titulus: MAGR PAVLUS OV _ _CA Z IOHE RU_ _ S SVIS PINXERVT hoc opus.

Type: Two-masted, lateen-rigged merchant ship (Type IIIb).

In the panel to the right of figure 93, the vessel of the *translatio* is depicted from the starboard stern (fig. 94). The ship is shown dramatically close to some treacherous rocks, which obstruct the bow and midships area, but the ship miraculously avoids shipwreck. St. Mark is portrayed in his coffin, balanced on the sheer strake; the saint also appears, effecting the miracle, at the quarterdeck.

Of the two masts, only the mizzen is completely visible, although both are clearly lateen and have crow's nests aft of the mast heads. Sails are still set; the mariners work frantically to lower the mizzen. The mizzen vang are nicely illustrated: lines from both port and starboard stern run up through their tackle and down again to the deck and up again. Above the tackle, at both port and starboard, the line continues up to tie off to the upper end of the *pennae* of the yard. The illustration thus accurately portrays a completely functional pulley system. Only two lines are depicted to secure the mast itself, and these are represented as passing behind the sail to the quarterdeck, not to either side of the sail, as would be for shrouds, so they are apparently backstays. In any case, the number of supports represented is insufficient.

Individual strakes at and below the main wale area finish into the sternpost. Those just above also terminate into the sternpost, but higher up they run parallel to it, sweeping upward to the base of the quarterdeck, forming an ample, rounded stern (see detail, fig. 95). Curved struts fastened to beams at the base of the bulwark in the stern support the quarterdeck.

Two asymmetrical quarter rudders are mounted to port and starboard, beneath the quarterdeck. A rudder hoist, passing around the rudder three times to secure it, is visible to starboard. Just forward of the rudder, a T- or crescent-shaped anchor with a fixed wooden anchor stock is shown hanging, crown aft, at the stern, ready to be cast.

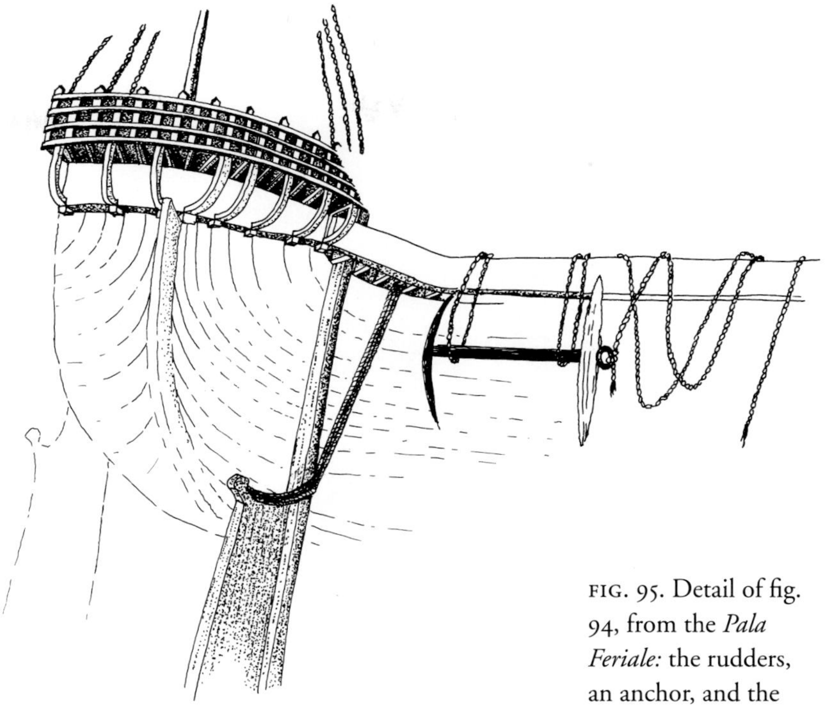

FIG. 95. Detail of fig. 94, from the *Pala Feriale:* the rudders, an anchor, and the configuration of the planking at the stern. *Helen C. Dewolf*

Figure 96

Theme: "St. Martin Saves a Ship in Distress."
Artist: Paolo Veneziano, or School.
Location: Polyptych, altar frontal, Oratorio di San Martino, Chioggia (Kaftal, 1978: fig. 897).
Date: First half of the fourteenth century (Pallucchini, 1964: 27).
Type: Two-masted, lateen-rigged merchant ship (Type IIIb).

This medium-sized round ship is quite similar in design to the vessels of figures 41, 54, 87, 93, 102, and 104. Both masts of the ship in figure 96 rake strongly forward, fortified at deck level with wedges. The foremast has snapped halfway up the mast from the strength of the storm winds. Sails have already been furled on their yards in

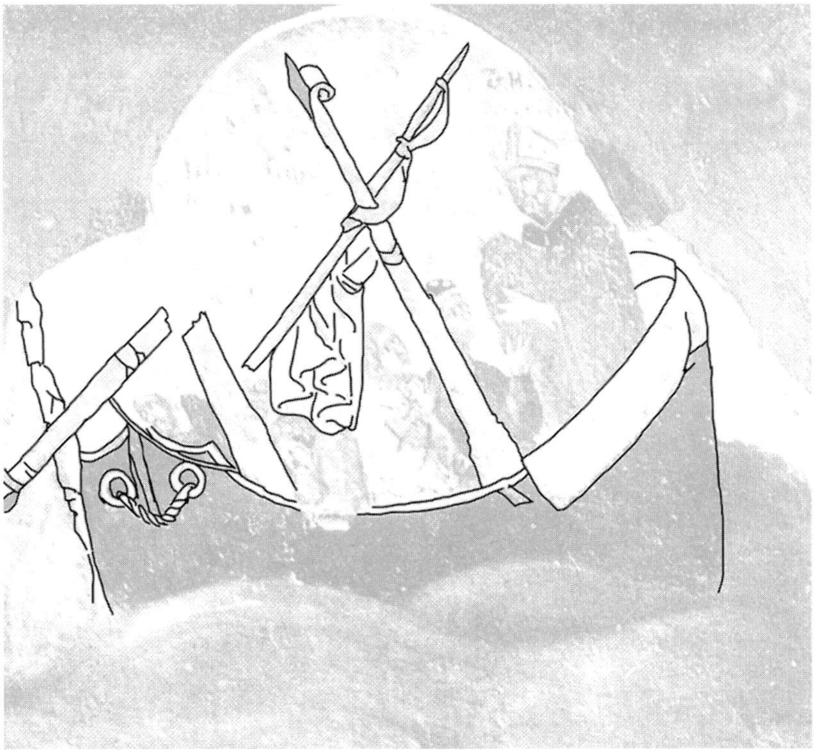

FIG. 96. "St. Martin Saves a Ship in Distress," first half of the fourteenth-century polyptych panel by Paolo Veneziano (or School), Oratorio di San Martino, Chioggia. *Helen C. Dewolf*

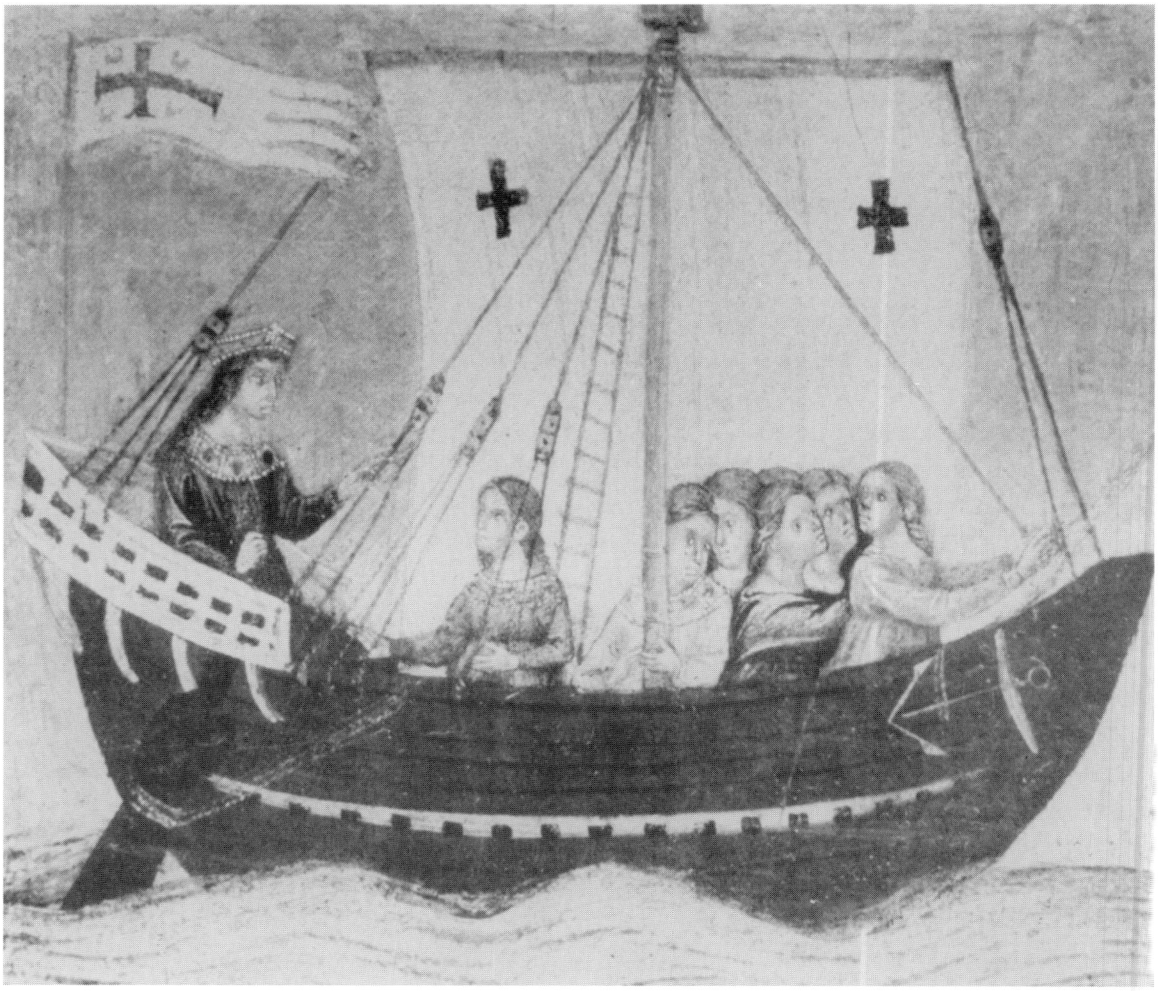

FIG. 97. Panel from *vita* of St. Ursula by Veneziano (or Veneziano School), first half of fourteenth century. *Muraro, 1970: pl. 88*

efforts to save the ship. In Kaftal's reproduction (1978: fig. 897) wedges around the mast at deck level and the *cholzexe* sheave blocks and crow's nest at the head of the masts are visible; however, details of the rigging are not discernible.

The hull is rounded, with a steep sheer at bow and stern. The bow shape is full, as described for the very similar figure 93. The stern appears slightly higher than the bow and has a quarterdeck apparently like figure 87.

Figure 97

Title: Legend of St. Ursula.

Theme: *Vita* of St. Ursula: "St. Ursula and Her Companions on the Ship."

Artist: Paolo Veneziano (Pallucchini, 1964: fig. 47) or Veneziano School (Muraro, 1970 145 and pl. 88).

Location: Originally an altar frontal, diptych, present location uncertain. According to Pallucchini (1964: p. 27 and fig. 47), this panel is in a private collection in Milan, while Muraro (1970: 145) records it as being in a private collection of Bergamo.

Date: First half of the fourteenth century (Pallucchini, 1964: 27).

Type: Single-masted, square-rigged merchant ship (Type IIId).

With the exception of its square sail, figure 97 is almost identical to the ships in figures 98–101 of the same theme and depicts a round ship (cf. a later square-rigged example, fig. 128, with a single stern rudder). It is likely a copy by artists within the Veneziano school. Certain details, however, especially rigging, tackle, and the bower anchor, are more clear in this image. Three shrouds or stays are tied from the head of the mast to the starboard bulwarks: the two forward of the quarterdeck may be shrouds, while the one secured to the quarterdeck is probably a stay. Braces with their tackle run from the ends of the yards both forward and aft: the forward brace runs through its single block tackle once, while the aft one passes through its double block tackle twice, for more advantage. A woman toward the bow hauls on a line that probably represents the halyard. A rope ladder behind the mast gives access to the crow's nest at the top of the mast.

The features of the hull and anchor are virtually identical to those described for figure 101. Sixteen protruding through-beams show the line of the deck within the hull. Through-beams are a typical medieval feature on round ships, inherited from ancient ship construction techniques. Like the ship in figure 42, the rudder appears to be mounted in a modified box mount and is further secured with a rudder hoist. The rudder shaft passes through the floor of the quarterdeck. An anchor is secured externally at the bow.

Figures 98–101

Title: St. Ursula polyptych, altar frontal.

Theme: *Vita* of St. Ursula.

Artist: Paolo Veneziano (Pallucchini, 1964: 26), or School (Muraro, 1970: 55).

Location: Panels 7–10 of polyptych; present location unknown; previously of G. Volterra Collection (Florence, 1959) and the Queiroy Collection (Paris, 1907).

Date: ca. 1335.

Types: Four versions of a two-masted, mixed-rigged merchant ship (Type IIIb).

This altar frontal depicting St. Ursula's *vita* includes four important maritime panels that are particularly interesting because they illustrate one ship's construction and first voyage. Reproductions of this series are small and dark. The details of the rigging and hull features in the original painting must be quite good—it is unfortunate that the frontal's present location is unknown. All four of the maritime panels in the polyptych portray a decked, two-masted, flat-bottomed round ship. The first (fig. 98) and third (fig. 100) maritime panels are in direct profile, while the second (fig. 99), just off true profile, includes a partial view of the bow, and the last (fig. 101), of the stern.

Each panel presumably depicts the same ship, built for and used by Ursula. The vessel was meant, then, to carry two masts of roughly the same height as that shown in figures 99 and 101, though the mizzen is omitted in figure 100, and masts are not yet stepped in the ship under construction (fig. 98). In figure 99 and 101, the mizzen is slightly aft of midships and rakes forward, while the foremast is extremely far forward, with an even stronger rake. All rigged masts depicted are lateen, and in the three versions where the sail is set, cross designs decorate the sail. Two spars are lashed together to form the long yards necessary for the lateen sails. A crow's nest atop each mast is reached via a rope ladder tied aft of the masts. Depicted rigging include stays, secured below the crow's nest, and vang and tack controlling the yards.

From figure 98, the construction scene, it is evident that, like Contarina I (ca. 1300), the round ship depicted is flat bottomed and built frame first. The shapes of the bow and stern vary slightly from panel to panel. As the series represents one ship during its construction, preparation, and voyage, these differences are explained by minute changes in the angle of view, each revealing slightly different characteristics of the hull.

Figure 98 shows a minor projection, the continuation of a wale, at both the bow and the stern. Figure 100 shows a similar projection at the bow. Figures 98, 100, and 101 similarly represent the

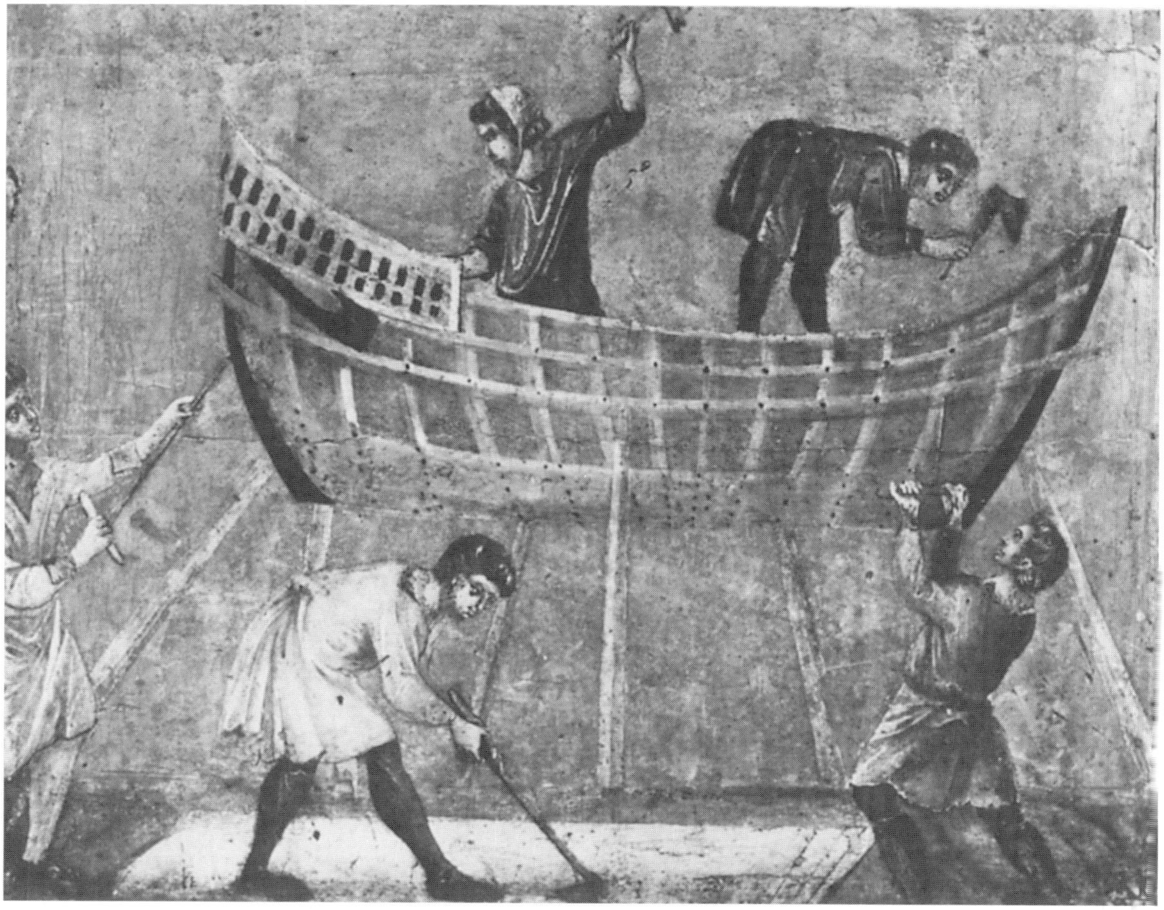

FIG. 98. A ship construction scene, seventh panel, *vita* of St. Ursula (ca. 1335), by Paolo Veneziano. *After Rubin de Cervin, 1985: 21*

stem rising sharply from the keel and ending in a pointed bow. Figure 99 shows a fuller bow area, with a more inward-curving stem (as in fig. 28), but because part of the port bow is represented in this view, the perspective is deceiving. Actually, the stern is fuller than the bow. Best seen in figure 101, the support system for the sterncastle of St. Ursula's ships illustrated by figures 98–101 appears to be similar to that for the ship in figure 94: the small quarterdeck's exterior is bolstered by supporting struts. Figure 100 minimizes this structure into a simple rectangle, resembling other representations of quarterdecks, such as in figures 37, 41, and 48.

In all cases, the ship has a fair curve in profile, and the stem finishes at a height slightly below that of the quarterdeck structure. Through-beams projecting at deck level along the line of the main wale are visible in figures 99 and 101, defining the location of the deck where the women stand. The main features of this decked round ship are comparable to Zibaldone's illustrations (figs. 62 and 63) and Veneziano's other polyptych panels (figs. 93 and 94).

In figure 98, a dark, curved, hook-shaped timber is visible at the stern just above the main deck level but beneath the quarterdeck. In the other scenes, the rudder passes inboard where this timber would be inside the ship. This hook-shaped timber is the structural timber that held the shaft of the rudder as it passed inboard and gave internal support to the rudder system. The rudder mount system's exterior is best illustrated in figure 99, where the rudder is seen passing inboard. Beyond the addition here of a supplemental rudder hoist, its characteristics are identical to those of the merchantman in the contemporaneous *vita* mosaic of St. Isidore, figure 26.

In figures 100 and 101, a crescent-shaped anchor is depicted, catted horizontally at the bow, crown aft, and secured over the gunwale to inboard. The projection of the wale beyond the stem visible in figure 100 may have served as a bitt beam to cat up the anchor.

Figure 98
Theme: "The Building of Ships for St. Ursula's Journey."
Location: Seventh panel.

Figure 98 shows the ship during the intermediate stages of frame-first construction: keel, posts, frames, and a main and secondary wale have been set, and a small quarterdeck built at the stern. (Figure 44 shows two smaller round ships in a subsequent stage of construction, with hull planking attached.) Two carpenters bore holes with their augers in the sternpost and a frame toward the bow; the shipwright between them sketches plans on the ground. From within the ship, two men employ adzes to finish off the timbers.

The sternpost curves slightly inward, while the stem rises more sharply from the keel. The frames are evenly spaced, although fourteen frames is too few for a ship this size. The comparable two-masted lateener, Contarina I, had a total of fifty-eight frames. Several of the lower strakes, running parallel to the keel, have already been attached to the framing with nails. The main wale projects slightly beyond both bow and sternposts. This short projection from the main wale at the bow may have served as a bitt beam to cat up the anchor (cf. fig. 100).

Figure 99
Theme: "St. Ursula and the Virgins Depart; St. Ursula Relates Her Vision to Her Companions."
Location: Eighth panel.

The next panel in the series shows St. Ursula and the virgins under sail. On the foremast, three rigging lines lead aft from the mast head; one stay works through tackle to the starboard gunwale, while another two to somewhere aft of the mast. One of the rigging lines closest to the mast must be the halyard, possibly doubling as a backstay: one line passes through the *cholzexe*, the sheave block at the head of the mast. From there, the line appears to run forward of the mast and down, to support the yard below. A rope parrel also can be discerned. The woman in the bow holds the tack of the foresail, carefully defined with its tackle, while St. Ursula works the vang, also defined with its tackle. Mizzen rigging lines include four lines from the mast head, those leading aft, the halyard, shrouds, and stays. The halyard passes through the *cholzexe* and on to the yard below. The tack is secured at the starboard gunwale, while the vang is tied off at the quarterdeck. Both lines run through tackle. Both masts have a rope ladder for access to the head of the mast, where crow's nests are positioned aft.

The shape of the starboard sides of the quarterdeck is identical to that seen in figure 26. The bow is the broadened type discussed for figure 28.

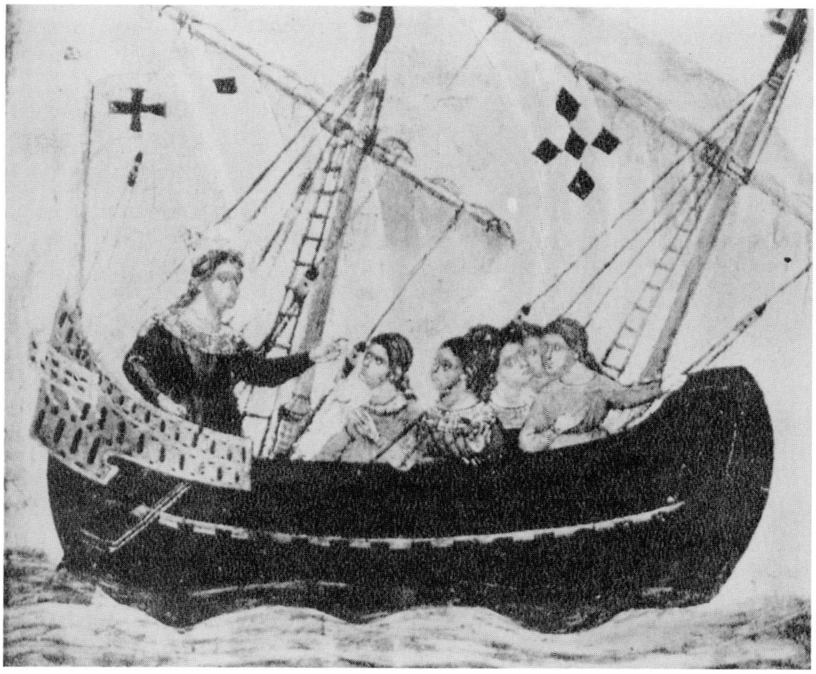

FIG. 99. Ship under sail, eighth panel, *vita* of St. Ursula: "St. Ursula and the Virgins Depart; St. Ursula Relates Her Vision to Her Companions" (ca. 1335), by Paolo Veneziano. *Muraro, 1970: fig. 87*

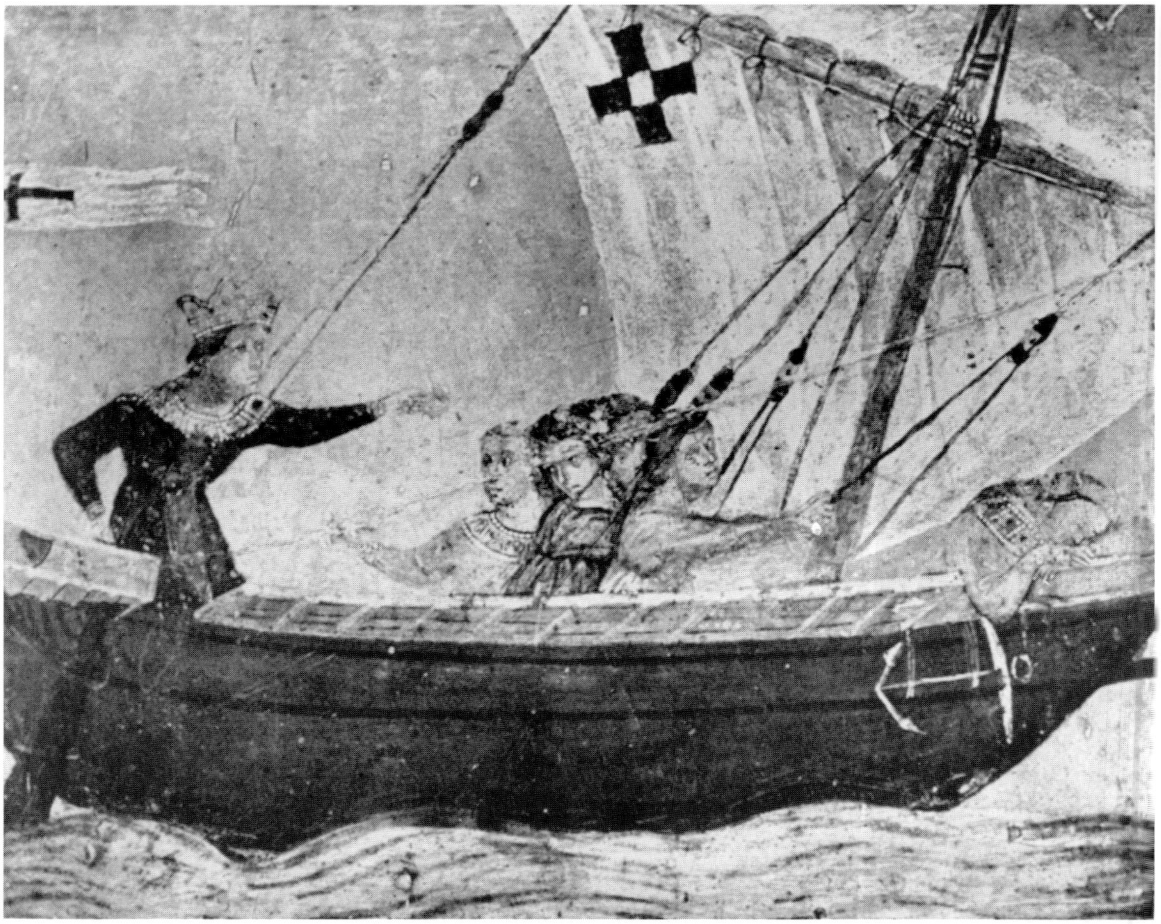

FIG. 100. Ship under sail, ninth panel, *vita* of St. Ursula: "St. Ursula Teaches the Virgins to Sail" (ca. 1335), by Paolo Veneziano. *Muraro, 1970: fig. 84*

Figure 100
Theme: "St. Ursula Teaches the Virgins to Sail."
Location: Ninth panel.

This version of the vessel has visible what, at first glance, appear to be inner frames, but their angle relative to the gunwale strake precludes that interpretation unless they are just drawn in an inaccurate perspective. They may create an outrigger structure like in figures 64 and 65.

The mizzen has been omitted in this version of the ship. Because a mizzen appears in both the previous and subsequent panels, and there is plenty of space aft for a second mast, this is probably simply an oversight on the part of the artist, or perhaps an intentional omission to emphasize St. Ursula giving orders from the helm. The single mast depicted supports a lateen sail with most of its essential rigging: halyard, three shrouds or stays, and both vang and tack lines, with tackle. The parrel is well defined, as are the robands and seam lines of the sail, and even the lines securing the stays or shrouds above the parrel.

Figure 101
Theme: "Approaching the Harbor at Cologne."
Location: Tenth panel.

As the maidens approach Cologne (fig. 101), the mizzen has been furled while the foresail is still open, and a cross decorates it. Where the lowered yard attaches to the mizzen, three rows of beads of the parrel are apparent. Above, the three lines around the mast are probably the upper ties of the three shrouds or stays leading aft. The halyard and its tackle can been seen aft of the mast leading through the *cholzexe* at the mast head, to below. The mizzen vang is tied off from the upper end of the yard to the end of the port side of the quarterdeck structure; the mizzen tack is hidden by the figures. Robands and seam lines are depicted. St. Ursula works the foresail vang, while another maiden controls the foresail's tack; the tackle of both lines is detailed. Only two shrouds or stays are visible on the foremast, behind the rope ladder.

The view depicts the starboard side, seen slightly from the stern; the end of the full stern is shown in perspective, revealing that the quarterdeck is supported by curved struts as seen in figure 26.

Figure 102
Theme: "St. Peter Walks on the Water."
Artist: Lorenzo Veneziano.
Location: Gemäldgalerie Staatliche Museum, Berlin.
Date: ca. 1368–72 (Pallucchini, 1964: 173–178).
Type: Two-masted, lateen-rigged merchant ship (Type IIIb) and fishing boat (Type Ib).

In figure 102, the two-masted round ship sails in strong winds. The mizzen is set slightly aft of midships; the foremast, set far forward. Both rake forward strongly. The lines girding the base of the foremast at deck level probably secured wedges. The base of the mizzen is blocked from view by a figure working the mizzen tack. Both

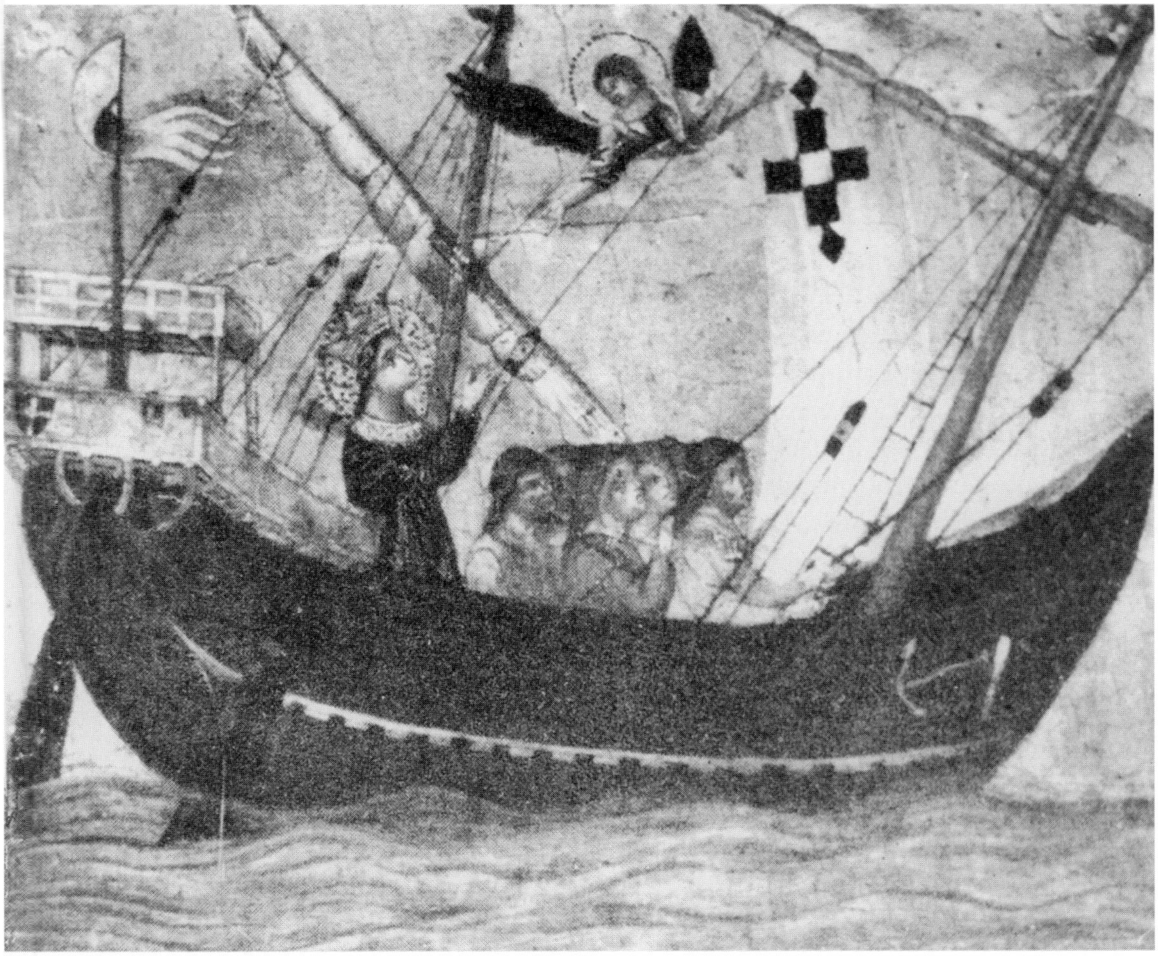

FIG. 101. Ship under sail, tenth panel, *vita* of St. Ursula: "Approaching the Harbor at Cologne" (ca. 1335), by Paolo Veneziano. *Muraro, 1970: fig. 84*

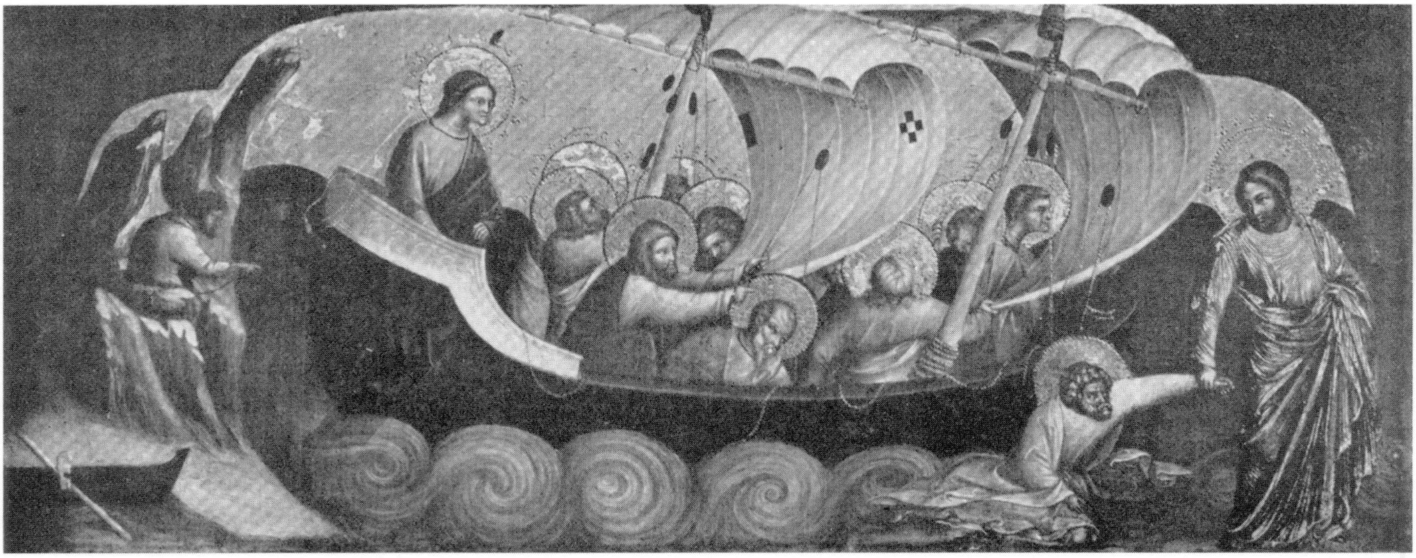

FIG. 102. "St. Peter Walks on the Water," by Lorenzo Veneziano, ca. 1368–72. *Courtesy Gemäldgalerie Staatliche Museum, Berlin*

yards are attached with parrels at the head of the mast. The unfurled lateen sails, hung on their yards with robands, reveal vertical lines, representing seams of the vertical bands of sailcloth. A cross decorates the mizzen sail. Opposite the heel of the sail is a rectangular patch. On both masts, three lines representing the halyard and shrouds, with tackle, are sketched running from beneath the mast head to the sides and aft. Vang and tack with their tackle are indicated for the mizzen sail, though that sail obscures the vang of the foresail. The foresail's tack, with its tackle, is depicted, secured at starboard bow.

The hull bottom is covered by waves. The stern (similar in shape to that seen in figures 54, 87, and 88) has a raised quarterdeck area and is slightly higher than the bow. A nicely defined swing rudder mount, though difficult to make out in the dark reproduction, is at the stern (see detail, fig. 148L).

In the left foreground is a small lagoonal craft identical to the fishing craft illustrated by the more detailed figure 103. An oarlock is fixed to starboard with the oar's slot forward.

Figure 103 (A: foreground; B: background, right; C: background, left)
Theme: "The Calling of the Apostles."
Artist: Lorenzo Veneziano.
Location: Gemäldgalerie Staatliche Museum, Berlin.
Date: ca. 1368–72 (Pallucchini, 1964: 173–78).
Types: Three fishing boats (Type Ib).

These small craft appear to be flat bottomed, with a gently rising stem. On the foreground vessel, figure 103A, a small foredeck is cross-planked. Details of the side planking are lost in the photograph of the painting; the original painting may be more detailed. The only visible feature of the hull side is the caprail, a lighter-colored wood. An oar is held by the apostle in the bow; it could be fitted into and held by the typically Venetian oarlock, here mounted to starboard with the oar's slot forward. The other apostle hauls in a fishing net.

Only the bow of a similar vessel appears in the background to the right (B); the rest of its hull is blocked from view by a rock promontory. The stem of this vessel is clearly visible. The oarlock is identical in shape to that on the foreground vessel.

In the background, left, is a rare depiction of a *marotta* (C), a *battèllo* hull with holes, a barge-shaped vessel in which fish were kept alive.[17]

FIG. 103. Fishing boats (A) foreground; (B) back, right; (C) back, left, in painting, "The Calling of the Apostles," by Lorenzo Veneziano, ca. 1370; (C) is a *marotto,* a specialized vessel with holes in the hull, used to keep fish alive. *Courtesy Gemäldegalerie Staatliche Museum, Berlin*

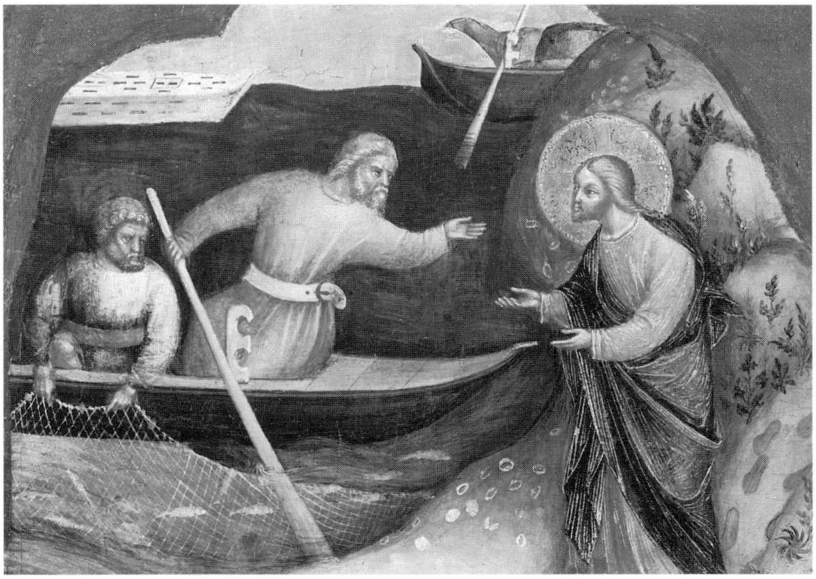

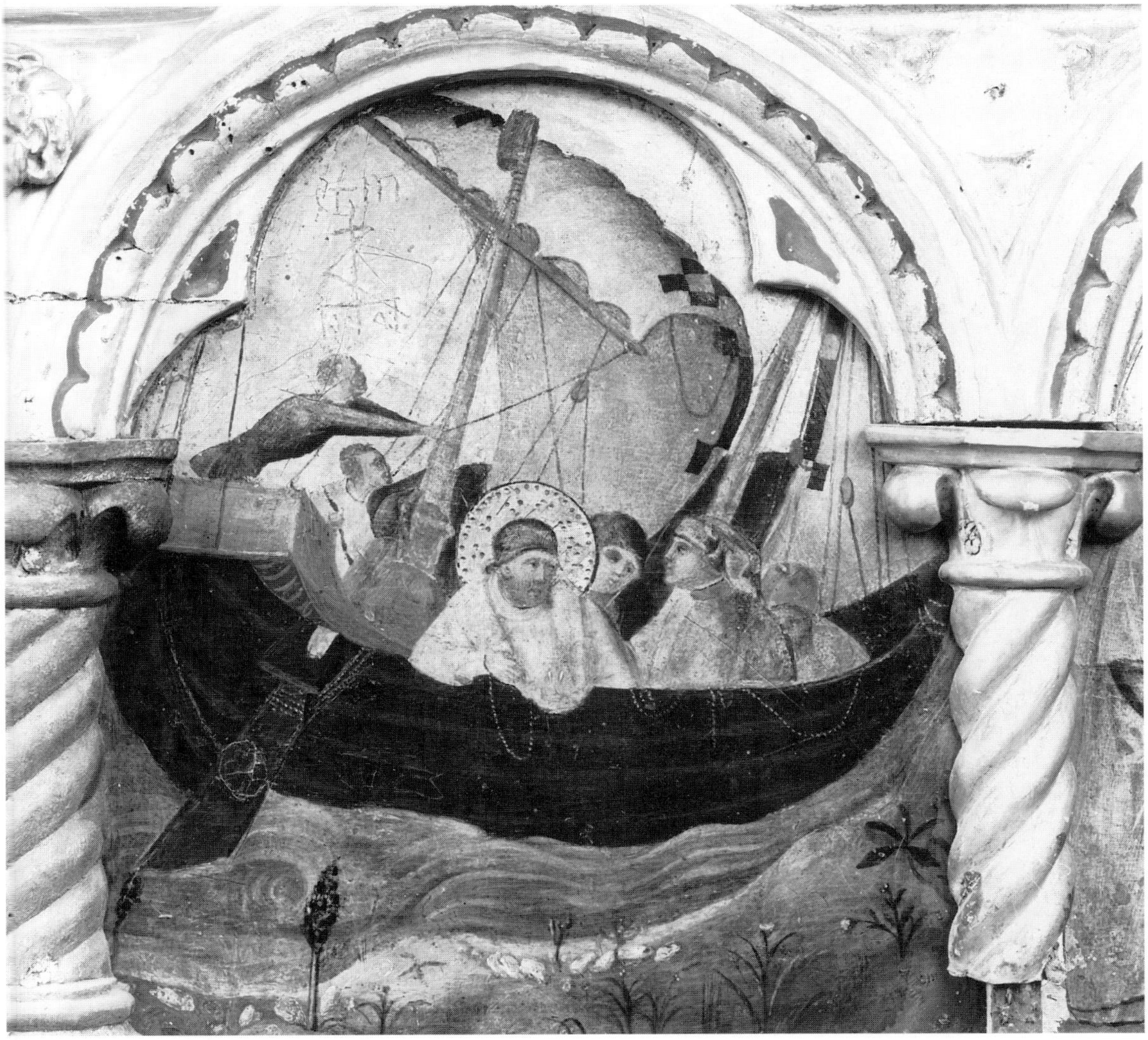

FIG. 104. "St. Thomas Becket Sails to France," by Stefano di Sant'Agnese (?), second half of fourteenth-century predella panel from San Zaccaria. *Courtesy Böhm*

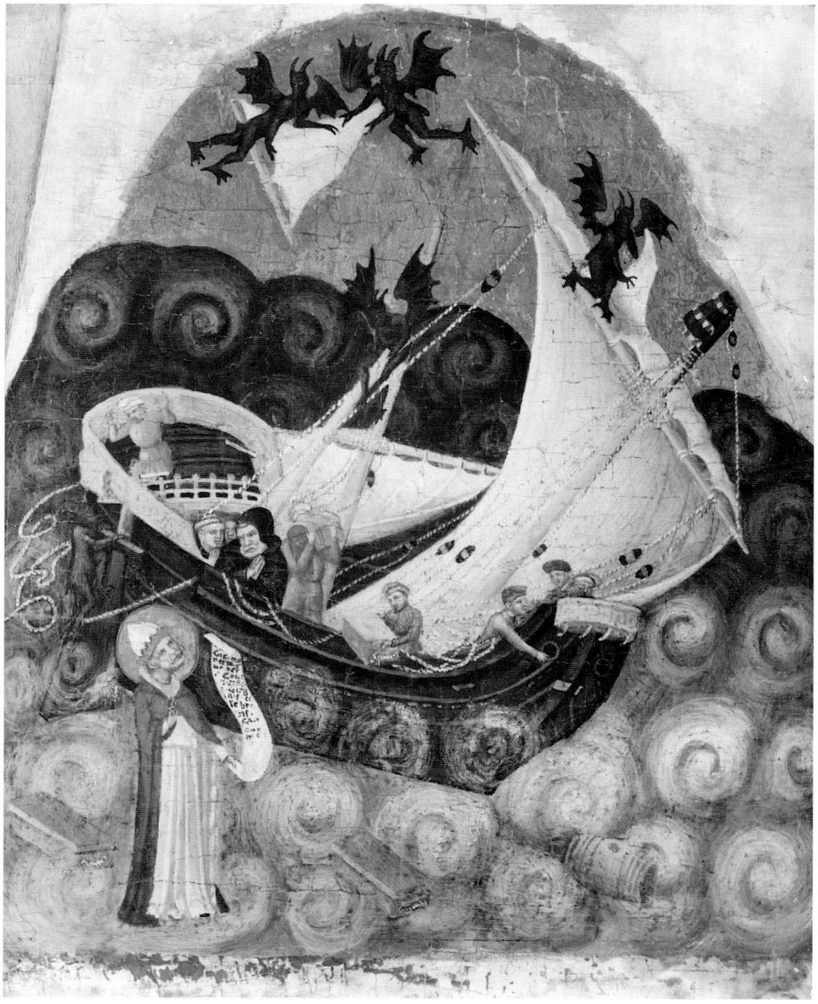

FIG. 105. A merchant ship in a storm, from the Altarpiece of the Virgin Mary. *Reproduced courtesy trustees of The National Gallery, London*

Figure 104

Theme: "St. Thomas Becket Sails to France."
Date: Second half of the fourteenth century (Pallucchini, 1964: 190–94).
Artist: Stefano di Sant'Agnese (?) (Kaftal, 1978: 1273).
Location: Predella panel, from San Zaccaria, San Tarasio Chapel, Venice, present location un known.
Type: Two-masted, lateen-rigged merchant ship (Type IIIb).

St. Thomas Becket sails in a two-masted round ship, figure 104. The arch of the predella cuts off the peak of the foresail and the top of the mizzen sail's yard. The extra-large figures on board also block the bottom of the foremast and some of the rigging details. The vessel is similar to the two-masted, lateen-rigged round ships depicted in figures 98, 99, and 101. Note the tackle of the foremast tack and the mizzen tack. On the mizzen, two pairs of lines attached to either side of the yard, near where the yard crosses the mast, may act as shrouds or stays. A crow's nest is set aft on the visible mizzen. The heel of the mizzen sail has a stylized cross decoration.

On the visible, starboard side, an asymmetrical rudder is attached through the hull secured with a modified box mount.

Figure 105

Title: Panel of Altarpiece of the Virgin Mary.
Theme: Miracles of the Virgin associated with Feast of the Conception (December 8): Helsinus, saved from shipwreck.
Artist: Venetian or Dalmatian School.
Location: From the Veneto or Dalmatia, now in the National Gallery of London (#4250).
Date: End of the fourteenth century.
Types: Figure 105: Two-masted, lateen-rigged merchant ship (Type IIIb).
Figure 106: Lagoonal craft (Type Ib).

This altarpiece includes two maritime images, figures 105 and 106. Figure 105, a dramatic scene depicting Helsinus and a few others aboard fervently praying to the Virgin as demons wreak havoc with their ship: masts and yards snap, and the sail is ripped. Several mariners toss cargo overboard in efforts to save themselves. Prelate Helsinus holds a scroll in the left foreground. Saved by the Virgin who heard his prayers, thereafter Helsinus preaches the celebration of the immaculate conception.

The foremast seems too strongly forward raking, accentuated by the angle of view. The lines around the mast at deck level probably secured wedges. A barrel-like crow's nest is fitted aft of the mast head, and a rope ladder leads up to it. Two spars lashed together form the yard. Robands are shown securing the lateen sail. Two tack and two vang run through blocks to port and starboard; the vang is secured aft near the quarterdeck. Three starboard shrouds with blocks are visible. The halyard is shown twisted rather loosely and precariously around the mast. Another line, passing through a series of two blocks, runs between the lowermost end of the yard and the forward upper side of the crow's nest. This is a unique depiction of this particular rigging in this position; it appears to be functioning as a lift to control the up and down movement of the yard (perhaps the medieval term *sachetus de gabia cum sua sagora* in Pryor's figure 13 (1984, no. 3; fig. 130N). The only other comparable depiction is in the left ship of a painting of the departure of Alatiel (fig. 108), where it is attached from the bottom of the crow's nest to the uppermost end of the yard.

The mizzen and its yard have both snapped in two. Part of the sail and yard are being carried off by demons in the sky. Tackle, and the shrouds or stays, where they tie off to the yard, are the only mizzen rigging visible.

The most prominent structural timbers of the hull are clearly recorded. The entire hull bottom is visible through the waves, revealing a flat bottom like Contarina I. The rake of the stem is strong, while the stern appears to be a full transom stern and slightly higher than the bow. Planking timbers are undefined, but pairs of parallel lines represent several wales. The lowermost one curves from the stem to midships; abaft it is obscured by Helsinus's scroll. Just beneath the main wale, visible as a row of small rectangles from amidships into the bow, are the ends of through-beams. This indicates a deck level. The bow is full, a small foredeck is supported externally by struts. A third wale above the main wale defines the lower side of the bulwarks.

The visible starboard quarter rudder is massive and has been mounted though a modified box mount, further secured with a rudder hoist. A demon clutching the rudder thwarts the efforts of the helmsman on the quarterdeck to control the course of the ship, who throws up his hands in despair.

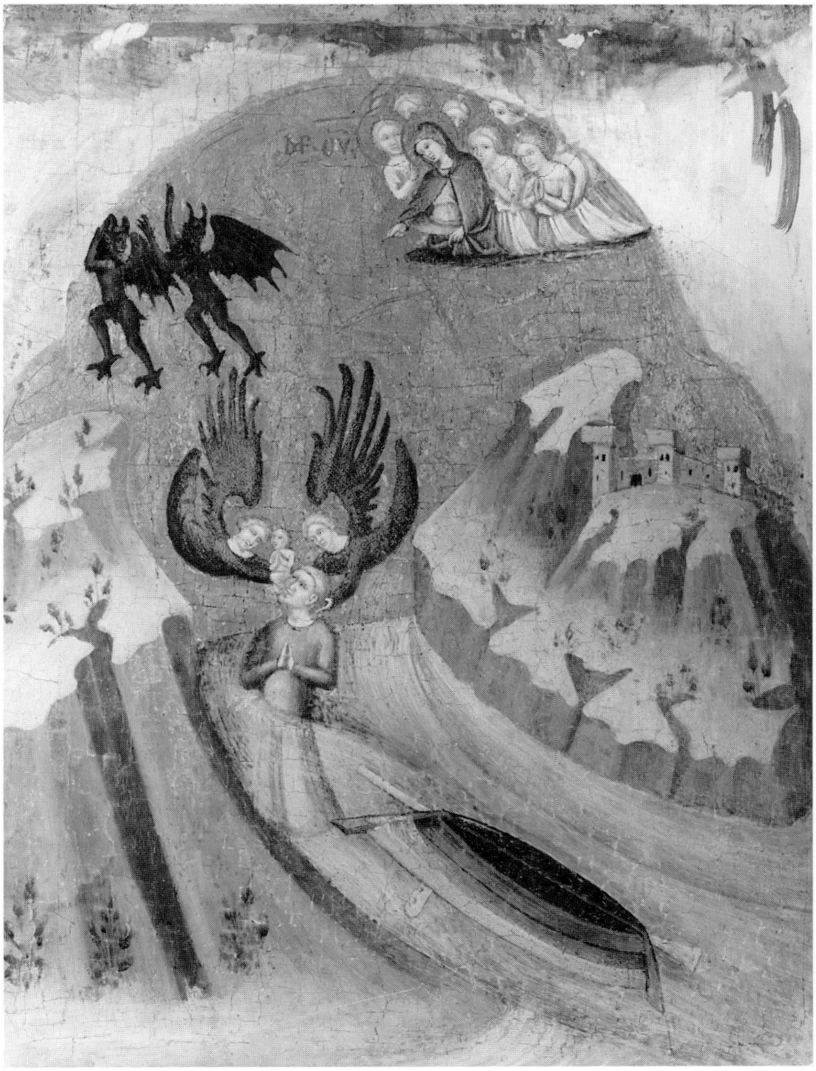

FIG. 106. A late fourteenth-century painting of a capsized gondola, from the Altarpiece of the Virgin Mary. *Reproduced by courtesy of the trustees, The National Gallery, London*

Figure 106

Theme: *The Golden Legend:* "The Virgin Saves a French Canon from Drowning by Devils."

Type: Lagoonal craft (Type Ib).

Figure 106 depicts the story of a French canon, who, while journeying down a river on his way home from adultery, is drowned by devils who capsize his boat. Two angels lift out his soul, but then the canon is miraculously restored to life by the Virgin, who has heard his prayers.

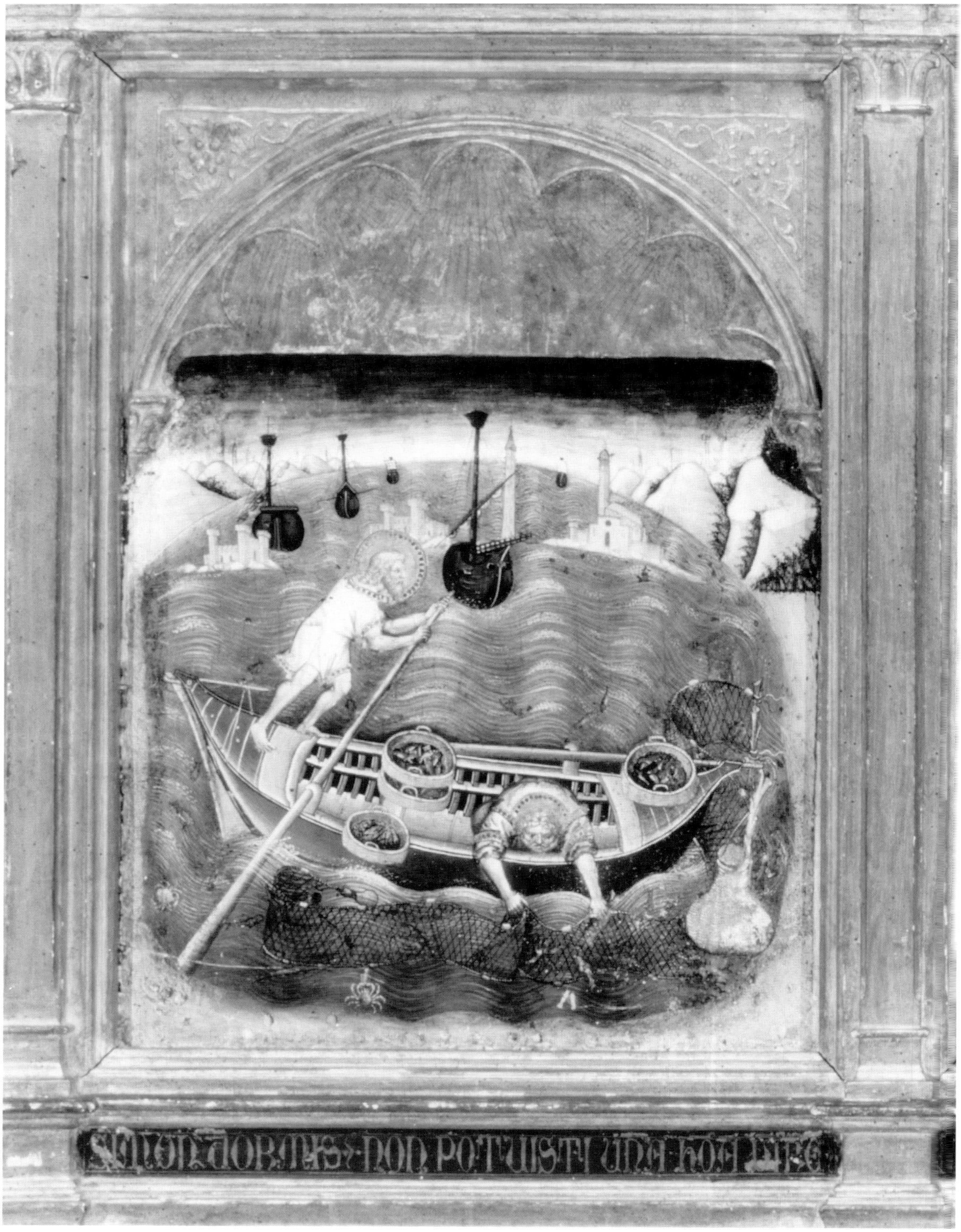

FIG. 107. “The Miraculous Draught of Fishes,” from a polyptych panel by Jacobello del Fiore, 1401–39. *Gift of the museum membership, Denver Art Museum Collection*

Although the boat is being used on a river, it closely resembles the small lagoonal craft of figure 77. The small craft is very clearly depicted, despite the fact that it must be mostly underwater. As the vessel is capsized, its flat bottom with a minimal keel is revealed. Posts rise sharply from the keel—the bow more steeply than the stern—and are very nearly straight.

Individual planking is not defined, but a main wale is shown finished into the posts. A wide sheer strake, the Venetian style *forcole* oarlock, and the steering oar, are yellow, while the rest of the hull is painted black.

Figure 107
Title: Altarpiece of St. Peter and St. Paul.
Theme: "The Miraculous Draught of Fishes."
Artist: Jacobello del Fiore.
Location: Polyptych panel, originally from the Veneto. Denver Art Museum (#1951.84.1–84.4).
Date: Early fifteenth century (Chastel, 1963: 135).
Types: Fishing boat (Type Ib), five single-masted, square-rigged merchant ships (Type IIId). [Related panels: "The Calling of Peter and Andrew" (Kaftal, 1978: fig. 1072); "Peter Walks upon the Water to Jesus" (Kaftal, 1978: fig. 1073). Two fishing boats (Type Ib); seven single-masted, square-rigged merchant ships (Type IIId) in background.]

In this polyptych panel, three lagoonal craft relate three different biblical stories with carracks in the background, but are nearly identical in their details of a fishing boat in the foreground. Two include only the bow, while one shows the complete vessel. Therefore, only the complete one, depicting "The Miraculous Draught of Fishes," has been reproduced in this catalog (fig. 107). The vessel type has a smaller foredeck, and also a more gradual sheer, but otherwise is quite similar to the *burchio* type seen in Menabuoi's fresco, figure 79; this may represent the smaller *burchièlla.*

The boats in the other panels show a square hole cut into the foredeck, where a removable mast could be stepped when sail power was desired. Figure 107 lacks this detail, although it is likely it too would have had a removable mast. Christ stands at the stern, working a steering paddle in the Venetian style *forcole* oarlock at starboard aft. A second paddle is stowed along the port gunwale, secured in another *forcole* oarlock near the foredeck.

The small vessel probably had no true keel. Stem and stern rise gently from the flat bottom and finish the double-ended hull with a bow and stern roughly equivalent in height. The angle of view depicted in figure 107 reveals part of the interior hull construction and shows a consistent room and space. Small decks at both bow and stern are cross-planked. Framing is fortified with an inner wale or clamp and a sturdy caprail. Ceiling planking has been set above the framing. A single rudder is hung on the sternpost. The loom is steadied under a rope tied to the sides of the vessel, holding a general course for the fishermen.

The sharp detail of this painting, its use of perspective, and the definitive affirmation of natural details, already seen in the similar craft of figure 79, make it another excellent point of reference for the small lagoonal fishing craft type.

Figure 108
Title: The History of Alatiel (Pataky and Marjai, 1973: pl. 7).
Artist: Maestro dei Cassoni Jarves.
Location: Museo Correr (Correr Museum), Venice (M. 4562).
Date: First half of the fifteenth century.
Type: Two single-masted, lateen-rigged merchant ships (Type IIIa) and two lighters (Type Ia).

In this diptych, figure 108, two round ships are shown in the process of loading, in preparation for a pilgrimage. It is difficult to interpret the details of either ship for two artistic reasons.

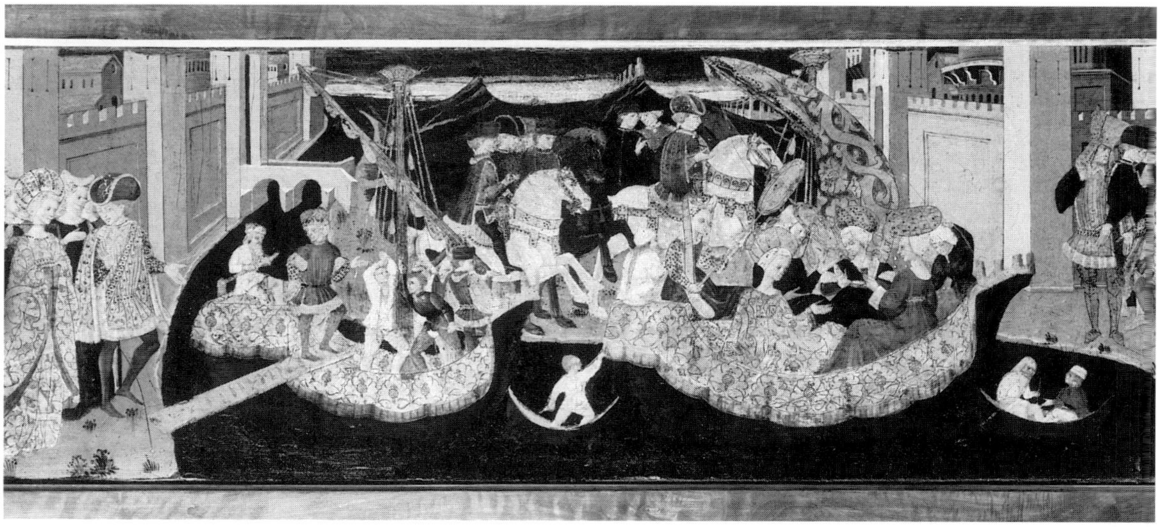

FIG. 108. The History of Alatiel, first half of the fifteenth-century painting by Maestro dei Cassoni Jarves. *Courtesy Museo Correr*

The first is that the emphasis on the people in the story has unrealistically obscured most of the vessels. The other difficulty is the highly ornamented and decorative nature of the painting. Although some nobles actually did gild the masts and decorate the sails of the ships they supported (Pataky and Marjai, 1973: pl. 7), this sumptuous portrayal by Maestro dei Cassoni Jarves certainly is exaggerated, and the gilding has supplanted other, possibly nautical, details.

On the right ship, five lines aft of the single mast may represent some stays or shrouds and the halyard. A vang line with tackle is depicted above the right horseman's head. Robands secure the elaborately decorated sail to the yard, which is made up of two sections. Part of the transom stern is barely discernible through the ornate fabrics draped along the gunwale. Four upright projections on the bow may have served as cleats or bitts.

The ship to the left is virtually identical but has its sail furled, and a few more rigging lines are defined. Two mariners amidships haul up the yard. Five other sets of lines to either side of the mast represent shrouds and stays. A rarely depicted feature is the *sachetus de gabia cum sua sagora*, a line running through tackle from the top of the mast to the upper end of the yard (similar to one in figure 105, where it runs to the lower end of the yard). A helmsman mans the tiller toward the stern.

The two lighters are very simply rendered with no details beyond a general banana-like hull.

Figure 109

Theme: "Madre di Misericordia, Mother of Mercy."

Artist: Unknown.

Location: Santa Maria Glorioso dei Frari, Venice.

Date: Fifteenth century.

Type: Two riverine cargo vessels (Type Id).

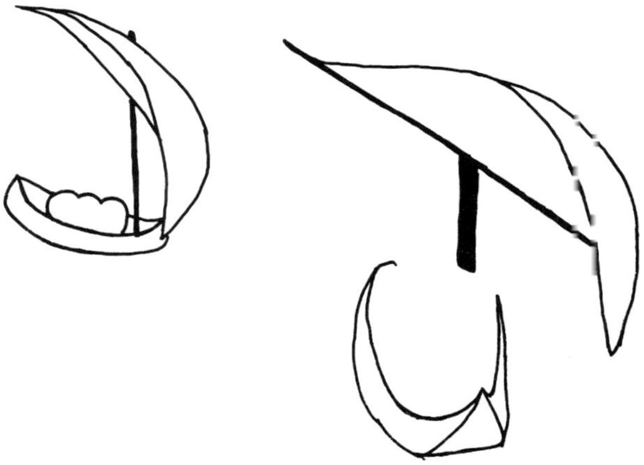

FIG. 109. Two river boats, from a fifteenth-century panel painting of the "Madre di Misericordia, Mother of Mercy," Santa Maria Glorioso dei Frari. *Dawn Hoyt Kidd*

Figure 109 is a painting of the "Mother of Mercy" protecting the friars. The figures stand on the banks of a river, and two river cargo boats sail in the background.

The boats are too small to recognize many details, but the basic type is that of figures 81 and 121, the single-masted, lateen-rigged, flat-bottomed river boat.

Figure 110

Title: *The Judgment of Paris.*

Theme: Careening scene in an imaginary harbor, Rome.

Artist: School of Sandro Botticelli.

Location: Private collection, Cini Foundation, Venice.

Date: ca. 1445–1510.

Types: Two three-masted, mixed-rigged merchant ships (Type IIIf).

[In background: Single-masted, square-rigged merchant ship (Type IIId)].

[Similar Botticelli work: Two three-masted, mixed-rigged merchant ships (Type IIIf) (Venturi, 1937: p. 17; pls. 37, 57)].

Figure 110 illustrates the unusual scene of a ship being careened in beautiful detail. The remarkable detail suggests a sketch was made from life, though we have no way of knowing whether in Venice or some other port of Italy. Botticelli (and his school) must have worked from notebook images, for a virtually identical ship careening detail was painted by Botticelli in his fresco for Pope Sixtus IV, made between 1481 and 1482 (*The Punishment of Korah, Dathan, and Abiram* in the Sistine Chapel; Venturi, 1937: p. 17; pls. 37, 57). Figure 110 illustrates the mixed rig becoming common in Mediterranean waters beginning in the first half of the fifteenth century (e.g., figs. 70 and 107), and even more so, during the second half (e.g., fig. 127) and in the following century, as the carrack type. No tumble home is indicated in figure 110; it is perhaps, like figures 56 and 60, an example of the Mediterranean-style *coche* and not quite a carrack.

Figure 110 includes just the stern of a ship to the left. The complete ship is listed over to port, revealing some of the inner hull construction as well as the upper deck of the ship. Figure 111 is a reconstruction by Artù Chiggiato, who based his proportions on the assumption that the ladder by the main hatch in the painting would have measured approximately .75 meters wide x 2.2 meters tall, with five rungs 32 centimeters apart, resulting in an overall length of 25.8 meters, deck length (quarterdecks included), 31.1 meters, and the maximum deck width of 7.9 meters (de Cervin, 1985, p. 23).

The mainmast, standing just forward of midships, rakes only slightly forward; the mizzen stands vertically—or even slightly aft—while a small mast for a foresail on the forecastle rakes strongly forward. The forestay of the main is secured near the base of the foremast; that mast's forestay is tied to a spar projecting off the bow. Both the mainmast and the foremast have centrally placed crow's nests. All sails are stowed. The mizzen's long lateen yard has been tied firmly to the base of its mast for storage, with one end supported by a transverse timber forming the upper bulwarks at the aft end of the sterncastle. Two other yards forming a near-vertical "X" have been tied about the mainmast to reinforce it while the ship is careened. Eight tackle and spars are visible amidst the numerous shrouds and stays bundled around the mainmast.

Hatches for loading cargo are cut through the deck forward of the central and mizzen masts. An additional smaller hatch for ventilation is aft of the mizzen. A small, triangularly shaped forecastle is higher than the transom stern, which has a raised quarterdeck. Along the port side, the tops of top-timbers are visible near where the parapet railing is set, and the corresponding top-timbers along part of the starboard show consistent room and space. The main deck planking runs along the length of the vessel, although decking on the sterncastle, the floor, and the after side of the forecastle is

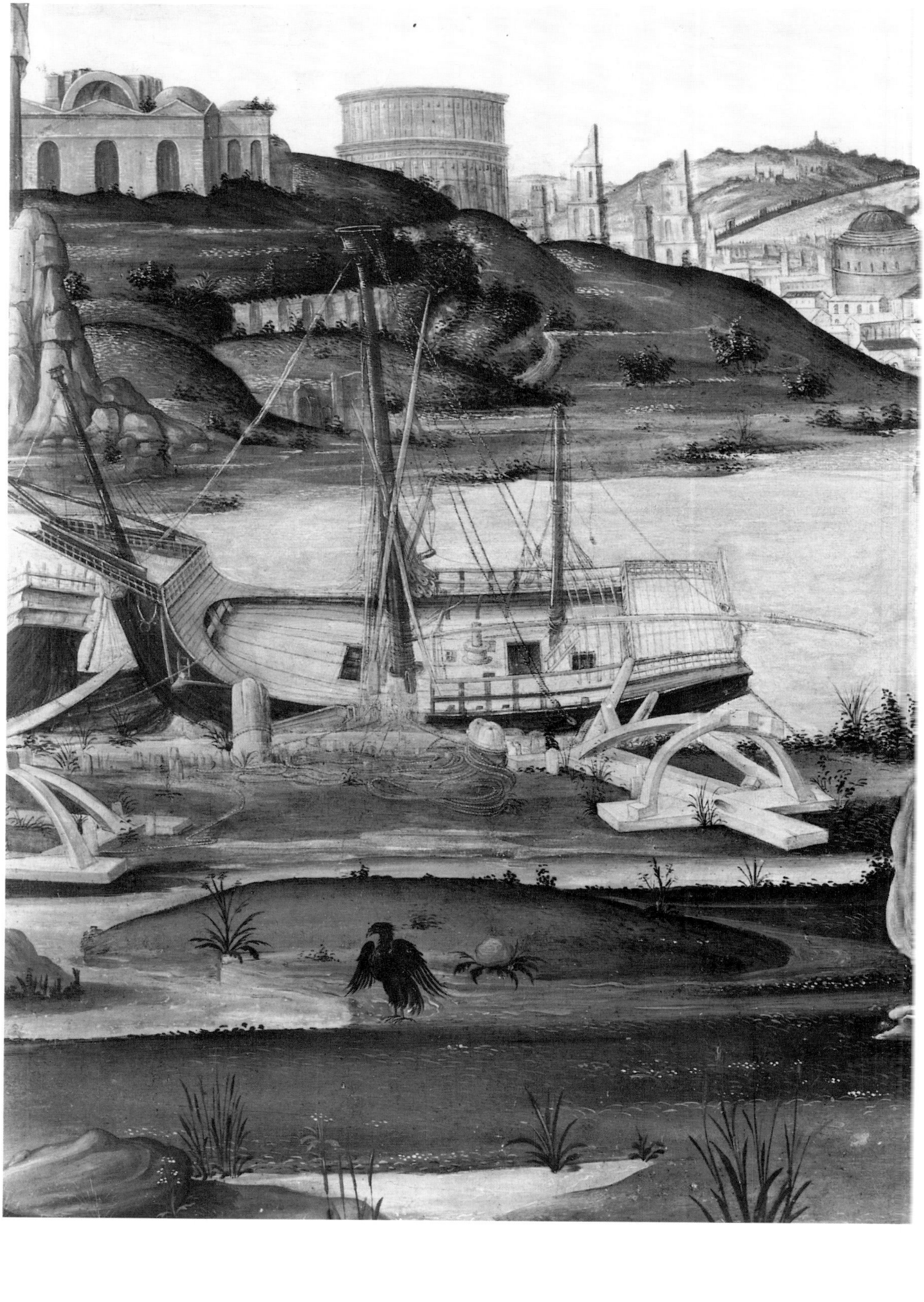

FIG. 110. School of Botticelli painting, *The Judgment of Paris* (ca. 1445–1510), depicting the careening of a ship. *Private Collection, Cini Foundation, Venice*

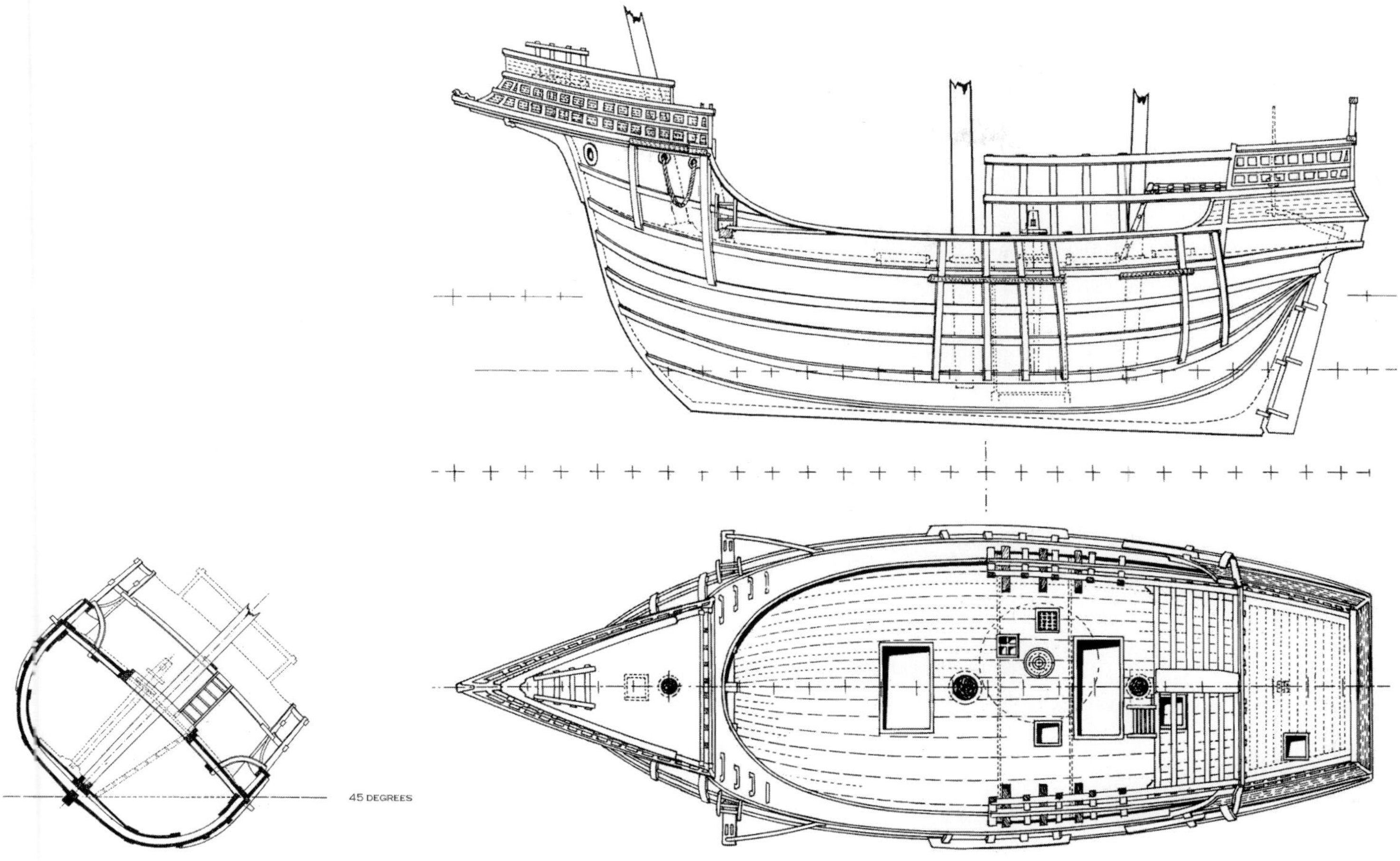

FIG. 111. Reconstruction of a fifteenth-century *coche* by Artù Chiggiato, based on Botticelli's painting, *The Judgment of Paris. After Rubin de Cervin, 1985: 10–11*

cross-planked. A typical arched opening gives access to the forecastle. Here, above the upper deck level, a thick horizontal beam projecting through the port side of the bow can be seen. This riding bitt, called the *arganellum,* was accessible via the small ladder and would have provided the mariners a place to secure the anchor after catting it. A capstan is on deck near midships.

This ship probably had a single stern rudder fixed to the transom stern as seen on the ship to the left. The open arrangement of the quarterdeck with a parapet and the placement of the mizzen's yard for storage (lashed to the bole of the mast and supported on a transverse timber at the stern) likely resemble dispositions used on earlier, completely lateen-rigged ships as well.

Sculpture

Figure 112
Theme: "James and John Cast a Fishing Net."
Location: Column of altar canopy (fig. 1G), San Marco, Venice.
Date: ca. seventh century?
Types: Fishing boat (Type Ib).
[Nearby on same column: Fishing boat (Type Ib)].

The northwest stone column of the altar canopy in San Marco has two small boats sculpted in high relief, relating the stories of James and John's "Miraculous Draught of Fishes," and "Christ Preaching to the Multitudes from a Boat." One boat is so simplified that it adds nothing to our understanding of Venetian

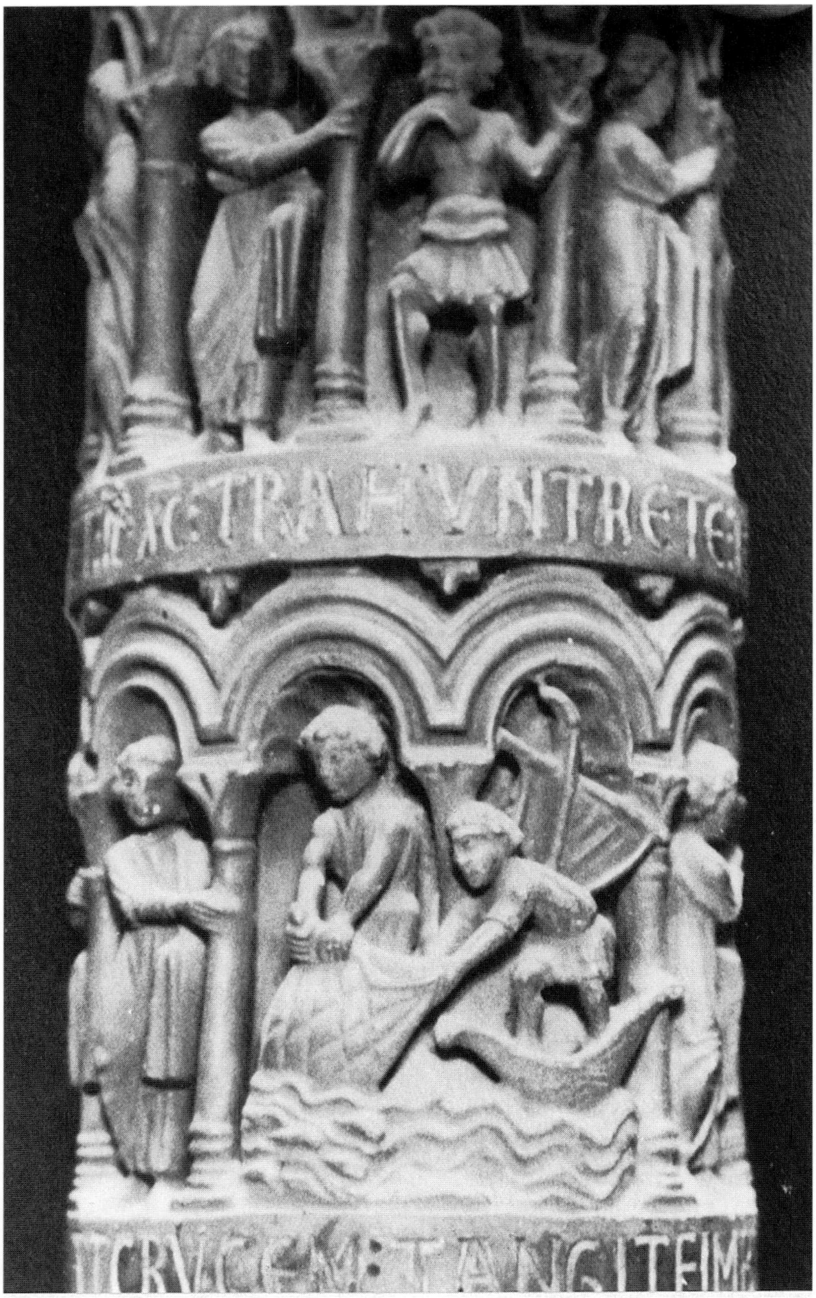

FIG. 112. "James and John Cast a Fishing Net": small craft scene from a sculpted column of the altar canopy (ca. seventh century?), San Marco. *Permission to photograph courtesy the Procuratóre di San Marco*

craft. It has a distorted saucer or inverted turtle-shell shape, with one wale and the caprail emphasized. The masted vessel is illustrated in this catalog as figure 112.

Figure 112 has an unrealistic banana-shaped hull, with its ends flaring outward. It is extremely shallow drafted. The scene depicts the two apostles drawing in their nets, though only one man, enlarged for emphasis, actually stands in the vessel. It is not clear what the other apostle stands on; perhaps he is ashore or on another craft. The most interesting aspect of the sculpture is the early style, hook-like mast head, like the one seen in figure 29. The sail is lateen, though no rigging is detailed.

Figure 113

Title: Bronze coin or medallion minted in honor of the Doge Peter Candianus.

Titulus: According to Jal, the legend around the ship reads: *PETRVS CAND. DVX CHELANDIA,* while above the ship is: *PORTIS,* and below the ship: *C. FECIT.* The reverse of the coin reads: *SECVRITAS VENETIAE* (1840: 247). Levi recorded the legend as *SECVRITATIS VENETIA, PETRVS CANDIANVS* (1892: pl. 13, fig. 2)

Translation: [Doge] Peter Candianus established *chelandia* at the entrance to the lagoons. Security of Venice.

Location: Present location uncertain (Levi, 1892: pl. 13, fig. 2).[18]

Date: 931.

Type: Riverine war craft (Type Ic).

The decked lagoonal and river war boat figure 113 was propelled primarily with oars: on the starboard side, three are mounted near the stern and four more, just forward of midships. Both Levi and Jal have interpreted what actually seems to be simply a mast set far forward as a defensive tower (Levi, 1892: pl. 13X, fig. 2, and Jal, 1840: 247).

It is likely this long, slender hull is flat bottomed. The sternpost rises steeply and is slightly higher than the stem. Two lines running parallel from stem to stern indicate an extra-wide sheer strake or the caprail. A decked cabin at midships extends about a third of the total length of the boat. Oarsmen, probably more numerous than indicated by the number of oars depicted, must have sat on benches between the cabin and the sides of the hull. The vessel has been much simplified to fit its small image space on the coin.

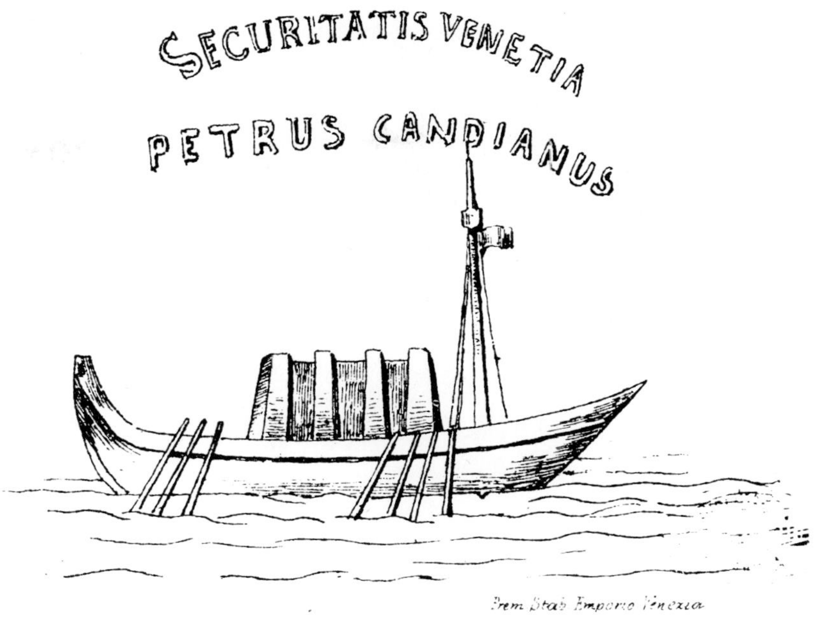

FIG. 113. Coin minted in honor of Doge Petrus Candianus in 931. *Levi, 1892: pl. 13, fig. 2*

Figure 114
Titulus: RESVLPASTORPCLARV MARE TRANSIT GEMINANUS.
Theme: "St. Geminiano's Voyage."
Artist: Maestro of St. Geminiano.
Location: Main door, Duomo, Modena.
Date: Twelfth century.
Type: Coastal cargo vessel (Type Id).

The hull of this small boat in figure 114 is simplified in a typically Byzantine style with a high stem and stern, the three figures exaggerated, and the mast too vertically set. The rope parrel at the mast head and lines attaching the upper part of the lateen sail to the yard are well illustrated. No other rigging lines are detailed. The helmsman works a symmetrical steering oar.

Figure 115
Title: "Labors of the Months: The Craftsmen."
Themes: Figure 115: "The Shipbuilders."
Figure 116: "The Fishermen."
Artist: Lombard-Emilian masons.
Location: Intrados of archivolt, main portal, San Marco, Venice.
Date: ca. 1250.
Types: Figure 115: Single-masted, lateen-rigged merchant ship (Type IIIa?).
Figure 116: Fishing boat (Type Ib).

The "Labors of the Months," thirteenth-century relief sculptures in the stone archivolt of the main entrance of San Marco, represent craftsmen of Venice. Included are shipbuilders, storekeepers, bakers, butchers, milk sellers, master builders, shoemakers, barbers, dentists, coopers, carpenters, blacksmiths, ironworkers, and fishermen. Among the sculptures, two scenes contain vessels, figures 115 and 116.

The construction scene portrays one man in the bow of a small round ship boring a hole with an auger (fig. 115). Another in the stern removes an adze from a tool basket. Two men working from below caulk with hammer and chisel or a caulking iron. A main wale and an upper wale or caprail just above the through-beams for a deck level are indicated. Strakes at the stem have been bound together with rope, probably only temporarily for construction purposes.

Figure 116
Title: "Labors of the Months: The Craftsmen."
Theme: "The Fishermen."
Artist: Lombard-Emilian masons.
Location: Intrados of archivolt, main portal, San Marco, Venice.
Date: ca. 1250.
Type: Fishing boat (Type Ib).

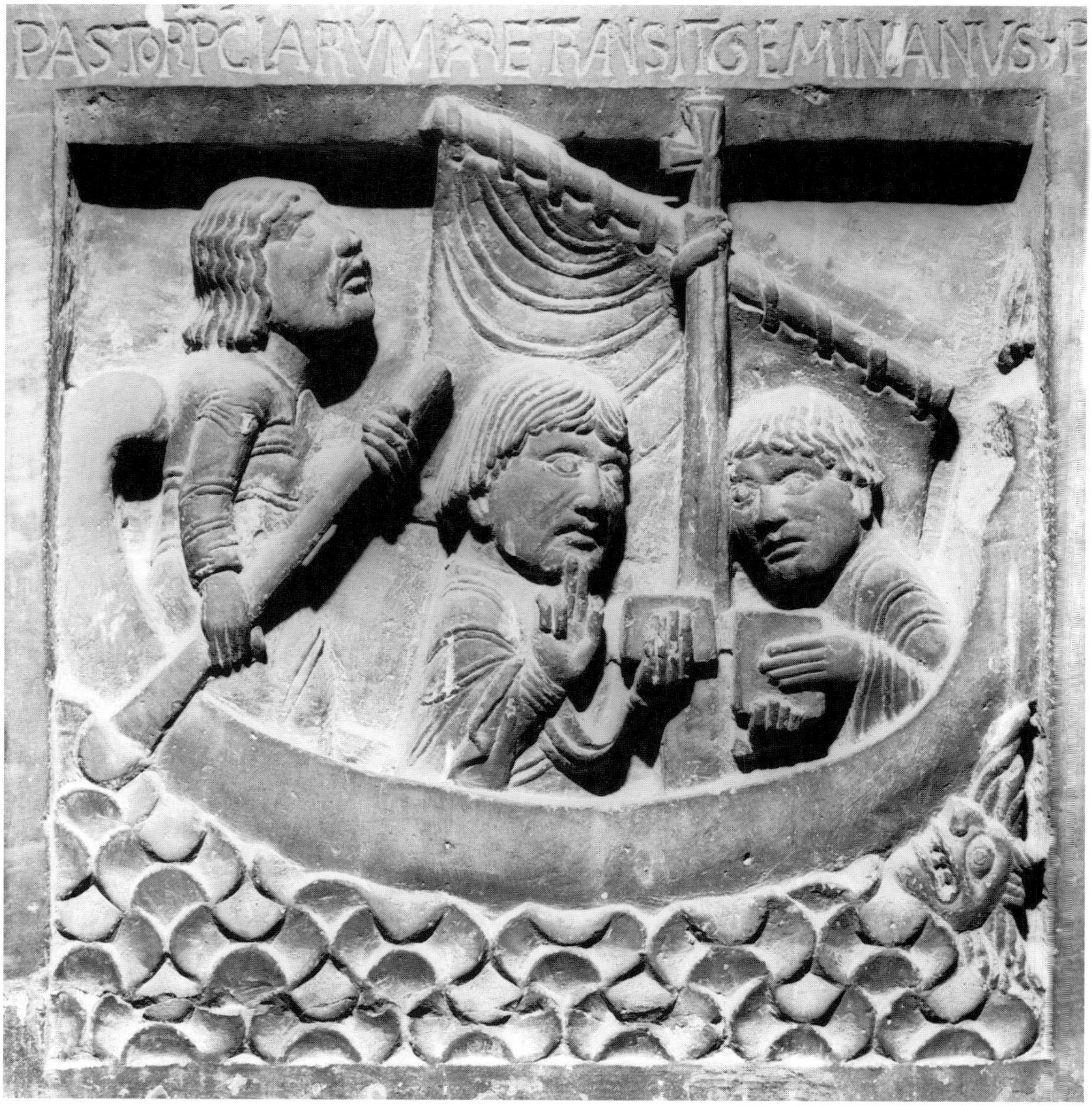

FIG. 114. "St. Geminiano's Voyage," twelfth-century sculpture on main door, the Duomo, Modena. *Courtesy Museo d'art medievale e moderna, Modena*

In this shallow relief sculpture of the stone archivolt, figure 116, a middle-aged and a young man, are engaged in two different shallow-water fishing techniques. The older fisherman, sitting toward the stern of the small boat, catches fish with hooks on a line weighted with a lead sinker. Perched on the rim of the vessel at the bow, the younger man has thrust a trident into a fish.

Except for the rise to the stem and sternposts, their small fishing craft has an almost horizontal sheer strake. Three horizontal lines represent the uppermost strakes, curving upward at bow and stern. A row of consistently spaced nails securing the strakes to inner frames are well indicated, although exaggerated in size.

Figure 117

Title: *Paliotto* (altar frontal) of San Marco.

Theme: *Vita* of St. Mark: "The Voyage to Alexandria."

Titulus: VALITIN ALEXANDRIA NAVIGIO VEHITVO.

Translation: Sailing to Alexandria.

Location: Treasury, San Marco, Venice.

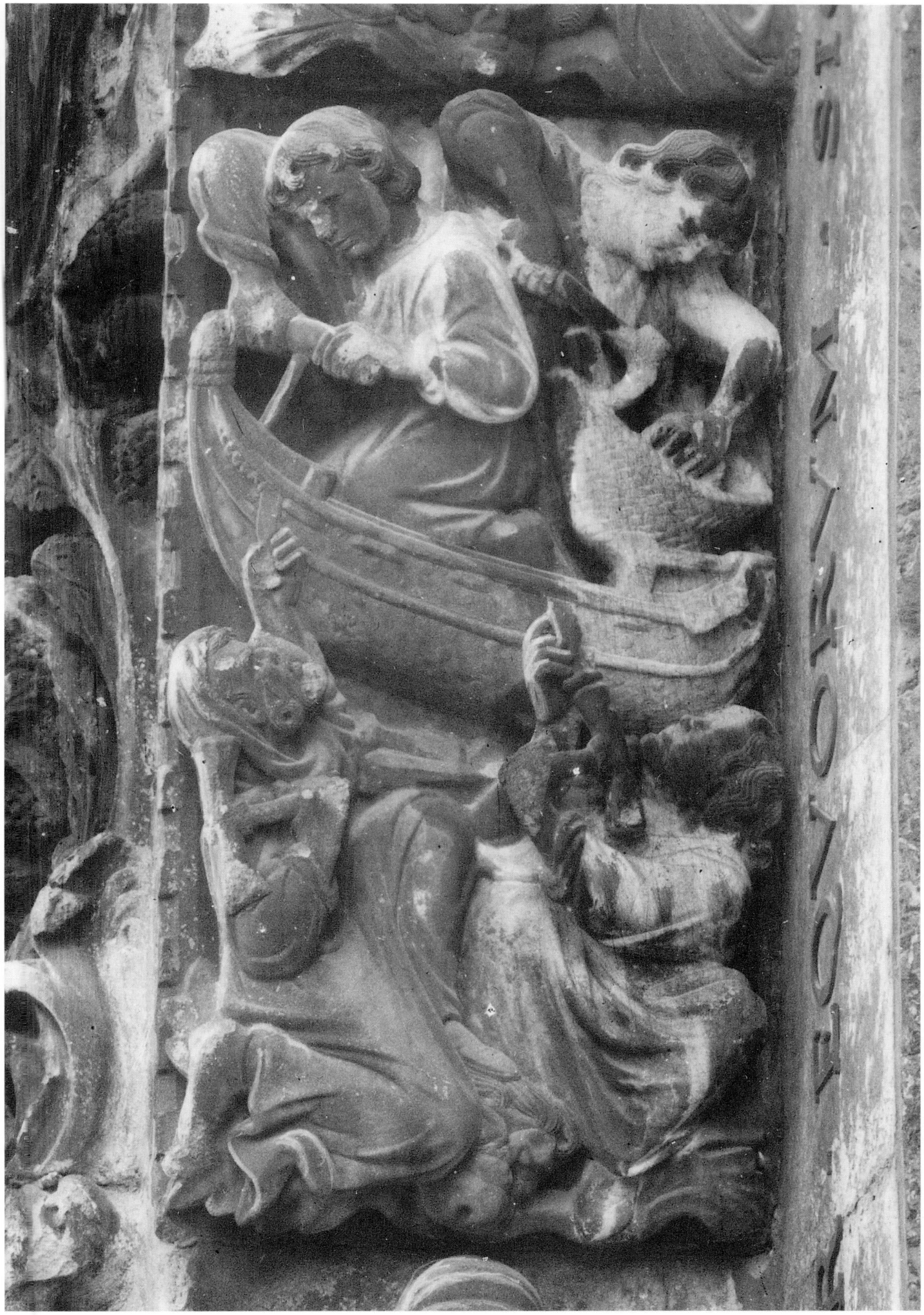

FIG. 115. "The Shipbuilders," stone sculpture on the main portal of San Marco, ca. 1250. *Courtesy the Procuratóre di San Marco*

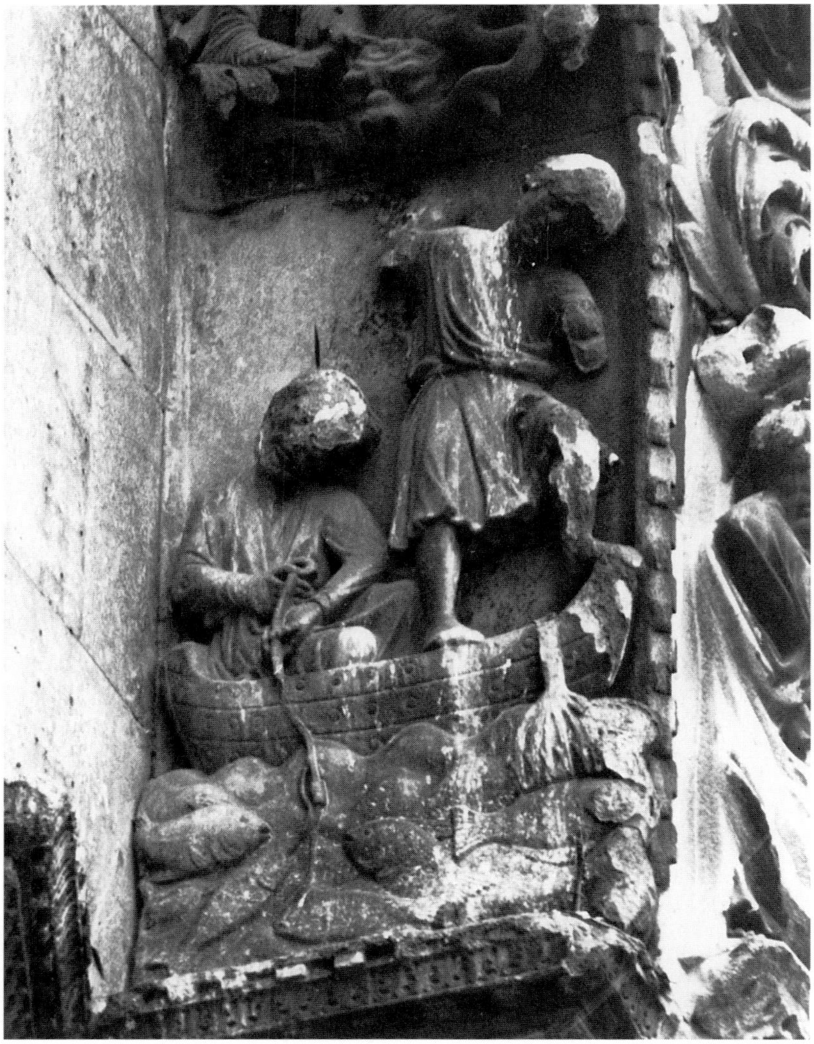

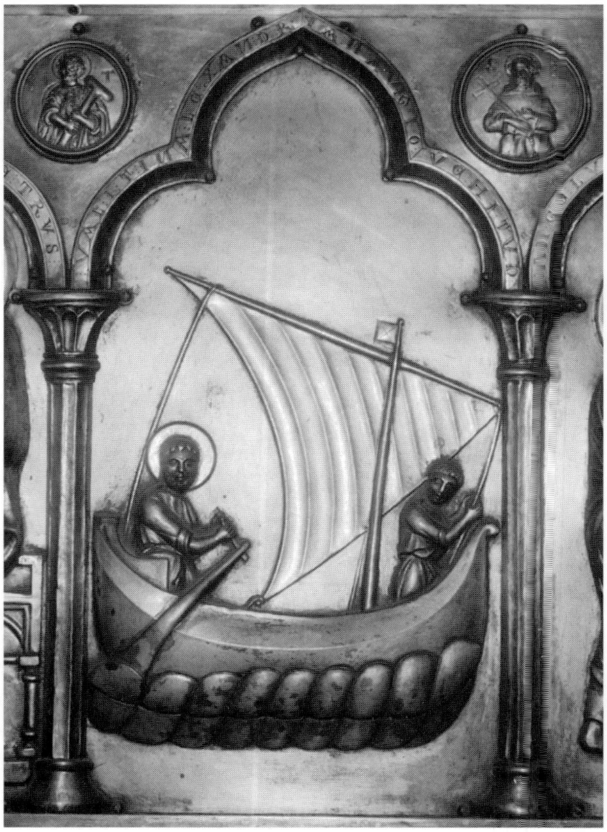

FIG. 117. Vermeil *Paliotto* of San Marco, thirteenth-century scene from the *vita* of St. Mark (the *praedestinatio*): during the Voyage to Alexandria. *Permission to photograph courtesy the Procuratóre di San Marco*

FIG. 116. "The Fishermen," stone sculpture on the main portal of San Marco, ca. 1250. *Courtesy the Procuratóre di San Marco*

Date: ca. thirteenth century (Sansoni, 1971: table 251).
Type: Single-masted, lateen-rigged merchant ship (Type IIIa).

The *Paliotto* figure 117 is a repoussé sculpture. The relief was originally vermeil, but now the silver is completely worn away, though the remaining metal is well preserved.

The single mast is set far forward at a slight rake. A small crow's nest, or possibly a pennant, is aft at its top. The unfurled lateen sail has vertical lines indicating its seams. Vang and tack are depicted at each end of the yard; a mariner at the bow hauls the tack, and the sheet is tied off slightly aft of midships. The hull is represented with minimal lines, indicating only the sheer, the stem and sternposts, and the wale. A very small quarterdeck with side railing offers the helmsman a seating platform like that seen in figures 25 and 115. The mariner seated here works the quarter rudder by its tiller.

Figure 118
Title: Silver chest of San Simeon of Zara.
Theme: *Translatio* of St. Simeon of Zara.
Artist: Francesco da Sesto.
Location: San Simeon, Zara, Dalmatian coast, Yugoslavia.
Date: 1377 (Nebbia, 1932: 48).

Types: Two-masted, lateen-rigged merchant ship (Type IIIb).
[Inside the lid of the chest: fishing boat (Type Ib) (Cecchelli, 1932: 109)].

This repoussé silver reliquary includes two maritime scenes. The fishing boat inside the lid is too simplified to be of much value and so is not illustrated here. Figure 118 is more interesting, depicting a round ship, its two masts, crow's nests, lateen sails, and rope ladders. This relief presents particular detail, however, of the hull's construction. The well-defined strakes of the side and bow area run parallel to the sheer, and are fixed with a regular nailing pattern. Presumably the stern would have been constructed like that of the similar ship seen in figure 94. Two rows of nail heads are depicted along nearly all defined strakes. The stem rises sharply from the keel. The quarterdeck has a structure to provide a temporary roof over the helmsman. A hole in the side of the hull allows the rudder stock to be passed inboard.

Instead of finishing into the stem to form a pointed bow, the sheer strakes finish at approximately the same height as the stem, but a short distance away, creating the broadened bow type seen in other representations and discussed in figure 28.

Figure 119
Theme: "The Calling of Peter and Andrew."
Location: Façade relief, Sant'Andrea della Zirada, Venice.
Date: Fourteenth century (Lorenzetti, 1982: 487).
Type: Lagoonal fishing boat (Type Ib).

A scene with a simple, open fishing craft decorates the stone façade of Sant'Andrea della Zirada, figure 119. It appears to be flat bottomed and ideally suited for lagoonal navigation. Strakes are indicated, as is the typically Venetian oarlock, with the oar's slot aft, and a thwart at just below the caprail amidships, between the two figures.

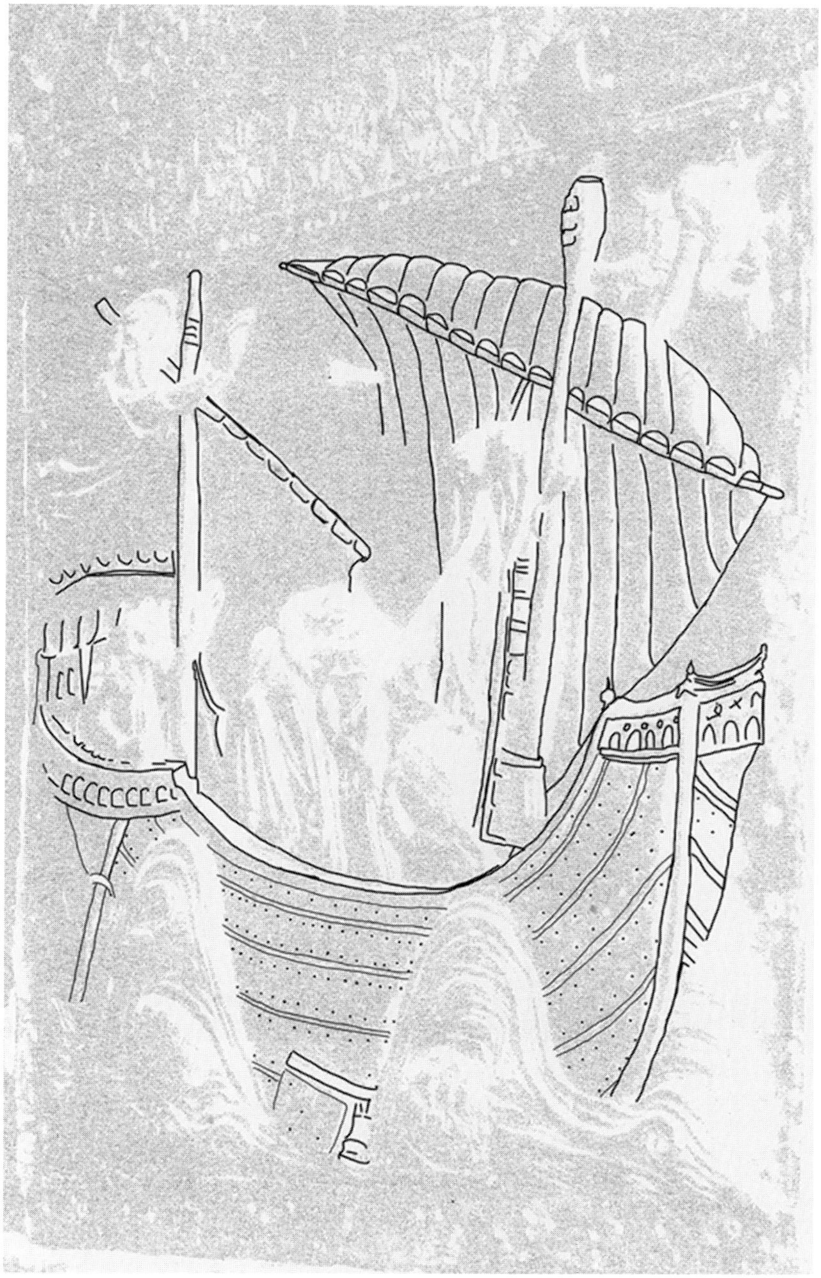

FIG. 118. *Translatio* of San Simeon, relief in side of a silver chest of San Simeon, Zara, 1377. *Helen C. Dewolf, after Nebbia, 1931: fig. 27*

Figure 120
Title: *Paliotto del Corpus Domini.*
Theme: "The Calling of Peter and Andrew."
Artists: Paolo and Canterina d'Andrea Bartolomeodi.
Location: Museo Correr (Correr Museum), Venice.
Date: Early fifteenth century.
Type: Lagoonal fishing boat (Type Ib).

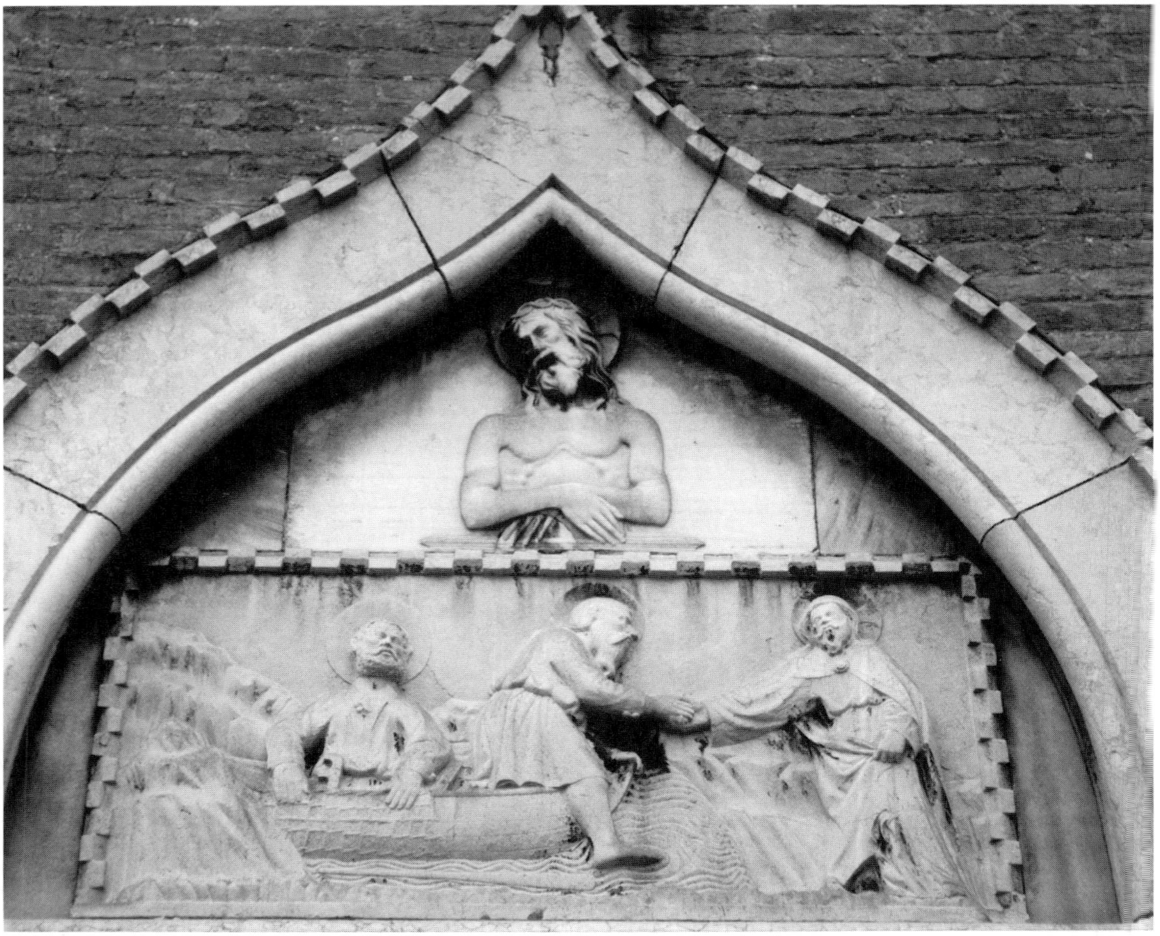

Fig. 119. "The Calling of Peter and Andrew," fourteenth-century façade relief, Sant'Andrea della Zirada

The gilded wood panel polychrome sculpture in figure 120 includes another small lagoonal craft. Besides the typically Venetian oarlock, with its oar's slot aft, nothing about this simple open craft is noteworthy. The artist has generically rendered only the main lines: the water line, sheer, stem, and stern; it looks very much like any rowboat of the present day. From amidships, Andrew works the oars as paddles freely, without engaging the shaft in the oarlock.

Figure 121

Theme: "Madre di Misericordia, Mother of Mercy" (between Saints James and John).
Artist: Bartolomeo Buon?
Location: Gothic doorway to *Corte Nuova della Scuola Vecchia delle Misericordia* (The new courtyard of the Old School of Misericordia).
Date: Early fifteenth century.
Type: Two riverine cargo vessels (Type Id).

These river boats in figure 121 are flat-bottomed, single-masted lateeners. The sculptor has simply defined basic details of the hull, gunwale, mast, sail, a vang, single rudder attached with pintle and gudgeon, and a load of wood cargo on deck amidships.

Figures 122–24

Theme: Ships at anchor.
Date: Mid-fifteenth century (?).
Artist: Anonymous; graffiti sketcher.
Location: Columns of San Marco façade, second portal (H, I, J).
Date: Mid-fifteenth century (?).
Types: Figure 122: Two single-masted, square-rigged merchant ship (Type IIId).

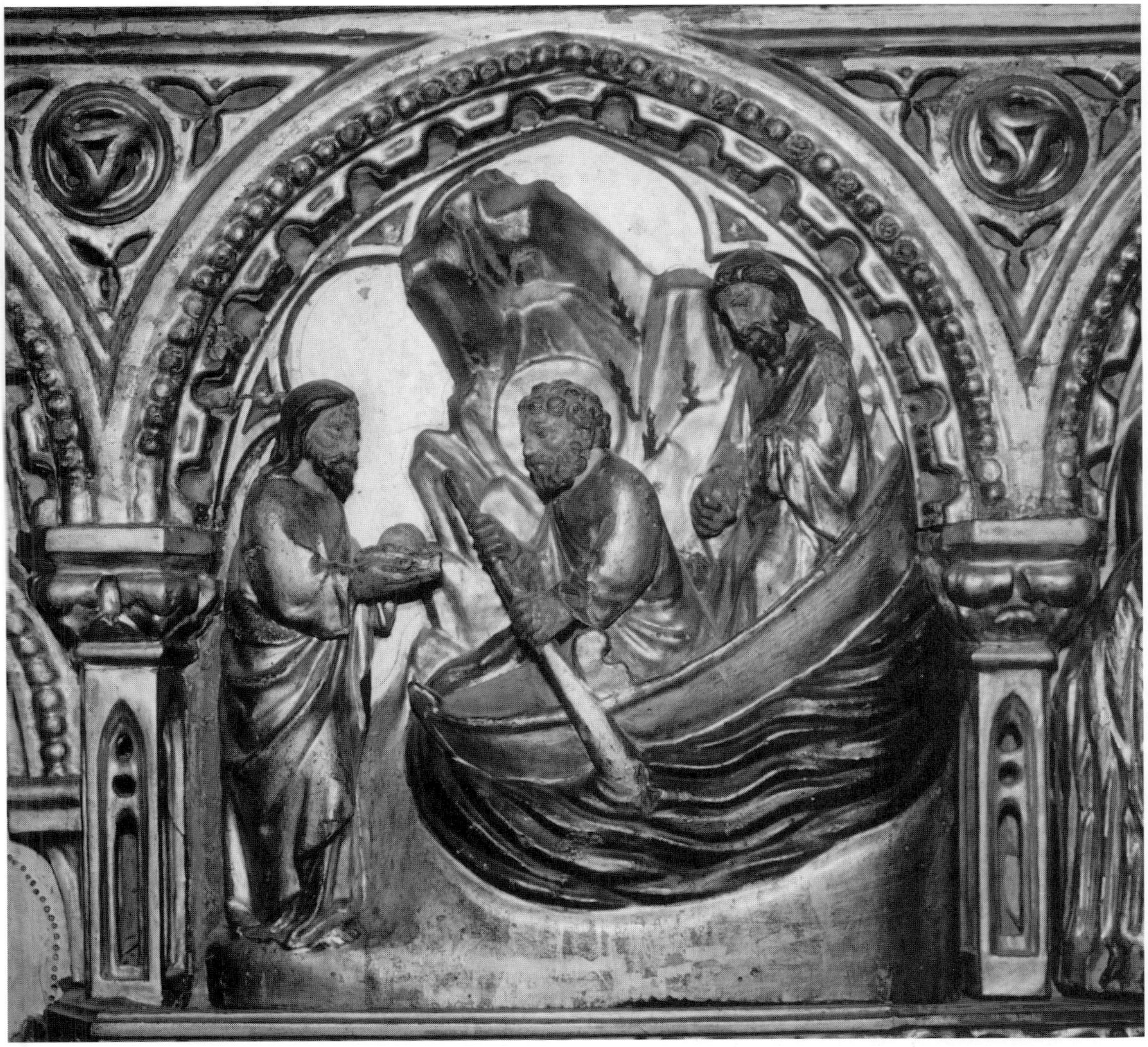

FIG. 120. *Paliotto del Corpus Domini,* early fifteenth-century polychrome sculpture by Paolo and Canterina d'Andrea Bartolomeodi, Museo Correr. *Permission to photograph courtesy the Museum*

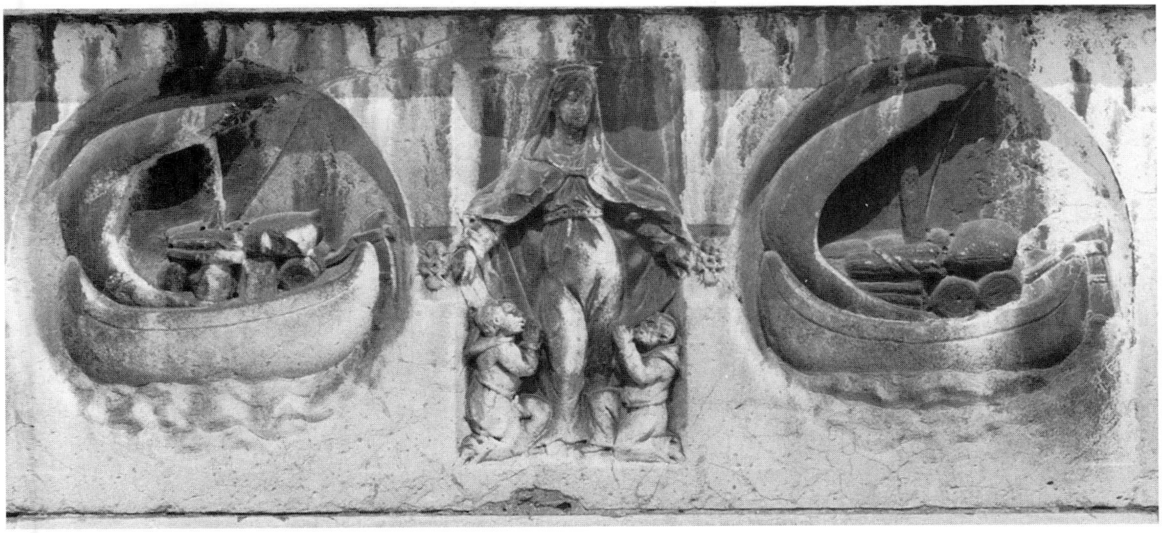

FIG. 121. River barges in a fifteenth-century sculpture, "Madre di Misericordia," by Bartolomeo Buon (?), from an exterior wall of the Scuola Vecchia delle Misericordia

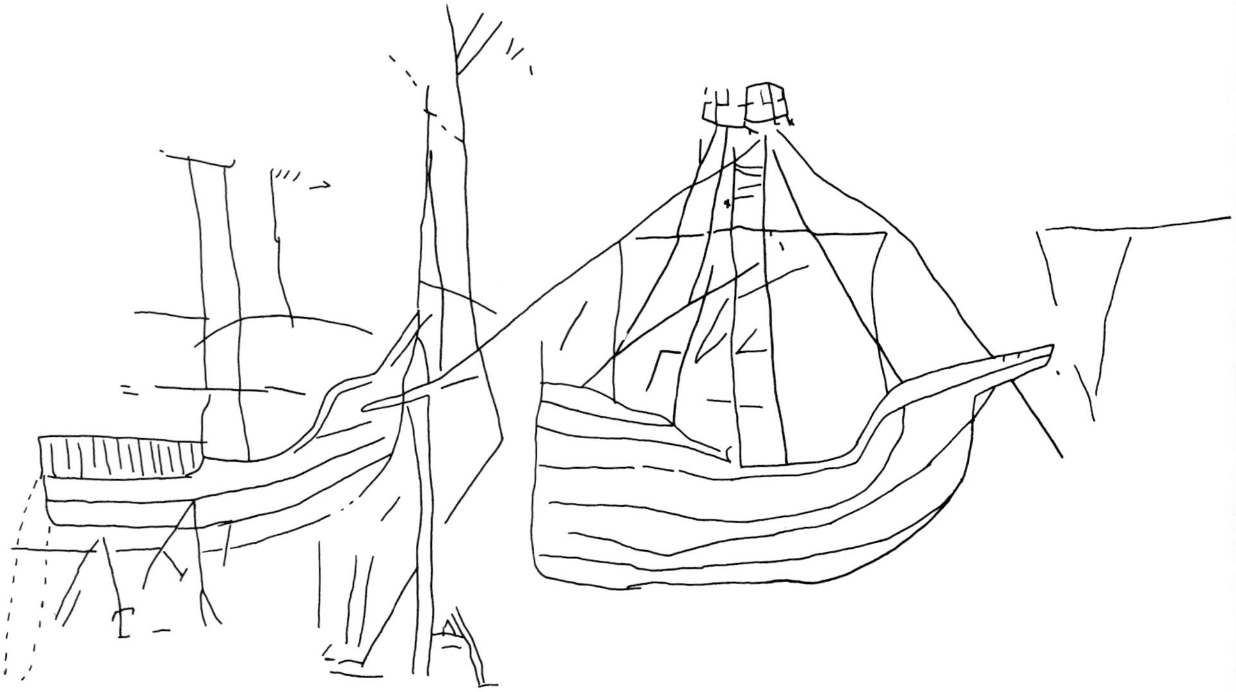

FIG. 122. Graffiti representing two ships, column of San Marco façade

Figure 123: Two-masted, mixed-rigged (?) merchant ship (Type IIIe?).

Figure 124: Single-masted, square-rigged merchant ship (Type IIId).

[Helms, 1975: Fig. 4, right: Single-masted, mixed-rigged merchant ship (Type IIId)].

Three groups of early ship graffiti were found on columns of San Marco's façade (figs. 122–24). In 1892, Levi published two: figure 122, right, and figure 123 (1892: pls. 33, 34). Another six graffiti were located in 1974 and published the following year (Helms, 1975). Helms observed some graffiti that I did not see (Helms, 1975: Figs. 2, no. 2; 4, no. 4; 7, nos. 5 and 7; and 11, no. 8); I located one (fig. 122, left), which he did not find, making a total of nine ship graffiti. Not much is recognizable in Helms's graffiti no. 2 and no. 5, making them of little value; his galley graffito no. 7 and hybrid graffito no. 8 most likely postdate this study, leaving a total of five images to consider here. Helms's graffito no. 4 is so similar to the ships of figure 122, that it has not been illustrated here.

Graffiti scratches are admittedly more difficult to decipher than the formal imagery of professional artists. Yet it is easy to imagine a bored mariner on shore leave, doodling, as he looks out to a harbor full of such ships! Graffiti are important forms of evidence, then, as they potentially visualize an actual ship type, as remembered by a common man, who quite possibly was actually looking at the ship while he drew.

The earliest façade of San Marco was brick, with a minimal amount of marble decoration. At that time, these marble columns were not yet in place. During a major reconstruction campaign between the end of the twelfth century and middle of the thirteenth century, marble columns and relief (much, spoils from the East) were incorporated into the façade. This embellishment continued through the first half of the fifteenth century, when another rejuvenation campaign peaked. Interestingly enough, some of the ship graffiti are inscribed toward the back side of the columns, making it fairly certain that these graffiti were done at some time when the column was not actually in place, conceivably while being transported by ship to Venice. It is also possible that during a phase of reconstruction of San Marco—after a fire or during some

later expansion or enrichment project—the columns were temporarily removed for renovations and the graffiti made at that time. The ship type represented by figures 122–24 and Helms's no. 4, first appears in the fifteenth century, and continues into the sixteenth. As these five are comparable to other fifteenth-century images of this catalog rendered in greater detail (e.g., figure 71, which dates to 1444), these graffiti have been assigned to the mid-fifteenth century.

Figure 122
Theme: Ships at anchor.
Location: Column of San Marco Façade, second portal, fourth column right of door (fig. 1H).
Type: Two single-masted, square-rigged merchant ships (Type IIId).

The two ships depicted in these most interesting graffiti, figure 122, are at anchor. The shapes of the hulls are similar to each other, to Helms's no. 4 (1975: fig. 4, right, and fig. 6) and to those seen in figures 56, 70, 71, and 129. On the ship to the right, a square sail seems to be depicted and also a centrally placed crow's nest; both ships have one vertical mast amidships and lines implying square sails. Both reveal the general hull shape of the *coche*, with a forecastle and sterncastle integrated into the lines of the ship, but no tumble home indicated. The left ship has a series of vertical lines on the sterncastle that probably indicate a parapet.

Figure 123
Theme: Carrack at anchor.
Location: Column of San Marco façade, second portal, third column right of door (fig. 1I).
Type: Two-masted, mixed-rigged (?) merchant ship (Type IIIe?).

This carrack, figure 123, has a square mainsail set on a vertical mast forward of midships. Vertical lines aft of the mainmast stepped at the forward side of the sterncastle likely represent a mizzen.

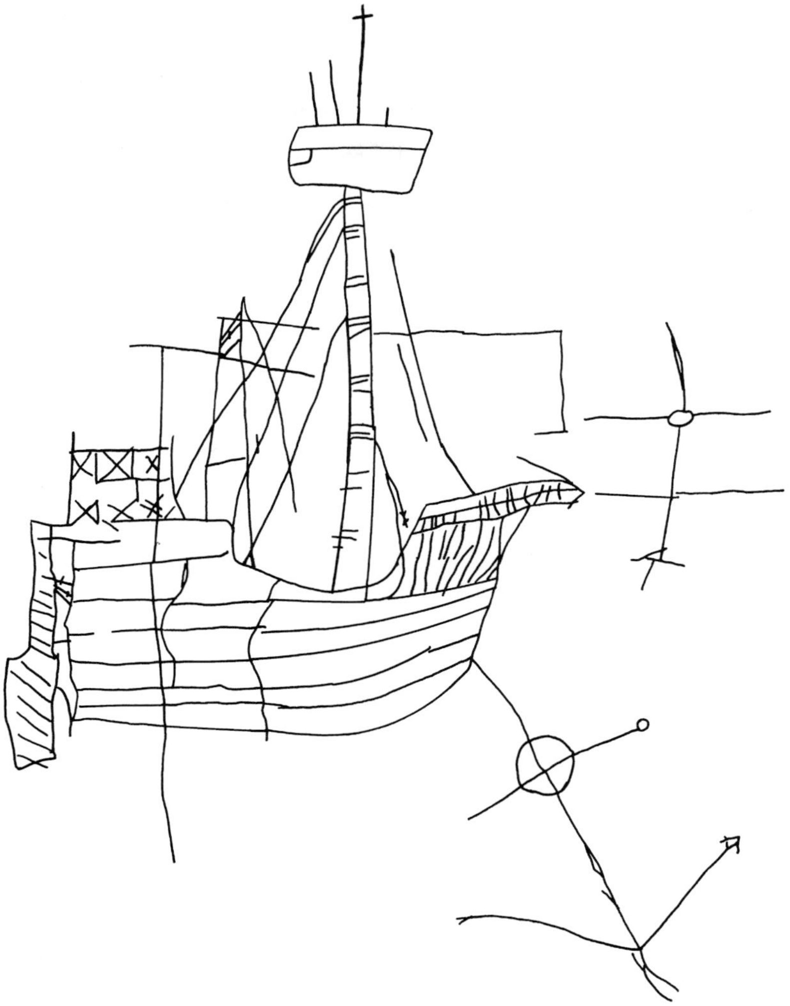

FIG. 123. Graffito depicting a carrack with a single stern rudder at anchor, column of San Marco façade

Sets of two to three horizontal lines spaced fairly evenly up the mainmast may also indicate wooldings. Where they match to rigging lines, they may also indicate the ties. The uppermost ones, just beneath the crow's nest, attach the stays to the mast head; lines run aft to the forward part of both port and starboard sterncastle bulwarks, and two fragmentary lines forward of the mast lead toward the foredeck, where one would expect the forestays to tie off. Another line beginning at the main deck bulwarks, leading to above the middle of the mast, aft, probably is a shroud, as are the two lines attached slightly lower but on the forward side of the mast. A large crow's nest is drawn at the head of the mast.

The basic carrack shape is quite well defined, and surprising detail of its construction are evident, giving clues to the shape of the hull, which compares to figures 70 and 71. The bow and sterncastle structures have X's and vertical lines to represent a lattice-work palisade and semivertical lines to indicate lapstrake siding on the forecastle. Horizontal lines along the hull show the run of strakes. Below and just above the widest area of the tumble home they finish into the stem and corner of the transom stern. The tumble home is emphasized by two curves drawn roughly perpendicularly to the hull planking aft of midships. Such girding timbers are evident in figure 71, and are even more clear in later paintings of carracks, such as in Vittore Carpaccio's paintings and in engravings by Breidenbach (e.g., fig. 127). The orientation of the relatively narrow strakes of the hull side changes dramatically in the area of the forecastle, indicating a change of construction, done by house carpenters, not shipwrights.

A horizontal line at the top of the rudder leads to the raised deck and may represent the tiller of the stern-mounted rudder.

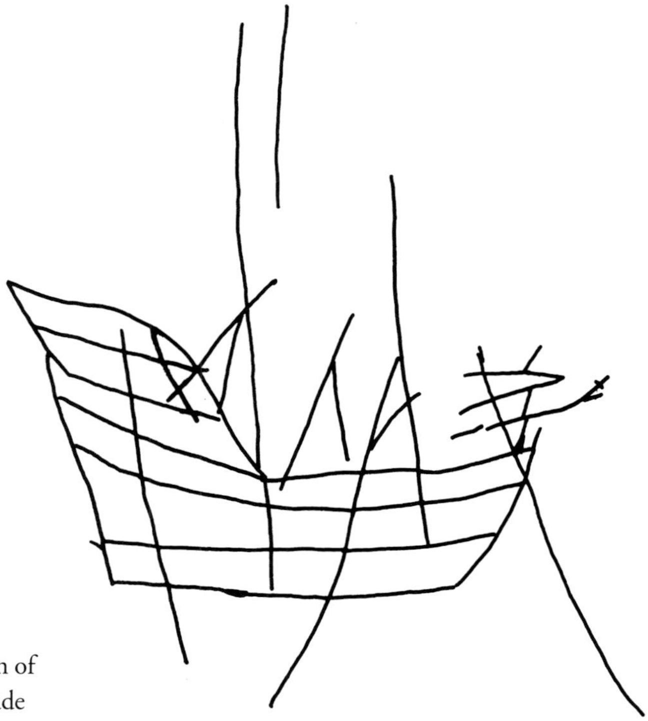

FIG. 124. Ship graffito, column of San Marco façade

Two crescent-shaped anchors are schematically rendered off the bow area.

Figure 124
Theme: Ship at anchor.
Location: Column of San Marco façade, second portal, fourth column left of door (fig. 1J).
Type: Single-masted, square-rigged merchant ship (Type IIId).

This graffito, figure 124, is the most simplified of the lot, with little of the rig defined. Still the hull is roughly carrack shape, but with a more pronounced sterncastle than forecastle. A pair of vertical lines represents one mast amidships. Three lines running forward at various angles may represent anchor or mooring lines.

Figure 125
Theme: Large galley.
Date: Mid-fifteenth century (?).
Location: Prison cell in Ducal Palace.
Type: Oared galley warship (Type IIa).

A bored prisoner whiled away some hours scratching this complex graffito on the walls of his prison cell. The ship in figure 125 represents a galley, with lateen sails on the two larger masts and a square sail on the foremast. Wind power would have been augmented by rowing.

The central mast is set forward of midships, and the mizzen, just forward of the quarterdeck; both are vertical with a small crow's nest centrally placed on their tops. The foremast, set as far forward in the bow as possible, inclines slightly forward. All three sails are shown furled, with the yards secured high on the masts.

Rigging details are incomplete, with only a vang and one shroud or stay apparent on the mizzen, but the mainmast has five shroud or stay lines with their pulleys and a fragmentary line for the vang. Four lines indicating backstays lead from the head of the foremast to the

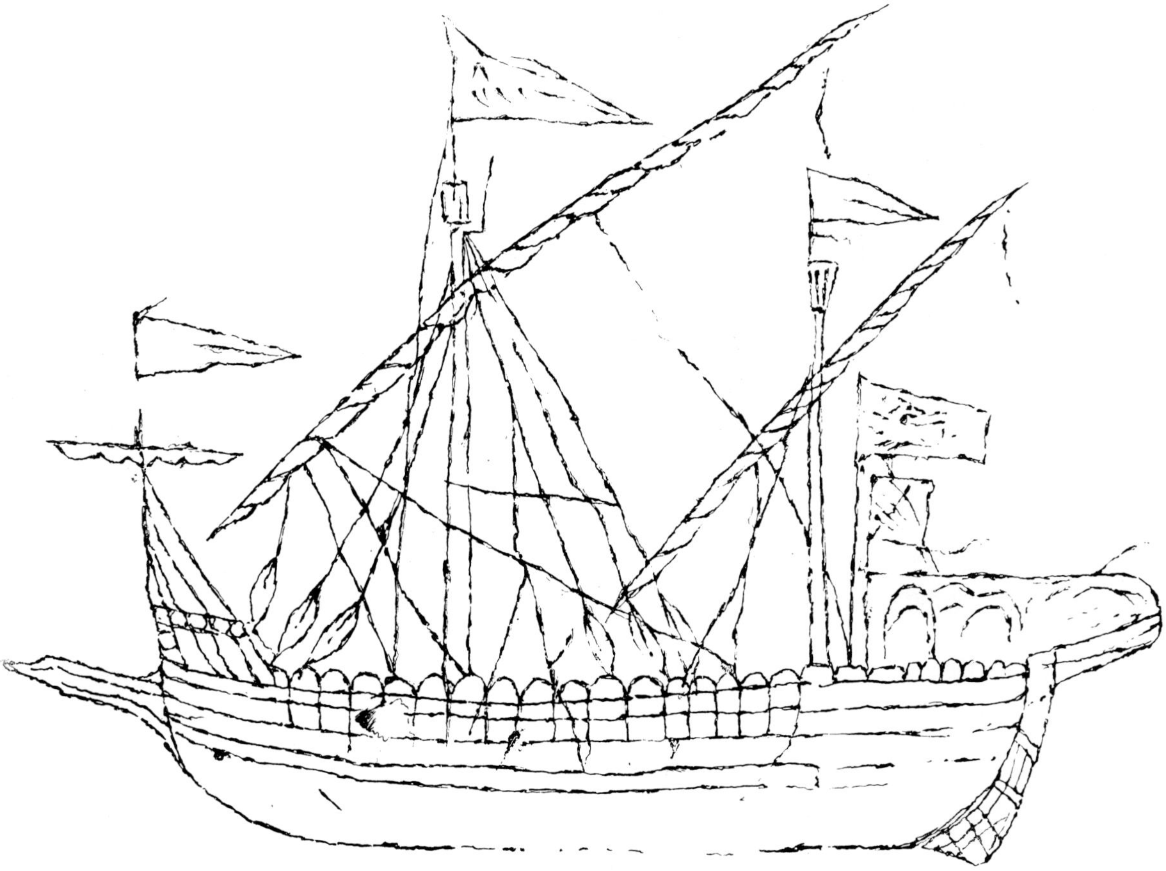

FIG. 125. Graffito of a large galley, from a prison wall in the Ducal Palace. *Levi, 1892: fig. 93*

foredeck. The hull, drawn with a straight keel, has a gradual rise at both bow and stern. The quarterdeck is arcaded at the stern. A single, curved rudder is fitted to the curved sternpost. A prominent beak projects from the bow. Similar in hull shape to figures 58 (1457–58), 68 (1444), and 69 (1444), merchant galleys with no beak at the bow, this graffiti is assigned to the mid-fifteenth century.

Prints from Engravings

Figure 126
Theme: Galley under sail.
Location: Museo Correr (Correr Museum), Venice (Levi, 1892: pl. 22, fig. 1).
Date: fifteenth to sixteenth century (?).
Type: Oared galley warship (Type IIa).

The date of this engraved metal plate is unknown, but the ship in figure 126 is represented as a lateen-rigged vessel with cannons, which were invented at the beginning of the fourteenth century. It seems to date to the fifteenth or sixteenth century. The ship represented has some features of early galleys, rarely illustrated. Because it lacks a firm date or a good parallel, it is excluded from the typology developed in the next chapter.

The galley is powered by approximately fifteen oars per side, supplemented by the lateen sail on the single mast. This mast is set toward the bow. The sail is attached to the yard with robands at the ends of each of the seam lines. On the more visible oars of the starboard outrigger, it can be seen that the oars are arranged all on one level, probably for groups of men to row *a scaloccio,* several men to a bench; an awning protects the rowers.

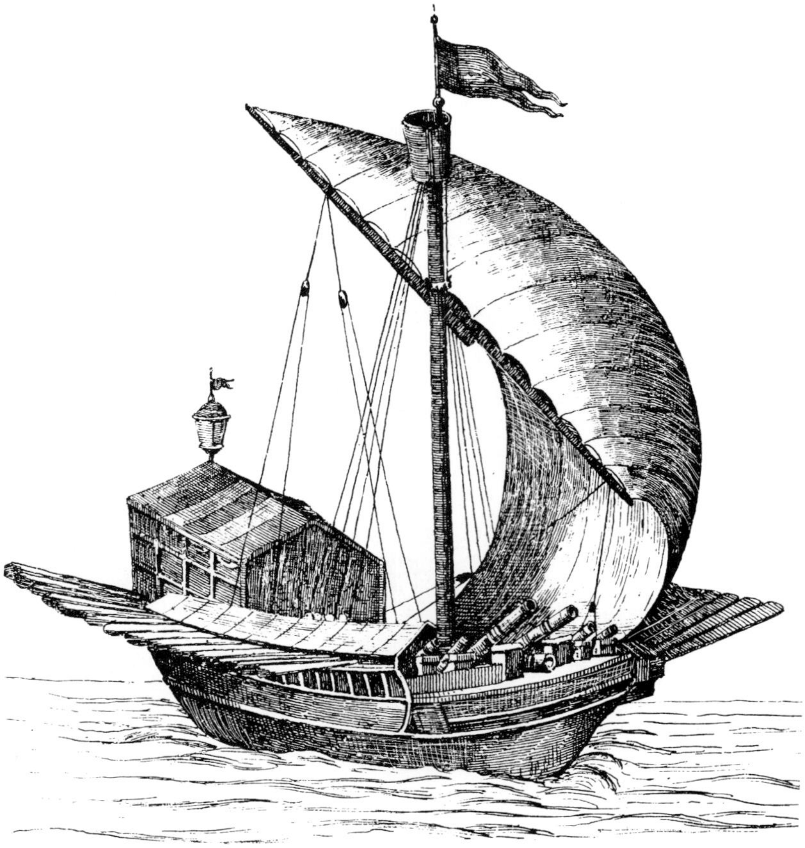

FIG. 126. Galley under sail, from an engraving of the Museo Correr. *Levi, 1892: pl. 22, fig. 1*

Four shrouds are shown to both port and starboard, and pairs of vang and tack with their tackle are clearly defined to both port and starboard. A line on the forward side of the mast depicts the halyard. The large roofed sterncastle has a lantern at the aft end of its roof. The vessel was apparently steered with a single stern rudder, not visible due to the angle shown. A large cannon is on the central gangway, and three smaller ones are mounted on the forward yoke of the rowing frame to either side.

Figure 127

Title: *De Perigrinationibus in Terram Sanctam (Perigrinationes).*

Theme: Bishop of Mainz's pilgrimage to the Holy Land in 1483: Venice city/harborscape.

Artist: Bernardus of Breydenbach and Erhart Reuwich.

Location: Biblioteca Nazionale Marciana, Magonza, xylograph, ff. 12–13, Venice.

Date: 1486.

Types: Figure 127: Three-masted (?), mixed-rigged (?) merchant ship (Type IIIf?), lagoonal vessel (Type Ib).

Figure 128A (front, right): single-masted, square-rigged merchant ship (Type IIId).

Figure 128B (back, left): Two-masted, mixed-rigged round ship (Type IIIe?).

[Other details: Sixty-five Type I small craft, (in cluding fifty-seven double-ended craft, three with masts, and only one transom stern ves sel), five Type II war galleys, and fifty-one Type III merchant ships].

Canon Breydenbach and the Dutch artist Reuwich accompanied the Bishop of Mainz on a pilgrimage in 1483. They documented what they saw along the way, creating a guide for pilgrims. In 1486, Erhard Reuwich made woodcuts of the original illustrations to create *Perigrinationes,* which popularized them. Breydenbach and Reuwich's work was first edited by Magonza as a xylograph, which was reprinted in various languages. The Biblioteca Nazionale Marciana of Venice contains a copy of the xylograph. Two interesting images from the scene of Venice, illustrated in the vibrant colors typical of northern art, are included in the catalog as figures 127 and 128.

Breydenbach and Reuwich visited Venice for twenty-five days in May of 1483. The cityscape view includes the Molo from the Riva degli Schiavoni to the Dogana Bridge taken from the southwest from the Lido. Figure 127 illustrates a large carrack being refitted along the Molo. There is a bowsprit on the forecastle. The masts have apparently been removed for the work in progress, as has the rudder. On the visible starboard side, men work from a floating platform, caulking the hull.

The well-defined hull has the characteristic carrack shape. Many bands of wales girdle the sides of the hull. Also clearly defined are the vertical external framing for the tumble home and

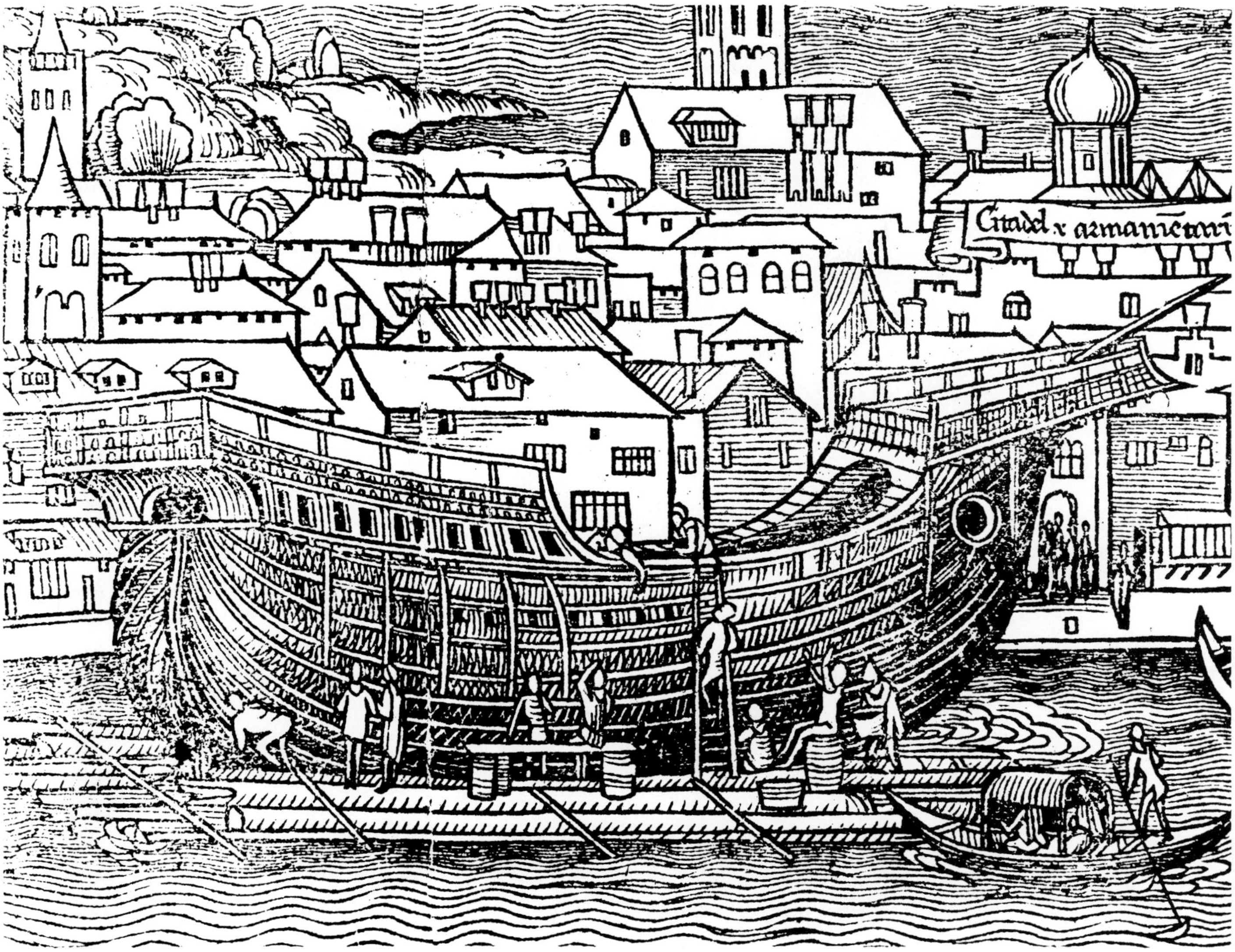

FIG. 127. A large carrack being caulked on the Molo, in a woodcut print of Venice's seascape, from *Perigrinationes* (1486), Biblioteca Nazionale Marciana. *Courtesy the Library*

the transitional timbers supporting the castle structures at the stem and stern. At the stern, lower hull planking fits into the sternpost, while upper planking fits into the bottom of the tragent. Curved struts support the after side of the quarterdeck, and there are window openings along the sides of the sterncastle. The aft side of the forecastle is cross-planked with an arched opening for access. At the bow is a hawse hole, and at the stern, a semicircular opening for the tiller, but no anchor or mooring lines are depicted. Large carracks become extremely common in art after the second half of the fifteenth century.

Approaching the bow of the large ship is a small cargo lighter, similar to those seen in figures 84, 109, and 121.

Figure 128

Types: A (front, right): Single-masted, square-rigged merchant ship (Type IIId).

B (back, left): Two-masted, mixed-rigged round ship (Type IIIe).

Figure 128 from *Perigrinationes* shows a detail of two ships moored side by side on the Molo. Most of the background ship, B, is hidden by the front ship, but a lateen mizzen yard, a verti-

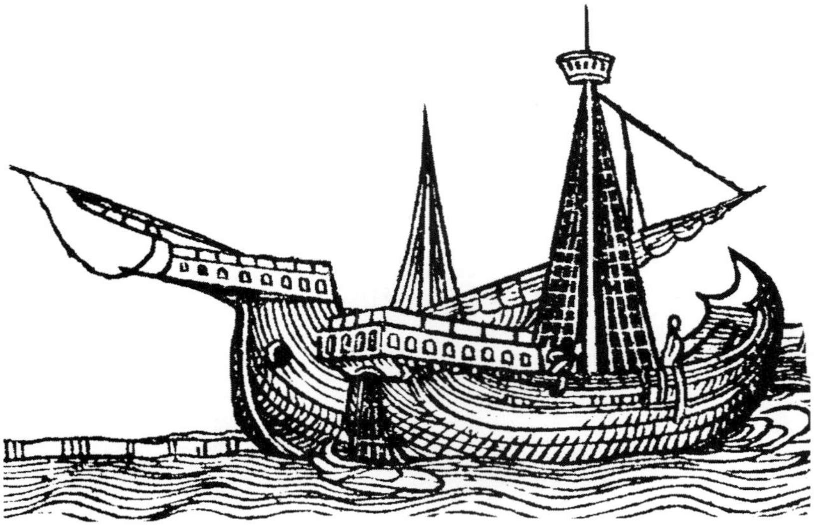

FIG. 128. Merchant ships moored side-to-side, detail of a woodcut print of Venice's seascape, after *Perigrinationes* (1486), Biblioteca Nazionale Marciana. *Courtesy the Library*

cal mainmast and bowsprit are visible. The medium-sized ship is two-masted, with a mixed rig. The bow shape appears to be the same as figures 110 and 127, with a large forecastle integral with the hull. Planking runs into the forecastle, which has arched openings.

Figure 128A, the foreground vessel, a Mediterranean-style *coche* round ship, is more interesting. A vertical mast amidships, with ratlines leading to a centrally placed crow's nest, indicates it would have supported a square sail. Chain plates, metal strips fixed to the side of a sailing ship to which the shrouds attached, are defined on the outside of the hull. Upper-hull planking runs into the sterncastle, which has arched openings. Purposeful vertical lines beneath the tragent probably indicate the stern rudder. Just above the opening for the tiller, struts support the after side of the castle, which has arched openings along the visible side and stern. One interesting detail may clarify other illustrations of the catalog: the termination of the bow and the shape of the stern. Note how the sheer strake sweeps sharply aft into points before terminating in the stem. Earlier images of round ships show a similar bow shape (figs. 28, 93, and 96), which might seem fanciful, yet it is clear Breydenbach, too, was intentionally defining something distinctive about the bow's shape.

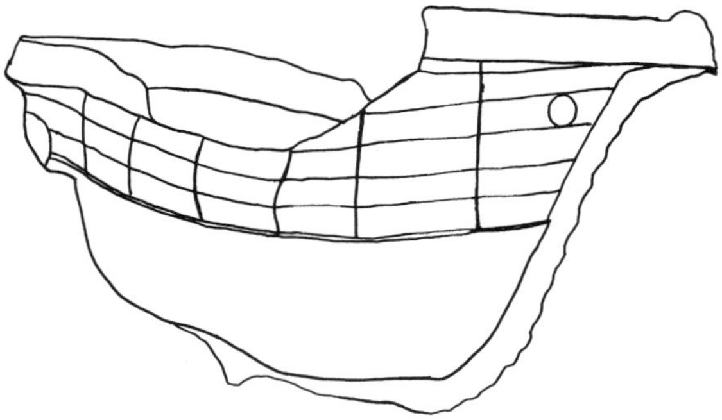

FIG. 129. Gilded silver and rock crystal votive of ship, made in Venice ca. 1440; kept in the Treasury of Toledo Cathedral. *Dawn Hoyt Kidd*

Metalwork

Figure 129
Theme: Votive ship.
Artist: Venetian.
Location: Treasury, Toledo Cathedral.
Date: ca. 1440 (Hahnloser, 1971, pl. 175).
Type: Two-masted, mixed-rigged merchant ship (Type IIIe).

Figure 129, three-dimensional sculpture, an open, votive bowl of gilded silver and rock crystal in the shape of a ship, was made in Venice in the early fifteenth century. A much more elaborate carrack-shaped silver reliquary in the Padova Cathedral Treasury (Nebbia, 1932: fig. 121) probably dates to the end of the fifteenth century.

No masts are present in the open bowl form, but the vessel is large enough in proportions to have had at least two masts. The hull's shape is similar to figures 70, 110, and 123.

Beneath the main wale, the lower part of the hull has been left plain, but above, strakes, including secondary wales, and the waterway are defined, as are the upright exterior braces seen on depictions of ships with tumble home. Like the vessel in figure 110, the ship's bow ends in a point, and has a high triangular foredeck, while the ample stern has a full transom. A decorative parapet runs around the foredeck and the quarterdeck.

Chapter Three

VENETIAN WATERCRAFT

Diversity to Meet Every Need

What then, can be determined about Venetian ships and boats? Analysis of the evidence and significant conclusions begins with a discussion of rigs and ship construction common to the Mediterranean, followed by the archaeological evidence of Venetia. This chapter describes attributes of Venetian craft evident in this catalog's representations, including stern variations, steering devices and their mounts, and anchor types. Finally, a functional typology is developed based on the textual and representational evidence for Venetian watercraft.

"Written records tell us the name of the vessel and provide a description of it; iconography shows the vessel (usually the part above the sea), but does not write its name; archaeology finds the bottom of the hull, but does not provide a name" (Ciciliot, 1996: 242). Ships and boats of the past are best understood by considering and integrating all forms of evidence for them: archaeological, textual, and pictorial.

Rig Types

As is typical of medieval Mediterranean sailed vessels, the majority of ships within this sample had lateen rigs (figs. 130 and 131), although the square rig (fig. 132) used by the Romans was depicted in the sixth century (fig. 8), and again, after its reintroduction to the Mediterranean, as early as the first half of the fourteenth century (fig. 97). Figure 133 graphs the type of rigs that occur in the representations through time, and, by the number of masts, provides an indication of the relative ship size. The largest seagoing ships—three-masted lateeners—first appear in early twelfth-century art. The three-masted, mixed-

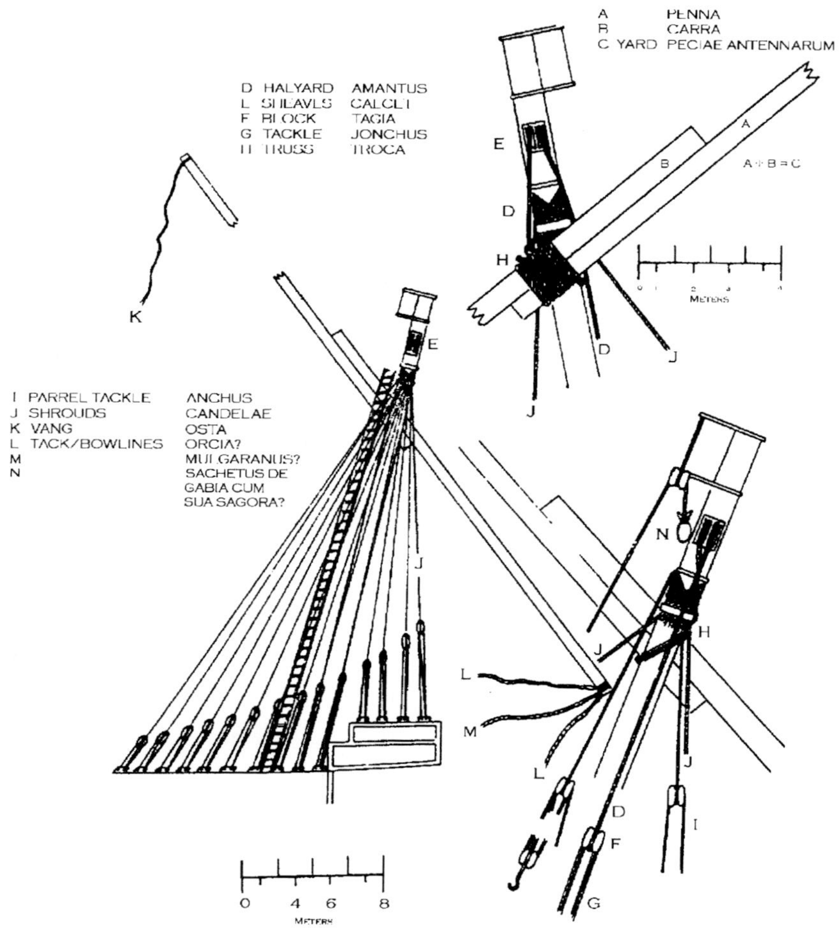

FIG. 130. Standing and running rigging of the lateen rig, and a suggested identification of some Italian medieval terms. *After Pryor, 1984, no. 3: fig. 13*

rigged type occurs by the mid- to later-fourteenth century (e.g., fig. 51), but it is not common until the middle of the fifteenth century.

Lateeners are characterized by huge triangular sails hung on long yards obliquely set on forward-raking masts. On multimasted lateeners, the foremast, set far forward in the bow, was almost always the tallest mast and also the mast with the strongest rake. Yardarms could be slanted and adjusted to the wind direction, and the yard itself provided the leading edge of the sail (Kreutz, 1976: 82). Yards, often longer than the overall length of the ship, were made up of two or more sections scarfed securely together. The upper spar was called the *penna* (plural *pennae*) in medieval Italian documents (fig. 130A), while the lower section was referred to as the *carra* (plural *cares,* fig. 130B); together they were known as *peciae antennarum* (fig. 130C).

The halyard, called the *amantus* (fig. 130D), passed through lateral sheaves in the *cholzexe* (Venetian dialect) or *calcet* (fig. 130E), "a massive piece of timber scarfed to the mast head and which had two lateral pulleys (the *pulezia*) inserted in it beam to beam by means of which the lateen yards were hauled up the sides of the mast" (Pryor, 1984: no. 3, 286). A block (*tagia* or *tabia;* fig. 130F) and tackle (*jonchus;* fig. 130G) facilitated hoisting and tightening by allowing the halyard rigging to pass through the block at least twice, which greatly increased the mechanical advantage. The yard and halyard were secured to the mast by a truss (*troca;* fig. 130H) with the parrel and its tackle, the *anchus* (fig. 130I), making the yard's position relative to the mast adjustable. The parrel reduced friction to prevent wear. After raising the yard, the halyard was rove off aft. It thus doubled as a backstay (*suste*). Forestays were not used on lateeners; they would have interfered during tacking and jibing. Numerous shrouds (*candelae;* fig. 130J), sometimes up to thirteen or fourteen per side on a mast (Pryor, 1984, no. 4: 365), were attached below the *cholzexe* sheaves and were made taut to windward with deadeyes so they could be quickly cast off when changing tack.

On medieval lateeners, the running rigging included a minimum of three lines, but they commonly had up to seven. The head of the sail, called the peak, was trimmed by one or two vangs (*osta;* fig. 130K), which were usually attached to the *penna* a bit in from its uppermost end. Having one vang to windward was essential; some depictions show another vang to leeward (e.g., fig. 94). The side-to-side movement of the heel or tack, the forward corner of the sail, was maneuvered by two lines, tack, which some call bowlines (*orcia;* fig. 130L)—attached to the lower end of the *carra,* running to both windward and leeward sides. Sometimes a third, heavy line rigged with a pulley block was attached to the

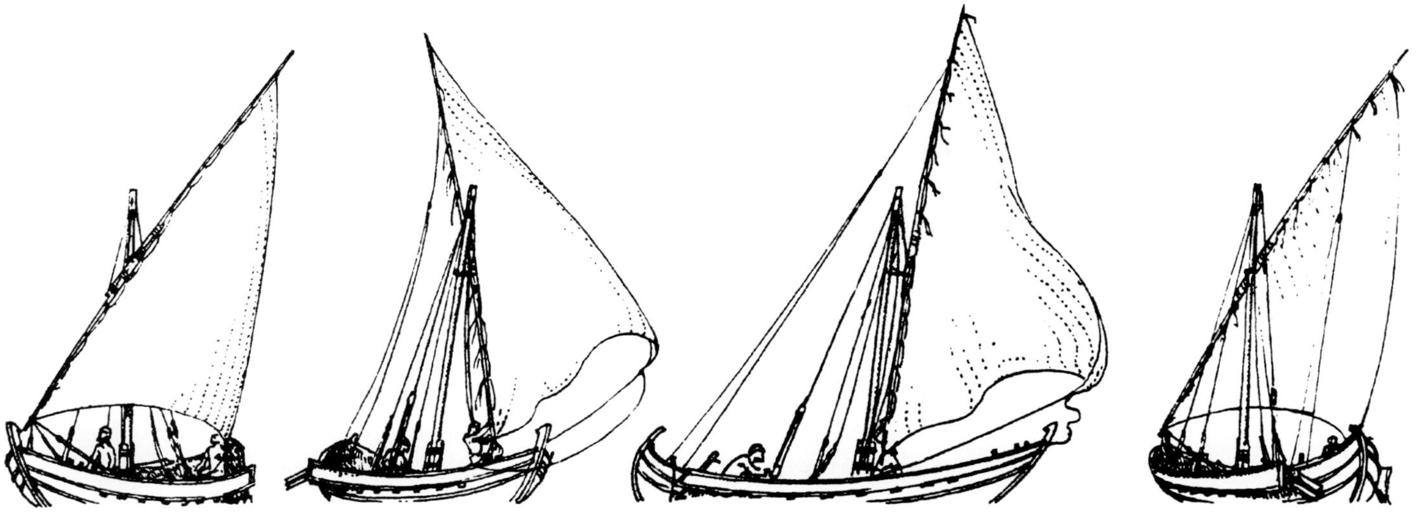

lower end of the *carra* (fig. 130M) to control the up-and-down movement of the yard, either while sailing to peak the yard to maximum efficiency or during tacking; this was perhaps what was called the *mulgaranus* or *marganàli.* Another line, called *de gabia cum sua sagora* (translated as "sock with a whip used to supply the top"), believed to have functioned as a lift to control the up-and-down movement of the yard, is perhaps what is seen in figure 105. The other low corner of the sail, the clew, was controlled by one or two sheet lines (probably the *pozia* or *pozal*). Larger ships needed two, one to port and one to starboard. Having two sheet lines made changing tack easier. Because the opposite tack's sheet was already set up, it was not necessary to lead the sheet around to the opposite side.

There is still uncertainty as to the exact function of some of the ancient terms; in particular, *pozia* and *orcia* are debated (Bellabarba, 1995: 139; Hocker, 1987: 367; Pryor, 1984: 214 and fig. 13; Pryor, 1990: 267–76; and Bonino, 1978b: fig. 1).

Several attributes of a medieval lateener minimized the awkwardness of its tacking maneuver. The masts all raked slightly forward, crow's nests were attached aft at the head of the mast, and shrouds were set up on lanyards and deadeyes. A forward slant to the mast and any projections at its top, as well as positioning the crow's nest aft, facilitated passing the yard and sail in front of the mast for a tack. Tacking a lateener was quite cumbersome and required a large crew. Landström has described and illustrated (fig. 131) the maneuver excellently:

> The lateen sail was hoisted outside the shrouds, and the leeward shrouds were slackened so that the yard could be trussed to the mast. If it was desired to tack when going to windward, it was necessary to fall off the wind (fig. 131A). The [vang][1] and sheet were made loose (fig. 131B), the parrel was slackened somewhat so that the yard was freed slightly from the mast, and then one of the crew hauled on the yard until it was vertical. The sheet was then transferred to the other side (when there was only one sheet) and the sail was allowed to blow forward (fig. 131C) while the shrouds now to windward were made taut and those to leeward were slackened. When the vessel began to turn into the wind the sail was sheeted home on the leeward side, the yard retrussed to the mast and trimmed with the tacks and braces for the new tack (fig. 131D). On ships as large as the crusader vessels it must be assumed that the yard was forced over with the aid of tack tackles (Landström, 1961: 83).

FIG. 131. A lateener tacking to windward: (A) falling off the wind; (B) freeing the yard, hauling it to vertical; (C) bringing the sail and sheet to the other side; (D) turning into the wind and trimming for the new tack. *After Landström, 1961: figs. 215–18*

The main advantage of the lateener was that it could sail a bit closer to the wind. Another advantage was that in a sudden storm, simply by loosening the main sheet, the sail could be deactivated quickly (Kreutz, 1976: 98). The major disadvantage of the medieval lateen sail was that it could not really be brailed; if the wind strength changed drastically, the yards had to be lowered and sails changed completely (Pryor, 1984, no. 4: 363).

A square-rigged ship was far easier to tack but likewise required yards and lines to raise and lower the sails and to control them. The basic rigging is shown in figure 132: the yard (fig. 132A, *antenna*); the halyard (fig. 132B); lifts (fig. 132C, *mantici*); shrouds (of various names, including *senali,* fig. 132D; *quinali,* fig. 132E; *quadernali,* fig. 132F; and probably *frasconi,* fig. 132G, as well). Besides being used as shrouds, *quadernali* were also used as loading tackle, to maneuver the sail, and probably even as buntlines (Bellabarba, 1998: 225). Forestays (fig. 132H, *stazi*) and backstays secured the mast fore and aft. The downhaul (fig. 132I) pulled the yard and sail down. Buntlines (fig. 132 J, quadernali? and fig. 132 K, *briol*) were used to brail it, and some ships also had a bonnet system to increase and decrease the sail size. Running rigging lines included the brace, tack and sheet, and bowlines. The brace (fig. 132L, *braze* or *braze d'antenna*) attached to the yard. Along the lower side of the sail, tack and sheet lines controlled the leading edge (fig. 132M, *scota?* and fig. 132N *contrascota?*). The other corner was controlled by one or two sheets (fig. 132O)—and sometimes a center sheet in between—and bowlines (fig. 132P, *borine?*).

The square rig required a dramatically smaller crew than lateen-rigged ships. Square-rigged ships could not sail as close to the wind, however, so even after the square sail became common again on large round ships, the lateen rig continued to be used on galleys (e.g., fig. 69) and small craft (e.g., fig. 121), and many ships were fitted with lateen sails on some of their auxiliary masts (e.g., fig. 51). The square sail was common on Roman-period ships, had lifts, could be brailed, and is likely the rig on the vessels of the Ravenna harbor mosaics dating to circa 650 (fig. 8), but it is not seen again for centuries (fig. 133). The earliest Venetian example (fig. 97)

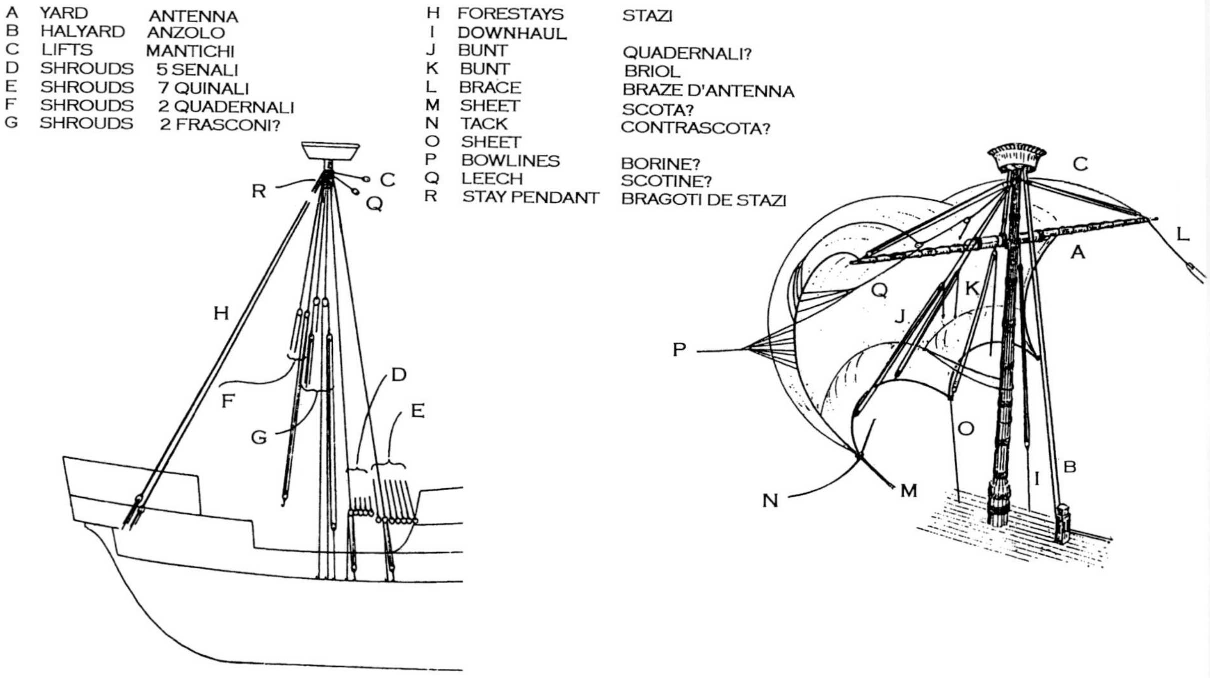

FIG. 132. Standing and running rigging of the square rig, and a suggested identification of some Italian medieval terms, based on the square-rigged ship in the *Fabrica di galere* manuscript. *After Bellabarba, 1998, figs. 14 and 15*

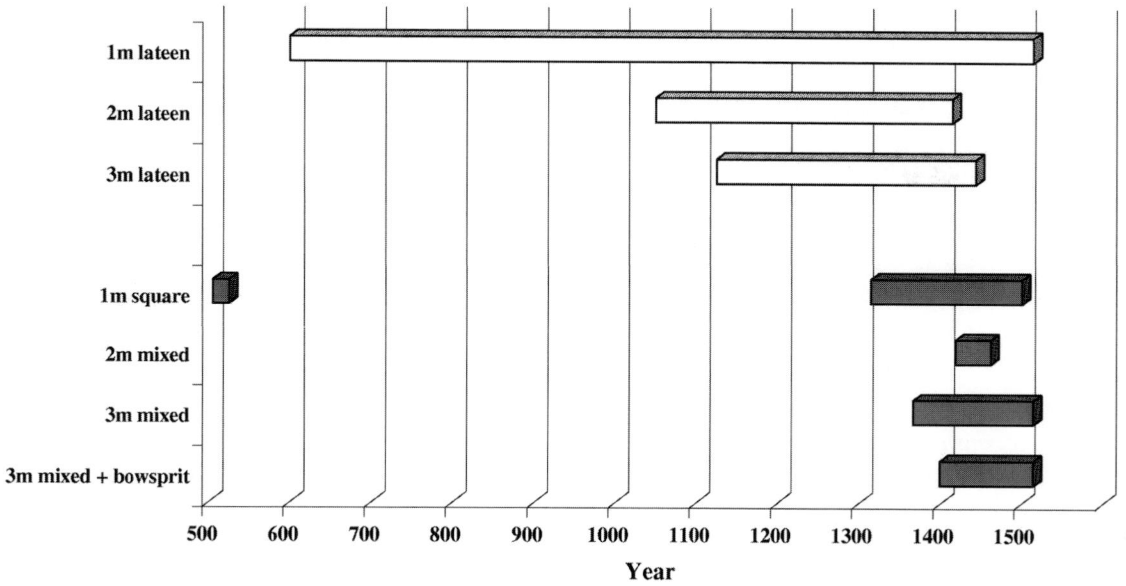

FIG. 133. Trends in rig types, as indicated by representational data. Early in the fourteenth century, the square sail appears again after eight centuries; by the middle of the next century, the lateen rig is no longer used as the main sail on large ships, and a mixed-rig becomes the norm.

shows the mast vertically set, with the crow's nest centered at its head. Later illustrations show that the lift had carried over from antiquity (fig. 67). Whether square, lateen, or mixed rigged, all ships waited for the right winds and steered with sail settings as much as by their steering apparatus (Pryor, 1984, no. 4: 377).

Ship Construction

Two basic methods of boat and shipbuilding are referred to as shell-first and frame-first (or skeletal) construction.[2] In building with the shell-first system, flush-laid, edge-joined planking forms the basic hull shape, and any reinforcing framing is inserted only after the hull is shaped. This is a very ancient and long-standing technique, with examples dating at least as far back as 2850 B.C., continuing in use throughout the medieval period on small craft.

As the name frame-first or skeletal construction implies, first an inner framework is set up to define the basic hull shape, to which the hull planking and inner planking are subsequently attached. This technique, possibly Greco-Byzantine in origin, was used throughout the Mediterranean. It is interesting to note that by the twelfth century, Venetian shipwrights were already considered superior shipbuilders, as witnessed by the fact that in 1187, the Byzantine emperor Isaac Angelus had Venice build ships for the Byzantine empire, and, previous to that, Byzantium had relied on the Venetian navy for maritime defense (Norwich, 1977: 121).

Initially, before they had formal plans, Venetian shipbuilders utilizing skeletal construction probably worked from a series of templates to determine the shape of the stem, sternpost, and the midships frame as is still done today in traditional shipyards. The ship's profile was defined by laying the posts and keel pieces; figure 134 illustrates a type of scarf with an ancient history still used to join keel sections in the fifteenth century. Next, control frames, the main points of reference amidships and near the ends, were set. Then flexible battens defining the wale lines were placed. Creating such a framework determined the shapes required for all the remaining frames, to which strakes were laid flush and nailed.

This proportional construction technique is the basis of that defined in Venetian treatises on ship construction from the fifteenth through seventeenth centuries. Once Venetians developed geometric methods to obtain the fair curves

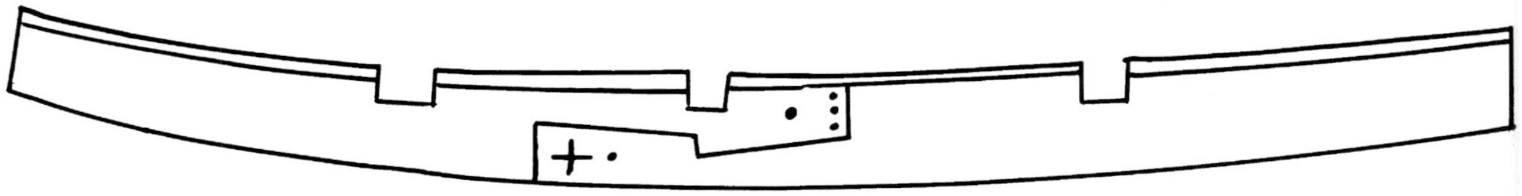

FIG. 134. Join between two sections of the keel, after folio 43 in the fifteenth-century book by Zorzi of Modon

required in shipbuilding, a reproducible hull was effected, and this meant that a naval fleet could be mass produced and maintained. Shipbuilding treatises lay out the theoretical, geometrical way to determine the shape of the frames, but, in practice, the shipwrights may still have done so through experienced approximation.

Skeletal Construction in Representations and Technical Treatises

The Venetian artistic representations that depict construction scenes (figs. 98 and 115) and two comparable French manuscript illuminations (figs. 44 and 45) all date to the first half of the fourteenth century and illustrate the skeletal system of construction in common use by that time in the Mediterranean. The most informative is figure 98, showing the early stages of construction. The primary and secondary wales have replaced the two flexible battens, and they run from stem to stern. Regularly spaced frames have been set within, and the first strakes applied. Technical treatises on ship construction and archaeological discoveries supplement the evidence from these few representations and confirm that the transition to this new approach to shipbuilding in fact occurred during the early medieval period, and in Italy probably as early as the tenth or eleventh century, though some small boats continued to be built shell first.

The earliest known Venetian technical treatises concerning ship construction appear in the last quarter of the fourteenth century, but the frame-first technique described reflects a simpler proportional technique that dates from a much earlier period and was passed down orally. Existence of a written form, defining a geometrical, reproducible way to build a ship, was key for the growth of Venice as a naval power. Because warships needed to be produced by the state rapidly and in great numbers, and consistency of their proportions therefore became more important, far more written documentation exists for galleys than for merchant ships.

Technical treatises include drawn plans of ship types and details for their construction. Sketches from *Zibaldone da Canale, Arte de far vasselli,* and the book by Zorzi of Modon contain profiles and dimensions, as well as illustrations of completed ships under way (figs. 62–65, 67–71).

Interpreting information given in technical treatises is challenging, because essential details were at times left out. Details of interest to us may have been left out for secrecy or were simply forgotten. They may have been taken for granted as being obvious to a shipwright. These treatises, really the first signs of a formal naval architecture, have been the object of many worthy studies to which the interested reader may refer.[3] Paramount are Alvise Chiggiato's papers on naval architecture. The first, a description of a Venetian galley, was published with the transcription of the entire *Ragioni antique* manuscript (Dosio, 1987: 57–79, tables B and C). Chiggiato considers his later work for a *galea rubea* (thirteenth-century records from Brindisi) the most accurate rendition, but his *galea tarida* (Naples) and the fifteenth-century merchant galley in *Fabrica di galere* are also interesting (Chiggiato, 1991).

Chiggiato's study and reconstruction of the flat-bottomed galleys described in the manuscript

Ragioni antique spettanti all'arte del mare et fabriche de vasselli (1470–1529) incorporates evidence from contemporaneous manuscripts and offers the key to understanding the language of Venetian shipwrights by visualizing their line of reasoning. In *Ragioni antique,* the galley's hull is succinctly defined by the *scheda,*[4] a brief list giving only seven statements and no more than eleven distances between specific points in the hull. The hull was conceptualized in three parts: the central body of the hull, where the bottom of the hull was almost completely flat, the bow, and the stern. The shipwright began with the *scheda*, and utilizing a *mezo redondo*[5] (Chiggiato, 1987: fig. 1), a special protractor tool used to obtain curves and distances based on projections of the Y-axis (the sinusoid), he set up a framework of geometrical functions that could produce any desired variations in size or shape. Aided in the shipyard by two pre-marked curved molds, called *sesti,* and two or three *stazze,* or pre-marked sticks, the *redondo* made it possible to reproduce a ship in the shipyards with the exactness of a modern shipwright's drawn plans. Such measuring tools are still used in Mediterranean shipyards today.

Almost all of the initial measurements derived from the *mezo redondo* are proportional figures based on the width of the *boca,* the midships beam. Proportional, mathematical controls were used throughout the ship. The shipwright used the *mezo redondo* to derive the ship's lines, the curvature of its main frames and that of the deck, and to determine the length of masts and yards. It was even used in the cutting of sails and rigging.

Chiggiato found that only two curves necessary to define the hull were not derived geometrically: vertical profiles and the *cantinaria.* The height of the frames was obtained by the *cantinaria*, a natural curve formed by a flexible chain hanging under its own weight: an oiled halyard was hung taut between the posts and giving it slack until it touched the tops of all the frames and the desired sheer was obtained. A series of parabolas (probably obtained by molds in the shipyards) was necessary to obtain vertical profiles (Chiggiato, personal communication). Chiggiato discovered that only a few corrective measures were necessary to obviate undesirable shapes in the hull (e.g., flats in the sides of the hull that could result by using the sinusoid alone to obtain the hull's tapering; Chiggiato, 1987: fig. 3). Chiggiato does not account for the way the length of the ship was calculated. The later Venetian manuscript, *La architectura navale,* by Stefano di Zuanne (1686), offers one answer to this essential determining factor. In this case, the length of the galley was determined from the number of benches and the *interscalum,* the distance between oars. From this, according to *La visione di Baldassarre Drachio* (1593), the two posts were set, and the midships beam was fixed at the midpoint in the overall length.[6]

Archaeological Remains Exemplify Both Shell-first and Skeletal Construction

Considering the variety of ship and boat types used by Venetians, relatively few remains have been discovered and excavated as yet: fewer than ten are known from Venetia and the Emilia-Romagna region. Boats found at Cervia, Pomposa, and Pontelagoscuro, ranging in date from the fourth through the eleventh centuries, exhibit the shell-first method of boat construction. The larger boats and ships (Contarina I and II, Porto Fuori, Logonovo, and the Lazise galley) are all frame-first construction; those found so far date from the beginning of the fourteenth century to the mid-sixteenth century.

The fourth to sixth-century hull remains found at Cervia (just south of Ravenna on the Adriatic coast) are now kept at the Museo Nazionale of Ravenna. They are apparently from a boat suited for either lagoonal or river navigation (fig. 135). The hull, approximately 12.5 meters

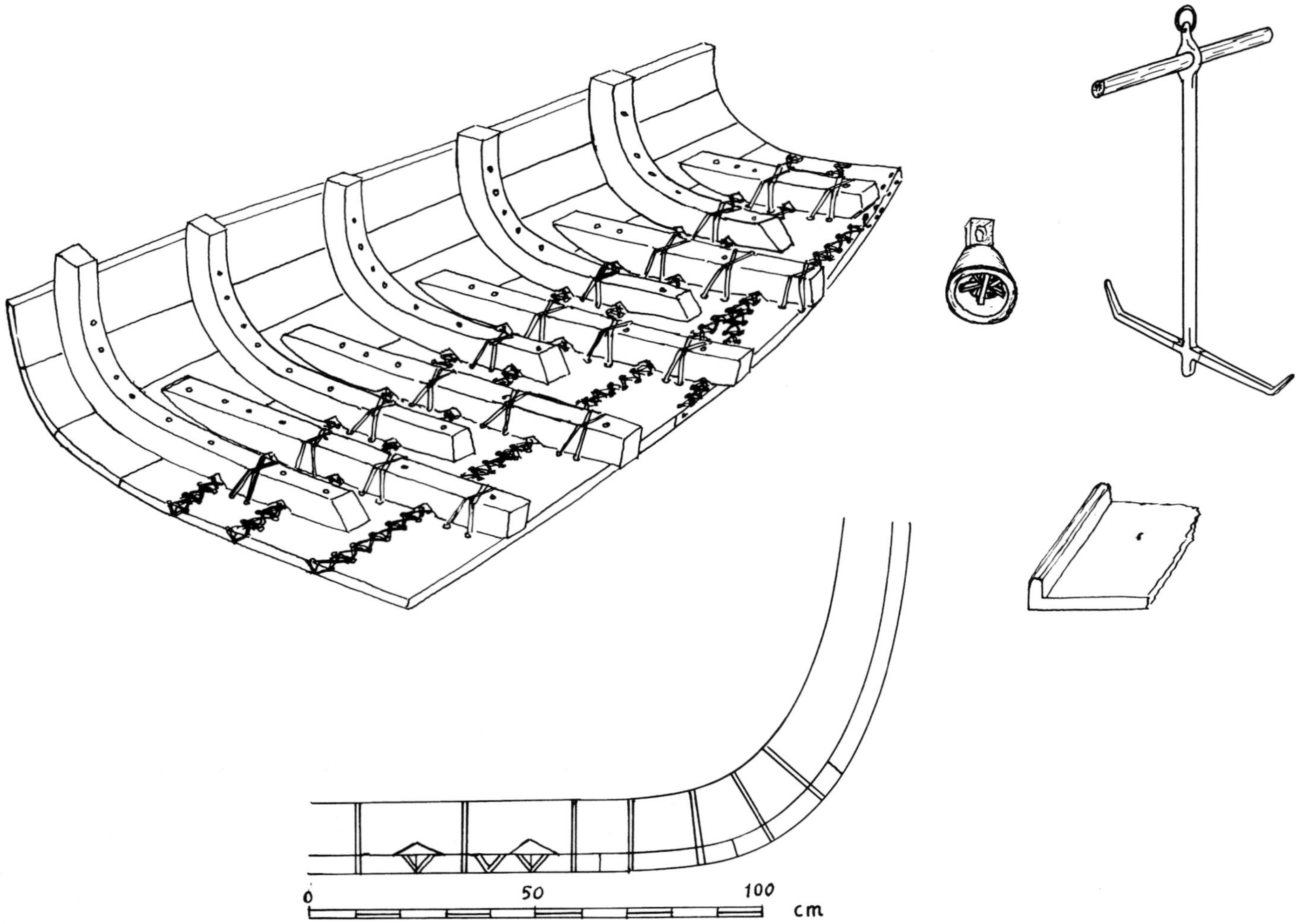

FIG. 135. Remains of the sewn boat and anchor from the fourth–sixth century found at Cervia. *Courtesy M. Bonino, 1991: fig. 3*

long with a beam of 3.5 meters, is built entirely of flush-laid oak planking. Bottom planking is sewn together through holes prepared by a drill or an auger (Bonino, 1978a: 40–41).

A boat of identical construction but much later in date (eleventh century) was found slightly inland at Pomposa (Borgo Caprile or Codigoro), north of Ravenna, on a tributary of the Po (fig. 136). It has yet to be excavated properly. As in the Cervia boat, oak strakes are edge joined and sewn. After the hull was shaped, the framing timbers were set inside approximately 40 centimeters apart. This flat-bottomed vessel has a gradually rising stem, and Bonino hypothesizes it may be of the *burchio* type, with an original size of 12–15 meters long and a beam of 3.5 meters (1978a: 53–54).

Part of the side and bottom of an eleventh-century (?) capsized boat was discovered at Pontelagoscuro on the Po River north of Ferrara. It is now kept at Museo Nazionale of Ferrara (fig. 137). A 7 x 0.9 meter section of oak planking was found, edge joined with deep mortise-and-tenon fastenings. The boat appears to have been about 15 meters long with a beam of 5 meters. The flat-bottomed vessel has a hard chine, and is believed to be a *sandòn,* or floating watermill. This type of watermill boat developed in the early Middle Ages for use on the Po and Adige Rivers (Bonino, 1978a: 54, 55, 212 and fig. 11; 1978b: 27).

Two round ships were found and excavated in 1898 at Contarina (Rovigo), south of Venice near what was in earlier times the mouth of the principal course of the Po River. The younger ship, referred to as Contarina II, dates to the mid-sixteenth century, and although not much of the hull bottom was preserved, a good section of the bulwark provides valuable evidence of that structure (see Bonino's reconstruction, 1978b: fig. 9). The medieval ship from Contarina, referred to as Contarina I (ca. 1300; fig. 138) is the best-documented discovery from the region and has proved to be an invaluable source of information for further details of the frame-first construction system not visible or measurable in representations. The hull bottom, including most of the port side, and the starboard side through the turn of the bilge, survived.

The wood was in excellent condition at the time of its discovery. Most of the iron fasteners had completely degraded, however, so the ship had to be excavated from within, allowing the external part of the hull to be supported by the surrounding sand. All timbers were carefully measured, photographs were taken of the ship *in situ* (figs. 139–41), and accurate plans were made and published (fig. 142; Relazione, 1901: 22–35, table 3 and Bonino, 1978b: fig. 4). The original hull, however, was destroyed. The Museo Storico Navale (Museum of Naval History) in Venice retains the original excavation report, photographs, and a 1:10 scale model of the ship. The model was built by Mr. Francesco Piccoli, a carpenter of the Venetian Arsenal, and is accurate to detail, except that the frames are proportionally shorter than they should be (Bonino, 1978b: 15).

Contarina I was an average-sized, two-masted, lateen-rigged round ship of approximately 75 metric tons, 20.98 meters in length, 5.2 meters in beam, and 2.46 meters high at midships (fig. 138; Bonino, 1978a: 62; 1978b: 13–15. Further details of her measurements are given in appendix 3). The discovery of both mast steps verifies the mast positions commonly seen in medieval representations of two-masted, lateen-rigged round ships: the mizzen was set slightly aft of midships, while the foremast was set extremely far forward with a stronger rake. Contarina I's rather squat, full shape made the ship well suited for large cargoes (fig. 142), while the dimensions of the mast steps indicate that she had tall, sturdy masts. These characteristics lead one to believe that this was an ideal vessel for coastal trade, although Pryor suggests that the characteristic shape, with inward-curving stern and stem, relatively flat bottom, and lateen sails, must have been awkward to handle (Pryor, 1992: 33). The hull is similar in shape to many illustrated round ships, such as those in the Zibaldone manuscript (e.g., figs. 62 and 63), the *Pala Feriale* (figs. 93 and 94), and in Veneziano's painted polyptychs (figs. 98–101).

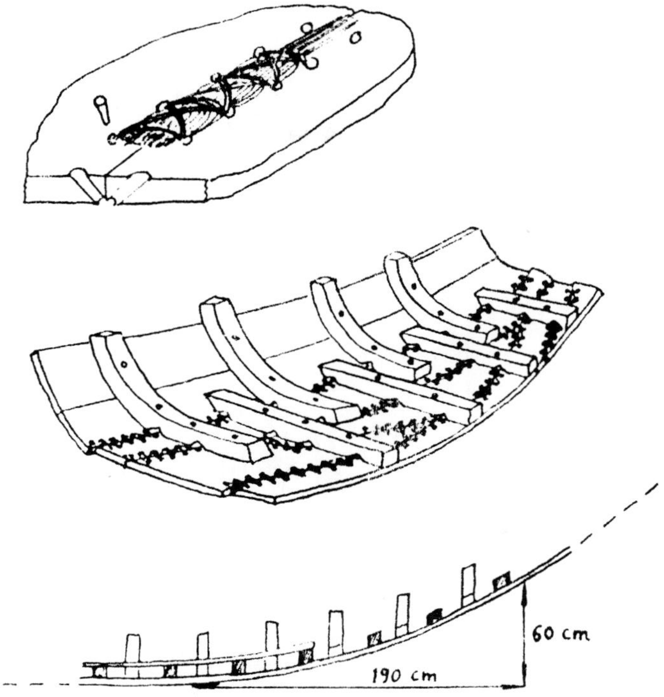

FIG. 136. Remains of the eleventh-century boat discovered at Pomposa. Top: detail of sewn hull planking. *Courtesy M. Bonino, 1991: figs. 6–7*

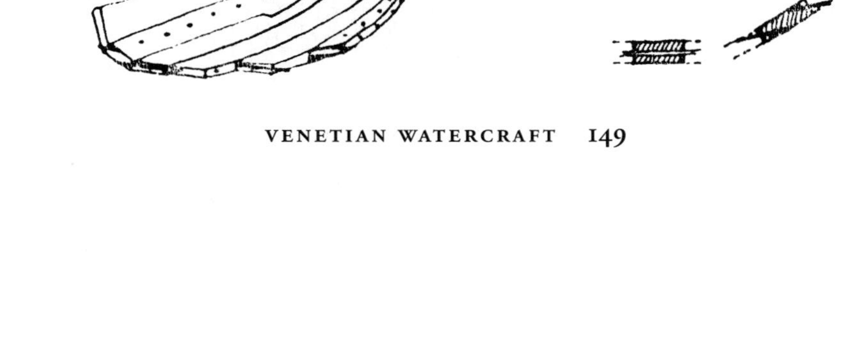

FIG. 137. Structural parts of the eleventh-century watermill boat found at Pontelagoscuro. *Courtesy M. Bonino, 1978a: fig. 11A*

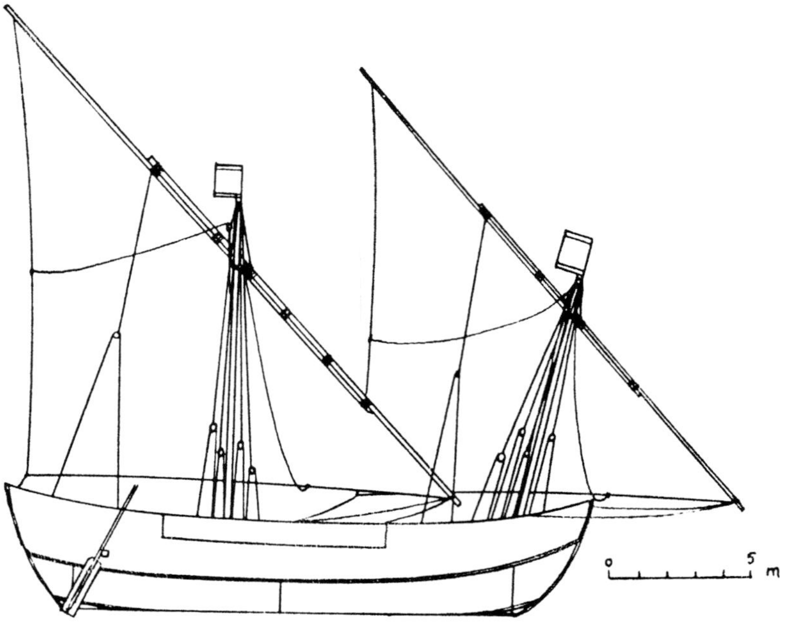

FIG. 138. Reconstruction of the Contarina I ship, ca. 1300. *Courtesy M. Bonino, 1978a: fig. 14A*

Except for the larch inner wales, all timbers of Contarina I were oak. Remains revealed that the shipwrights exclusively utilized the natural curvature of timbers for posts and framing (Relazione, 1901: 25). Iron nails were used throughout; there was absolutely no evidence found for mortise-and-tenon joints. The basic frame-first construction technique was followed: first, setting up the keel, posts, and midships frame as main reference points. Next, temporary battens were attached to define the shapes of the remainder of the frames. After these battens were removed, exterior hull planking was applied to the frames. Clamps and foot wales were set inside the hull to reinforce frame overlaps, and wales, bilge keels, clamps, and foot wales were added (Steffy, 1994: 93).

The keel consisted of two sections scarfed together, 15 centimeters wide with an overall length of 16.5 meters. Its height or thickness at midships was 7 centimeters, but this increased to 10 centimeters where it was attached to the posts. Only the lowest sections of the stem and sternpost were discovered, but these abutted the ends of the keel and were fixed with two iron bolts. There was evidence for a simple scarf join at the posts' upper ends. Where the posts extended from the keel, their profiles were straight for a bit over a meter, after which they became inward curving. The posts were trapezoidal in section, with

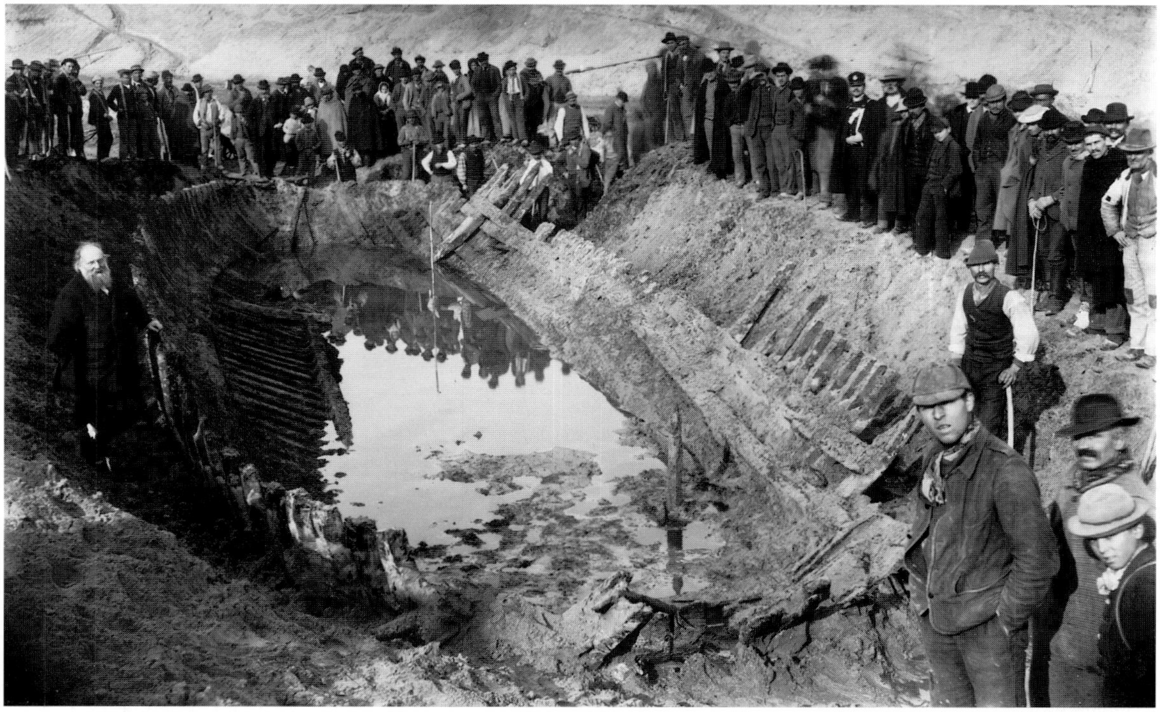

FIG. 139. Contarina I (ca. 1300), seen from the bow. Photographed *in situ* during the excavation in 1898. *Courtesy Museo Storico Navale*

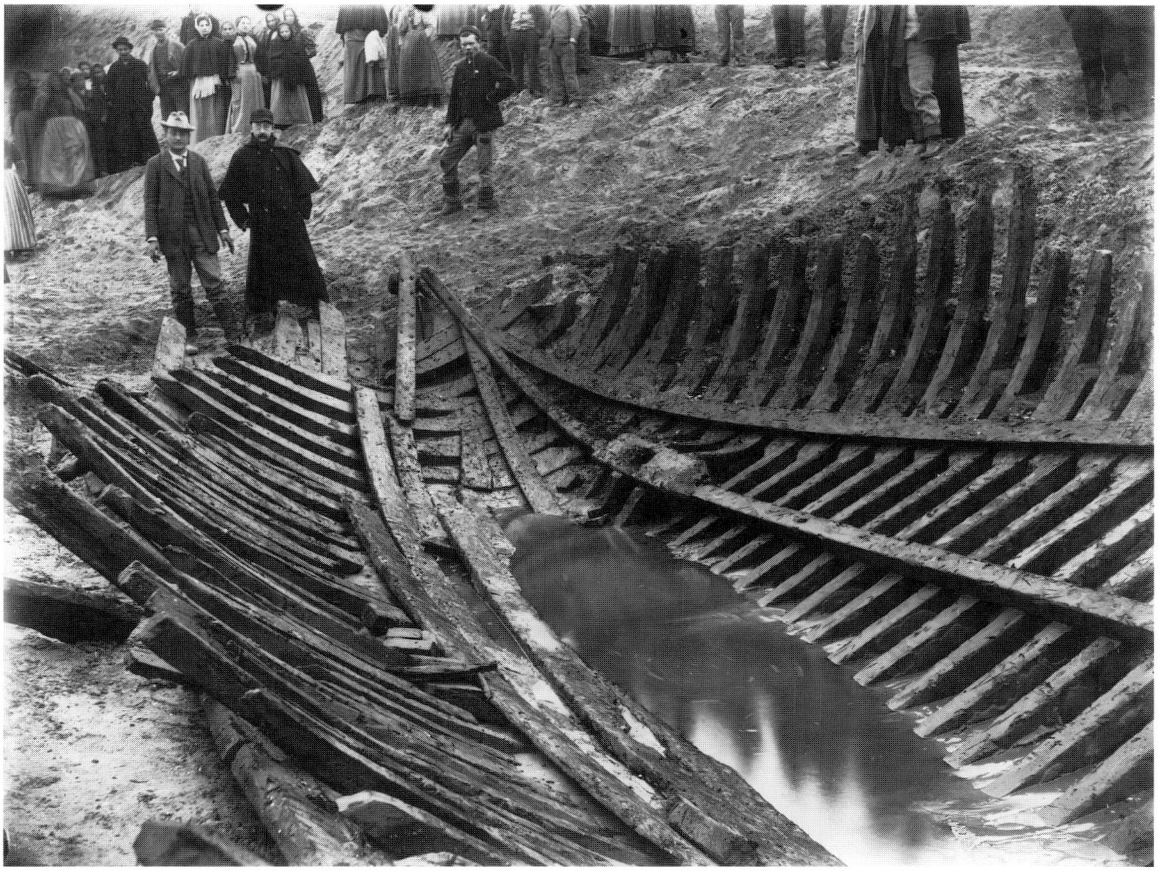

FIG. 140. Detail of the bow of Contarina I (ca. 1300), showing the foremast mast step, photographed *in situ.* *Courtesy Museo Storico Navale*

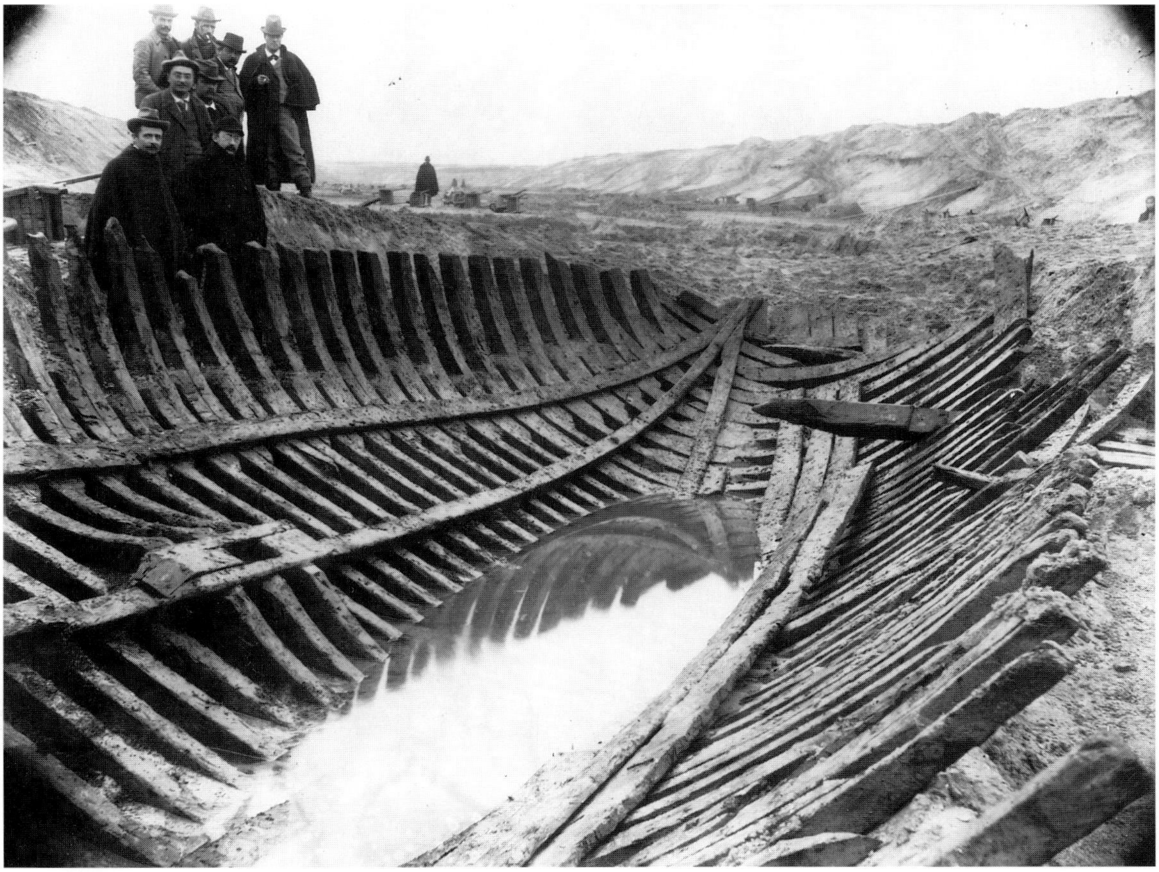

FIG. 141. View of the stern of Contarina I (ca. 1300), photographed *in situ,* showing the mizzen step and a port through-beam. *Courtesy Museo Storico Navale*

dimensions diminishing toward their upper ends. There were neither rabbets on the keel nor the posts (Relazione, 1901: 24–25).

Including the midships frame, fifty-eight frames were set perpendicularly to the keel, regularly spaced 28.2 centimeters apart (fig. 142A–C). They were composite frames made up of five timbers (a floor timber [*madiere* in Italian], two half-frames and two top timbers [in Italian *scalmo;* plural *scalmi*]), with at least a 50 centimeters overlap where three iron bolts (1.3 centimeters in diameter) fastened them together. Each floor timber was made of a single piece of wood usually of constant dimensions although those under the mast steps were thicker, presumably to provide additional support and partly butt up against the mast steps (Relazione, 1901: 29; see mast steps in figs. 140, 141, and 142E and F). In the twenty-nine frames forward of the mizzen step, the floor timber and the top-timber were attached to the futtock (*stamenale* in Italian) on its after side. This was reversed in the twenty-eight frames aft of the mizzen, where the floor timber and the top-timber were attached to the futtock on its forward side. The midships frame was unique in that it had two half-timbers abutting one floor timber (fig. 142B and C at position labeled 2). Both the floor timbers and futtocks measured 12 x 12 centimeters in section. Top-timbers had a constant sided dimension of 12 centimeters but reduced their molded dimensions toward their upper ends.

Except for the control frames at midships and either end of the keel, which had to be fastened to the keel before the keelson was installed (Steffy, 1994: 93), each floor timber was joined to the keel with a single 1.5 centimeter bolt that passed through the keelson and the keel and was

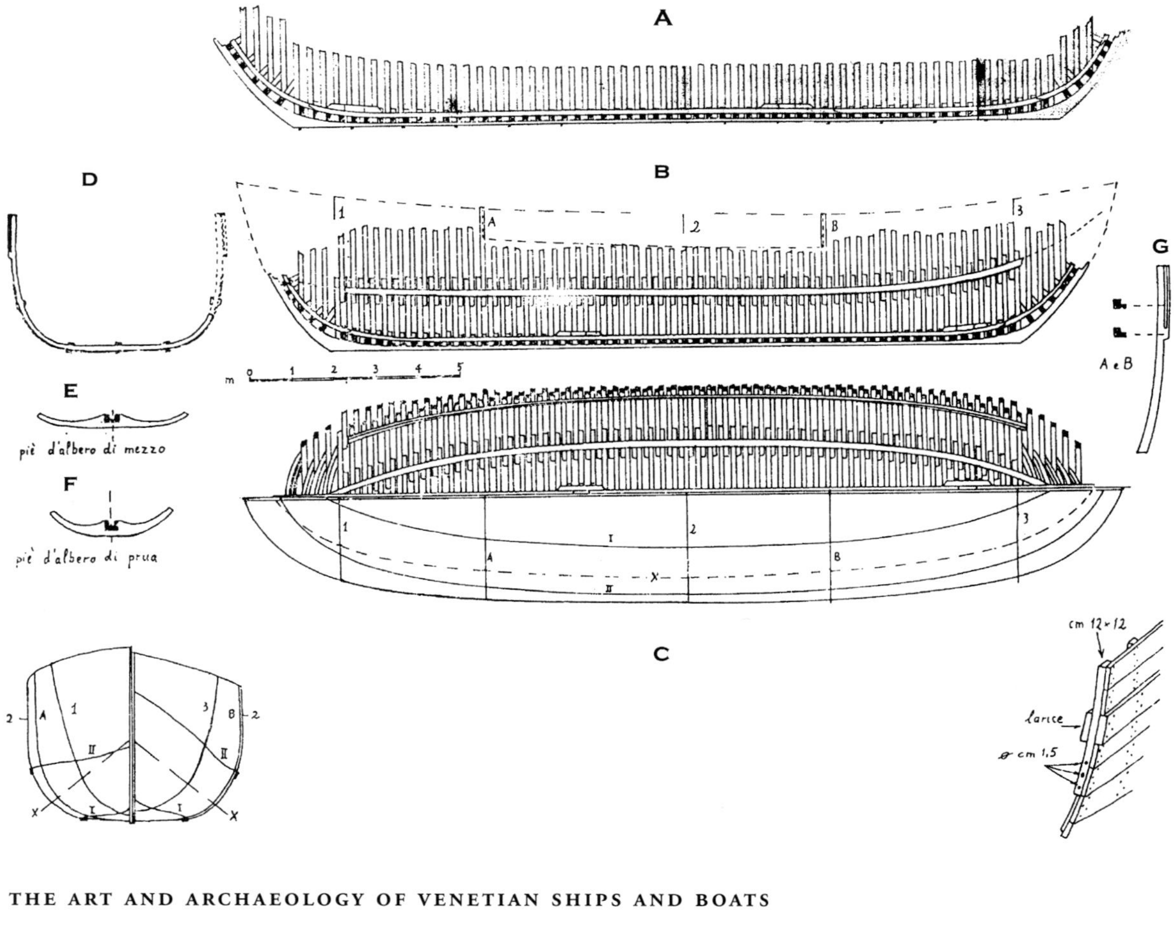

FIG. 142. Details of Contarina I (ca. 1300). (A) Port profile; (B) Starboard profile; (C) Horizontal projection; (D) Midships section; (E) Frame with foremast mast step; (F) Frame with mizzen step; (G) Detail of side showing groove for movable side planking. *After Relazione, 1900: table III; courtesy Museo Storico Navale, and Bonino, 1978b: fig. 4, courtesy M. Bonino*

clenched over the keel's lower surface. A small groove, about 2 centimeters in diameter, was cut into each floor timber's outer face to allow the bilge water to flow freely under the frames to a central sump for pumping or bailing.

The framework of the bow and stern areas was quite similar: four frames at the bow and three at the stern were fitted at their heads to transom knees (*gaisoni* in Italian) that were bolted through the posts (fig. 142C). Like all other frames, these measured 12 x 12 centimeters and were set with the same frame spacing.

Strakes forming the courses of external hull planking averaged 4 centimeters thick, and were usually between 30 and 40 centimeters wide. Toward the bow and stern, where they converged, they narrowed to roughly 13 centimeters. The plank scarfs were rather short and of irregular form; some were hooked and others were just a simple diagonal scarf. Hull planking was joined to frames with square iron nails, countersunk. According to the excavators, the garboard strakes were simply fitted to the keel, without any fastenings (Relazione, 1901: 28).

To strengthen the hull, clamps—or stringers—and wales were placed inside and out at the weak juncture of the floor timbers and the futtocks, and where half-frames and top-timbers overlapped. The wales, made up of two pieces scarfed and secured with two nails, were fixed firmly to the frames with four nails per frame and were worked into the posts just like any strake. Bonino noticed that the first wale lay exactly three Venetian *piede* above the keel, and he believes that this reflects the *trepie,* the most important standard shipbuilding measurement routinely specified in fifteenth to seventeenth-century Venetian treatises, indicating the shape of the frames at the point of maximum curvature at the *boca* (Bonino, 1978a: 62–64, 213).[7] In any case, at least on the Contarina I ship, the measure seems to have defined the location of the primary wale, positioned along the line of the overlap between the floor timbers and the futtocks and providing indispensable reinforcement along the length of the hull.

The excavators believed that the keelson, or inner keel, was an ineffectual structural element of the Contarina I ship, because the keelson consisted of six pieces, joined with scarfs secured with only one peg at each join. These joins were always placed by a floor timber to which the peg was secured. Along the central third of the ship, the keelson was sunk 8 centimeters into the top of the floor timbers. Fore and aft of this section, it sat directly upon the floor timbers (Relazione, 1901: 26–27). The keelson must have contributed at least some longitudinal rigidity to the hull.

Two robust mast partners were formed from two timbers, 10 centimeters wide, 20 centimeters tall, and long enough to cover five frames. A cavity formed the mast step itself, 24 centimeters long. The upper face of the floor timbers supporting the mast steps curved upward and abutted the mast steps on either side to provide additional strength.

Evidence for a superstructure was entirely lacking (Relazione, 1901: 30), although the ship probably had at least a small quarterdeck and might have been completely decked. Three facts indicate that the vessel was probably stripped and burned soon after sinking: evidence of burned timbers, the fact that no beams remained, and the discovery of so few associated artifacts (Relazione, 1901: 24). A rudder pintle and degraded iron nails were found, completely encrusted with sand and shells. The pintle's encrustations have verified that the vessel was indeed seagoing. Its encrustations contained coastal mollusks that had attached, while alive, to the iron pintle (Relazione, 1901: 42). The report makes no mention of anchors, but as the ship was apparently salvaged and burned, it is likely the anchors had been recovered.

Several features of Contarina I provide unique pieces of evidence for medieval ships. These include a through-beam and unusual details of the side planking along the port's bulwarks that should be interpreted, respectively, as the mount for the quarter rudder and movable side planking.

At the stern, between the fourth and fifth frame on the port side, a large beam projected from the hull below the deck level (fig. 141). At the time of excavation the beam was interpreted to be intrusive. In fact, it probably was in situ, a through-beam to provide the mount for the port quarter rudder or steering oar, as has been suggested (Pryor, 1984, no. 1: 181, and Bonino, 1978b: 13–17).

The fortuitous preservation of a section of the port's bulwarks explicates the irregular sheer line conspicuous in figures 14, 41, 44, and also in a fresco by Andrea da Firenze in Pisa (Nebbia, 1932: fig. 17). Futtocks A and B, labeled in the starboard profile drawing of figure 142B, and sketched as the detail, G, have a unique feature: the molded dimension at their upper end was increased on their outer face so as to accommodate a vertical slot running through them in the forward-aft direction just inboard of the outer face (Relazione, 1901: 29). Movable bulwark panels located along the central portion of the hull could apparently be slid forward and aft within these slots, thus making an opening in the bulwark. This has been interpreted as proof that the Contarina ship must have at times been rowed (Relazione, 1901: 34). I believe it facilitated boarding and loading.

In the winter of 1979, during the excavation of Murina cave, fragments of an old boat were recovered. The place of discovery, near Ravenna between Porto Fuori and Lido Adriano, had been a makeshift harbor from the Middle Ages through Renaissance times. Bonino has studied these boat remains, now disassembled in storage in the Museo Nationale of Ravenna, and has drawn a reconstruction of the boat's bow. He presented his study at a convention in Cattolica in 1981, but no acts from the conference have been issued, and he graciously offered to let the information be published first here. Bonino's interior and exterior sketches are included as figure 143, and line drawings and construction and framing details, as figure 144. Bonino recommends reassembly and restoration of the boat to allow a more detailed examination of the remains.

The Porto Fuori boat has the same basic construction as the Contarina I ship and both date to ca. 1300. The boat's overall length was probably about 17 meters, smaller than Contarina I's 21 meter length. The hull is made entirely of oak, except for the wales, which seem to be pine. Two types of iron nails were used. Some, round in section (10 or 15 millimeters in diameter), were apparently nailed into pre-drilled holes and connected structural parts of the hull (e.g., floor

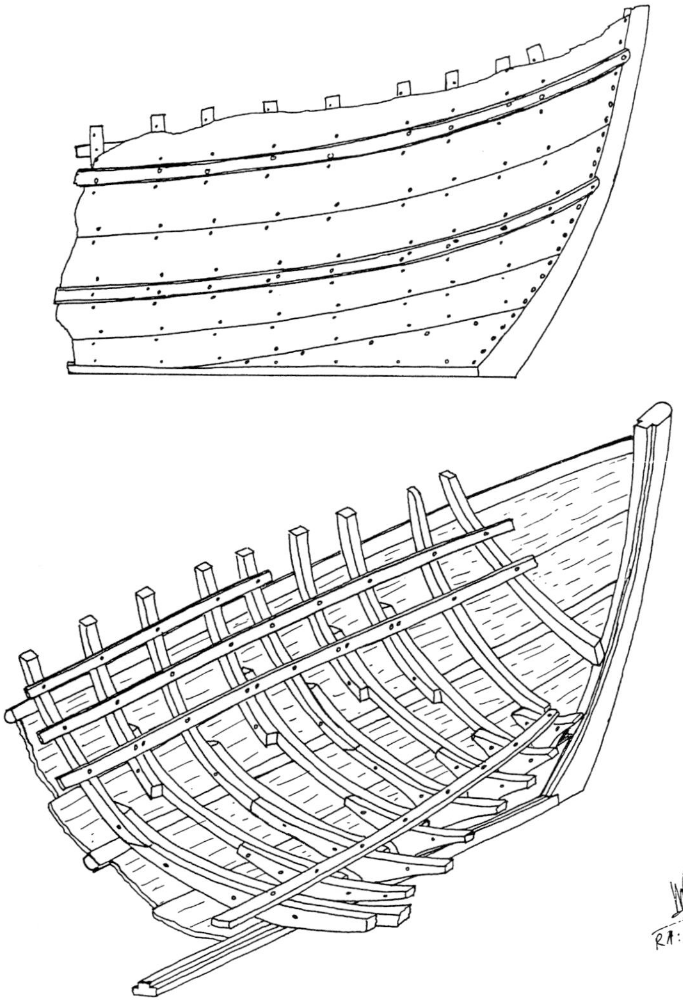

FIG. 143. Reconstruction of the bow of the Porto Fuori boat (ca. 1300). *Courtesy M. Bonino*

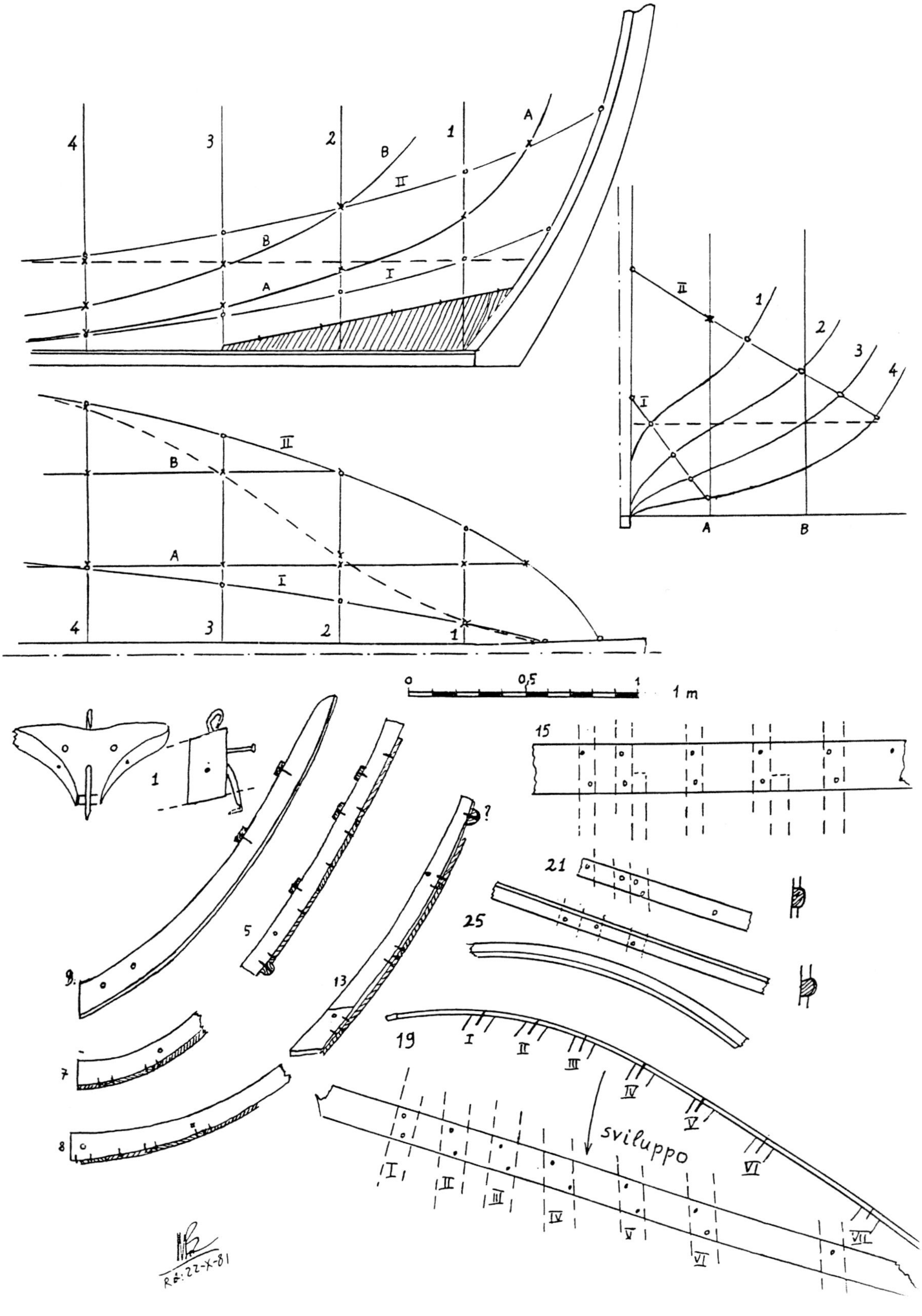

FIG. 144. Framing and construction details of the Porto Fuori boat (ca. 1300). *Courtesy M. Bonino*

timbers to futtocks and to the keel, and stringers to frames). Others, square in section (10 x 10 millimeters or 7 x 7 millimeters), secured the strakes to the frames and the inner keel, and in some places, joined the composite framing timbers to each other. These were driven directly into the wood; there are signs of cracking in the surrounding wood. The keel had rabbets for the garboard strakes. Both the first floor timber and the inner keel were fitted to the stempost. Frames were made of five sections. On either side of the hull's interior were three clamps or stringers, not always complete, and on the outside at least two wales.

The boat was found in poor condition, with no rigging or other equipment. It seems likely that, like Contarina I, the wreck was probably salvaged soon after sinking. Less of the hull is preserved, however, because the boat at Porto Fuori was subsequently demolished by continual dredging to keep the entrance to the harbor clear. Recovery of wrecks from beaches is documented in Ravenna archives (1468), while Venetian laws mandated that any ships wrecked in canals had to be removed in order to maintain navigability of the lagoon. It is likely that Ravenna had similar customs. The remains of the vessel showed no signs of repair, and, caulked only twice during her life, apparently was not old when she sank.

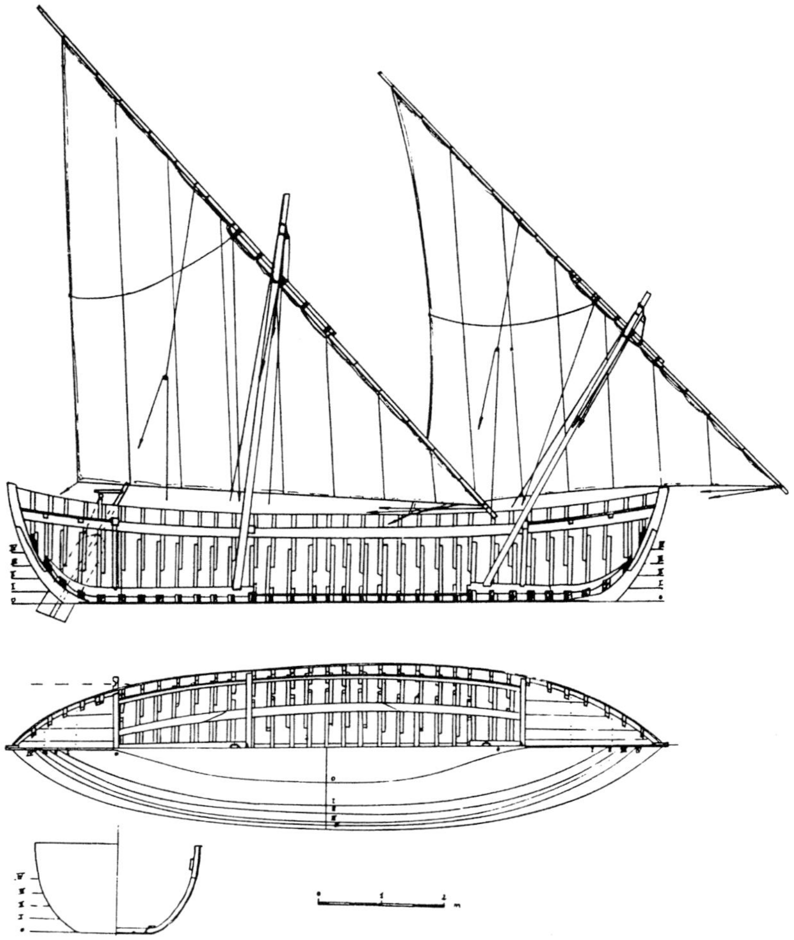

FIG. 145. Reconstruction of the Logonovo boat (ca. 1400), now in the Museo Nazionale di Ferrara. *Courtesy M. Bonino, 1978a: fig. 16*

Another vessel very similar to the Contarina ship in its construction, though considerably smaller, is the Logonovo boat, a two-masted, lateen-rigged boat discovered in 1958 at Lido di Spina, near Ferrara (fig. 145). Much of the hull was well preserved, though part of the stern, beams, decks, and upper stringers had been destroyed. It has been dated to ca. 1400. As in the Contarina ship, the keel, posts, and midships frame were set as the main points of reference, with the rest of the framing determined by temporary battens. Joins were made on each overlap of the frame assembly, not with iron bolts, but with two 1.5 centimeter treenails. Because it was smaller, no transom knee framing was needed in the boat's bow and stern areas.

The Logonovo boat had no true keel nor keelson, just an extra-heavy central plank, and a heavy inner timber along the forward part of the hull (Steffy, 1994: 93). After the hull planking was attached with iron nails, the entire hull was covered with pitch. A flat bottom and sharp turn of the bilge led Bonino to classify the vessel as a river craft of the *marciliana* type, and, in his estimation, the vessel must have measured approximately 10.05 meters long, with a keel length of 8.65 meters, a beam of 2.55 meters, and a height at midships of 1.14 meters (Bonino, 1978a: 63–64, 72–73; Steffy, 1994: 93). The remains were restored and are now housed in the Museo Archeologico Nazionale in Ferrara. The stern was missing, and the boatbuilder who reassembled the vessel formed a traditional craft with a rectilinear sternpost. Bonino (1978b: 15) points out that the hull should instead be double ended, the profile typical of lateen-rigged medieval ships. Like all of the vessels discovered in this region so far, the hull was almost entirely oak. Larch wood was used only for the mast steps and stringers.

During the Republic of Venice's struggle with the Duchy of Milan over territory around Lake Garda in 1509, the southern riverine route was blocked, so Venetians actually transported four *fuste,* twenty-five *copani,* and two to six galleys over the mountains to the north side of the lake. One of these sixteenth-century galleys has been found at Lazise, Lake Garda, and was investigated in 1962. The extremely light construction of galleys as compared to round ships makes the find of a galley exceptional. The galley measured 39.6 meters with a beam of 4.9 meters. Scantling dimensions include an average planking thickness, 2.9 centimeters; frames (molded) 8.9 centimeters; frames (sided) 7 centimeters; keelson (molded) 9.8 centimeters; and keelson (sided) 12.1 centimeters. Oars were 32 feet long, with heavy weights in the handles to counterbalance them (Scandurra, 1972: 209–10; figs. 3–5 and plates 10–18).

These eight discoveries attest to intense and diverse navigation within the region, which is also well documented in notarial and pictorial documents of this period. The construction, size, and features of Venetian vessels varied greatly depending on the intended use. Several small boats found show evidence for shell-first construction, while larger vessels were constructed frame first. Oak was used almost exclusively to build these vessels, except for a few special elements, such as the mast step, stringers, and wales, which utilized larch or pine. Oak is a sturdy wood that does not warp with humidity and is less susceptible than other woods to worm attack, making it an excellent choice for coastal vessels.

Attributes of Venetian Craft: Stern Details

Stern shape is significant because it affects the hydrodynamical design of a ship. It also correlates with rudder type and placement. Broadly speaking, sterns are either *double ended,* with a "pointed end" roughly equivalent in shape and space to the bow, or have a stern fuller than the bow, either *rounded* or *transom,* a flat termination to the stern. With both forms, the ends of the hull could have an outward rake or inward curve. Obviously, either design is a compromise: a transom stern makes a more capacious hull but negatively affects the laminar flow; a *double-ended* hull of the same length is more efficient in the water but holds less cargo.

The relatively narrow hull of *double-ended* Venetian type has a minimal deck at the bow or stern, if any at all. The symmetrical ends of the *double-ended* hull either rake outward (as in figs. 84, 103, 107, 112, 113, 115, and 116) or curve inward (as in figs. 5, 8A, B, and C, 23–25, 31, 35, 36, 120, and 121). One small boat type seen in figure 84 resembles the ancient burchio and modern *rascòna* types (fig. 152), showing a flat bottom continuing into a flat, panel-like bow. In a double-ended hull, the strakes generally run parallel to the keel and converge to finish at the stem and sternpost. Many of the double-ended vessels represented are small boats. Archaeological evidence provides examples of double-ended boats and an example of a large double-ended hull in the medieval ship discovered at Contarina; there were probably many large double-ended ships.

Characteristics of vessels with the stern fuller than the bow differ depending on the size of the craft. Byzantine manuscripts contain numerous examples of small craft with two or three tine-like features at the stern (as in figs. 32, 33, and Matthews, 1983: figs. 22–24 and 29). This seems to indicate the presence there of a fuller, open stern area finished in a relatively flat end. This is clearly depicted in figure 32 (detail, fig. 146A),

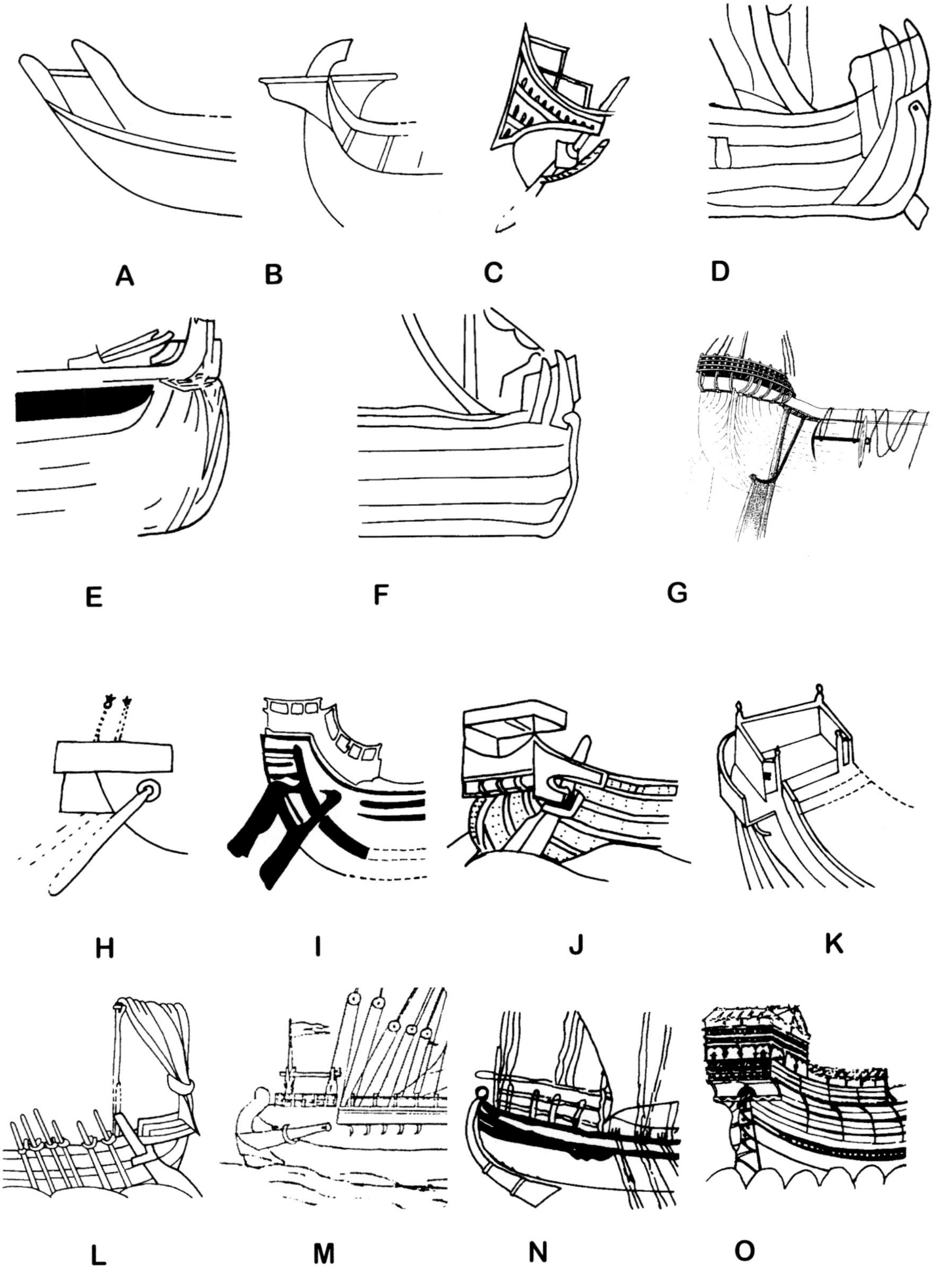

FIG. 146. Stern configurations. Details from (A) fig. 32, (B) fig. 31, (C) fig. 25, (D) fig. 18, (E) fig. 45, (F) fig. 21, (G) fig. 95, (H) fig. 12, (I) fig. 37, (J) fig. 26, (K) fig. 87, (L) fig. 27, (M) fig. 65, (N) fig. 69, and (O) fig. 70. *Rob Barras, Helen C. Dewolf, and Lillian Ray Martin*

which shows the inside of the stern: two sturdy stanchions, upright timbers, capped by a cross-timber frame a flat-ended stern. Other small boats with flat-ended sterns include figures 2, 16, 17, and 117, and, with extra high stems, figures 3, 4, and 17.

Larger ships had a quarterdeck or sterncastle structure and, to support it, they needed a structurally strong and fuller-shaped stern, which could be rounded or transom. This was accomplished by working the straking at the stern into both the sternpost and a tragent,[8] a horizontal beam astern (e.g., figs. 146G and O), or by laying stern planking perpendicularly to two strong stanchions at the stern above the tragent (e.g., figs. 146D and I). The rounded style created ample space for a small quarterdeck area (e.g., figs. 146J and K, 54, 73, 95, 102, 105, and 118), while the transom supported a more substantial sterncastle structure (e.g., fig. 146O).

Smaller, rounded-stern ships with inward-curving sterns had a small afterdeck, in art characterized in profile by a roughly triangular form on the quarters as in figures 146C, 23, 39, 40, 115, and 117 (cf. Matthews, 1983: 30, fig. 10); this may illustrate part of the rudder mount system.

Medium-sized ships with a rounded stern show more substantial structures of various shapes supported at the stern. What appears as a parallelogram on stern quarters in profile representations of round ships (figs. 146H, 41, 48, and 49) as well as galleys (figs. 146L, 47, and 125) is a simplified portrayal of the type of stern and rounded quarterdeck better seen in figures 54, 95, 97, 100, 102, and 105. Figure 41 shows the support struts for a rectangular enclosure on the quarters; in figures 97 and 146K, it can be seen that these struts continue around the stern to support the aft end of the quarterdeck as well as its sides. Frequently, people are depicted standing or sitting in this area (e.g., figs. 41, 47, 48, and 97). If there is ample space for a human in this area, the hull cannot possibly narrow as does a double-ended craft; the stern shape must be more rounded and full. Furthermore, if the sterns of three painted versions of the same vessel (figs. 99, 100, and 101) are compared, then it becomes obvious that ships with quarterdecks depicted in profile as a simplified rectangle, and others more accurately representing details of an inverted J-shaped rudder mount system integrated into the quarterdeck structure (e.g., figs. 146J and 99), have the same shape stern. The difference reflects the artist's perspective and degree of accuracy.

A transom stern is strong enough to support the largest sterncastle structures (e.g., fig. 146O). Several variations depicted reflect differing hull shapes that accommodate different rudder mounts. A sketch made by Zorzi, figure 68, illustrates the stern of merchant galleys like figures 146M and N: a flattened wing transom stern curves gently as it narrows to the keel, and to this, a curved stern rudder was affixed. Mediterranean-style *coche* round ships and carracks seem to have sterns with a flush transom to which a straight stern rudder could be affixed (figs. 146O, 56, 61, 67, 70, 71, 110, 122–24); on some, the sterncastle projects aft of the hull proper.

Some ships with transoms but fitted with quarter rudders reveal three posts at the stern, two projecting strongly above deck flanking the sternpost below (fig. 146D–F). The area between the two upright timbers and a horizontal tragent is filled in with planking, perhaps like that on the ship discovered at Pantano Longarini (Throckmorton and Throckmorton, 1973: fig. 10–11). The continuations of two wales, usually shown originating low in the hull (figs. 146D and I, 42, 62, and 63) or from the uppermost wales or sheer strake (fig. 146E) sweep upward at the stern, projecting above deck level. When originating low in the hull, these seem to form the outermost port and starboard frames of the transom and support the after end of the sterncastle.

Probably the most enigmatic feature in medieval ship representations are these curious posts, usually inward-curving timbers, which project above deck level at the stern (e.g., figs. 146D–F, H, and 10, 11, 13, 29, 42, 62, 63, 153[9] and Landström 1961: figs. 221–23). Perhaps these were the *ali* or "wings" mentioned in textual sources. These two upright timbers, seen inward curving or outward raking and at times flanking a center sternpost, varied among differing ship types but existed on all sized vessels. When projecting above the deck, the two timbers seem to define the outermost limits of the castle, or, when lower in the hull, to provide the structural timbers associated with a transom-like stern. On larger ships, these important structural timbers may have had an additional specific function, while in smaller vessels (such as those depicted in figures 29, 33, and 42) they probably represent simply one of several methods used to construct a flat-ended or transom stern. Whatever the case, a pair of upright timbers depicted at the stern indicates that the vessel had an ample area astern.

These timbers most likely had secondary uses and were not strictly structural features. Four possibilities include the *ali* and *spontalos* described in medieval texts, tent poles, or fortifying structures for horse ports. Medieval documents mention a feature called *ali*, which can be translated as "wings." According to Pryor, *ali* initially finished into the quarterdeck, but, "by the great age of the maritime republics, the wings themselves no longer terminated at the after-castle but were swept upwards and backwards through it. In imagery, they were depicted as extensions of the hull above the uppermost complete deck. From a point somewhere abaft amidships the hull of the *corridoria* and bulwarks must have separated into hull proper and wings which remained . . . outboard of the former." Pryor suggests these wings had two functions: to support the yards when lowered with their furled sails and to provide a platform from which to sling the steering oars over the side (1984, no. 3: 276). Bonino concurs that the wings formed part of a platform for lowering yards (1978: 9). Zeno's maritime code of 1255 specifies that the *tarrete* ship type had to have at least three *spontalos* on either side and two in the poop. Lane (1966: 163) presumed "these *spontalos* were frames or slings of some sort, used to propel stones," which may be another viable interpretation for these commonly depicted inboard-curving posts. One certain use for some uprights is as tent poles, as evident in figures 45 and 153. Other tent supports, though not integral with the stern structure, are defined in figures 146L, M, and N.

The posts seen on at least some of the larger round ships used as crusader transports, such as figure 146D, and the merchantman, figure 146I, may have been jambs, the fortifying structure making possible a horse or loading port at the stern. Thirteenth-century archival evidence and a manuscript illumination illustrating the landing of Turkish forces at Famagusta, 1571, from the Topkapi Palace Museum (Pryor, 1990: fig. 1) corroborate this as a position for the horse port, although the horse port could have been positioned at other parts of the ship in other cases or at other times. Records from the archives in Sicily (which were destroyed in World War II) included some letters dating from 1270–1300 by Count Charles of Anjou, specifying details for the construction of his taride at Brindisi. On May 1, 1278, he wrote:

> . . . there should be ports on the deck above just as is suitable and as is the custom in other *tarida.* Item, there should be one port at the stern of the *tarida* for embarkation and landing of men and horses; which port should be eight and a half *palmi*[10] high and five and a half *palmi* wide. That port should be able to be closed with two very strong doors and those doors should have false beams so that where the *tarida* is weak because of the large openings of the ports, it should be strong because of the beams. And that port at the stern of the *tarida* should [have] a good strong swinging door. Item, at the stern in the space where it is usual

to stow things, the deck beams should be doubled and six quite strong ones should be built in made of good oak or ash or elm; which beams are *syonte* as the Provençals say.[11] Item, it should be rounded at the stern so as to allow a horse to be able to embark and land saddled and armed. (Sicily Reg. Ang. 1 [1268, A], fols. 112r and 153r–v, as translated by Pryor, 1982, no. 2: 115).

From this document, and several others almost identically worded, it is certain that the horse transports at least in the time of Count Charles I had their horse ports as part of a specially constructed stern, which was to be fortified with two "false beams" (Pryor, 1982, no. 2: 106), and, given that the doors could have been larger than five and a half *palmi* on other ships, these may well be the posts depicted in some of these representations. The stern ports were closed with inner and outer doors, which opened vertically. The inner door, called a *bactiporta* or *battiporta,* was hinged at the top and locked by a bar on the inside (Pryor, 1982, no. 2: 119). The outer door was probably also hinged, but at the bottom; after being pulled closed, it was caulked to make it watertight. The upper continuations of the posts may have been used to facilitate closing the port (Concina, personal communication). Stern horse ports could have been used for beach landings on any vessel that was rowed or had sweeps; certainly at times transports would have loaded and unloaded horses at a wharf (Pryor, 1982, no. 1: 13).

The inward-curving features of medieval depictions may have had any or all of these functions. In some cases they are structural timbers that framed a squared, transom stern, at least some of which incorporated horse ports; others, as Pryor and Bonino have hypothesized, framed a squared quarterdeck to which the rudders could be slung and provided a support onto which furled yards could be stowed.

Another stern feature described in written documents of the medieval period is an area called *bellatorium* in Latin, and *ballador* or *ballaor* in Venetian. It projected over a meter beyond the poop of large merchant ships and was used as a fighting platform (Pryor, 1984, no. 3: 279 and fig. 9; Laughton, 1956: 278). The ships detailed in figure 15 offer examples of this fighting deck, including the weaponry. Zeno's code of 1250 required that each crew member carry *"balistam de cornu cum centum quadrellis habeat"* (Predelli and Sacerdoti, 1903: 96, code 27), that is, a crossbow with 100 bolts. The simplest crossbows were called either *a crocio* (cross type) or *a gancio* (hook type) and launched short bolts with triangular iron tips, like those seen in figure 15B (top and second from bottom) and in figure 15C (the lower three).

Attributes of Venetian Craft: Steering Devices and Their Mounts

The ability to steer is obviously necessary for any watercraft. Integral parts of a steering device include a blade (shape varied), a loom, and, at least on all larger craft, a system for mounting the steering device securely to the hull while still allowing it to be controlled. In addition to their normal rudders,[12] large oars at the bow, called bow sweeps, were sometimes used on sailing vessels to help the bow across the wind while tacking. Small craft cruising the shallows of lagoons and rivers could be controlled by hand with oars or punting poles, maneuvered from any area of the boat, without the advantage of a fulcrum, but oarlocks and thole bights were common. The size and weight of the rudders affected the strength and type of the mount required.

Distinct systems of mounts were in use at different times, and several at any one time (graph, fig. 147).

Figure 148 illustrates a wide range of the steering devices and mounting systems represented in this pictorial catalog. Three basic mount

FIG. 147. Use of steering mount types through time, from representational data. Three basic mount systems for quarter rudders (Q. R.) include: (A) variations on the box mount, the modified box, collar, or *luctatorio;* (B) brace mount; (C) swing mount; the stern mount varied to fit the shape of the stern, either curved or straight.

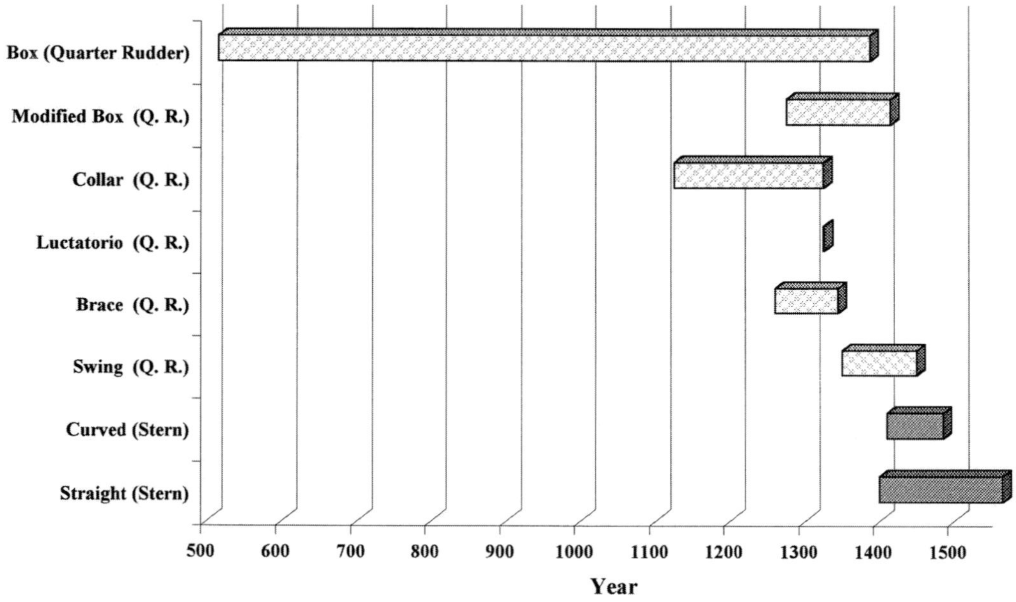

systems for quarter rudders are illustrated. These include the Roman-type box mount (modified, collar mount, and *luctatorio*), the aft or brace-mounted system, and the swing mount. Some mounts brought the loom to the caprail (e.g., figs. 148B and 5), while others passed the loom through the side of the hull (figs. 148G–I), or through the floor or sides of the quarterdeck (figs. 148C–E, J–M), and the tillerman steered from the quarterdeck or sterncastle. Another system, for a single stern rudder hung on iron pintles and gudgeons on the stern, had appeared in northern Europe by 1200 and was introduced to the Mediterranean by the fourteenth century. Initially Mediterranean ships retained their quarter rudders as well (figs. 148N), but the effective stern rudder had completely replaced them by the middle of the fifteenth century (figs. 148O, P).

SHAPE OF THE STEERING APPARATUS

A pair of steering oars or rudders, called *temone,* were set on the quarters of all but the smallest medieval vessels. Steering was accomplished by

FIG. 148. *(right)* Examples of rudder mounts. Box-type rudder mount of (A) fig. 8, (B) fig. 24 and modified box mounts, all with rudder hoists (C) fig. 25, (D) fig. 105, (E) fig. 26, and (F) fig. 104. C has a balanced rudder, while B, D, and E have unbalanced rudder blades. The looms pass through to be handled from the quarterdeck. (G) Symmetrical quarter rudder or steering oar of fig. 14, mounted through hull by a *luctatorio,* a wood or iron ring set into the hull, through which the loom passes inboard, forming the lower mount point, and perhaps also the gasket, to seal the port in the hull. (H) The standard medieval quarter rudder type, with intentionally unbalanced blades of foil design, from fig. 10, mounted through a port in the hull. Note the rudder hoist looped about the port rudder. (I) Another example of the *luctatorio,* from fig. 48. (J) A brace mount, from fig. 63; the loom passes through the floor of the quarterdeck. (K) An unbalanced quarter rudder blade aft-mounted to a through-beam, from fig. 42. (L) Detail, fig. 54, depicting a swing mount system, with asymmetrical blades shown in a reversed position. (M) Another swing mount, complete with rudder tackle, from fig. 102. (N) A swing-mounted quarter rudder to supplement the new type stern rudder, from fig. 65. (O) A curved stern rudder, fitted to the stern from fig. 68. (P) A single straight stern rudder on a transom stern, from fig. 70. *Rob Barras, Helen C. Dewolf, and Lillian Ray Martin*

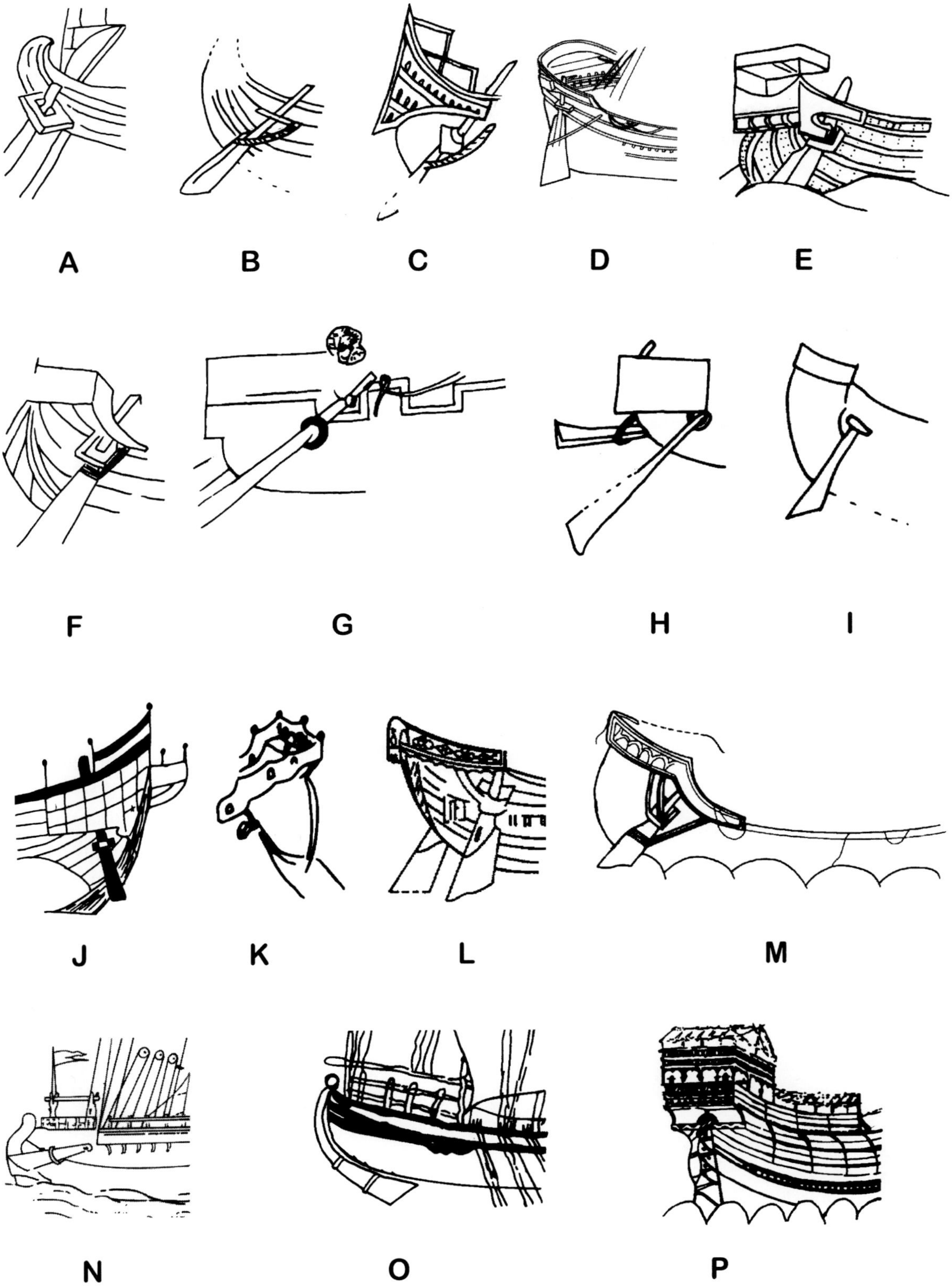
A
B
C
D
E
F
G
H
I
J
K
L
M
N
O
P

setting the quarter rudder blades in contrasting positions. Presumably most rudders would have had a tiller to facilitate their control, although this detail is often omitted in pictorial images.

A quarter rudder blade can be symmetrically balanced, either elliptical or rectangular in shape, or unbalanced, having the part of the blade aft of the shaft much larger than the forward part. Up to a certain size, above which the rudder becomes difficult to manage, the unbalanced blade is advantageous for a vessel with quarter rudders. This submerged foil-designed blade, which was developed during the medieval period, can equalize to a neutral position from most angles more easily than can a balanced blade, thus increasing the force of the rudder (Mott, 1991: 34 and 41).

Medieval quarter rudders were rather large and also functioned as leeboards. The *Fabrica di galere* (ca. 1410 material) defines the proportions of *temone* for the lateen-rigged ship described in the manuscript: the total length was equal to a third the length of the keel, or 4 *passa*. The shaft and the blade were equivalent in length at 2 *passa* each, and the width of the blade at its bottom was to be 4 *piede* (1.39 meters) (Bonino, 1987: 53 and 54).

All paddles and oars seen in smaller craft are balanced, figures 2–5, 16, 29, 32, 34, 74, 79, 103, 106, 109, and 120. Most are elliptically shaped blades, though those in figure 5 are rectangular. Among larger vessels, there is one elliptically shaped bow sweep (fig. 29) and a few symmetrical quarter rudders, (figs. 12 and 25), but most numerous are examples of asymmetrical, unbalanced quarter rudders (e.g., figs. 10, 26, 27, 38–42, 48, 53, 54, 65, 94, 99, 100, 101, 104, 105, and 118). The shape of the unbalanced foil design rudder is best seen on the ships of figures 10 and 54, and in a twelfth- or thirteenth-century atrium mosaic of St. Phocus in San Marco (fig. 149). Positioning the major part of the blade aft of the shaft increases the rudder's force while decreasing its drag.

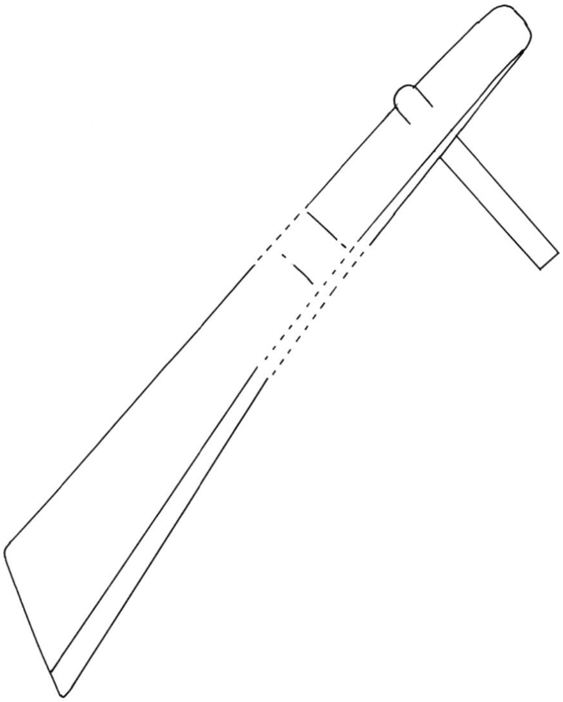

FIG. 149. Detail of an unbalanced quarter rudder, from a twelfth- or thirteenth-century atrium mosaic of St. Phocus holding a rudder, San Marco

MOUNT SYSTEMS

A system for mounting the steering rudders has three basic requirements. The system must hold the rudder in place at two points, permit its being dismounted, and allow either rudder to be moved in a direction parallel to the axis of its loom in order to control the depth and angle of the blade in the water. To adjust the rudder, tackle could be just a simple line attached to the blade of the rudder or a more complex system of block and tackle. One common arrangement consisted of two sets of tackle: the rudder hoist, used to raise the rudder, and the rudder pendant, which prevented the rudder from swinging out too far from the side of the hull. In figures 148B–D, the rudder pendant is depicted leading to the trailing edge of each rudder. A simple arrangement, a line looped around the rudder with both ends leading up to deck, is nicely illustrated on the port rudder of figure 148H.

The last requirement for the mount of a steering rudder partly applies to steering oars and paddles, the steering devices used on smaller craft, as well. Controlling a smaller blade in the water can be accomplished manually (e.g., fig. 74). The oar could also be secured at just one point by means of a thole bight hung on thole pins or be supported by an oarlock. Examples of smaller craft with their paddles hung via thole bights on thole pins include figures 5, 16, 17, and, on a larger vessel, figure 27. Small craft with a typically Venetian oarlock, called *forcole,* include figures 24, 46, 74, 79, 80, 103, 106, 107, 119, and 120. Ships, however, require strong structural mount systems for their heavy steering devices. The earliest system represented, the box mount (deriving from the Roman mount) was formed by adding a crosspiece upon two through-beams set near the waterline (figs. 148A, B, D–F, 8C, 27, and 104). The rudder shaft passed through the box and was either lashed to the caprail, as must be the case in figure 148B, or passed inboard through the hull, as in figure 148D. This system confined the rudder firmly. The rudder could not swing up if it hit shallows, and so the rudder could break if the bottom of the blade were not set sufficiently above the level of the keel (Mott, 1997: 33). A variation of the box mount common on oared ships utilized the outrigger rather than constructing a separate mount along the sides of the hulls; the shaft of the rudder passed through the outrigger, and the rudder could be worked from the quarters (fig. 153 and possibly fig. 8B [the mosaic has undergone extensive modern repair]).

Similar and functionally identical to the box mount was the wooden collar, a solid piece of wood with a circular hole for the rudder shaft (Mott, 1997: 74–77). This mount is illustrated by figures 148C and G–I, as well as 38–40, 47 and 89. The rudder shaft passed through the collar and then to a second mounting point inboard (Mott, 1997: fig. 2.1). This was a sturdy arrangement and would have allowed the rudder to be raised as necessary, but it also monopolized much hull space. The hole cut through the hull must have been sealed with some sort of gasket. This detail is illustrated in figures 148G and H, 11–13, 37, and 47–49, first seen in the twelfth century, though no more visual examples of this system were found after 1350 (c.f., Mott, 1997: 87–89). This arrangement seems to have taken at least two forms, depending on vessel size.

On smaller vessels, representations of a modified box mount show the rudder shaft passing through the hull just forward of a roughly triangular-shaped feature of a small quarterdeck (e.g., figs. 23, 25, and 40). The triangular feature was apparently an intrinsic part of the rudder mount system added after the hull was almost completely constructed. This is evident through comparison of two figures that represent the same basic vessel type: figure 115, a vessel under construction, and figure 25 (detail, fig. 148C), a vessel completely constructed and under way. In figure 115, no triangular rudder mount system has yet been attached, while in figure 25, a nearly triangular-shaped outboard of the loom appears to be part of the mount system. The thirteenth-century figure 25 is the earliest example located of a fixed mount using a wood collar (cf. Mott, 1997: 75, where a twelfth-century date is incorrectly given).

On larger ships, the triangle-shaped feature is altered and enlarged, encompassing an inverted J shape turned on its side. Here, too, it appears to be part of the mount system where the shaft of the rudder passes inboard to the quarterdeck (figs. 148E, 94, 97–101, and 104). Compare figure 98, a ship under construction, with the following figure 99, the same ship shown under way. In the construction scene, another J-shaped inner brace is depicted in a perfect position to act as the counter brace to the external feature of the ship's bulwarks defined in figure 99; it was here the rudder passed through the hull and needed structural support. In figures 92, 94, and 97, the quarter rudder is secured through the quarterdeck in a similar system of interior bracing.

A second system exemplified in this sample

entails two forms of exterior bracing. With the aft-mount system (fig. 148K), the rudder shaft was mounted on the after side of a strong through-beam. Figure 42 is the sole example in this sample of the aft-mounted system. The brace mount, shown by figure 148J, had two through-beams appropriately spaced so the rudder shaft could pass between them (Mott, 1997: fig. 2.1).

The swing mount derived from the aft-mounted system (Mott, 1997: 84; figs. 148L–N). The swing mount was another vast improvement, because it allowed the rudder to pop up instead of breaking should it hit an obstacle. Fourteenth- and fifteenth-century examples figures 54, 58, 65, and 102 exemplify the swing mount system.

Until fifteenth-century mariners came to trust the pintle and gudgeon–mounted stern rudder, ships with the newfangled stern rudder of the north retained their quarter rudders (e.g., fig. 148N). The new steering device, called *alla bavonesca* in Venice (Bonino, 1987: 67), was possibly absorbed in the Mediterranean along with the square sail. Functioning like most modern rudders, stern-mounted rudders are of a completely different design and shape, either curving to fit a curved stern (figs. 148N and O, 56, 57, 69, and 125) or straight, along a transom stern (figs. 148P, 55, 58, 60, 67, 71, 91, and 123). The straight stern rudder was eventually preferred, because the curved stern rudder could break quite easily.

Attributes of Venetian Craft: Anchors and Mooring

The mooring methods utilized by medieval seafarers are quite similar to those used today. Figure 24 illustrates a technique still characteristic of the shallow waters of Venice: the boat is tied off to a piling set in the lagoon. The ship in figure 71 is secured to heavy moorings fixed ashore, just as in modern harbors. The most common mooring method represented or implied, however, is anchoring. Anchors were used at sea, in protected harbors, and, in conjunction with bow and stern lines, when moored at dock. Thus a seagoing ship needed several anchor types, including kedge anchors, small anchors used to keep a ship steady in harbor or to maneuver the ship to and from dock; bowers; sheet anchors, a ship's largest, extra-heavy anchors, which were thrown only in an emergency (Tinniswood, 1945: 87); and some spares. As a general rule, the anchor's particular form or shape does not clearly identify its function (Keith, 1988: 119), and so, unless clarified by the representation's theme, it is not possible to determine the specialized use of anchors depicted.

Sixteen images of the catalog illustrate one or more of their ships' anchors. Three basic anchor shapes are exemplified: stone, hook, and grapnel. Only one of the anchors is made of stone; the remainder, of iron and wood. Iron anchors had existed in the Mediterranean at least as early as the fifth century B.C. (Stophanes's description of the Battle of Plataea in Herodotus, Book 9: 76). The forge welding of iron was a long-established method that continued until late medieval times: anchors from both the seventh-century Yassi Ada and the eleventh-century Serçe Limanı ships were made by forge-welding together many small iron pieces (van Doorninck, 1984: 3–4; van Doorninck and Steffy, in Bass and van Doorninck, 1982: 121–43; Moriarty and Marshal, 1965: 7). Stocks were either wooden or wood sheathed in iron (Moriarty and Marshal, 1965: 6); the stock caused the anchor to cant and set itself into the sand as illustrated by figure 150M.

The anchors in the catalog can be classified into five shapes of three basic types, illustrated in figure 150: (1) the round stone, or millstone anchor (fig. 150A); (2) the grapnel anchor (fig. 150B–D); (3) three varieties of the hook anchor: the cruciform hook anchor (fig. 150E), the V-shaped hook anchor (fig. 150F–G), and the

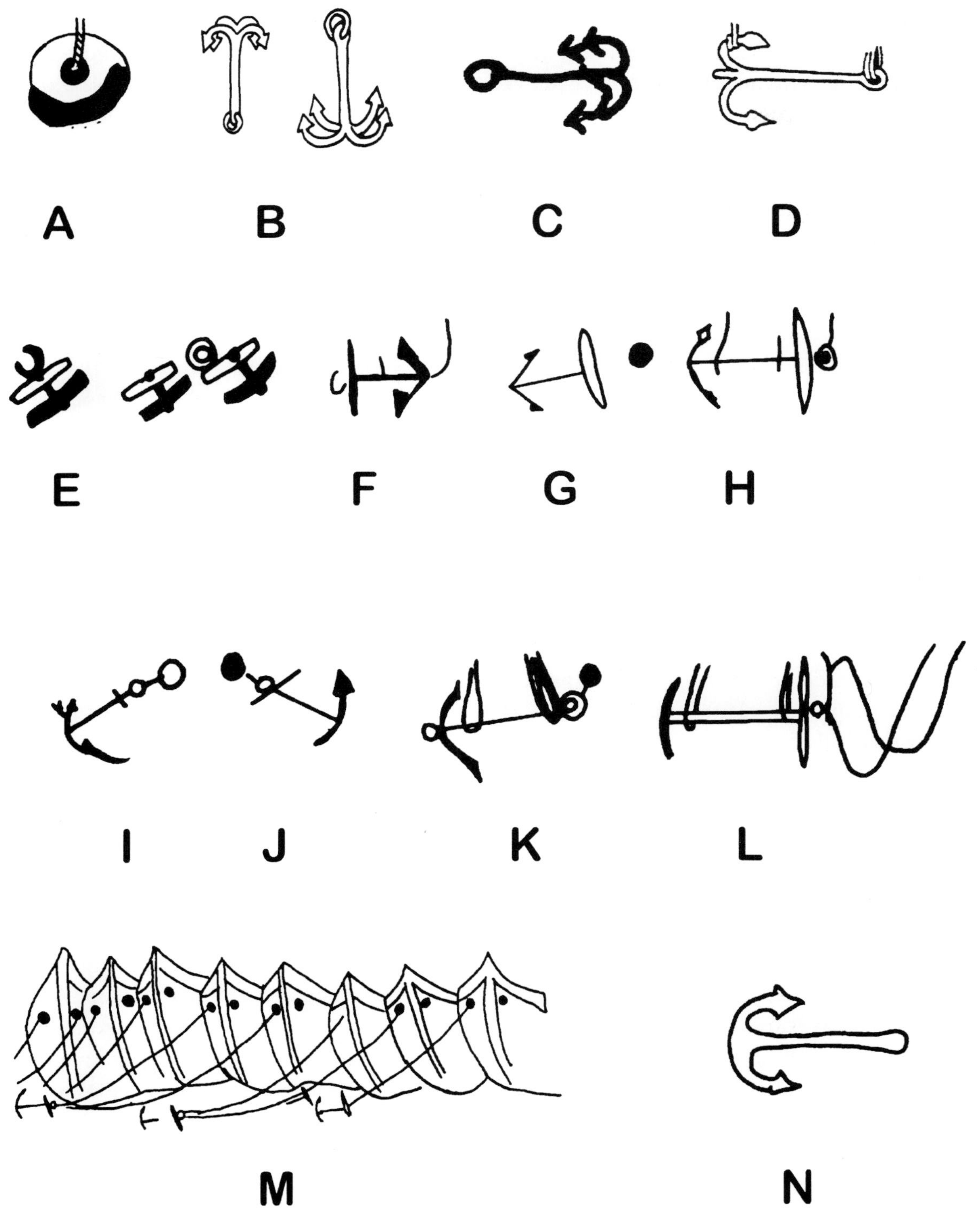

FIG. 150. Examples of anchor types. (A) Millstone anchor of fig. 46 (fourteenth century). Examples of the grapnel anchor, (B) from the fifteenth-century *Art de far vasselli* material, folio 14r, (C) from fig. 66 (fifteenth century), (D) fig. 86 (fifteenth century) (E) Cruciform-shaped hook anchors of fig. 14 (twelfth century). V-shaped hook anchors of (F) fig. 37 (1255), and (G) fig. 97 (fourteenth century). Crescent-shaped anchors (fourteenth century): (H) fig. 100, (I) fig. 41, (J) fig. 42, (K) fig. 26, (L) fig. 94, (M) fig. 43, (N) after Moll, 1927: pl. 22, fig. 2.

crescent-shaped hook anchor (fig. 150H–N). There is archaeological evidence from the Serçe Limanı shipwreck and elsewhere for a fourth variety of hook anchor, the Y-shaped anchor, and although it was probably used widely in the Mediterranean from the tenth through thirteenth centuries, no examples of it occur in this representational sample. Both the cruciform and Y-shaped hook anchor types apparently disappeared during the Renaissance (Bonino, personal communication). Each anchor type represented will be discussed in ascending order of frequency.

Millstone anchors (fig. 150A). A manuscript illumination from the first half of the fourteenth century illustrates St. Clement being drowned with a stone anchor tied to his neck. The millstone anchor, approximately twice the size of the saint's head, has a centered hole about one-third the total diameter of the stone. Millstone anchors were used on small craft of the Mediterranean and northern Europe from as early as the early Bronze Age through at least the end of the medieval period (Moriarty and Marshal, 1965: 10).

Grapnel anchors (figs. 150B–D, 70, and 86). The grapnel anchor is characterized by four arms with flukes; one original use of the anchor was for hooking onto an enemy vessel prior to boarding. A small grapnel—with no flukes—was found with the seventh-century ship at Yassi Ada, probably an anchor for the ship's boat (van Doorninck and Steffy, 1982: 140). This is perhaps the earliest known example of a grapnel in the Mediterranean, though the type was probably used throughout the Greco-Roman period. It continues in use today as a sand anchor. An early representational example is seen in figure 77, a fourteenth-century fresco recorded by Levi. *Arte de far vasselli,* fifteenth-century material, contains sketches of grapnel anchors on folio 14r (fig. 150B). Fifteenth-century ships with a grapnel hung horizontally at the bow include those shown by figures 65 (crown forward; anchor detail, fig. 150C) and 86 (crown aft). In figure 70, a grapnel is hung off the bowsprit by a ring at the anchor's crown. Grapnel anchors now kept in the Museo Storico Navale were raised from the sixteenth-century Lazise galley (Scandurra, 1972: 220, with figs. 16 and 17).

Cruciform hook anchors (fig. 150E). Three hook anchors hung at the bow of the twelfth-century round ship in figure 14 are the earliest representations of anchors in the catalog. Although possibly very schematized portrayals of either the V- or crescent-shape of anchor, they seem to be of the cruciform variety. If so, they constitute the only examples of this type seen in our sample of representations. The foremost anchor is secured at the bow through the hawse hole; the other two are fastened inboard, with their cables running over the gunwale. The stock of these anchors is depicted as being slightly shorter than the length of the two arms together. The shank is also short relative to the stock, at roughly three-quarters the length of the stock instead of equal to it. More reliable proportions for the cruciform anchor are known from one discovered with the fourth-century Cervia boat (fig. 135): although the stock was not found, the shank length is more than a third longer than the combined lengths of the arms. Its iron shank is circular in section and the arms, square. Cruciform anchors were found on the fourth-century Dramont F wreck, the seventh-century ship at Yassi Ada (van Doorninck and Steffy, in Bass and van Doorninck, 1982: 121–43), and they are seen in other representational examples, such as an eighth-century Byzantine relief at Karabagla, and a later Italian example (ca. 1300) at San Eustorgio of Milan (Bonino, 1978a: 41); clearly the type was widely used.

V-shaped hook anchors (figs. 150F and G, 81, and 100). Four examples dating from the thirteenth–fourteenth centuries illustrate the V-shaped hook anchor, sometimes referred to as a long plan anchor (Moriarty and Marshal, 1965: fig. 10C). This type derived from Mediterranean iron anchors of the Hellenistic period, which are characterized by a rectangular shank (Kapitän, 1984: 43). The type was gradually phased out of use in the Mediterranean, but it appears to have been reintroduced to the region by the year 1000 (Moriarty and Marshal, 1965: 7).

The anchor in figure 37 is hung horizontally at the bow, crown forward (anchor detail, fig. 150F); its flukes seem excessively large. Two fourteenth-century depictions (figs. 150G and 100) also show a V-shaped hook anchor hung horizontally at the bow but with the crown swung aft. All three portray a stock fitted at the head of the shank. Use of fixed-stock anchors reflects little concern over space on board, and therefore probably indicates a trend toward heavier and fewer anchors on larger-capacity ships.

Crescent-shaped hook anchors (figs. 150H–N and 123). This type is the most common anchor represented in this sample; all examples date to the fourteenth century. Some crescent-shaped anchors were apparently stock-less or had removable stocks (as in fig. 26), but most show fixed stocks at the tops of their shanks (as seen in figs. 42 and 150M).

In figure 42, of a crescent-shaped anchor with a fixed stock (detail, J), the hawser runs from the ring of the anchor through a hawse hole. Two lines loop around the shank of the anchor in figure 94 (detail, fig. 150L), while a hawser leads inboard from the loop at the top of the shank. Figure 150M offers a valuable example of medieval harbor mooring techniques: eight vessels are secured in harbor, sharing four anchors between them. The shanks lay horizontally upon the top of the sand, and one arm of the anchor is imbedded into the sand. Nine hawsers and hawse holes are visible. The vessel closest to shore has both port and starboard hawsers utilized.

These anchor representations provide other useful information, such as the most common visible storage locations and orientations of anchors and hawse holes, as well as some technical details of the anchors. Generally, representations show only one anchor of a particular vessel. Maritime codes and archaeological evidence, however, demonstrate that there were at least several, if not many, anchors on board all ships. Some were stored on deck or below deck, or possibly on the far side of the ship, positions that would not necessarily be visible in a portrayal of a ship.

One frequently depicted practice was to hang anchors ready at the bow. The method of securing an anchor with a fixed stock can be seen in figure 151, a detail from Carpaccio's painting (ca. 1490), "St. Ursula's Arrival at Cologne." In the background, the bow of a carrack is shown in profile. A hawser tied through the hawse hole loops around this ship's anchor shank just below the stock, and another line, secured at the base of the shank just above the attachment of the arms, runs over the gunwale to be affixed inboard; thus, the anchor is fixed roughly horizontally in place. On the foreground vessel (viewed directly from the bow), one cable, running from the port hawse hole, already secures the vessel, probably to the dock. Two anchors hang ready, one at starboard with its cables secured through the hawse hole to somewhere inboard; one to port, simply over the gunwale. Mariners commonly hung anchors horizontally at the bow, ready to cast (e.g., figs. 26, 41–43, 86, 97, 101, and 102). A bower is usually hung horizontally at the bow with the crown aft. Two examples (figs. 37 and 65) show the anchor hung horizontally at the bow with the crown forward. In figure 14, three anchors are represented hanging at the bow neither vertically nor horizontally but with their crowns angled forward. Figure 94 shows an anchor hung just forward of the rudder at the quarters, but it too is hung horizontally, crown aft. Similarly, the stock-less anchor in figure 26 is supported horizontally by two lines tied inboard. The lines pass over the gunwale and loop around both the upper and lower shank. A hawser leads from the ring at the upper end of the shank through the hawse hole inboard. At the crown end of the anchor is

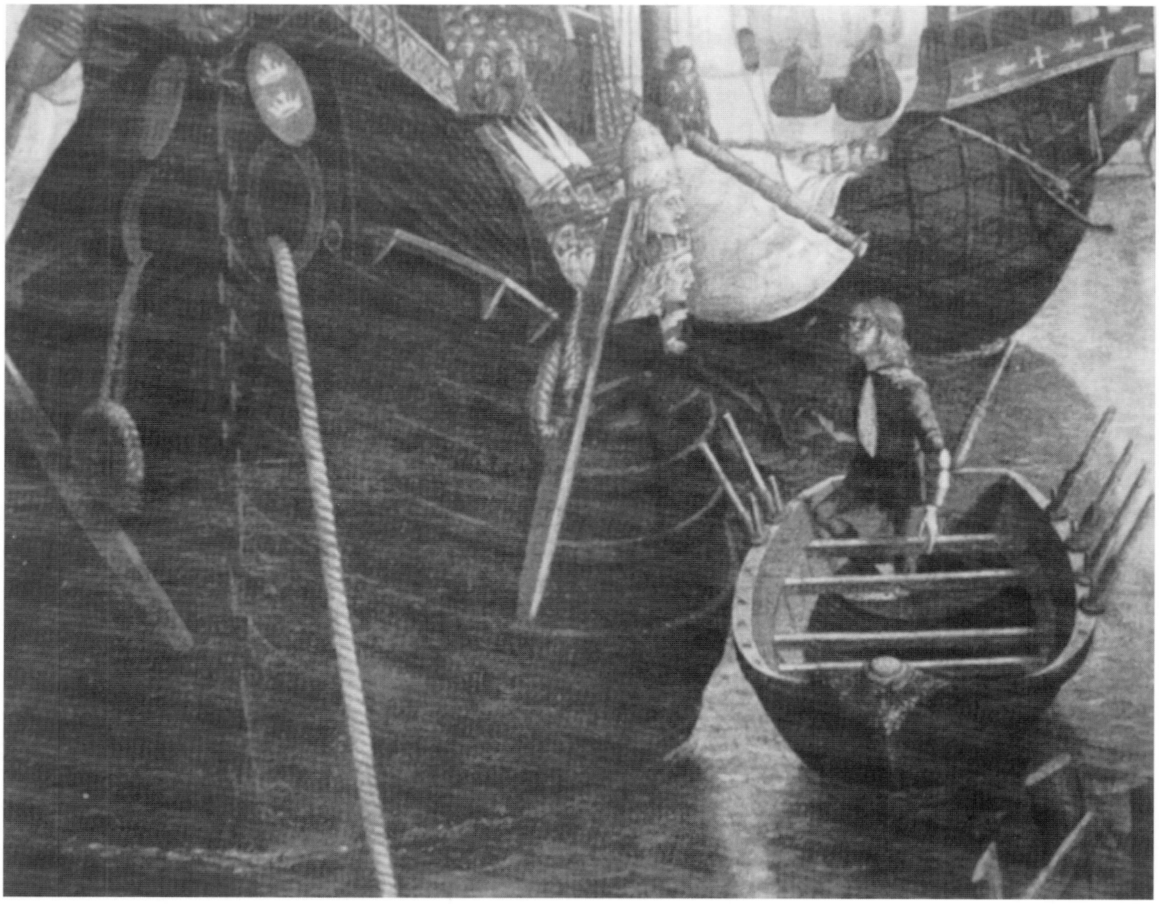

FIG. 151. Anchor secured at the bow, detail from the late fifteenth-century painting by Carpaccio of the St. Ursula *vita* cycle: Arrival at Colonia, Galleria dell' Accademia. *Permission to photograph courtesy the Museum*

another ring; a buoy could be attached to this end and the cable used to facilitate freeing and hauling the anchor. Ropes hung over the gunwale support the anchor in figure 41, and a hawser runs from the anchor ring through the hawse hole. Figure 70 shows a grapnel anchor hung off the bowsprit, useful for boarding enemy ships.

In many depictions, the stock is drawn as if it were in the same plane as the arms (e.g., fig. 150E–H and L). Unless these anchors were merely weight anchors rather than the more effective canting anchor, the proper perspective of the stock in relation to the shank is rarely accomplished in medieval art. The stocks would have had to be set perpendicularly to the shank, as shown in perspective like in figure 150J, in order for the anchor to cant. Assuming the majority of the anchors we see depicted with a stock were in fact canting anchors, most anchors appear to have been drawn in a contorted perspective, in attempts by the artists to define both the arms and stock clearly. Sometimes no foreshortening is indicated; the artist just gives us a more or less accurate "profile view" of all the anchor parts, the arms, stock, and shank.

The flukes that are recognizable in the representations are the spade or herreshoff type (Moriarty and Marshal, 1965: fig. 17) and are shown as roughly an equilateral triangle, half as long as the length of an arm.

Many figures include a hawse hole at the bow (e.g., figs. 26, 28, 37, 41–44, 48, 49, 51, 58, 70, 71, 77, 93, 96, 99, 100, 101, 105, 110, 126, 127, 128, and 129). Once ships became larger and their anchors so heavy that it was less feasible to heft them overboard, the hawse hole developed (Moll, 1927: 304); a hawser ran through it into the ship's hold. The San Isidore chapel mosaics (ca. 1300) include the earliest represented examples of hawse holes (figs. 26 and 28). The ship in figure 37 shows vertical bitt beams serving to bitt the hawser (Pryor, 1984, no. 3: 277).

The Venetian maritime statutes collected by Predelli date to 1227 (Ziani), 1229 (Tiepolo), and 1250 (Zeno). The information concerning anchors given in these codes is tabulated in appendix 4. Ziani's statutes of 1227 make no mention of anchor requirements. Both Tiepolo and Zeno's statutes, however, define requirements for vessels from 200 to 1000 *migliariis,* reflecting a slight increase in the number of anchors, buoys *(indigarios),* and hawsers *(canapos* or *canouos)* from 1229 to 1250. A rather large number of anchors was required, indicating anchors were still relatively small and light. Zeno's statutes also make a distinction between *nave* and *tarrete* not made in the earlier statutes. A *nave* was required to carry more anchors and hawsers than the *tarrete*; obviously heavier ships needed additional anchors. It would be helpful to locate maritime codes from the following century. An increase in anchor weight occurred late in the thirteenth or early in the fourteenth century, and as the anchors were made heavier, one would expect to see a decrease in the number required by law (van Doorninck, personal communication).

Textual Evidence for a Functional Venetian Ship and Boat Typology

To develop the most accurate picture of medieval Venetian watercraft possible, evidence gleaned from textual sources, pictorial evidence, and nautical archaeology must be integrated, because each contributes different kinds of information. For example, details of superstructure, rigging, and sails are rarely preserved in the archaeological record, but they are commonly part of depicted images or are described in textual sources. Some ship and boat measurements are specified in written records (see appendix 3); one needs precise figures of overall dimensions to determine length-to-beam ratios, which quickly identify a vessel's carrying capacity versus its speed through the water. Ships and boats suitable for carrying cargo have a 3:1 or 4:1 length-to-beam ratio. If the dimensions given can be believed, the ninth-century *ippagoghi* had a squat 2:1 length-to-beam ratio; this vessel would take a great deal of wind power to move through the water, but it could be heavily laden. Galleys ranged between a 7:1 and 9:1 length-to-beam ratio; these sleek-shaped vessels could move faster through the water with less wind or rowing power but had far less carrying capacity. Archaeological examples are rarely intact, and—although their overall dimensions must be estimated—they confirm these ratios. The boats and round ships of Cervia, Pomposa, Contarina I, and Logonovo had a length-to-beam ratio of 4:1; the Pontelagoscuro vessel and Contarina II ship were slightly beamier at 3:1; the Lazise galley, 8:1.

Integrating all the evidence helps to compensate for the fact that each source of evidence has a preponderance of certain types of ships over others. For example, literary sources tend to describe function more than details of form and offer evidence for warships that is scant in the artistic and archaeological records, especially in the earlier periods. In contrast, representational evidence predominantly portrays the merchant ship types not emphasized in the textual sources. Written records from the eighth to the thirteenth centuries mention warship names such as *navi lunghe, dromone, galere,* and *trierio* but provide few other ship names besides the ambiguous term *nave.* Until the thirteenth century, the word *nave* was used so generically that it has little meaning beyond "vessel capable of navigation." Beginning in the thirteenth century, however, written records began making a greater distinction of ship types. Thus, we find, for example, Zeno's code of 1255 divided into two sections, clarifying regulations for two distinct merchant ship types, the *nave* and the *tarrete.*

Even so, a serious problem to be faced in interpreting the textual evidence is that "writers virtually never give the characteristics of the ship types they mention," and, because one term can refer to more than one vessel type, "ship type designations can be . . . misleading" (Kreutz, 1976: 94). Another limitation of textual evidence is that it primarily concerns military exploits, giving far less emphasis to mercantile ships and smaller lagoonal and fishing craft. Round ships were less regulated, so they are less well recorded in textual sources (Lane, 1963: 194). Archaeology is likewise limited in what it offers. To date, fewer than ten of the numerous vessel types known to have existed have been brought to light: a few small open boats; larger, two-masted, lateen-rigged boats and merchantmen; a floating watermill; and only one warship galley.

This section presents a descriptive inventory of ship and boat names in Venetian textual sources by century. The compilation is based on two detailed surveys of the primary sources, Casoni's *Venezia e le sue lagune* (1847) and Bonino's *Archaeologia e tradizione navale tra la Romagna e il Po* (1978a). The vessel terms occur in written sources including nautical codices, shipping contracts, government records, and chronicles, graphed in figure 154. Some are Venetian or northern Italian dialectical versions of common Latin names. In the interest of brevity and clarity, each vessel name is placed in the century of its earliest documented occurrence and is repeated only if the use of the term changed at a later time.[13] This arrangement does not mean to preclude the indisputable certainty of cases where a vessel type continued to be used in the following century or centuries. Along with the previously discussed examples from the archaeological record, this textual evidence well supplements the typology developed with the pictorial catalog to follow.

Initially, Venetian trade was conducted on the rivers of northern Italy, key rivers that led inland to the trans-alpine trade routes. It is therefore not surprising that most of the vessels mentioned in the earliest Venetian documents of the fifth and sixth centuries, such as the *campolo* and *cursorie,* were trading vessels of modest size suited for river navigation. Both the *campolo* and the *scrilla* ran the local commerce within the lagoon and to nearby river destinations. Cargoes were frequently transshipped as they went upriver: they were reloaded, as necessary, onto vessel types appropriate to the local navigation conditions. Two other fifth- and sixth-century types, the *acazie (acates, acate),* a vessel used as both a cargo ship or a war transport, and the *liberniche,* primarily an oared warship but occasionally used also for commerce, were employed on rivers as well, and all must have had a fairly shallow draft.

Written records of the seventh century identify five riverine commercial ships, the *marciliane, magne marciliane, varchette, pandora,* and the *tarete (tarede, taride),* and one warship, the *nave lunghe. Marciliane* traded foodstuffs. The larger *magne marciliane* reached up to 120 tons in size. Both the *pandora* and the *tarete* were used as military transports and carried two masts to supplement rowing. The *tarete,* approximately 180 tons, a cross between a long ship and a round ship, was a small ship well adapted for coastal trade (Unger, 1980: 125), although somewhat difficult to defend due to its low sides. The *navi lunghe* "long ships" were primarily rowed warships that could have one mast for auxiliary sail power.

The eighth-century Venetian texts show a slightly greater diversity of uses, although vessels were still relatively small and shallow-drafted riverine craft. An example of the *sandòn,* a flat-bottomed vessel used as a floating watermill on the Po and Adige Rivers, was excavated at Pontelagoscuro (fig. 137). Another type of river craft was the *scafa,* a small cargo boat that was towed behind a larger vessel. The *cymba (cumbus)* was a medium-sized sailing boat, while the *carabus*[14] was a larger type of round ship suitable for coastal as well as riverine trade. The generic term *navis (naves, nave),* along with many etymologically related permutations, often meant simply anything that was navigated. Salt traders from Comacchi are described as *naves* in the *Capitolare of Liutprando* (715); they had the monopoly of river commerce on the Po and carried the equivalent of 8.3 tons of salt. These boats must have been relatively small riverine sailboats (approximately 21.5 tons) with flat bottoms, similar to the later *burchi.* The *bucintoro* of eighth- to fourteenth-century texts refers to a strong war galley and not to the ceremonial barge of Renaissance Venice.

In the ninth century, Venice began trading in the Levant, and a formalized military fleet was formed. Texts of this century primarily specify warship types, reflecting growing concern in Venice for military protection against pirates and competitors. Their transports include the *nave oneraria, usiache (usie),* and *ippagoghi (ippegi, hippagmi).* The very spacious *nave oneraria* carried foodstuffs, ammunition, and luggage while in convoy with war expeditions, but it would also serve as a merchant ship. *Ippagoghi* and *usiache* were beamy and high-sided horse transports. One source describes that a door for the horses was set at waterlevel at the stern and caulked after loading. *Ippagoghi* are recorded as being 29.9 meters long, with a beam of 13 meters. Oared warships, of numerous variations and capacities, were called by many names: the *panfile, galee, navi belliche, navi castellate, pistro, nave grossa, nave turrita (tarida), trierio, dromado, dromone, dromone proprio, dromone nave, dromone nave lunga* (Bonino, 1978a: figure 8B) and the *chelandia.* The *dromone* (dromon in English), a bireme long ship, was rowed from two levels. Rowing supplemented one to three lateen sails; the panfile was a smaller version of the *dromone.* The *galee* were fast and long warships, while the *navi castellate* were well fortified with castles at bow and stern. A heavy fighting vessel mentioned specifically as guarding the lagoons of Venice from the Saracens was the *chelandia (chilandre, chilandrie).* Like *nave,* this term has many variations, including *galandrie (ghelandre, galandre, gagiandre), zelandie (zenlandrie), palandarie (palandrie, palandarie), salandre (salandrie), celandrie (celindrie), chelijs, chelandie panfile, chelandie usiache (chelandie usie),* and *chelandie galee.* Some of these names give a definite clarification: the *usiache* indicates that the ship was used as a horse transport, while *galea* meant that the vessel was rowed; but clearly the name *chelandia* is one with many meanings. The basic *chelandia* type probably had a second deck or some sort of protective structure (Lane, 1973: 27–29), and the range of subtypes included transports, oared galleys, and—very likely—commercial ships as well.

A few new ship names recorded in tenth-century documents are likewise primarily warships and transports. Those mentioned include the *usserii (uscieri, uschere)* and the *arsilii,* horse transports, and the *cumbarie (gumbare, gambarie),* one-masted, oared, and used for war or riverine and coastal trade. *Arsilii* were sometimes used for trade as well. In this period, the term *chelandia* sometimes referred to a flat-bottomed military river boat like the one seen in figure 113, but it also was still used to designate a larger, sailed transport ship.

Although Venice was certainly a seagoing nation by the year 1000 (Lane, 1973: 1), eleventh-century texts still specify more lagoonal and river craft than seagoing ships: the *battàna* was a lagoonal vessel, the *burchio, burchièlla (burchela),* and *battèllo* types (Bonino, 1978a: figs. 24A and B) were used in river and lagoonal trade. What is believed to be an eleventh-century example of the *burchio* has been excavated at Pomposa (fig. 136). Two types of bows characterized these river and lagoonal craft: the bow of the *burchio* river boat, like that of the *burchièlla,* the riverine warship *chelandia* (fig. 113), and the modern *rascòna* (fig. 152), with a flush bow rising from a flat bottom (Bonino, 1978a: figs. 20B–D and fig. 25), while bows of double-ended vessels, including

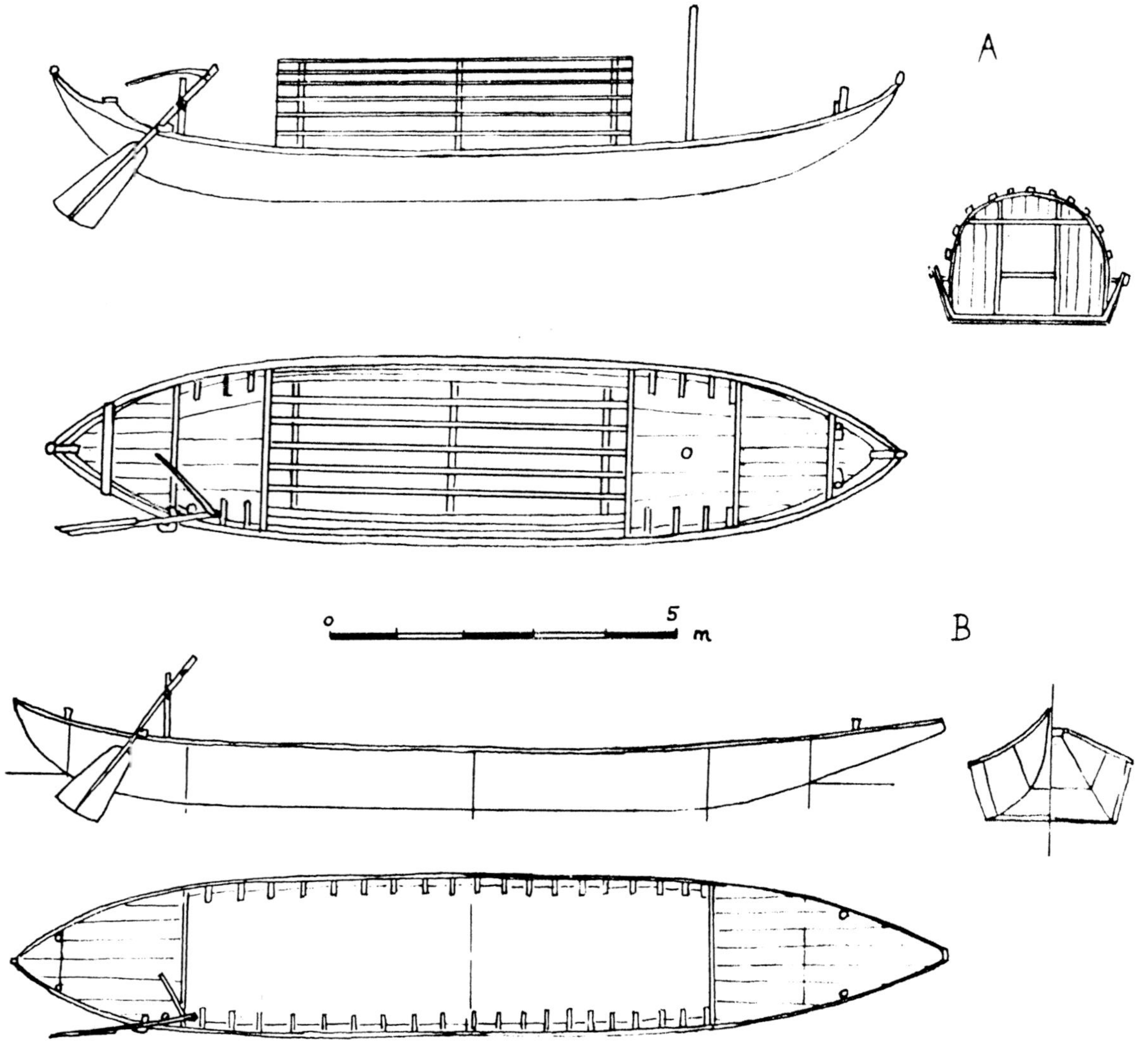

FIG. 152. The flat-bottomed *rascòna* type, a derivation of the ancient *burchio* type. (A) Eighteenth-century example; (B) twentieth-century example. *Courtesy M. Bonino, 1978a: fig. 26*

the *battèllo* and *battàna*, were pointed (Bonino, 1978a: 24C). The *galea lunga*, a fast bireme warship, and the *saica,* a transport, are first mentioned in documents of this century.

Written documents of the twelfth century report only three new vessel types: the *seole* boat, which served for inland navigation, and the *paroneno* and the *brulotto,* as seagoing war vessels. The *brulotti* warships were used in expeditions to the Holy Land and were regularly armed with *sifoni,* with which Venetian and Byzantine mariners launched the devastating "Greek fire." This was a secret chemical substance that, once ignited, would not easily extinguish, even with water. In the twelfth century, several very large *nave* round ships were built, whose "personal" names were recorded: the *Mondo,* the *Auila,* the *Paradiso,* and the *Pelligrina.*

Not only do the writings of the thirteenth century make more distinctions in ships than ever before, they also give more details. *Battelli* were ships' boats of 30 *piede* (10.4 meters), and *gondola,* 24 *piede* (8.35 meters). Another ship's boat strong enough for use at sea was the small *schifo.* The *piatta (piatto, plato), piatterella,* and *piatta alla mantovana,* flat bottomed and very stable, were used for heavy loads, both in lighterage and lagoonal to inland trade. *Sandali* and *plactae* were river barges, hauled by another vessel.

Medieval writings up to this time had been using the term *nave* very generally to mean any floating vessel. Finally in the thirteenth century, the term gains clarification. The *nave latine* indicated a relatively large lateen-rigged ship used primarily as a merchant ship but also as a war transport. Minimum proportions for a small *nave* are specified in the maritime code of January 7, 1229 (Predelli and Sacerdoti, 1903: 51). The keel length had to be 56 *piede* (19.5 meters). The *"lanzar in delfinis,"* the *slanzo* was to be 34 *piede* (11.83 meters), making an overall length of 90 *piede* (31.3 meters). The *lanzo* or *slanci,* called rake in English, is the difference between the maximum length of the vessel and the length of the keel (Bonino, 1978: 71). It can also be defined as the horizontal distance from where the stem and stern posts start to rise to a vertical dropped from the top of that post (Chiggiato, personal communication). The *boca*, or beam, measured at the maximum curvature amidships, had to be 24 *piede* (8.35 meters); the height at midships, 9 *piede* (3.13 meters). The patron could decide the width *in fundo,* the hull width of the bottom's flat part. Minimum proportions of a later, similar-sized *nave latine* are given in the fifteenth-century material of *Fabrica di galere,* as follows: In a one-decked ship with a *colomba,* or keel, of 12 *passe* or 60 piede (20.86 meters), the *boca* was 24 *piede* (8.4 meters); the *trepie* (molded beam, or hull width not including the outer planking), measured at 3 piede above the keel, was 16 *piede* (5.6 meters); and the width of the floor, 9 *piede* (3.13 meters). The height up to the deck at midships was 9.5 *piede* (3.3 meters). The overall length of the ship, when including the *slanzo* (rake) at bow and stern, was 16 *passe* or 27.8 meters (Bonino, 1978b: 10). *Boca, colomba,* and *lanzo* are Venetian dialect.

The thirteenth-century terms *banzonus, buzo nave, buzus,* and *buzusnavis* are found without distinction in the early statutes and are etymologically related to the word *nave.* All refer to the same basic ship used as either a merchant ship or transport and seem to indicate slight variations based on size or function. A *nave buzzi (buzusnavis),* for example, was larger and stronger than the *buzo.* Another dual-purpose ship of the thirteenth century is the *tarrete,* and for the first time in Zeno's code of 1250, the various *naves* are differentiated from the *tarrete*; the statutes specify different regulations for the *tarrete.* Apparently the ta*rrete w*as a smaller, more slender type of lateen-rigged round ship (100–400 tons), sometimes oared, with probably only one deck and mast, while *naves* were two-masted, beamy lateeners with high sides, at least two decks, a sterncastle, a forecastle and a fighting top (Lane, 1973: 46), ranging in size from 200 to 600 tons.

Warships recorded are the *salandria, nave quadre, nave usseria,* and *navi veliere,* the oared *galea,* the *galere grosse,* and enlarged *dromoni.* The *nave usseria* was a horse transport; the *salandria, nave quadre,* and *navi veliere* were transports, although *navi veliere* were used by merchants as well. Louis IX of France commissioned crusader ships to be built in Venice in 1268; the strongly fortified *Roccaforte* was a Venetian-built *nave* quadre, which held a square sail on the mainmast and a lateen on the mizzen. *Salandria* is etymologically related to the Byzantine term for an oared warship, *chelandion,* but the Venetian *salandria* relied solely on sail power—it had no oars. It was used for crusader and horse transport, but there are no specifications in contracts for the provision of special stern ports or oars on *salandria*; they could not, then, have been useful in assault landings (Pryor, 1984, no. 2: 200; no. 4: 377 and fig. 15). *Galere grosse,* large galleys measuring about 115 meters with approximately an 8:1 length-to-beam ratio, employed both oars and sails, with a shelter along its middle for the soldiers, and was used mostly for war, though at times for commerce. In the thirteenth century, an enlarged bireme *dromone* long ship was characterized by two banks of oarsmen seated within the hull, two lateen-rigged masts, fighting castles at bow and stern, a *sperone (spiron)* projecting from deck level at the bow), and *ali* projecting upward and inboard at the stern. The next evolutionary stage raised both decks: oarsmen on the lower level pulled oars that pivoted on the sheer, and an upper level of oarsmen pulled against an outrigger (illustrated by an early southern Italian example, fig. 153).

Approximately at the turn of the fourteenth century, a lower and more seaworthy hull was developed by placing the oarsmen all on the same level within the hull on diagonally set benches. The men sat, two to three on a bench, in an arrangement called *a zenzile* or *a terzaurolo* (e.g., figs. 27 and 58). Because their oars pivoted on an outrigger, the oars had to be lengthened. Naval historians have differing opinions concerning the rowing system of Venetian triremes and argue over the number of men per bench. According to Rubin de Cervin, Fincati spoke the final word on the matter when he pointed out that Venetian documents from the thirteenth through mid-sixteenth centuries always specify *"galee da tre remi e tre homini per banco."* These triremes, then, were rowed with three men to a bench, each man with his own oar (Rubin de Cervin, 1985: 31–32). The resulting system clustered the oars in groups of two (biremes) or three (triremes) and made rowing from a completely seated position impossible (Casson, 1964b: 72). The design offered a lower center of gravity without decreasing power, and the lengthened oars provided greater leverage. This meant that these vessels were actually faster given the same man power. The lower hull, with fewer decks, proved to be less top-heavy, and therefore more seaworthy as well.

Documents of the fourteenth century specify an even greater number of distinct vessels, including some specialized lagoonal craft and buoys. The *gagiandra (gajandra),* a stationary buoy supporting a chain, protected the port of Venice in 1355 during war with Genoa. Flat, robust buoys called *pontoni* floated the equipment used to remove mud accumulated on the bottoms of canals, and were indispensable to maintain navigable depths in the lagoon. The shallowness of the Venetian lagoon may have limited the size of Venetian ships, but it also provided a unique protection. The largest Venetian ships could only be floated into port with *cammelli* (camels), flat-bottomed rafts that tied to a ship's port and starboard in order to lift its hull and thus reduce its draft; no large enemy ships could reach the city without these *cammelli.*

Other fourteenth-century lagoonal vessels are the *gripparia, ganzaruolo, galaldelo, perischermo, piattoni (peatoni, plates), scafa (scafo, scafe, scafi),* and *tartanelle peschereccie.* The *ganzaruolo, galaldelo,* and *perischermo* were racing craft sometimes used as ships' boats for large warships. The *piattoni* were ceremonial lagoonal boats; the *scafa* were armed vessels that patrolled the lagoons. *Tartanelle peschereccie* were two-masted fishing boats.

Coastal and river craft include the *marano,* built to transport stones for the breakwater at the Lidi; and the *burchi,* flat-bottomed cargo boats of roughly 13 tons that carried salt, oil, and wine cargoes up the rivers (Bonino, 1978a: 69 and fig. 20C). *Burchi* had an open deck, with small half decks at bow and stern, and a small sail. A smaller version of the burchi were the *burchiele (burchièlle);* these had four oars and one lateen-rigged mast. The average *marsiliana,* or *barca marsiliana,* a small type of *navi latine* first mentioned in the fourteenth century, carried food supplies upriver. It was about 10 meters long and 1.9 meters in beam. The Logonovo boat (ca. 1400) may be an example of this type (fig. 145).

Among fourteenth-century oared warships and transports are the huge *galera cetea;* the fast *galeotte,* which had one mast supplementing between sixteen and thirty oars of manpower; the *nave uselleria (nave uscheria),* a horse transport;

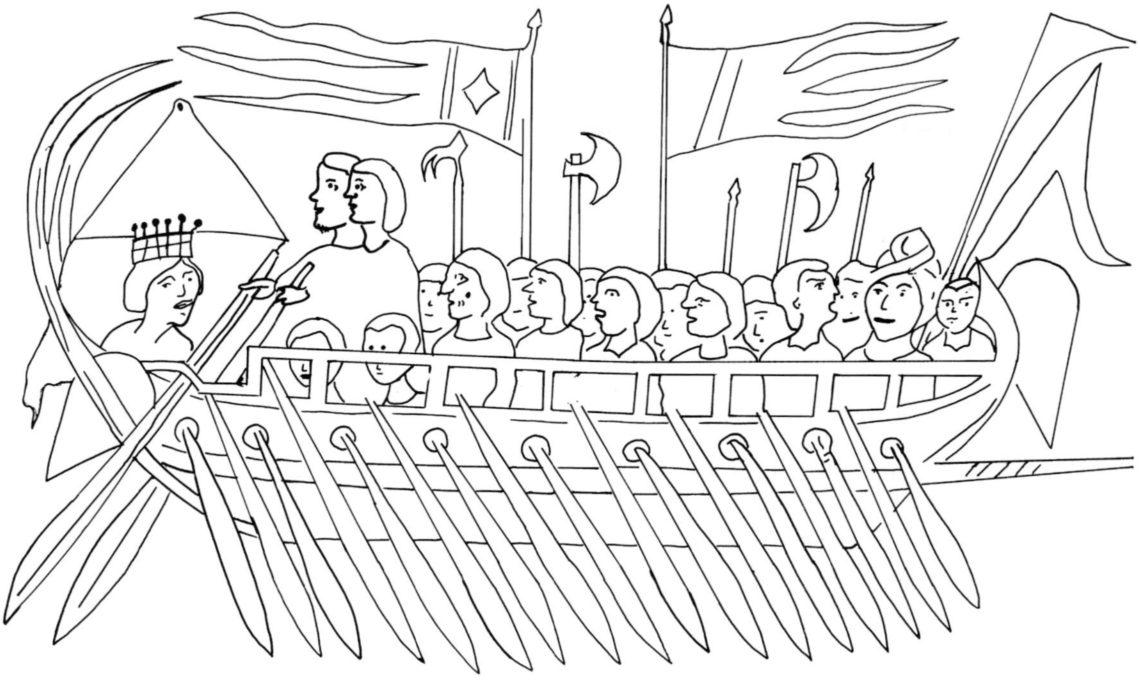

FIG. 153. A dromon or bireme galley under oars, from the south Italian twelfth-century manuscript, *Liber ad Honorem Augusti* by Pietro di Eboli. *After Bragadin, 1974: 28*

and the *lembo (libo),* a shallow-drafted, flat-bottomed, large transport used in shallow coastal regions.

Before 1318, there is "no clear evidence . . . of a differentiation between galleys designed for trade and those designed for war or patrol" (Lane, 1963: 202, note 110). Between the 1290s and 1320, however, Venetian long ship galleys were enlarged, and the trireme gradually replaced the bireme arrangement. The resulting merchant galleys were increasingly used for commercial luxury cargoes, and by the 1330s, several types were distinguished, one for patrol use and others for trade. One light galley type was built to patrol the gulf, and there were also galleys especially designed and dimensioned for voyages to Flanders, Romania, Trebizond, or Alexandria (Lane, 1973: 122; 1963: 202 and note 110). Several ship types used for both cargo and warfare were the oared *galere da mercanzia, galeazza da mercanzia, galea grossa (galere grosse),* and the sailed transports—the *navi marani, parentarie (parendarie), tartane, grosse tartane, navi rotonde,* and the *cocche (cocha).* The *galeazza da mercanzia* was a large seagoing trireme with two to three vertical masts. A *tartane* normally had two lateen-rigged masts, but some *tartane grosse (tartana da guerra)* had three.

Venetian texts first mention the *cocha* (also called *navi rotonde*) in 1315 (Lane, 1973: 123), although the type was seen in the Mediterranean as early as the end of the twelfth century (Pryor, 1992: 39). By the second half of the fourteenth century, *cocha* became the common term for a large round ship, having replaced the *buzo navis* lateener in importance. The *cocha,* called cog in English, was a relatively flat-bottomed and high-sided round ship rigged with a single square sail, steered with a single rudder attached at the stern. It ranged in size from 120–720 tons. A type with the same English name originated in the tidal areas of the North Sea, where it was clinker built, flat bottomed, with a straight stem. Some say this northern cog was introduced in the Mediterranean around 1300, and soon "cogs" with stern rudders and square sails were being built in the Mediterranean but adapted to the Mediterranean frame-first tradition (Scandurra, 1972:

187 and 214; Bonino, 1978a: fig. 17). According to Bellabarba, true cogs were, in fact, never constructed in the Mediterranean. What Venetians called *cocha*, then, were simply large round ships built in the traditional Mediterranean way, but with a central stern rudder and a single square sail (1988: 236).

The medieval lateen-rigged ship with side rudders endured in Venice longer than in other areas of the Mediterranean, and the number of *coche* built by Venetians was actually rather negligible. The influence of the northern cog in the Mediterranean did, however, have significant repercussions on the history of seafaring. A ship with stern rudder and square sail was far easier to handle than lateen-rigged ships with two quarter rudders, and a square-rigged ship therefore required a smaller crew. A ship rigged with the lateen sail was well adapted for coastal sailing under diverse wind directions, but one with a square sail was better suited for traveling with a following wind. A good compromise was reached with the mixed-rigged type, by rigging a large square mainsail, a smaller lateen-rigged sail aft, and a small foremast at the bow. The most notable significance of the cog in the Mediterranean is that it influenced the development of mixed-rigged ships with a stern rudder, and eventually, ships capable of ocean navigation (Bonino, 1978a: 74 and 94).

Fifteenth-century texts refer to *edifizi per cavare il fango de'canali,* designed to remove the mud from the canals of Venice. Other lagoonal vessels recorded are the *copano* and the *burchioni.* The *copano*, nicknamed *per far acqua,* meaning "to supply the drinking water," was similar to the *schifo* lighter of the thirteenth century. The *burchioni* were riverine and lagoonal traders but larger than the *burchi* of the fourteenth century. Riverine warships included the *barbotte, fusta, radeguarda, ganzara,* and *barche lunghe.* Lighters or ships' boats included the *batel, gondola,* and *lauto* (Bellabarba, 1988: 117).

Fifteenth-century warships specified are the long ships *galera mezzana,* the *barzotto,* the similar *barche falcate, bombarda, bregantini (brigantini), fregata, saettia (saittia, sagitta, sagetia, saggottaria), galea sottile, galea leggera,* and the *trireme veneziana minore.* Transports included the *schierazzo (schirazzo)* and the *caravelle* (one specified at 300 *botti,* or 180 tons), which was also used for cargo. Another cargo and transport ship was the *grippi,* which had only one mast and a capacity of 1200 *staja* (87 tons).

Besides the *grippi* and *caravelle,* fifteenth-century round ships were the *berlingher* (with one example of 250 *botti,* or 150 tons mentioned in 1499), and the very common *caracca* (carrack). The carrack, larger than the *cocha,* had at least three masts rigged lateen or mixed, pronounced castles at bow and stern, and tumble home in the side of the hull, which lowered the center of gravity of the huge ship, making it more stable. A foremast for a square sail was placed on the forecastle, which was higher than the sterncastle. *Galea* and *galera mezzana* were oared and sailed ships used commercially.

This completes the overview of vessels named in textual sources through the fifteenth century. In summary, this textual information would lead one to believe certain generalizations. Figure 154 reflects the variety of types mentioned in textual sources, but in no way does it define the frequency of any type, nor the actual number of ships in use. The graph is of value in indicating the range of new Venetian ship and boat types, as revealed by textual evidence, as compared to the numbers illustrated by art (fig. 155).

During the earliest phases of Venetian seafaring, when Venetian merchants were primarily occupied in river trade (fifth–sixth centuries), the majority of the vessels mentioned were lagoonal and river craft, as would be expected. Most types recorded by the ninth and tenth centuries were warships; reflecting a growing concern for protection, necessary to ward off the feuding lords along inland rivers, and the Saracens along the coasts of the Adriatic (Lane, 1973: 6). This

TRENDS BASED ON TEXTUAL EVIDENCE FOR SMALL CRAFT, WARSHIPS AND MERCHANT SHIPS

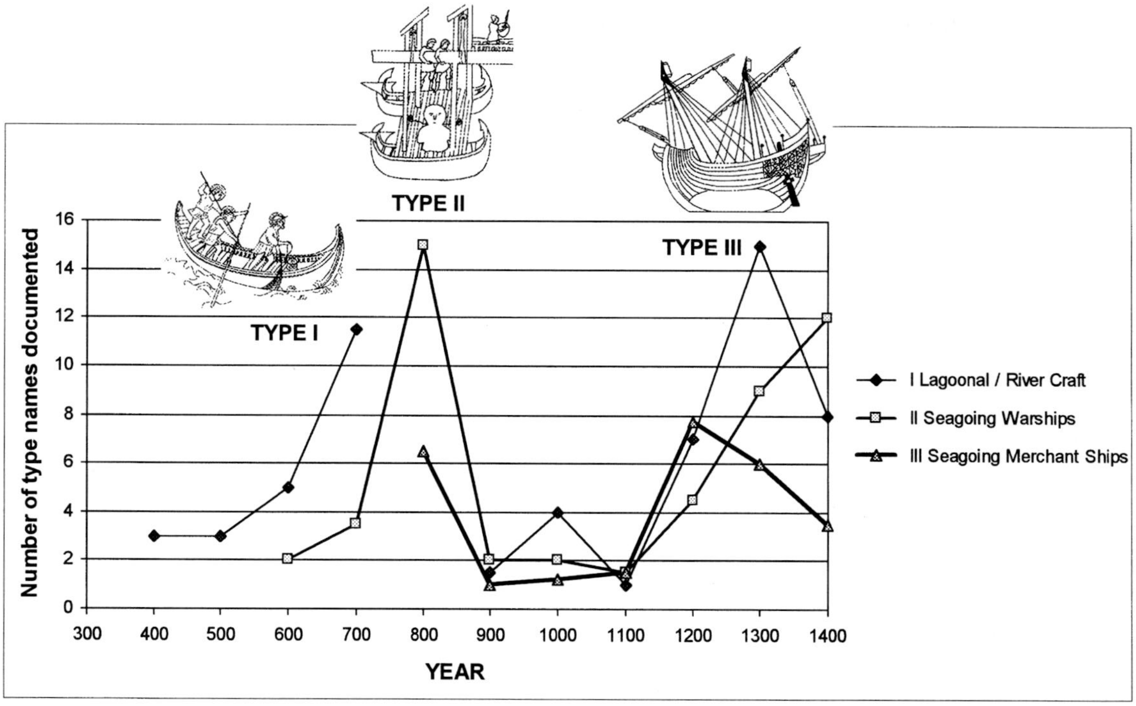

FIG. 154. Trends in Venetian vessel types referenced in textual evidence of each century

TRENDS BASED ON REPRESENTATIONAL EVIDENCE FOR SMALL CRAFT, WARSHIPS AND MERCHANT SHIPS

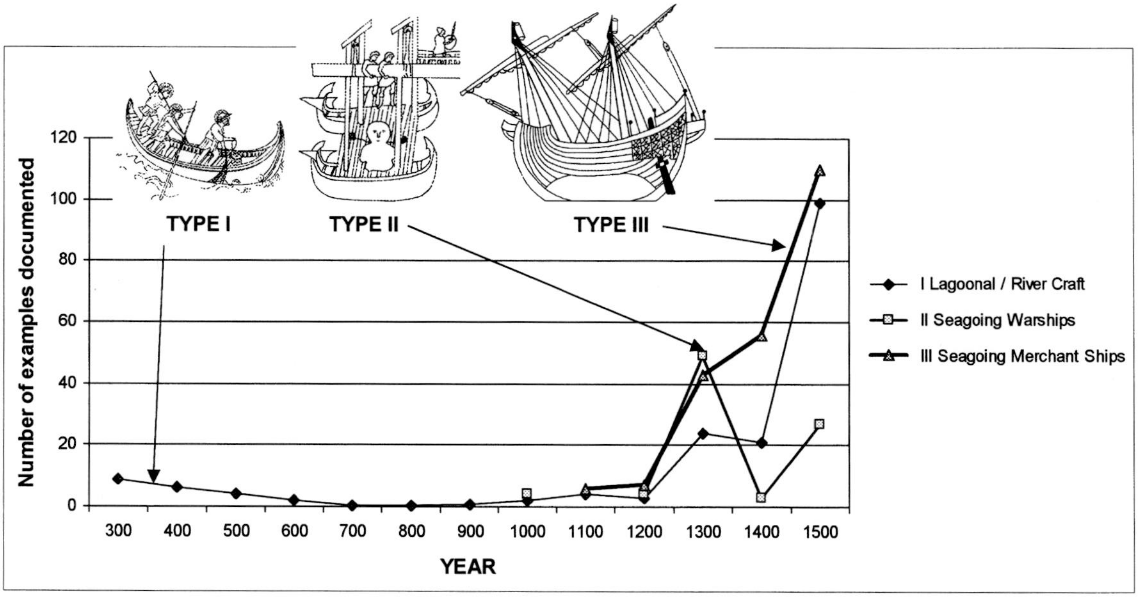

FIG. 155. Trends in Venetian vessel types as indicated by the representational evidence

resulted in the formalizing of a Venetian military fleet. Piracy was subdued in the eleventh century, but by the end of the twelfth century, piracy had again become a serious threat to Venetian seamen, who were now regularly navigating Mediterranean waters for overseas trade in seagoing round ships (Lane, 1973: 35). The importance of the Fourth Crusade to Venice is reflected by the jump in named warships in thirteenth-century texts (fig. 154), which continued to rise with the subsequent conflicts with Genoa. By the fourteenth century, a far greater diversity of all the types were distinguished in the texts—river and lagoonal craft, and larger ships. Most large ships were warships or dual-purpose merchant/warships, with a smaller increase in strictly merchant ship types. This reflects the interrelationship between trade and war.

It is helpful to look at these trends, but one must consider how accurately the distinctions given in the documentary evidence reflect the wide range of watercraft types actually in use at any one time. Shortcomings are inherent to the documentary sources, because the texts utilized numerous synonyms for various ship types, making it difficult to distinguish between similar types and equivalent types. A second problem is that the descriptions given are usually generalized, and thus lack the desired clarity necessary for interpretation (e.g., the generic term nave). Finally, government records comprise a major part of the textual evidence; these focus on the planning and recording of military exploits. Naturally, such sources, biased as they are toward naval affairs, mention a preponderance of warship types and merchant ship types suited for adaptation to military use. They mention other types of watercraft infrequently, if at all.

Fortunately, analysis of the artistic record allows the further development of a functional typology, expanding the picture of medieval Venetian vessels. Watercraft in the catalog are divided into three types, with subtypes defined by relative size, number of masts, or use for a specific task.

Representational Evidence for a Functional Venetian Ship and Boat Typology

To identify conclusively an unlabeled ship representation with a historical name is unfeasible, yet identifying a type based on its use is possible. This survey evaluated a sample of more than five hundred ship and boat images dating to the end of the fifteenth century. Nearly half of these are Venetian images dating before the middle of the fifteenth century. Several viable approaches to create a typology are possible, though in any typology some overlap and exceptions will occur. One approach could be to set criteria on form or ship construction distinctions, resulting in groups of small craft, long ships, and round ships. The variety of shapes found among the small craft alone illustrates the complexity of this approach. It would place a war transport among the round ship merchantmen, and the merchant galley (which occurs late in this sample), among long ships, traditionally used for war. Trying to combine this approach with textual and representational evidence is difficult, because early written descriptions rarely indicate a ship's shape, but they usually identify its function and name. Representational images can be deceiving in regard to the vessels' form, particularly in the most common side views. Because the art often illustrates identifiable stories, it is usually quite easy to interpret the vessels' intended functional type.

The typology used here more meaningfully reflects how vessels were used. Vessels are classified as small craft, lagoonal, or river boats (Type I), seagoing warships (Type II), and seagoing merchant ships, generally called round ships (Type III). Subtypes of the smaller vessels include lighters (Type Ia), fishing boats and lagoonal craft (Type Ib), and river boats, either riverine war craft (Type Ic), or riverine cargo boats (Type Id). Subtypes in the seagoing warship category include long ships, oared galleys designed primarily for war (Type IIa), and war transports, which can resemble round ships (Type IIb).

The merchant ship (Type III) category is further subdivided by rig type and relative size as indicated by the number of masts. In the fourteenth and fifteenth centuries, texts provide evidence for new capacious ships—round-hulled *coche* and carracks and long ships used as merchant galleys. Because very few images are ever labeled with ship names, and these were ships of trade, they are categorized as Type III. Subtypes for merchant ships include single-masted lateeners (Type IIIa), two-masted lateeners (Type IIIb), three-masted lateeners (Type IIIc), single-masted square rigs (Type IIId), two-masted mixed rigs (Type IIIe) and three-masted mixed rigs (Type IIIf).

In a few cases, a vessel could be interpreted as either of two types, and it must be remembered that ships and boats were in fact multipurpose. Merchant galleys, transports, and round ships were used both for war transport and trade as required. This typology, especially when combined with results of textual analysis (fig. 154), provides a good overview of trends and a general reflection of medieval Venetian vessel types. Figure 155 illustrates the frequency of the three basic vessel types in this catalog. Figures 156–58 plot subtype distribution.[15]

Type I: Flat-bottomed lagoonal and river boats (fig. 156)

Lagoonal and river craft were relatively small, flat-bottomed vessels, usually undecked, although some had a small deck at one or both ends. These boats were small enough to be maneuvered easily by hand-held steering paddles or oars, though oarlocks or thole pins could be installed to offer a fulcrum point. Lagoonal and river craft constitute a large part of the catalog, with representations dating as early as the fourth century. Archaeological examples of boats have been excavated at Cervia (fig. 135), Pomposa (fig. 136), Pontelagoscuro (fig. 137), Ravenna (fig. 144), and Logonovo (fig. 145).

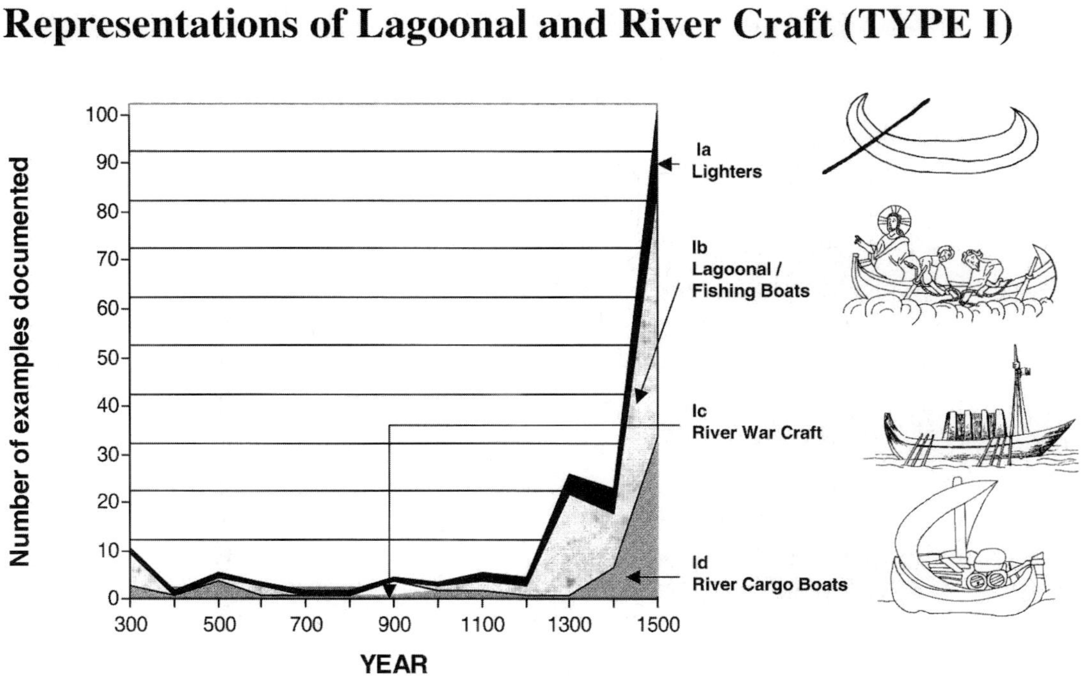

FIG. 156. Type I. Small craft, lagoonal or river boat types, trends in the representational evidence. Type Ia—lighters; Ib—lagoonal craft and fishing boats; Ic—riverine or coastal war craft; Id—riverine cargo vessels

Most lagoonal craft were suitable for many daily tasks and were multifunctional as they are in Venice today. Any smaller craft would have been useful for lighterage and fishing as well as to ferry people along the canals of Venice. Larger lagoonal craft used for cargo shipment had a small sail. These vessels would have encountered at least some river navigation, traveling partway upriver until different navigational conditions, such as large marshes, rivers, or alpine lakes, prompted transference of cargo to another ship type. Conversely, riverine vessels could work the lagoonal coastal environs around Venice. River craft could be larger vessels than lagoonal craft.

The lagoonal and river craft are subdivided as follows: (Type Ia) lighters, (Type Ib) lagoonal craft and fishing boats, (Type Ic) rivergoing war craft, and (Type Id) rivergoing cargo boats.

Type Ia: Undecked lighters (e.g., figs. 10, 49, 61, 87, and 108, for a total of twenty-four Venetian examples)

Art depicting stories such as the embarkation of the relics of a saint (figs. 10 and 87) or other portrayals of loading scenes (figs. 49, 87, and 108) clearly are illustrating small service boats or lighters. The examples represented resemble each other in the shape of their bows and sterns; all are small, open, undecked boats.

Type Ib: Lagoonal craft and undecked fishing boats (e.g., figs. 2–5, 16, 17, 24, 36, 46, 72, 74, 75, 79, 80, 83, 88, 102, 103, 106, 107, 112, 116, 119, 120, and 127, for a total of ninety-eight Venetian examples)

Like the gondolas of today, boats of this type were used primarily for transport within the lagoons. However, they also could have been used as lighters or for fishing. Figure 119, a boat viewed slightly from above, displays the inner hull construction of that boat and reveals one strengthening thwart at about midships. The vessel in figure 24 is slightly larger than other examples. Figure 107 has a half deck at bow and stern.

Venetian lagoonal craft utilize a uniquely shaped oarlock, called forcole in Venetian. This feature is visible in figures 24, 46, 74, 80, 102, 103, 106, 107, 119, and 120, dating from the thirteenth through fifteenth centuries. A *forcole* is carved out of a single block of walnut (Rubin de Cervin, 1985: 106) and is still used on gondolas of the lagoon. The placement of the oarlock is not consistent in the actual boats nor in the images of them.

As the themes of the following relate to fishing, the boats depicted are intended to represent fishing boats: "The Miraculous Draught of Fishes" (figs. 16, 107, and 112), "The Calming of the Storm" (fig. 17), "Peter Walking on the Water" (figs. 5 and 102), "The Calling of the Apostles" (figs. 75, 83, 103, 119, and 120), or fishermen (figs. 2–4, 36, 79, and 116).

These fishing vessels show vast diversity. The earliest examples, which date to the sixth century, are two types of Roman fishing craft (figs. 2–4). The smaller vessel in figure 2 has a flat bow and inward-curving stern, features characteristic of the *horeia* type (Casson, 1971: fig. 137, no. 20). The other two (figs. 3 and 4) illustrate another distinct type: the stem ends in the typically Roman swan's head (cf. Throckmorton, 1972: fig. 2). A banana-like hull shape is seen in the very stylized figure 112. Another more realistic fishing boat type (figs. 16 and 17) is characterized by a flush or flat end. The number of oars employed varied depending upon the size of the vessel and the needs of the particular journey.

The next group of small fishing craft is exemplified by figures 5, 32, 36, 103, 116, 119, and 120. Dating through seven centuries—the sixth through the fifteenth—these representations attest to the continuation of a simple, small, undecked, multipurpose type craft. The only visible difference between the Byzantine and early medieval boat type is that the Byzantine figure 5 has three through-beams at the sheer strake; such strengthening of the later boats, if it existed, was not indicated. Otherwise, these vessels are nearly identical and reflect the known characteristics of the sixth-century *scrilla*, which could be fitted with a lateen sail when needed, and the thirteenth-century lagoonal *battèlla* or *gondola*.

The final variation of the fishing vessel category is exemplified by the boats of figures 79 and 107. Characterized by an afterdeck (fig. 79) or a deck at either end (fig. 107), these are among the larger fishing craft in the catalog and were propelled by rowing, punting, or a small lateen-rigged sail positioned far forward toward the bow (fig. 79, foreground).

Type Ic: Riverine war craft (fig. 113; the sole example)

Figure 113 shows a tenth-century example of a river and lagoonal war craft. Either a watch tower or a single mast is set far forward and a cabin or tented area amidships. The three oars shown aft on the starboard side, with four more set amidships, must have made this craft quite maneuverable in lagoonal and river navigation. The legend under the craft labels it as a *chelandia*, an oared warship used to patrol the lagoons. In many respects, and especially the profile of the bow, this *chelandia* resembles the *burchio*, a flat-bottomed lagoonal and river cargo vessel frequently depicted in later Venetian art (e.g., an early fifteenth-century fresco, fig. 84). The eleventh-century boat discovered at Pomposa (fig. 136), is believed to be of the *burchio* type because the profile of the bow: the flat bottom curves smoothly up into a flat bow.

Type Id: Riverine cargo boats (e.g., figs. 8, 35, 58, 84, 88, 109, 114, and 121, for a total of forty-six Venetian examples)

The three vessels in figure 8, from a sixth-century mosaic depicting the Port of Classis represent a type of medium-sized cargo transport, perhaps the *rascòna* type, which accomplished river trade on the Po. These vessels have a single mast amidships. The one unfurled sail is difficult to interpret, but the overall shape is square. The craft in figures 35, 84, 109, and 121, all with a single lateen-rigged mast, are probably also medium-sized river craft, which one would expect to have a relatively flat bottom.

Evidence for a type of river craft not represented in this sample has been discovered at Pontelagoscuro (fig. 137). This boat with a flat bottom and sharp rise of the stem, used as a floating watermill, was of the *sandòn* type.

Type II: Warship types: galleys or transports (fig. 157)

The most basic functional distinction to make between the remainder of the vessel types is that of the seagoing warship (Type II) and the seagoing merchantman (Type III). Although their shapes differed, their functions at times merged: all ships were used as warships when the need arose, and some rowed galleys were employed to carry precious merchandise when speed and security were desired.

Medieval warships can be divided into two functional subtypes: oared galleys (Type IIa), long ships propelled primarily by oar; and war transports (Type IIb), which used mainly sail power or were towed into position by oared galleys (Marzials, 1965: 37). Transports were similar in hull shape to the beamy round ship, while—except for the bow—the medieval war galley resembled classical period galleys with a length-to-beam ratio of about 8:1. The bow of the medieval warship galley had a projection or beak that the Venetians called *sperone* or *spiron*. One purpose of this projection on a sailed galley was to haul the foresail even farther forward, thereby improving the vessel's sailing qualities by making the ship more weatherly (Rubin de Cervin, 1985: 30). The projection also served as a boarding platform, essential because boarding had become the primary offensive tactic.

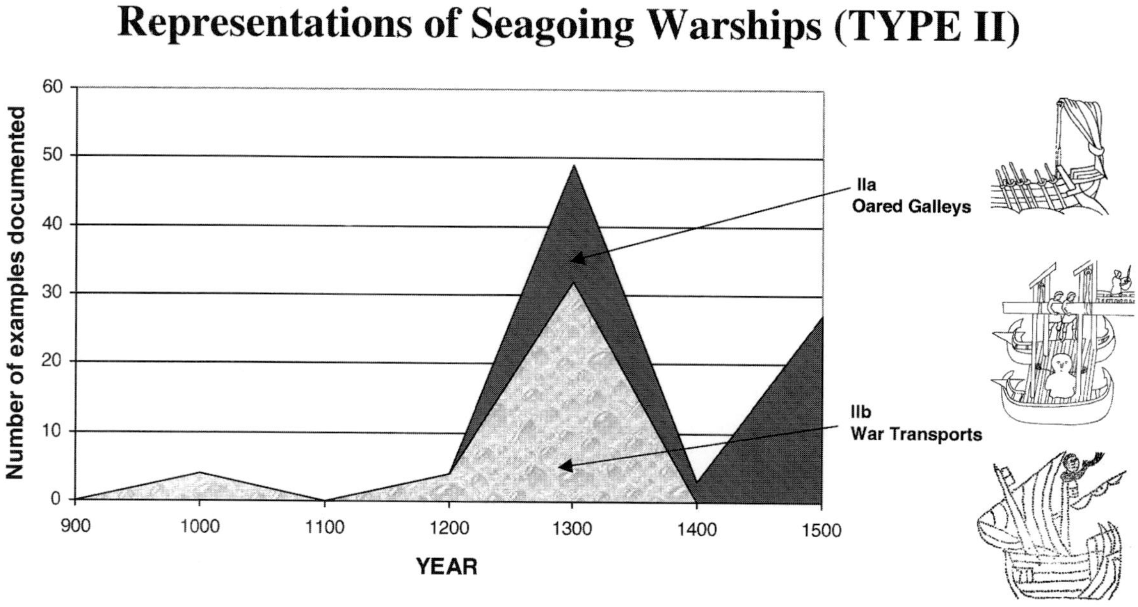

FIG. 157. Type II. Seagoing warship types, trends in the representational evidence. Type IIa—oared galleys; IIb—war transports

Type IIa: Oared galleys (figs. 27, 38, 39, 47, 57, 58, 88, 125, and 126, for a total of forty-seven Venetian examples)

Half of the warships in this catalog are oared galleys dating as early as the eleventh century. The textual evidence shows that there were numerous named warship types throughout the centuries of this survey. Considering the political situation of Venice and her frequent need to engage in naval battles, it may seem surprising that not more maritime images are warships, but mercantile themes were very popular. It must also be emphasized that Venetians employed their high-sided merchant ships as warships, and most of the vessels categorized as Type III could have been converted for martial use.

The earliest examples of long ships are quite stylized. The Byzantine figure 34 portrays two double-ended, small, oared vessels with rounded hulls, propelled with eight and ten oars per side arranged in one level. Probably the best early Italian galley illustration was made in southern Italy by Pietro di Eboli (from Eboli, near Salerno) in 1195. Figure 153 (his illumination in *Liber ad Honorem Augusti;* Stadtbibliothek, Berne, Cod. Berne 120, fol. 119) depicts the Empress Constance traveling from Salerno to Messina, Sicily, on a typical twelfth-century bireme galley or dromon. Here is illustrated the first of a two-step development in warship design involving the utilization of an outrigger; warship design evolved again toward the end of the following century. In figure 153, the oars are arranged in two levels. The lower nine oars pass through ports just above the main wale of the galley, and another eight rest above on what may be an outrigger that runs the full length of the ship. The hull bottom appears completely flat. A main wale and the sheer strake run parallel to it. The main wale continues horizontally, projecting from the bow, forming the boarding bridge. The stem rises in a straight line from the keel at about forty-five degrees, then curves inboard, flaring to finish like the stem seen in figures 13 and 31. At the turn of the fourteenth century, the a zenzile or a terzaurolo arrangement had developed (illustrated by figs. 27 and 58, respectively). The oarsmen, all sitting at one level on the same bench far inboard in a lower hull, worked their oars in pairs, *a zenzile*, or in groups of threes, *a terzaruolo*. All oars pivoted on the outrigger.

Figure 27 (ca. 1351) shows a small oared galley, oars arranged a *zenzile*. Figure 47 (early fourteenth century) shows a similar-sized galley during battle; its *sperone* at the main wale level projects at the bow. As the fighting occurs on deck, the oars have apparently been stowed away. No masts are indicated in either figures 27 or 47. Small galleys of figures 38 and 39 each have one bank of oars. Figure 38 has no *sperone*, but it does have a fighting deck. Figure 39 has a *sperone* but no fighting deck. Similar galleys with *sperone*—rowed either *a zenzile* or *a terzaruolo* with the possibility of raising one to three lateen sails to augment rowing—are illustrated in figures 57, 58, and 88, although, as Pryor has noted, the low freeboard necessary for oared ships made them extremely susceptible to being swamped in any sort of sea, which also meant that they could not set sails to maximum efficiency (1992: 35).

A galley was found at Lazise (fig. 137).

Type IIb: War transports (e.g., figs. 18–21, 31, 40, 48, 49, and 54, for a total of forty-six Venetian examples)
Transports and merchantmen were both designed to maximize capacity. As a result, transports closely resemble round ships and visually it can be difficult to distinguish them in representational images. The themes of figures 18–21, 40, 48, 49, and 54 make it clear that the vessels depicted are in use as war transports. Some ships specifically designed for warfare had horse ports. According to some sources, these were opened and a bridge was let out, allowing knights to land mounted (Marzials, 1965: 68). The mosaics, figures 18–21, illustrate crusader transports (ca. 1235); distinctive inward-curving projections at the stern visible in figures 18, 20, and 21 delimit a very full stern, which could well accommodate a horse port, although there is what has been interpreted as a horse port at the bow of the vessel depicted in figure 18. (Figure 19 has a similar feature.) This large ship type was excellent for siege warfare; the spars have been employed to form "flying bridges" or scaling ladders (Lane, 1973: 40; Marzials, 1965: 70).

Figure 31 (eleventh century) represents four two-masted warships in the midst of the siege of Constantinople. The double-ended hulls are similar in shape to Byzantine illuminations of small boats, figures 33 and 36. The war transport images date between the eleventh and fourteenth centuries.

Type III: Seagoing merchant ships (fig. 158)
Seagoing merchant ships make up the majority of the catalog, with the earliest dating to the twelfth century. These include both round ships and merchant galleys, but, as defined by this typology, they are subdivided by rig and number of masts, not by their form.

A majority of the ships in this catalog are some form of the round ship. They were primarily employed as merchant vessels, although in times of need served well as transport warships. The early medieval round ship has characteristics that link it to its bulky predecessor, the Roman *corbita.*

Type IIIa: Single-masted, lateen-rigged merchant ships (e.g., figs. 25, 29, 52, 65, 76, 85–90, 108, 115, and 117, for a total of seventy-five Venetian examples)
Single-masted lateeners constitute many of the representations in this catalog. Figure 117 (thirteenth century) represents a small lateener with a quarter rudder shown at starboard. Its small size is indicated by the fact that it has one mast and is manned by just two mariners. Although the boat of figure 115 does not yet have a mast in place, the similar shape of its hull probably indicates it, too, would have been fitted with a mast. A larger, single-masted vessel type is shown by figure 29 (ca. 1105).

This classification system makes distinctions based on the number of masts (which generally equates to a vessel's size) and type of rig. The basic hull shape and stern configuration of the single-masted ship in figure 25 and the two-masted ship in figure 23 (both of which date to ca. 1270) show that these two vessels are really

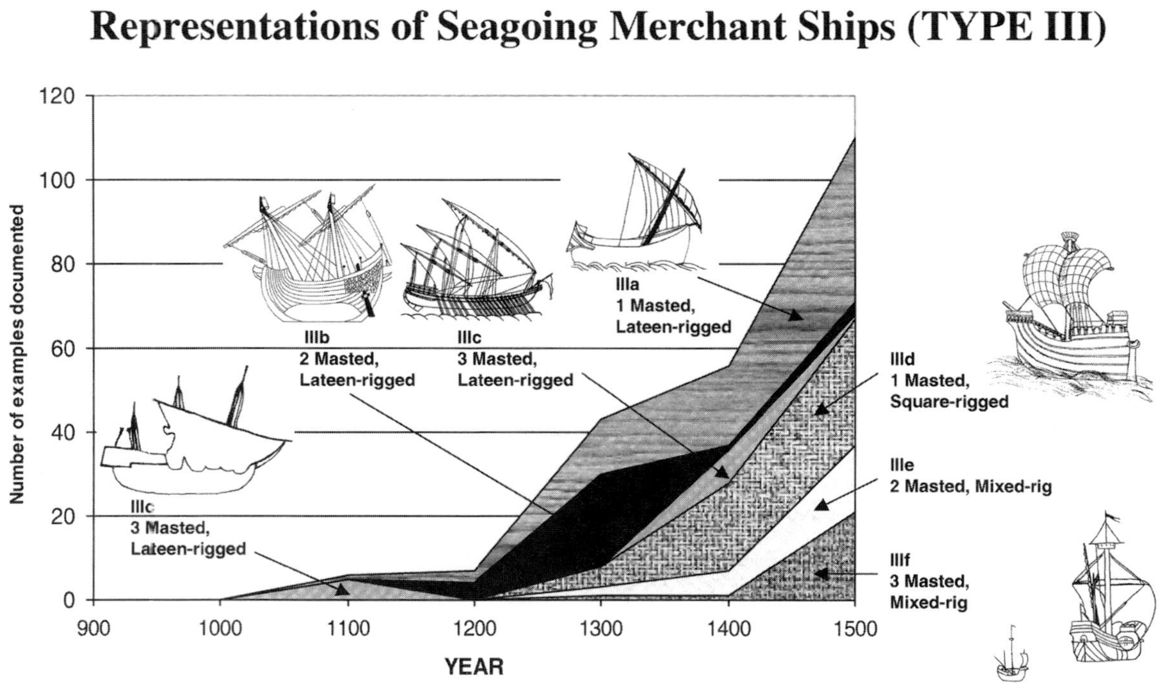

FIG. 158. Type III. Seagoing merchant ships, trends in the representational evidence. Type IIIa—single-masted lateeners; IIIb—two-masted lateeners; IIIc—three-masted lateeners; IIId—single-masted square rigs; IIIe—two-masted mixed rigs; IIIf—three-masted mixed rigs

of the same general form; one is just slightly larger than the other, requiring more sail power. Masts for the vessel of figure 115, a construction scene, were not defined by the sculptor, but the railing of the small quarterdeck and the general shape of the hull resemble figures 25 and 117; it appears to represent a similar, small, single-masted vessel. A larger, single-masted lateener is seemingly exemplified by figure 88. Although still completely lateen rigged, the early merchant galley figure 66 has a curved stern rudder attached to the stern, as well as two quarter rudders.

Type IIIb: Two-masted, lateen-rigged merchant ships (e.g., figs. 23, 26, 28, 37, 62, 63, 73, 78, 91–94, 96, 98–102, 104, 105, and 118, for a total of thirty Venetian examples)

An excellent example of the two-masted, lateen-rigged round ship was found at Contarina (fig. 139).

The first subcategory of Type IIIb is characterized by common bow and stern shapes. The stern is somewhat flat, a type of transom stern with two upright framing timbers and a tragent, the transverse beam, to support the large sterncastle. Figures 26 and 28 (ca. 1300), two illustrations of one story or theme, portray the same ship, as do figures 93 and 94 (ca. 1345), and figures 98–101 (1318–58). It is very informative to see the ship from different viewpoints. Figure 98, the construction scene, shows the inner skeletal framing system used.

A second subcategory of two-masted, lateen-rigged round ship is illustrated by figures 23, 87, 96, 102, and 104. These ships are characterized by a substantial quarterdeck with a rounded parapet, and a full, rounded, hull shape. The quarterdeck's construction can best be understood from figure 87. The angle of view depicted in this fresco clearly shows the arrangement: a rectangular section is partitioned off and decorated with finials at each corner. Outside of this, the rounded parapet completely surrounds the quarterdeck.

The final subcategory of two-masted lateener is exemplified by figure 23, which closely resembles the rounded hull shape of the smaller ship figure 25 with one mast.

Type IIIc: Three-masted, lateen-rigged merchant ships (e.g., figs. 10–14, 60, 68, and 69, for a total of fourteen Venetian examples)

Three-masted lateeners are one of the largest ship types represented, yet they are among the earliest representations in this catalog. Figures 10–14 date to the twelfth century. Far more common though, are smaller, single- or two-masted ships.

The ships of figures 10–14 are almost identical round ships. One perceivable difference is that a section of the side of the ship in figure 14 is lowered; this probably facilitated unloading. The foresail is the primary sail in these three-masted ships and is generally the tallest and largest. Confusion on the part of the mosaicists or of later restorers is likely the explanation for the inconsistent relative mast heights seen in the San Clemente series (figs. 10–13).

The other three-masted lateeners located, figures 60 and 69, are large, fifteenth-century merchant galleys, which were rowed and sailed.

Type IIId: Single-masted, square-rigged merchant ships (e.g., figs. 53, 56, 60, 67, 71, 82, 97, 107, 110, 122, 124, and 128A, for a total of fifty-six Venetian examples)

Square-rigged round ships, fitted with a single stern rudder and rigged with a square sail, made their appearance in Venetian images as well as in the Mediterranean in the fourteenth century. The first known Venetian examples, from the fourteenth century, are figures 53, 82, and 97, but these have a round hull shape very reminiscent of the lateener and retain quarter rudders. A later, stern-rudder example is seen in figure 128A.

More characteristically *coche*- or carrack-shaped hulls have the sterncastle integrated into the hull. The less well-defined *coche* might include figures 56, 60, 67, 110, and 122. These examples show no evidence of tumble home but have integrated castle structures.

The well-known carrack type is better defined, characterized by even larger castle structures integrated into the hull design, plus a pronounced tumble home, fortified with girding timbers and prominent wales. Single-masted examples are seen in figures 71, 107, and 122.

Type IIIe: Two-masted, mixed-rigged merchant ships (e.g., figs. 51 [right], 58, 59, 77, 83, 123, 128B, and 129, for a total of twenty-four Venetian examples)

Soon after the northern cog was introduced in the Mediterranean, the mixed rig evolved, combining advantages of both the square and lateen systems. A few fourteenth- and fifteenth-century examples are seen in the catalog, and the basic round form seems to have changed completely to the *coche* or carrack shape. Figures 58, 59, 77, 128B, and 129 have no indications of tumble home, while figure 123 shows the vertical girding timbers characteristic of a carrack.

The only record of figure 77 has been drawn with two lateen sails, but its hull shape and other features make it more likely that the main sail was originally square. This vessel is provided with a forecastle and a large enclosed quarterdeck at the stern.

Type IIIf: Three-masted, mixed-rigged merchant ships (figs. 30, 51 (left), 61, 72, 110, and 127, for a total of twenty-three Venetian examples—only two date prior to 1450; sixteen ships date earlier than 1486)

The ship of figure 51, dating to 1367, is an early example of a very large, mixed-rigged type, with huge castles at bow and stern. Fra Mauro showed an unusual four-masted variety on his *Mappamondo* (1459). This ship with four masts (fig. 61) is not illustrated elsewhere in this period, though four-masted ships occurred more commonly by the following century.

Figure 72 seems to have a transom stern, and neither it, figure 30, nor 110 indicate tumble home. Figure 127 has vertical girding timbers indicating its tumble home. Abundant examples of carracks appear in art of the second half of the fifteenth century, and they are even more numerous in sixteenth-century art (not covered by figure 158).

Certain vessel types dominate the art of any given period. The early Venetian art is filled with small craft for riverine and lagoonal environments. Until the eleventh century, Venetians didn't have large seagoing vessels, and their art reflects this fact. Later, vessel types connected with mercantile activities seem to have been more appropriate for the purposes of their art; "apparently ship meant commerce, not war, to the average citizen of the medieval world" (Kreutz, 1976: 109). Hagiographical cycles were popular themes in medieval art, thus merchant ships rather than warship types were frequently illustrated. Saints would usually have traveled on merchant ships and not warships. The Venetian artistic record cannot reflect an exact count of the different types actually in use at any given period. Textual evidence for ship and boat types fills out the story, and the archaeological record will hopefully do so even better as future sites come to light. Perhaps more accurate proportions could be gleaned from a study of city seascapes, which became popular beginning in the second half of the fifteenth century and contain numerous vessels in just one image. For example, one xylograph, the cityscape of Venice, from *Peregrinationes* (1483), contains a total of sixty-six Type I small craft, five Type II war galleys, and fifty-four Type III merchant ships (two details illustrated by figs. 117 and 118). Though not so prolific, the medieval artistic record of Venice provides diverse pictorial examples of many of the ship and boat types commonly used in Venice.

Further Research

There is a clear need for additional work in this new research field of maritime images. A database should be established for all known maritime art with a standardized format for criteria. Existing index catalogs, such as the Princeton Art Index (copies at the Vatican and Princeton University Libraries), must be consolidated with the few published surveys of maritime art such as Moll (1920); those on Italian naval art by Nebbia (1932), Levi (1892), Vocini (1950); Villain-Gandossi on medieval miniatures (1979 and 1985); and Delouka, on Byzantine ship graffiti from the churches of Aegina, Greece (1990). New surveys must be made in selected geographical areas, and especially in coastal regions, and integrated into the database. A survey of subsequent Venetian art would be an extremely profitable endeavor, especially because Renaissance art becomes more accurately detailed. Many prints of cityscapes (e.g., Jacopo dei Barbari's plan of Venice in 1500; Museo Storico Navale, inv. 1044) and paintings of naval victory scenes exist that incorporate hundreds of ships and boats in merely one image. Many victory paintings still hang in the Ducal Palace. A survey of the art from the Dalmatian coast and Venetian colonies throughout the eastern Mediterranean would likewise be informative. As Marco Bonino suggested in this volume's foreword, Tuscany would provide a complimentary study for Italian nautical history.

Graffiti that still remain on monuments, especially frequent on church portals and icons and in castle prisons, must be located and documented. Their documentation now is of the utmost importance—otherwise evidence will be lost. Greek churches, for example, are continually whitewashed. Castles, fortifications, and other buildings are falling into ruin.

The present study has resulted in the accumulation of new and valuable information concerning medieval Venetian shipping and, indeed, medieval vessels generally. Artistic representations of ships and boats cannot resolve all questions, and they can be problematic. Nonetheless, it is hoped that this comprehensive survey of the Venetian depictions, despite their inevitable limitations, has demonstrated that there is much to be learned from a systematic approach to the study of maritime images. These images become even more meaningful when their details can be corroborated by similar images, as well as by the evidence found in textual sources and archaeological examples. Surveying maritime art in other regions will result in a more complete understanding of seafaring and ship construction and will provide ready sources for comparison when new shipwrecks do come to light.

APPENDIX I

Museums, Libraries, and Church Sites Surveyed

The following museums, libraries, and churches were inventoried for possible maritime images. Medieval or early Renaissance ship or boat images were located in the sites marked with an asterisk (*), and images from these sites have been included in the catalog and typology graphs unless otherwise indicated. Entries defined by brackets are not illustrated but are included in the typology graphs.

Museums Surveyed

The exhibited material of these museums of Venice was completely surveyed; however, collections in storage were not.

Archaeological Museum *
[3 Type Ib, 2 Type Id, 4th-century seascape mosaic (Correr inv. 53)]
Civico Museo Correr *
Franchetti Gallery at the Ca' d'Oro
Gallerie dell'Accademia, Sopraintendenza ai Monumenti *
[Vittore Carpaccio's paintings, ca. 1460–1526, "Votive Ships in Church": Type IIa, 2 type IIIf); St. Ursula's *Vita:* Type Ia, Type 2 IIa, Type 6 IIIf)]
Gallerie della Fondazione Querini-Stampalia *
Museo dell'Estuario, Torcello
Museo Diocesano di Arte Sacra (Cloister of Sant'Apollonia, Museum of Diocesan Sacred Art)
Museo Dipinti Sacri Bizantini *
[* Three ship images in background of a Byzantine icon.] Not permitted to photograph; not included in catalog or typology.
Museo di Seminario Patriarcale
Museo Fortuny
Museo Marciano *
Museo Storico Navale *
Museo Vetrario di Murano
Palazzo Ducale
Scuola di San Giorgio degli Schiavoni *
[Vittore Carpaccio's painting, ca. 1460–1526, *St. George Slays Dragon:* 2 Type IIIe]
Scuola Grande di San Rocco
Under restoration; unable to visit.

Libraries Consulted

Library collections containing medieval Venetian manuscript material offer an almost inexhaustible source of maritime images. The following libraries have been utilized to inventory the primary Venetian collections and specifically Venetian material:

Archivio di Stato, Campo dei Frari *
Biblioteca Classense, Ravenna *
Biblioteca del Civico Museo Correr *

Biblioteca della Fondazione Giorgio Cini
Biblioteca della Fondazione Querini-Stampalia *
Biblioteca della Seminario Patriarchale *
Biblioteca Museo Storico Navale *
Biblioteca Nazionale Marciana *
[6 war transports (Type IIb), 15th-century manuscript, *Miscellanea Varia* [Biblioteca Marciana Cod. Lat. Z. 339 (=1550) cc. 43^{v}–44^{r} (Zorzi, 1988: 132)].
Bodleian Library, Oxford University *
Art Index, Princeton University *
Houghton Library, Yale University *

Churches Inventoried

This list of churches in Venice was the initial basis for selection for on-site research. Promising targets included all the extant medieval churches of Venice; unless otherwise noted, these were thoroughly surveyed on site. Churches built after the fifteenth century were not all surveyed on site, because it is unlikely much medieval or early Renaissance art exists in them. Dates and information on status is based on Lorenzetti (1982), Umberto (1976) and author's research in Venice during 1989 and 1994.

Information for the churches is given in the following format, although not all information is available for each church:

Each entry is entitled by San/Santa/Sant' or Chiesa di before the name. Alternate and full forms of the name or location details are given as parenthetical information.
Foundation/Built
b. = beginning of
f.h. = first half
m. = mid
s.h. = second half
e. = end
c. = century
Renovation History, Status, or Presence of Maritime Art

Agnese
10th–11th c.
Rebuilt in 12th, 16th, 17th, and 18th c. Defunct, 1810.

Agostin
s.h. 10th c.
Demolished.

Alvise
1388
Renovated in 17th–18th c. Closed; unable to view interior. No medieval or early Renaissance maritime art found on visible exterior.

Andrea (on Chioggia)
13th c.
Rebuilt in 1743.
Andrea della Zirada
*1329
Medieval or early Renaissance maritime art found on façade. Unable to view interior; privately owned and not open to the public.

Angelo Michele (in S. Marco)
920
Demolished.

Angelo (in Giudecca)
1555
Demolished.

Angelo Raffaele
7th c.
Early church burned. Rebuilt in 9th, 12th, and 17th c.; present building 1735.

Anna
1240
Reconstructed in 1634.

Antonin (in Castello)
4th c.
Rebuilt in 12th, 14th, and 17th c. Demolished.

Antonio
1346
Deconsecrated; deprived of all art work, demolished.

Appollinare (Aponal)
11th c.
Restored in 12th, 13th, and 15th c. Deprived of all art in 1810.

Apollonia (cloisters)
14th c.

Apostoli
9th c.
Restored 11th, 12th, 17th, and 18th c.

Ascensione (S. Maria in Broglio)
9th–10th c.
Demolished.

Barnaba
9th c.
Rebuilt in 11th and 14th c.; present building 1749.

Basegio (Basilio)
10th c.
Demolished.

Bartolomeo (Bortolomio)
9th c.
Reconstructed in 12th, 17th and 18th c. Closed indefinitely; unable to view interior.

Basso
1076
Reconstructed 12th c. Burned and rebuilt 1661.

Benedetto
11th c.
Rebuilt in 13th, 17th c. Locked; unable to view interior. No medieval or early Renaissance art found on visible exterior.

Biagio e Cataldo (in Giudecca)
10th c.
Rebuilt in 18th c. Demolished.

Biagio (in Castello)
11th c.
Rebuilt 14th, 15th, and 18th c. Locked; unable to view interior. No medieval or early Renaissance art found on visible exterior.

Boldo (Ubaldo)
10th c.
Demolished.

Bonaventura (dei Riformati)
1620
Demolished.

Ca' di Dio (S. Maria della)
13th c.
Rebuilt in 1544.

Canciano
9th–10th c.
Possibly reconstructed in 11th–12th c. Rebuilt in 14th, 16th, and 18th c.

Cappuccine
1612–14

Carmini
1286
Renovated in 16th and 17th c.

Cassiano
9th c.
Rebuilt in 11th, 13th, 14th, 17th, and 19th c.

Catecumeni (S. Giov. Battista, in Dorsoduro)
f.h. 16th c.

Celestia
e. 12th c.
Demolished.

Caterina
11th–12th c.
Rebuilt in 14th and 15th c. Under restoration; unable to view interior. No medieval or early Renaissance maritime art found on visible exterior.

Caterina, Mazzorbo
14th c.
Deconsecrated; unable to visit.

Chiara
f.h. 13th c.
Demolished.

Convertite
m. 16th c.
Corpus Domini 1366 Demolished.

Cipriano, Murano
1108
Demolished.

Clemente (on island)
15th c.
Unable to visit island.

Cosma e Damiano (in Giudecca)
1481
Deconsecrated; not open to the public.

Croce (in Giudecca)
13th c.
Reconstructed 14th c., renovated in 15th c., and totally rebuilt in 16th c. Unable to view interior. No medieval or early Renaissance maritime art found on visible exterior.

Croce degli Armeni
1496
Reconstructed in 1682.

Croce (in S. Croce)
8th–9th c.
Demolished.

Daniele
5th c.
Demolished.

Domenico
1312
Demolished.

Domenico (on Chioggia)
1200
Rebuilt in 14th c.

Elena
s.h. 12th c.
Rebuilt in 1435. Many treasures were removed in 1807.

Eremite
1693

Elisabetta (on Lido)
16th c.
Enlarged in 1620.

Eufemia (in Giudecca)
s.h. 9th c.
Reconstructed in 14th c., restored in 18th c.

Fantin
9th c.
Renovated in 12th and 13th c. Demolished and totally rebuilt in 1507.

Fava (S. Maria della Consolazione)
e. 15th c.
Oratory built in 15th c.; church added in 1704.

Felice (S. Maria della Fava)
10th c.
Renovated in 13th c. and totally rebuilt in 1531.

Filippo e Giacomo
f.h. 12th c.
Demolished.

Fosca (in Cannaregio)
10th c.
Rebuilt in 12th, 13th, 15th c. and again in 1679 and 1733.

Fosca (on Torcello)
11th–12th c.
Drastically restored.

Francesco del Deserto
15th c.
Unable to visit island.

Francesco di Paola
s.h. 14th c.
Rebuilt in 16th c.

Francesco della Vigna
1253
Reconstructed in 1534.

Gallo
1581
A hostel erected in S. Marco in 976–78 was transferred to this location in 1581. The oratory was built in 1703.

Geminiano
6th c.
Demolished.

George's (Anglican)
1892
Previous Venetian chapel, San Vio, demolished.

Geremia
11th c.
Reconstructed in 13th c. and again in 1753–60.

Gesu' e Maria (in S. Croce)
b. 17th c.
Demolished.

Gesuati (Maria del Rosario, in Dorsoduro)
1668
Rebuilt in 1724.

Gesuiti (in Cannaregio)
m. 12th c.
Possible 13th c. renovation? Reconstructed in 18th c.

Giacomo (in Guidecca)
9th–10th c.
Reconstructed in 14th, 17th c. Demolished.

Gioacchino (in Castello)
1418

Giacomo dell'Orio
9th c.
Reconstructed in 13th, 14th, 15th, and 16th c.

Giacomo di Rialto (Giocometto)
5th c.
Rebuilt and restored in 16th and 17th c.

Giobbe (in Cannaregio)
1378
Enlarged in 15th c.

Giorgio dei Greci (Greek Orthodox)
1539

Giorgio degli Schiavoni (scuola)
1451

Giorgio Maggiore
966
Rebuilt in 1566.

Giovanni (Giov.) Battista (in Giudecca)
1340
Demolished.

Giov. in Bragora (Battista, in Castello)
8th c.

Restored in 9th c.; rebuilt in 11th, 12th, 15th c. and again modified in 1728.

Giov. Crisostomo
11th c.
Rebuilt in 1497–1505.

Giov. dei Cavalieri di Malta (dei Furlani or del Tempio)
11th–12th c.
Restored in 1451. Complete reconstruction in 1565.

Giov. Elemosinario
9th–10th c.
Totally destroyed by fire in 1167 and 1513, rebuilt in 1180 and 1527–29. Closed for restoration; unable to view interior. No medieval or early Renaissance maritime art found on visible exterior.

Giov. Evangelista
970
Rebuilt in 12th and 15th c. Restored, 17th c.

Giov. Laterano
1504
Oratory built in 1504; church added in 1573. Partially demolished in 1810.

Giov. Novo (in Oleo)
9th–10th c.
Reconstructed in 12th c., and completely rebuilt in 1762. Closed indefinitely; unable to view interior. No medieval or early Renaissance maritime art found on visible exterior.

Giov. e Paolo (Zanipolo)
m. 13th–15th c.
Rebuilt in 1660.

Girolamo
e. 14th. c.
Burned and rebuilt in 1456 and again in 1705.

Giuseppe di Castello
1512

Giustina
7th c.
Rebuilt in 12th, 15th, 16th and 17th c. Closed in 1810.

Gregorio
806
Renovated in 14th c. and rebuilt in 15th c. Defunct, 1775. Stripped of all art in 1806.

Incurabili (Santissimo Salvadore)
b. 16th. c.
Demolished.

Lazzaro dei Mendicanti
1601–31

Lazzaro degli Armeni (Armenian monastery)
1717

Leonardo
11th c.
Reconstructed in 14th and 18th c.

Lio (Leone)
9th c.
Rebuilt in 1054, much restored in 15th and 17th c., and again in 1783.

Lorenzo
6th c.
Rebuilt in 1140, 14th, 15th, 16th and 17th c.; completely stripped of art.

Luca
11th c.
Restored in 13th and 14th c., rebuilt in 16th and 18th c., and again in 1832.

Lucia
12th c.
Reconstructed Palladian. Demolished.

Madonna dell'Arsenale
s.h. 16th c.
Demolished.

Madonna dell'Orto (Cristoforo)
s.h. 14th c.
Rebuilt in 15th c.

Marco *
832
Built on foundation of 6th c. Church of Holy Apostles. Burned in 976 and 1063, rebuilt in 978 and 1094.

Marcuola
9th–10th c.
Rebuilt in 14th and 17th c. and again in 1728–36.

Margherita
m. 9th c.
Reconstructed in 17th c. Defunct; now in use as cinema. Unable to view interior. No medieval or early Renaissance maritime art found on visible exterior.

Maria degli Angeli (on Murano)
12th c.
Rebuilt in 16th c. Locked; unable to view interior. No medieval or early Renaissance maritime art found on visible exterior.

Maria Assunta (on Torcello)
639
Radically reconstructed in 863 and 1008. Further expanded in 11th c.

Maria Assunta (Maria del Rosario, Gesuiti)
1668
Rebuilt in 1714–29.

Maria della Carità (Carità)
1116
Reconstructed in 15th and 16th c. Defunct; now part of *Accademia.*

Maria del Carmelo (Cármini)
1286
Partially rebuilt in 16th c. Seventeenth-century monument to naval captain with maritime art.

Maria Celeste (Celestia)
e. 12th c.
Demolished.

Maria dei Derelitti (Ospedaletto)
1662
Almshouse founded in 1527, church in 1662. Rebuilt in 1674.

Maria e Donato (on Murano)
7th c.
Restored in 9th c., rebuilt in 12th c.

Maria Formosa
7th c.
Rebuilt in 12th c., in 1492, and again restored after 1916.

Maria del Giglio (S. Maria Zobenigo)
10th c.
Burned and rebuilt in 966 and 1105. Altered in 14th c., and rebuilt in 17th c. Baroque façade with ships in Mediterranean harbors.

Maria Glorioso dei Frari (Frari)
1250
Early church demolished and building expanded in 1340, again rebuilt in 1445. 16th c. reliefs of battleships on tomb sculpture.

Maria Maddalena (Convertile)
16th c.

Maria Maggiore
e. 15th c.
Defunct; stripped of all art. Now a prison. Unable to visit.

Maria Mater Domini
960
Rebuilt in 11th and 16th c. Closed for restoration; unable to view interior. No medieval or early Renaissance maritime art found on visible exterior.

Maria Nova
s.h. 10th c.
Demolished.

Maria dei Miracoli
1481–89

Maria della Misericordia * (scuola)
936
Reconstructed in 13th, 15th, and 17th c. Stripped of most art in 19th c. Locked; unable to view interior. Early Renaissance maritime art found on exterior.

Maria del Navicella (on Chioggia)
Demolished.

Maria di Nazareth (degli Scalzi)
1654–58

Maria delle Pentienti (in Cannaregio)
1703

Maria del Pianto
1647–59
Abandoned and closed indefinitely.

Maria della Pietà
15th c.
Rebuilt in 1745.

Maria della Presentazione (Zitelle, in Guidecca)
1570

Maria della Salute
1631–81

Maria dei Servi
14th c.
Demolished in 1862.

Maria della Visitazione (in Dorsoduro)
1493
Now used by orphanage.

Marina
f.h. 11th c.
Demolished.

Martino * (on Chioggia)
Ancient
Rebuilt in 1380. Now used as a storehouse; unable to survey on site. Maritime art located through published material.

Martino (in Castello)
593
Partly rebuilt in 10th c. and completely in 1540.

Marta
b. 14th c.
Reconstructed in 15th and 16th c. Now a railway warehouse; unable to survey.

Maurizio
9th c.
Rebuilt in 12th c. and in 1590. Demolished and totally rebuilt in 1806.

Marziale (Marciliano)
9th c.
Rebuilt in 12th and 17th c.

Mattio (Matteo Apostoli)
1156
Reconstructed in 1735. Demolished.

Michele (on island)
10th c.
Suppressed in 19th c.; now again in use as cem-

etery church. No medieval or early Renaissance maritime art found in church or on graveyard monuments in cemetery.

Miracoli
1481–89

Moisé (Vittore)
8th c.
Rebuilt in 9th c., burned and rebuilt in 12th c., restored in 13–14th c., and again in 1632.

Nicoletto della Lattuga (Nicolò dei Frari)
1332
Demolished.

Nicolò al Lido
1043
Rebuilt in 16th c.

Nicolò da Bari
1470
Possibly built on earlier church foundations. Destroyed by Napoleon for public park.

Nicolò dei Mendicoli
7th c.
Rebuilt and altered in 12th, 14th, and 16th c.

Nicolò da Tolentino
1528

Nome di Gesù
1815–34

Ognissanti
e. 15th c.
Reconstructed in 16th c.

Pantalon
9th c.
Reconstructed in 13th and 17th c.

Paternian
9th c.
Demolished.

Penitenti
1703

Pietà (S. Maria della Visitazione, in Castello)
m. 14th c.
Church added in 1744.

Pietro (in Castello)
7th c.
7th c. church dedicated to SS. Sergius and Baccus. Church rebuilt in 817–30 and dedicated to St. Peter. Burned and rebuilt again in 1120, and restored in 14th, 16th, and 17th c. Completely rebuilt in 1596. Damaged in World War I.

Pietro Martire (on Murano)
1348
Almost completely rebuilt after 1474 fire.

Pietro in Volta (on Pellestrina)
17th c.

Polo
9th c.
Reconstructed in 12th and 14th c. Radically altered in 1804.

Provolo
9th c.
Demolished.

Rendentore
1577

Rocco
1489
Almost entirely rebuilt in 1725.

Rocco e Margherita
1488

Salute
1631

Salvatore
7th c.
Rebuilt in 12th, 14th, and 15th c. and again in 1506.

Samuele Profeta
10th–11th c.
Burned and rebuilt in 12th c. Restored in 14th–15th c., and much rebuilt in 1685.

Scalzi
1649

Sebastiano
m. 14th. c.
Present church 1505–45.

Sepolchro
s.h. 16th c.
Demolished.

Servi (in Cannaregio)
1330
Demolished.

Servolo (on island)
8th c.
Present church 1734–59.

Severo
9th c.
Demolished.

Silvestro
9th c.
Reconstructed in 15th c. Stripped of art and entirely rebuilt in 19th c.

Simeone Grande (Simeone Profeta)
967
Reconstructed in 12th, 13th, and 17th c. Many modifications.

Simeone Piccolo
10th c.
Reconstructed in 1718.

Soccorso (S. Maria Assunta, in Dorsoduro)
1590
Now part of girl's school.

Sofia
9th c.
Reconstructed in 13th c., renovated in 15th c., and again rebuilt in 17th c.

Spirito (on island)
Destroyed in 1656.

Spirito Santo
1483
Stripped of art in 1806. Defunct.

Stae (Eustachio)
966
Reconstructed in 15th, 16th, 17th c., and 1710.

Stefano
1294–1325
Rebuilt in e. 14th c., burned and rebuilt in 1529.

Stin (Stefano Confessore)
10th c.
Demolished.

Teodoro (in S. Marco)
1486

Teresa
s.h. 17th c.

Ternita
11th c.
Demolished.

Tolentini
1591

Tomà
10th c.
Reconstructed in 1395 and 1742. Closed for restoration; unable to view interior. No medieval or early Renaissance maritime art found on visible exterior.

Trinità
11th–12th c.
Demolished.

Trovaso (Gervasio e Protasio)
9th c.
Rebuilt in 1028, destroyed by fire in 1105. Soon rebuilt. This structure fell down in 1583 and was immediately rebuilt again in 1585.

Umiltà (S. Maria della Umiltà)
b. 16th c.
Demolished.

Vergini
12th–13th c.
Demolished.

Vio (Vito e Modesto)
10th c.
Demolished.

Vitale (Vidal)
1084
Rebuilt in 12th, 14th, and 17th–18th c. Defunct; now used for exhibitions.

Zaccaria *
9th c.
Rebuilt in 10–11th c., and again in 1444–1515; early Renaissance maritime art found through published material.

Zan Degolà (S. Giov. Decollato or Zuan Degolà)
8th c.
Modified and altered many times. Defunct, 1818. Closed; unable to view interior. No medieval or early Renaissance maritime art found on visible exterior.

Zulian (Giuliano)
m. 9th c.
Rebuilt in 14th c. and again in 1553.

Sources in Other Cities

Aquileia
Aquileia Cathedral *
313
Early Christian maritime art found.

Belluno *
Early Christian maritime art found.

Ursula *
Medieval or early Renaissance maritime art found.

Bologna
Petronio *
1390
Not surveyed at site; maritime art located through published material.

Francesco *
Not surveyed at site; maritime art located by Dr. Marco Bonino.

Bolzano
Domenico *
14–15th c.
Medieval or early Renaissance maritime art found.

Dalmatia *
Not surveyed at site; maritime art located through published material.

Faenze
Imola *
Not surveyed at site; maritime art located through published material.

London, England
National Gallery *
Medieval or early Renaissance maritime art found.

Lucignano
Misericordia *
Not surveyed at site; maritime art located through published material.

Milan
Private Collection
Not surveyed at site; maritime art located through published material. [Type Id, Ferrarese school painting, ca. 1450, St. Jerome has monastery built; illustrates barge used for transporting construction materials (No. 226; Kaftal, 1978: fig. 620)].

Paris, France
Musée des Artes Décoratives *
[Type IIId, St. Elpidius Polyptych panel, ca. 1430, Veneto-Margian school (Kaftal, 1978, fig. 347).

Padua
Antonio
1232

Baptistry of Duomo *
13th c.
Medieval naval art found.

Duomo *
Reconstructed in 1552. Maritime art located through published material. [Two-masted, mixed-rig merchant ship (Type IIIe), Late 15th-century silver reliquary, Padova Cathedral Treasury (Nebbia, 1932: fig. 121)].

Sofia
9th c.
Rebuilt in 11–12th c.

Parma
Parma Cathedral *
Not surveyed at site; maritime art located through published material.

Piacenza
Antonio *
Not surveyed at site; maritime art located through published material. [Type Ib, predella panel, 1420–30, St. Antonius's boat (Kaftal, 1978: fig. 102).

Pomposa
Pomposa Abbey *
Not surveyed at site; maritime art located through published material.

Ravenna
Apollinare Nuovo *
504
Early medieval maritime art found.

Apollinare in Classe
535–38
Neoniano Baptistry
5th c.

Galla Placidia
5th c.

Giovanni Evangelista *
5th c.
Medieval or early Renaissance maritime art found.

Rimini *

Agostino *

Medieval or early Renaissance maritime art found.

Not surveyed at site; maritime art located through published material.

Toledo, Spain

Toledo Cathedral *

Not surveyed at site; maritime art originating from Venice located through published material.

Udine

Udine Cathedral *

Not surveyed at site; maritime art located through published material.

Francesco *

Not surveyed at site; maritime art located through published material.

Vittorio Veneto

Andrea *

Maritime art located through published material. [2 Type Ib, Type IIIb, St. Andrew frescoes, ca. 1500, Chapel of Madonna of Battuti, by Antonio Zago].

Verona

Anastasia *

1290–1323

Medieval or early Renaissance maritime art found. [2 Type Ib (one with a "bird's head" sternpost), 2 Type IIa, 4 IIId, end 15th-century frescoes in Lavagnoli Chapel by Francesco Benaglio and Michele da Verona].

Maria della Scala *

Medieval or early Renaissance maritime art found.

Zara

Simeone *

Not surveyed at site; maritime art located through published material.

APPENDIX 2

Chronology of Venice

Compiled from the following histories of Venice: Fasoli (1978); Lane (1974); Norwich (1977); and Langer (1940).

5th and 6th centuries: Venetian lagoon settled. Trade concentrated within lagoons and up riverine system of northern Italy.

A.D. 568: Lombard invasion of Italy.

697: Venetians elect first doge.

9th century: Still active in riverine trade; influence spreading (Romagna region). Trade extended beyond Adriatic to Levant.

828: Appropriation of St. Mark's relics.

830s: Formalized Venetian military fleet.

992: Venetian trading privileges in Constantinople (chrysobull of Basil II).

1000: Dalmatian piracy subdued.

1054: Final schism.

1063: First three Crusades resulted in more Venetian trading rights.

1082: Byzantine emperor grants commercial privileges (including immunity from excise taxes) in exchange for naval aid against Normans.

1099: Commercial treaty with Imola; still involved in riverine trade.

1102: Venice conquered Sidon.

1123: Venice conquered Tyre.

1170–77: Byzantine emperor arrested all Venetian traders in Constantinople. Venice conquered Ragusa and Chios.

1201–1204: Fourth Crusade.

1202: Venice excommunicated by Rome for attacking a Christian city.

1204: Constantinople sacked; Byzantine empire divided. Venice obtained Crete, plus chain of colonies from Venice to the Black Sea.

1253–1268: First Genoese War; struggle over Black Sea and Levantine trade.

ca. 1270: Compass came into use in Mediterranean. Other improvements in the technology of navigation as well as shipbuilding.

1271–92: Marco Polo's journey to China and back.

1289–1311: Second Genoese War; War of Ferrara.

1291: Genoese eliminated Muslim control over straights of Gibraltar; Italian ships faced no obstacle in reaching North Sea. Beginning in 1314, state-subsidized merchant galley convoys to Flanders/northern Europe, Syria/Cyprus, Romania (Black Sea), and Alexandria.

1343–54: Third Genoese War; Venice defeated.

1347–54: Plague, first attack of Black Death.

1378–81: War of Chioggia; Genoa defeated.

1388: Treaty with Ottoman Turks.

1404–1406: Vicenza, Verona, and Padua submit to Venice (much needed mainland food supply).

1416: First of series of wars against Ottoman Turks.

1463–79: Great War against the Turks; Venice lost. Subsequently paid annual tribute for Black Sea trade.

1489: Acquisition of Cyprus.
16th century: Decline of Venice.
1500–73: Discovery of new route to Indies undermined prosperity of Venice.
1537–40: War with Ottomans.
1570: Turks attacked Cyprus.
1571: Battle of Lepanto; Venice won but to no long-term avail.
1573: Venice abandoned Cyprus to Turks.

APPENDIX 3

Representative Ship and Boat Measurements

Data for the types *magne marciliane, tarete, ippagoghi, battelli, gondola, buzi,* the thirteenth-century *nave quadre, tarrete,* and *galere grosse,* and the fifteenth-century *barzotto, berlingher, caravelle, coche* (Mediterranean "cog"), and great galley comes from Casoni (1847: 190–210), the *Comacci nave* from Bonino (1978a: 52); the fourteenth-century *burchio* and the *barca marsiliana* from Bonino (1978a: 213); the nave of 1229 from Predelli (1903: 51) and Lane (1973: 46); the thirteenth-century tarrete and fourteenth-century Mediterranean "cog" from Lane (1973: 46 and 123); the fourteenth- and fifteenth-century great galleys, light galleys, and the fifteenth-century *nave latine* and square-rigged round ships, from Lane (1934: tables B and C). Lane's lengths are measured at the uppermost deck level, while the other lengths are measured from end to end. These conversion factors were used to determine modern equivalent measures: 1 *piede* = 34.7735 cm; 1 *botti* = 0.6 tons; 1 *milliarium* = 0.47 tons.

Vessel type and date	**Height at midship (meters)**	**Beam (meters)**	**Length (meters)**	**Tonnage**
Textual descriptions / technical treatises				
Magne marciliane (7th c. rivergoing cargo boat)	2.8?	8?	17.4	120
Tarete (7th c.)				180
Comacchi nave, Capitolare of Luitprando (715)	1.35	2.7	15	21.5?
Ippagoghi (9th c. horse transport)	10	13	29.9	
Lateen-rigged *nave,* measurement decreed in maritime code of 1229	3.13	8.35	31.3	200–500
Battelli (13th c. ship's boat)			10.4	
Gondola (13th c. ship's boat)			8.35	
Buzi (13th c. round ship)				140–280
Nave quadre (13th c. square rigged round ship, such as the Louis IX's *Roccaforte,* 1268)	13.5	14.25	38.25	550

Tarrete (13th c. lateen-rigged round ship)				100–400
Galere grosse (13th c. long ship galley)	2.4	5.2	40	600
Great galley, for Cyprus voyage, 1318		5.33	40.4	
Great galley, for Flanders voyage, 1320		5.6	40.3	
Nave of 1380	1.5	4.16	13.9	224
Burchio of 1365	1.8	3.5	15	12
Barca marsiliana of 1357	1	1.9	10	6.7
Light galley, "galley of the guard," *Fabrica di galere* f. 77, material ca. 1410		4.4	38.8	
Nave latine, two-masted lateen-rigged round ship, *Fabrica di galere,* f. 33, material ca. 1410	3.3	8.4	27.8	
Square-rigged round ship, *Fabrica di galere,* f. 88, material ca. 1410	3	9.4	33	300 tons
Great galley, ca. 1445, described by Trombetta		5.9	48.3 ?	600
Light galley, ca. 1450, described by Trombetta		4.9	40.9	
Round ship, ca. 1450, described by Trombetta	4.2	11.8	29.6 + *slanci*	600
Cocha or *navi rotonde* (14th c. Mediterranean cog)				120–720
Cocha, ca. 1445, described by Trombetta		6.4	20.9 + *slanci*	120
Barzotto (15th c.)				120–720
Berlingher, ca. 1499, described by Sanudo				150
Caravelle				180

Reconstructions of illustrated vessels				
Figure 7, Longidieno, Roman boat relief (1st c. B.C.)(Bonino, 1991: 35)	1.2	2.5	9.7	5
Figure 8, Port of Classis riverboat mosaic (504–26) (Bonino, 1991: 35)			27	
Figure 18, Crusader round ship mosaic (1202) (Bonino, 1991: 35)	5.3	9.6	33.2	
Figure 79, Menabuoi fishing boat fresco (14th c.)	1.6	3	10	

Shipwrecks	**Height at midship**	**Beam**	**Length**	**Tonnage**
Cervia (4th–6th c. boat) (Bonino, 1978a, appendix 2, 212–13).	1.5	3.5	12.5	
Pomposa (11th c. *burchio*) (Bonino, 1978a: 54, appendix 2, 212–13).		3.5	12–15	13

Pontelagoscuro (*Sandòn* of ca. 11th c.?) (Bonino, 1978a, appendix 2, 212–13).	2?	5?	15?	
Ravenna (Bonino, personal communication)			17?	
Contarina I (Two-masted, lateen-rigged round ship, ca. 1300) (Bonino, 1978a: appendix 2, 212–13, and 1978b: 13–15)	2.46	5.2	20.98	75
Logonovo (Two-masted, lateen-rigged boat, ca. 1400) (Bonino, 1978a, appendix 2, 212–13).	1.14	2.55	10.05	
Lazise (early 16th c. galley) (Scandura, in Bass, 1972: 210)		4.9	39.6	
Contarina II (1550) (Bonino, 1978a, appendix 2, 212–13).	3.1	6.3	20.5	

Contarina I (ca. 1300) detailed ship measurements

These data include timber dimensions of the remains discovered (Relazione, 1900: 23–28), and the calculations for original dimensions by Pryor (1984: 180) and Bonino (1978 B: 12), set in parentheses.

Timber	Dimensions (centimeters)	Dimensions (meters)
Maximum overall length remaining		19.62
Estimated total length		Bonino (20.98)
Maximum beam (excluding external planking)		5.2
Boca width excluding frames		Bonino (5.12)
Width *in fondo*—the flat part of hull bottom		Bonino (2.63)
Width of floor		Bonino (2.63)
Beam at *trepie*		Bonino (4.44)
Depth from floor to gunwale		Pryor (2.9)
Keel length		Pryor (14.01) Bonino (16.5)
Keel, molded at midship	7	
Keel, molded at extremities	10	
Keel, sided	15	
Keelson length		Pryor (16.64)
Keelson, molded at midship	10	
Keelson, molded at extremities	8	
Keelson, sided at midship	14.5	
Keelson, sided at extremities	9	
Sternpost section where it joins the keel Both the stem and sternposts are trapezoidal, with dimensions (exterior side x interior side x thickness) which change continuously.	13.5 x 15 x 12	
Sternpost section at upper edge	8 x 9 x 11.7	
Stem section where it joins the keel	13.5 x 15 x 10	
Stem section at upper edge	8.2 x 10 x 16.8	
Frames, molded	12	
Frames, sided	12	

Exterior hull planking, average width	4
Run of planking varies amidships	30–40
Run of planking, toward posts	13

Lazise galley (1509) detailed measurements

Measurements from Scandurra, 1972: 209–10; figures 3–5 and plates 10–18.

Timber	Dimensions (centimeter)	Dimensions (meters)
Overall length		39.6
Beam		4.9
Planking thickness	2.9	
Frames, molded	8.9	
Frames, sided	7	
Average frame spacing	25.4	
Keelson, sided	12.1	
Keelson, molded	9.8	

APPENDIX 4

Anchor Requirements in Thirteenth-Century Maritime Codes

Tonnage given in *milliariis;* 1 *milliarium* = 0.47 dead weight tons (Lane, 1934: 248). The thirteenth-century Venetian maritime codes specify the mandatory number of *ancoris* (anchors), *indigarios* (anchor buoys), and *canapos* (hawsers). The vessels were required to have a certain number of new hawsers and a certain number of others in good condition.

Statutes of Doge Jacopo Tiepolo, June 1, 1229 (Predelli and Sacerdoti, 1903: 54–57; [a: 8–16]):

			Hawsers:	
Tonnage	Anchors	Buoys	new	good condition
200–99	6	6	6	5
300–99	10	10	8	12
400–99	12	12	11	13
500–99	14	14	13	15
600–99	15	15	14	16
700–99	16	16	15	17
800–99	17	17	17	17
900–99	18	18	18	18
1000	20	20	20	20

Statute on the *nave,* by the Doge Rainieri Zeno, August 6, 1250 (Predelli and Sacerdoti, 1903: 83–86; [8: 1–9]):

			Hawsers:	
Tonnage	Anchors	Buoys	new	good condition
200–99	7	7	7	7
300–99	10	10	10	10
400–99	13	13	13	13
500–99	15	15	15	15
600–99	16	16	16	16
700–99	17	17	17	17
800–99	18	18	18	18
900–99	19	18?	20	20
1000	20	20	22	22

Statutes on the *tarrete,* by the Doge Ranieri Zeno, August 6, 1250 (Predelli and Sacerdoti, 1903: 170–71 [7–11]):

			Hawsers:	
Tonnage	Anchors	Buoys	new	good condition
200	6	6	6	3
250	7	7	7	4
300	8	8	9	4
350	9	9	9	5
400	10	10	10	5

NOTES

Introduction

1. The earliest known Italian manuscript dealing with ship construction is not from the Veneto; it is a notarial document from Brindisi (1275). Based on the data found in this document, Alvise Chiggiato made line drawings of a typical thirteenth-century Italian galley, the *galea rubea* (1989 and 1991). The earliest known Venetian document is *Zibaldone da Canal* (ca. 1310–50), a mercantile manuscript containing seven illustrations of lateen-rigged merchant ships (represented by figs. 62 and 63; Stussi, 1967). The earliest surviving technical treatise, *Michele da Rodi* (1401), covers galleys of Flanders (North Atlantic journeys), Romania (east Mediterranean journeys), *galea sottile*, and *navi*, but has been in a private collection since 1966 (Chiggiato, pers. comm.). The contents of the first available technical Venetian manuscript, *Fabrica di galere* (the making of galleys), probably date to ca. 1400–20, although one extant version of the manuscript was actually rewritten at least seventy years later, and another version, *Arte de far vasselli,* dates to the early sixteenth century. These nearly identical manuscripts primarily describe the merchant galleys of the state-regulated Flanders voyages and include descriptions of a lateen-rigged ship fitted with both quarter and stern rudders (figs. 65 and 66; Anderson, 1945: 161) and a square-rigged *nave* ship, carrack in form (fig. 67; Bellabarba, 1988: 113–30 and 225–40). The technical book by Zorzi da Modon, also called Trombetta or Timbotta of Modon (ca. 1444–49), discusses a contemporaneous galley (fig. 68), a three-masted lateener (fig. 69), a large, mixed-rigged carrack (fig. 70), and a single-masted, square-rigged carrack (fig. 71). *Ragioni antique* (ca. 1470–1529; Dosio, 1987), another technical manuscript presenting a method of construction probably already in use during previous centuries, provided part of the evidence from which Alvise Chiggiato has mathematically reconstructed a fifteenth-century galley, and "visualized the line of reasoning used" (Dosio, 1987: 57–79, and pers. comm.).
2. The most important shipping contracts are those St. Louis negotiated with Venice and Genoa for crusader transport. There are three printed texts of the contract he made with Venice in 1268: Du Chesne, 1841–48, "Contractus navigii domini regis cum Venetis factus anno Domini M.CC.LXVIII" in *Historiae Francorum scriptores,* 5 vols. (Paris), vol. 5, pp. 435–37; Manuscript, late sixteenth–early seventeenth century, Bib. Nat., Paris [MS Lat. 5955: *Contractus navigii Ludovici IX, Francorum regis, cum Venetis factus pro passagio ad Terram Sancam, anno 1268];* Von Leibniz, 1693, "Contractus inter regem Galliae Ludovicum Sanctum et Venetos . . ." in *Codex juris gratium diplomaticus,* Hanover. St. Louis's contracts provide us with contemporaneous terminology used for various parts of a ship, including the masts, spars, sails, rigging, cabins, and other features of a medieval crusader ship (see Pryor, 1984; 1990 and Jal, 1840). Thirteenth-century Venetian maritime codes offer an idea of vessel size based on specifications for the number and weight of anchors required for various ship types, and specify maximum dimensions (Predelli and Sacerdoti, 1903; see appendix 4 for anchor specifications).
3. The graffiti that have good parallels indicating they could date to approximately the mid-fifteenth century are included in the catalog, while those with no parallels are omitted.

Chapter 1. A Brief Overview of Venetian History and Art

1. The major riverine systems of Europe during the medieval period were the Danube, Rhine, Ebro, Garonne, Loire, Val Padana or Padània (Po system), Rhone, Rodano, and Saône. Most important to Venetians were the deep rivers of the Po system: the Livenza, Piava, Sile, Brenta, Bacchiglione, the Adige, and particularly the Po, especially the deep Po of Primaro and the Po of Volano (Fasoli, 1978: 567–92).

2. Many scholars maintain that before 1204 Venice was denied access to the Black Sea, although Martin has shown that in fact, at least a century previous to the Fourth Crusade, Venetian merchants were already trading in the Black Sea (1979: 113); certainly they did so more intensely after the Fourth Crusade.
3. The existing wall paintings in the Ducal Palace postdate the fifteenth century.
4. **St. Andrew.** First-century apostle.
St. Elpidinus. Second-century knight.
St. Eustace. Placidus, Roman soldier for Emperor Hadrian. Died ca. 118.
St. Geminian. Deacon to bishop of Modena. Died 348.
St. George. Roman soldier martyred in 337 during the Diocletian persecutions. Legendary warrior saint included in *The Golden Legend* as the story of George and the dragon, a variant of Christ's triumph over the devil.
St. Jerome. One of the Four Fathers of the Western Church (ca. 345–420), he revised and translated the Bible from its Greek and Hebrew sources into the Latin Vulgate. He lived the ascetic life for a time at Aquileia, then, after 386, he founded Jeronymite/Hieronymite Order in Bethlehem. Cardinal in 420. His story, retold in *The Golden Legend,* was a popular subject in medieval art.
St. John. John the Divine, first-century evangelist and apostle.
St. Martin. Martin of Tours (ca. 316–97). Soldier who cut his cloak in half to share with a poor beggar in the freezing cold. That night he had a dream of Christ wearing his half cloak, after which he converted to Christianity. Bishop of Tours, 371.
St. Nicholas. Bishop of Myra. Regarded as patron saint of sailors. Died ca. 350.
Blessed Odoric. From Podenone, Friuli (1285–1331), Blessed Odoric became Franciscan, spent some years as a recluse, then as a missionary to Asia. Died at Udine.
St. Petronius. Bishop of Bologna. Died ca. 450
St. Simeon. Simeon of Padolirone, an Armenian hermit who went on pilgrimage to Jerusalem, Rome, Compostella and St. Martin of Tours. Renowned for the miracles he worked on these journeys. Settled in Cluniac Abbey of Padolirone, near Padua. Died 1016.
St. Thomas Becket. St. Thomas à Becket (1118–1170), archbishop of Canterbury and chancellor of England.

Chapter 2. Catalog: Venetian Maritime Images

1. The *titulii* of both ship mosaics of the south wall have been lost, and the one on the west half of the vault has been altered. This explains the discrepancies in the interpretation of their themes. According to Levi (1892: table 42, fig. 1), figure 12 represents a scene from the *vita* of St. Mark, his voyage from Aquileia to Alexandria. Other sources have inaccurately identified this mosaic as St. Mark's dream, the *vita praedestinatio* (Pataky and Marjai, 1973: 3) or St. Mark approaching Egypt (Casson, 1964a: fig. 97). Both Lorenzetti (1982: 208) and Demus (1984: 66) concur that all four mosaics in this cycle depict the *translatio.* The *vita praedestinatio* scene is depicted in the roughly contemporaneous mosaic of the vault (fig. 14) in San Pietro chapel, across the altar from San Clemente chapel (fig. 1B).
2. I am indebted to Tom Oertling for this interpretation.
3. Many thanks are due to Nicolle Hirshfeld for Latin translations.
4. The cliffs now bear the *titulus ESTUARIE,* but the inscription was altered by the restorers of the 1870s, and originally read *STROALIA,* for the island of Strofadi, where the near-shipwreck was supposed to have occurred (Demus, 1984: 68). According to legend, during the voyage to Venice, St. Mark appeared to the monk Stauracius and warned, *"Surge et dic hominibus istis Veneticis ut citius vela deponant ne patiantur naufragium quia terra non longe est."* The mariners were warned to take in their sails to avoid shipwreck, because the coast was near.
5. According to code, by 1255, two trumpeters were required to accompany all Venetian ships larger than 188 dead weight tons going beyond the Adriatic (Zeno's code 22, Predelli and Sacerdoti, 1903: 93).
6. 1 *milliarium* equals 0.47 dead weight tons (Lane, 1934: 248).
7. In later documents, the curved stern was referred to as a stern *alla Faustina* (as per Stefano de Zuanne, 1686). Because a curved stern rudder broke quite easily, a supplemental quarter rudder, called *zanca* was needed (as per Christoforo Canale in *Libri quattro, Della milizia marittima*). The rudder on a straight stern *alla Ponentina* (as per Stefano de Zuanne, 1686) broke less easily yet steered effectively (Bonino, 1987: fig. 1F; personal communication).
8. The *modulo* is the longitudinal distance between two frames' axes.

9. Both are necessary, because together they will constitute the baseline for the *partixon del ramo,* a secondary sinusoid which corrects the result of the first two, which is too flat.
10. The sinusoid, applied on the bottom of the hull, to reduce regularly to zero a 1/10 of the width of the main frame, the *bocha.* It begins at frame #1 and ends at the *codere chorbe.*
11. The sinusoid, applied at deck level likewise.
12. The sinusoid, 1/20 of the *bocha.* Its maximum value is centered on the *chodera chorba.* It leads against the *partixon del mader de bocha* between the main frame and the *chodera chorba,* and against the parabolic mold between the *chodera chorba* and the ends of the deck. The parabolic mold of the deck is built on two segments: 1/3 (of the overall length of the deck) x 1/9.
13. The sinusoid. The lateral profile of a frame is determined by a variable mold. The mold is composed by two identical but inverted parabolic molds, that move, one in respect to the other with a rule. The parabolic half-molds have the segments: 2/3 (of the *bocha*) x 4/9.
14. The *chorbe de mezzo* is a block of four frames they built together to have a solid base for beginning the work, which varies from boat to boat.
15. 1 *botta* equals approximately 0.6 dead weight tons (Lane, 1934: 249).
16. 1 *piede* equals approximately 0.347735 meters.
17. Dr. Marco Bonino identified this unusual vessel (personal communication).
18. Recorded as belonging to the Zoppetti collection of the Museo Correr, Venice (Levi, 1892: design 30). Personnel of the Correr Museum were unable to provide a photograph nor confirm it is in their collections. Dr. Marco Bonino saw the medallion in the coin collection of Museo Archeologico in 1966, but he could obtain no record or photograph of it (personal communication).

Chapter 3. Venetian Watercraft: Diversity to Meet Every Need

1. The term brace is usually used to refer to the upper rigging of square-rigged ships. On lateeners, the lines controlling the peak of the sail are more commonly called vang.
2. Tables in appendix 3 compile measurements from textual specifications, archaeological examples, and reconstructions based on representational evidence.
3. Lane (1934 and 1973), Bonino (1978), and Steffy (1994) discuss many of the treatises; Laughton (1956), on the Roccafortis of 1268; Pryor (1984) on merchant ships *(navis),* based on the crusader contracts of the thirteenth and fourteenth centuries, as well as various technical treatises; Jal (1840) on medieval warships and merchant ships; Anderson (1925) on the manuscript of the Venetian merchant, Giorgio Trombetta of Modon of 1444; Anderson (1945), Jal (1840) and Bellabarba (1988) on the anonymous fifteenth-century *Fabrica di galere.* Chiggiato offers an explanation of the system of shipbuilding described in *Ragioni antique spettanti all'arte del mare et fabriche de vasselli* (1480–1529; Dosio, 1987), as well as for the Naples (1268), the Brindisi (1275) and the early fifteenth-century Venetian *Fabrica di galere* materials (1991).
4. The *scheda* evolved from an early methodology of verbally transmitted messages, simplified to seven essential statements and eleven measurements (Chiggiato, personal communication).
5. This geometry tool was called *mezo redondo* by Zorzi da Modon, *mezzo tondo* by the author of *Fabrica di galere* and *mezzaluna* by Crescenzio.
6. I am indebted to Dr. Ennio Concina for this insight.
7. According to Pryor, in at least two documents, the *Fabrica di galere* and Trombetta's commonplace book, the *trepie* is specifically measured from the keel and not the floor. He implies that Bonino has misinterpreted the evidence by measuring it from the floor (1984: 190). However, in Bonino's original publication on the Contarina I ship, he states, "In the first ship of Contarina . . . the first wale lies exactly three Venetian *piede* (1.041 meters) above the keel (not the floor). The *trepie* was always indicated as a reference measure in all the Venetian treatises from the fifteenth to seventeenth centuries, which indicated the *boca,* the exact width of the midships section at three feet above the keel" (1978a: 62; author translation). In fact, in the earliest documents (including the *Fabrica di galere*), the *trepie* is the molded beam at a height of three Venetian feet, but, by later treatises (including Trombetta's), it became a generic term for the second of three primary widths defining the shape of a particular section (Fred Hocker, personal communication).
8. The term tragent *(trigànte)* occurs in the contracts St. Louis made with Genoa in 1246, which were quite similar to those he arranged with Venice in 1268. The tragent is "a lateral beam set into the top of the sternpost to provide the base for the after-castle" or *castellum* (Pryor, 1984, no. 3: 278).

9. Other interesting examples can be seen in a miniature of a Genoese ship departing for the Holy Land in 1178, from Codice N of Caffaro (1187; Bragadin, 1974: 39), in a painting by Ambrogio Lorenzetti of "St. Nicholas of Bari" (1348; in the Uffici Gallery, Florence, inv. 1890 no. 8348–49), and a manuscript of 1571 in the Topkapi collection showing a horse port with fantastic-looking "wings" (Pryor, 1990: fig. 1).
10. In the thirteenth century, the Neapolitan *palmi* was equivalent to 0.262 meters (Pryor, 1982: no. 2, 118).
11. See Pryor's later discussion on the translation of *syontus* or *syonatus* as "a scarf or joint in a beam," as well as single and double stern port design variations (Pryor, 1990: 255–73).
12. The development of the rudder during the medieval period has been thoroughly studied by Mott (1997) in *The Development of the Rudder: A Technological Tale,* to which interested readers may turn for further information.
13. Variations that are obviously different spellings of the same name are put in parentheses, with all variations counted as one type in the graph, figure 154. Etymologically related names that seem to indicate a subtype are grouped together, but each possible distinction is counted as another type for the graph. Etymologies are not explored further, because expected results of such analysis would be indefinite and of limited value to this study. Names that indicate dual-purpose vessels are counted half in each category.
14. The term *carabus,* from the Greek, *karavion,* also refers to an early primitive skin boat (Bonino, 1978: 18; fig. 1).
15. These graph the actual number of examples of each type that was located through this study of Veneto art. This includes all versions of aggregates (where the artist has depicted more than one version of the same ship to relate a story), images discussed but not illustrated in the catalog, and those listed in appendix 1. Date ranges are averaged for the purposes of the graphs, and mid-century dates are assigned to the first half of the century. The cut-off date used for the graphs is 1500; however, data from the second half of the fifteenth century is incomplete, especially for the years after 1486. That half-century's total data remains unknown and therefore is not precisely reflected in the graphs. However, the tallied results up to the year 1486 indicate that exponentially more art exists for this later period. Combining all tallied examples of Venetian maritime art between the years A.D. 300 to 1450 totals 239 vessels. In just the following dozen years, that number increases by almost 100 images; that total nearly doubles by the year 1486.

ENGLISH AND LATIN/ VENETIAN NAUTICAL GLOSSARY

[Based on Steffy, 1994, *Wooden Ship Building and the Interpretation of Shipwrecks;* Guglielmotti, 1899, *Vocabulario marino militare;* Corazzini, 1900, *Vocabulario nautico Italiano;* Bathe, 1978, *The visual encyclopedia of nautical terms under sail;* Gill, Claude S., 1982, *Steel's elements of mastmaking, sailmaking and rigging;* Pryor, 1984, "The Naval Architecture of Crusader Transport Ships: A Reconstruction of some Archetypes for Round-hulled Sailing Ships," *Mariner's Mirror* 70: figs. 7, 9, and 13.]

abaft: Further aft of; toward the stern relative to some other object or position.

adze: An ax-like tool with its blade at right angles to the handle, used for shaping and dressing wood.

after mast: The third, aft-most mast of a three-masted lateener, also called the mizzen.

amantus: Tie for the yard; the halyard (lateen rig).

amidships: The middle of a vessel, either longitudinally or transversely.

anchor: A wooden, stone, or metal device that, when connected to a vessel with a cable or chain, is used to secure the vessel to the bed of a waterway to prevent it from drifting.

anchus: Parrel tackle (lateen rig).

antennae: The yard (lateen rig).

apron: A curved piece of timber fixed to the after surface of the stem or to the top of the forward end of the keel and the after surface of the stem; an inner stempost.

arbor de medio: Middle mast.

arbor de prora: Foremast, mast at bow (sometimes known as *artimonum* or *artimon*), which was taller than the others and raked forward.

artemon: A sail used on the foremast or the *arbor de prora* for medieval lateen-rigged ships. Foresail.

astern: Behind the ship.

athwartships: Across the ship from side to side; perpendicular to the fore-and-aft line of the ship.

auger: A tool used for boring holes.

backstay: A stay leading from the head of the mast, aft, to support it.

balanced rudder: A rudder whose stock is placed aft of its leading edge so that the water pressure is approximately equal on its forward and after surfaces; balanced rudders require less turning power than conventional rudders.

balustrade: Railing of small pillars, frequently employed to form an open parapet to fence around an upper deck.

batten: A thin plank or strip of wood bent around molds or frames of a ship's hull, used to determine hull curvatures or to temporarily connect timbers during construction.

beam: A timber mounted athwartships to support decks and provide lateral strength. The width of the hull, which is technically the length of the main beam.

bellatorium/ballador: Fighting gallery behind the *paradisi* at the stern of some Crusader transport ships, perhaps in part to provide protection for the vital, but vulnerable quarter rudders. *Ballador* is the Venetian form of the Latin term *Bellatorium*.

bitt: Strong upright post (usually set in pairs) that projected above the deck of the ship, used for belaying cables, lines, etc. A frame composed of two upright pieces of timber, called the pins, and a cross piece fastened horizontally on top of them. Bowline and brace bitts were set near the bowlines and the masts; riding bitts, the largest bitts in a ship, were those for the anchor cable.

blade: The flat, immersed, turning portion of a steering oar or quarter rudder.

blocks: One or more freely rotating, grooved pulleys, set in a separate housing, about which ropes passed to form a hoisting or hauling tackle.

bowline: On a square sail, the line controlling the upper corners of the sail. Also, the tack, or line attached to the heel, or forward, lower corner of a fore-and-aft sail.

bowsprit: Spar that projects from the very front of the vessel.

brace: On a square-rigged ship, the lines controlling the upper yard.

brails: Ropes to truss up a square sail.

bulwark: Solid structure or stanchions with railing that extended above level of deck to protect persons or objects on board.

bunt: In order to hold more wind and thus work more effectively, sails are cut not flat but in such as way that the middle section bellies out. This belly is known as the bunt, and the lines that pull it forward, bunt lines.

calcet/cholzexe: Heavy piece of timber scarfed to the mast head that had two lateral pulleys inserted in it side to side and by means of which lateen yards were hauled. May have also been the structure to which the crow's nest was attached.

candela/ae: Shroud/s.

cant timber: A framing member that was mounted obliquely so that its cross-section would remain more nearly rectangular along the in-curving ends of the vessel.

capstan: A spool-shaped vertical cylinder, mounted on a spindle and bearing, turned by means of levers or bars; used for moving heavy loads, such as hoisting anchors, lifting yards, or careening vessels.

careen: To list a vessel deliberately so that part of its bottom was exposed for caulking, cleaning, repairing, etc.

cares/cara/carra: Heel, or lower section, of a two-piece yard.

cathead: A stout beam, projecting from the hull (in the bow), used to raise and store the anchor.

caulk: To insert oakum or other material between planks to make watertight by filling the seams.

central mast: The mast closest to midship on a three-masted lateener.

chine: The angular junction of the bottom and side of a vessel; usually found on flat-bottomed hulls, or those with little deadrise.

cholzexe: Venetian dialect for *calcet*.

clench: To secure a nail or bolt by bending or flattening its projecting end over the surface it last penetrated.

clew: The bottom corner of a sail. On a square sail, there are two clews; on a fore-and-aft sail (e.g., lateen), it is the after, lower corner controlled by the sheet.

clinker: Planked so that one plank laps over the next. Lapstrake.

coffa/cheba: Crow's nest.

crow's nest: Platform, basket, or box at the top of a mast where a lookout can be posted. *Cheba*.

crutch: A forked stanchion used as support.

deadeyes: A block without a sheave; flat rounded blocks fixed in the channels, and having eyes for the lanyards by which the shrouds are set up.

deadrise: The amount of elevation, or rising, of the floor above the horizontal plane.

double-ended hull: A hull that is nearly symmetrical about the midship transverse plane, and pointed at bow and stern.

fall: The rope that connects the blocks of a tackle. The fall sometimes implies only the loose part that is pulled upon to produce the desired effect.

finials: In architecture, the decorative upper termination of a pinnacle; a pointed ornament.

floor timber: Any framing timber that crossed the centerline of the keel and whose arms extended far enough to traverse one or more planking strakes on each side of the keel.

flukes (of anchor): The palm of an anchor. The broad, holding portion that penetrates the ground.

flush-laid planking: Planking in which adjoining strakes are abutted, edge joined, and do not overlap.

fondo: Bottom of ship.

forecastle: A short, raised foredeck.

foremast: The mast nearest the bow on vessels with more than one mast. On a lateen-rigged ship, it is generally the tallest mast for the main sail, and has a strong forward rake. Also called *arbor de prora, arbor di proda, artimon* or *artimonum.*

foresail: The sail of the foremast.

forestay: A stay leading from the head of the mast, forward, to support the mast.

frame-first construction: Skeletal construction.

frames: Single or composite members (floors, futtocks, half-frames, and top-timbers) attached to the inner side of the hull planking mounted more or less perpendicularly to the keel, whose function was that of strengthening the hull and maintaining its shape.

freeboard: The vessel's side, between the sheer plank and the waterline.

futtock: A frame timber other than a floor timber, half-frame, or top timber; one of the middle pieces of a frame.

garboard: The lowest outer hull strake, with its lower or inboard edge attached to the keel.

grapnel: A small anchor with four or more flukes arranged in a circular manner.

grommet: Originally, strands of rope in the form of a ring, used to secure sail to yard, oars to pins on the gunwale, etc.

gudgeon: A socket attached to the stern frame of a vessel, for holding a pintle of a rudder.

gunwale: Upper edge of the hull of an open boat.

half-frame: A framing member that commenced at or near the keel and spanned both the bottom and part of the side of a vessel. Half-frames were single timbers used in lieu of floor timbers and futtocks and were normally employed in pairs.

halyard: Ropes or tackle employed to hoist or lower sails and yards. On medieval lateen-rigged ships, it served a double function in that it secured aft, acting as a backstay.

hawse hole: A cylindrical hole in the bow through which the anchor cable or mooring line passed.

hawser: A strong rope used to tow or tie up a vessel.

iconography: the study of the meanings attached to pictorial representations, including signs, symbols, attributes, and emblems.

keel: The main, lowest longitudinal member of a hull, upon which the frame's deadwoods and ends of the hull were mounted; the backbone of the hull.

keelson: An internal longitudinal timber mounted atop the floor timber frames along the centerline of the keel, that provided additional longitudinal strength to the bottom of the hull; an inner keel, whose function was to stiffen the bottom structure.

lapstrake: Having overlapping strakes: clinker built.

lateen rig: The arrangement in which a three-cornered sail is attached to a yard that obliquely crosses a low, forward-raking mast.

leeboards: A board lowered on the leeside of a flat-bottomed vessel to act as a temporary keel in avoiding leeway, preventing the vessel drifting to leeward.

lifts: The ropes, wires or chains used to hold the yard up to the masts.

lines: The various shapes of a hull; expressed graphically, a set of geometric projections, usually arranged in three views, that illustrates the shape of a vessel's hull.

loom: The shaft or inboard part of the oar or rudder; a pole-like supporting axis for the blade.

luctatorium: Collar through which the loom of the rudder passed, attaching the rudder to the hull.

mast crutch: The forked pole, or cradle, on which an unstepped mast was supported.

mast step: A mortise cut into the top of a keelson or large floor timber, or a mortised wooden block or assembly of blocks mounted on the floor timbers or keelson, into which the tenoned heel of a mast was seated.

midship: A contraction of amidships and consequently, in a general sense, it refers to the middle of the ship. In construction, however, it is often used as an adjective referring to the broadest part of the hull, wherever it may be.

mizzen: On a lateen rig, the mast directly behind the mainmast, called *di mezzo* in Venetian. This is the aftermost mast on three-masted lateeners, and the mast closest to midship on a two-masted lateener.

mold: A pattern used to determine the shapes of frames and other compass timbers. Molds were usually made from thin, flexible pieces of wood.

mortise: A cavity cut into a timber to receive a tenon.

mortise-and-tenon joint: A union of planks or timbers by which a projecting piece (tenon), was fitted into one or more cavities (mortises) of corresponding size.

mulgaranus/*marganali*: Heavy rope attached to base of yard that controlled its fore and aft movement, and was rove through a block on the deck. Could be taken in to peak the yard either while sailing to obtain maximum efficiency, or when tacking.

orant [from Latin *orans*, "praying"]: Figure shown praying in art, with hands raised to the level of the shoulder or the head, with palms turned upward.

orcia: Tack (lateen rig).

osta: Vang (lateen rig).

outrigger: A structure built out from the hull proper to improve the efficiency of the oar system.

parrel: A sliding ring or collar of rope or wood that confined a yard to the mast but allowed its vertical movement; tackle that fit the yard to the mast and reduced friction so that it could be hoisted or lowered with facility. In the medieval period, a rope truss, or parrel trucks, was used.

parrel tackle: Line that tightened the yard to the mast at the parrel, belayed at the bulwarks.

parrel trucks: Round balls of wood with a hole through the middle in which a rope was reeved, to form low-friction parrel.

peak: The upper corner of a fore-and-aft sail (e.g., lateen), controlled by the vang.

peciae antennarium: Upper and lower sections of the yard.

peg: A tapered wooden pin driven into a pre-drilled hole to securely fasten two members or lock a joint.

pendant: Free line that led to a block; for example, large,

but short, ropes that went over the mastheads, to which were hooked the main and fore tackles, and served to transmit the effort of their tackles to some other object.

pennae: Upper section of the yard.

piede: Ancient Italian measurment, "foot," equivalent to 0.347735 meters. In Venetian documents, *pie, pe`*, and finally *pede* were used.

pintle: A vertical pin or bolt, especially one on which something turns, as the gudgeon of a hinge.

pozia/pozal: Sheet? (Lateen rig).

predella: A strip under or beside an altarpiece, containing small paintings of subjects closely related to that of the altarpiece itself; hence, sometimes used in art for a small picture connected with, and in the same frame as, a larger work.

quarterdeck: The after part of the upper deck, from the mainmast to the poop.

quarter rudder: A steering device that was securely attached to the side of the stern of a vessel. The flat immersed portion is called the blade. It was affixed to the stock or loom, a pole-like vertical member that pivoted within a collar or other supporting fixture attached to the hull. A tiller, the handle by which the rudder was turned, was perpendicularly attached to the upper end of the stock. In all cases, quarter rudders were solely designed for steering purposes and required secure attachment to the hull.

rabbet: A groove cut into keel (or other member) for purpose of seating planks.

rake: The inclination of the stem and sternpost beyond the ends of the keel; also, the inclination of the masts from the perpendicular.

riding bitt: Strong, upright timbers in the bow of a ship, to which anchor cables and hawsers were secured.

rig: The arrangement of masts, sails, etc., on a vessel. To put in proper order for working use.

robands: Small lengths of line passed through at the head of a sail to attach it to the yard. Used to fasten the head of the sail to the yard. Also known as rovings.

rocker: Fore-and-aft curvature of the keel of the bottom of vessel.

rockered keel: A keel that is curved longitudinally so that it is deeper at its middle that at its ends.

room and space: Average of the distances between frame centerlines throughout the hull. A more definitive designation for ancient ships is average frame spacing.

rudder: A timber, or assembly of timbers, that could be rotated about an axis to control the direction of a vessel underway.

rudder blade: The flat part of the rudder that diverts the water.

scarf: An overlapping longitudinal joint used to connect two timbers or planks without increasing their dimensions.

senali: Shrouds (lateen rig).

sheave: Pulley for hoisting or hauling.

sheer: The fore-and-aft curve of the hull at the main deck or bulwarks. The longitudinal sweep of the caprail or the top of the hull.

sheer strake: The top strake of planking at the level of the main or upper deck of a vessel.

sheet: On a lateen rig, the line that controls the clew of the sail, to retain clew in any direction. On a square sail, lines that control the bottom corners of the sail.

shell-first construction: A modern term used to describe the process by which all or part of the outer hull planking was erected before any frames were attached to it. In pure shell-built hulls, outer hull planking was self-supporting and formed the primary structure; the framework fastened to it formed the secondary, or stiffening, structure.

shrouds: Lines that lead from the mast head to the sides of the vessel, set up with deadeyes and lanyards, which support the mast athwartships. The shroud assembly includes the pendant and block runner through which a runner tie is rove and tightened by means of a deadeye at the gunwale. Medieval terms believed to identify various parts of the shroud assembly: *senali, chinali, poppeso, prodón a prodesso, quarnale, quinali, quadernali, frasconi.*

skeletal construction: Frame-first construction. A modern term used to describe the procedure in which hulls were constructed by first erecting frames and then attaching the outer skin of planking to them.

spar: A long wooden beam, generally rounded, and used for supporting the sails or rigging. It assumes various functions and names—mast, yard, boom, gaff, sprit, etc.

speron: Boarding platform.

stanchion: An upright prop or support; a piece of timber used to support the deck, the quarter rails, awnings, etc.

stays: Fore-and-aft mast support lines: *suste*. Ropes that lead from the mast head forward and aft to support the mast.

steering oar: An oar used to steer a small vessel, either from the side or the stern, consisting of the blade, or turning surface; the loom, a pole-like supporting axis for the blade; and sometimes a tiller, or turning arm, attached to the upper end of the loom. Steering oars could be used singly or in multiple, along the sides or astern of the vessel. While steering oars might have been collared or otherwise attached to the hull in some cases, they were lighter and much more portable than the permanently mounted quarter rudders used on larger vessels.

stem: A vertical or upward-curving timber or assembly of timbers, scarfed to the keel or central plank at its lower end extending forward from the keel and forming the upright post to which the two sides of the bow were attached.

sternpost: A vertical or upward-curving timber or assembly of timbers stepped into, or scarfed to, the after end of the keel.

stops: Bindings that attach the furled sail to the yard.

strake: A continuous row of planking, either made up of one piece, or several pieces scarfed together, extending from bow to stern.

stringer: Foot wale; thick ceiling planking at turn of bilge.

suste: Stays.

tack: The line to the heel, the forward, lower corner of a fore-and-aft sail (e.g. lateen), to maneuver side-to-side movement of the base of the yard; also sometimes called bowlines. The forward, lower corner of a fore- and aft sail. On a square sail, the line used to control that corner of the sail closest to the wind. On a square sail, the running rigging line to the leading edge of the sail.

tackle: A combination of ropes and block, for hoisting, lowering and shifting yards, sails, and objects; purchase.

thole/thole pin: A pin, or one of a pair or pins, set vertically in the gunwale to serve as the fulcrum for an oar.

through-beam: An athwartships beam that penetrated the outer hull planking and supported the quarter rudders or provided athwartships stiffness to the upper part of the hull.

thwart: A transverse plank in a boat or a galley; used to seat rowers, support masts, or provide lateral stiffness.

tiller: Handle, attached perpendicularly to the loom, by which the rudder is turned.

top-timber: Timber that formed the uppermost component of frame that extended to the rail cap or sheer.

tragent: *Trigànte*. Heavy transverse beam at upper end of sternpost that provided support for cabins in the sterncastle, on a wing transom stern.

transom: One of the beams fastened across the sternpost, which strengthened the stern and gave it a fuller shape or a flat stern. The deck transom held the ends of the lower deck planking; above it was the highest transom, the wing transom. The curve described by the transoms as they narrow in and down toward the keel is called the flight of the transom.

transom knee: An angular, horizontal reinforcing timber bolted to a transom and the side.

trigànte: Tragent.

troca/ trozza: Truss that held the yard to the mast; fitted with parrel trucks to prevent wearing and to reduce friction.

truss: A device that supports a standing yard. A pivot allowed the yard to swing horizontally when braced.

tumble home: The inward curvature of a vessel's upper sides as they rose from the point of maximum breadth to the bulwarks. Tumble home reduced topside weight and improved stability.

vang: A sail shaping line, which runs to near the top of the *penna* of the yard, permitting trimming of the peak. The *osta*.

wale: A heavy piece of outer planking, or a belt of thick planking strakes, strategically placed to gird the upper part of the hull. The wales acted as bands that bound the upper part of the hull together.

wedges: Fortification at girth of mast that immobilize the partner and help set the mast vertically.

whip: A small single tackle, formed by connecting the fall to a single block or with two blocks (one fixed, one movable), used to hoist things.

whipstaff: A piece of wood fastened to the helm, which the helmsman/steersman holds in his hand to move the helm and turn the ship.

wooldings: Windings of several close turns of rope in a tight manner around masts and yards that are made of several united pieces to strengthen and confine the same together. Wooldings girded the mast at fixed intervals.

yard: A long spar, supported more or less at its center, to which the head of the sail is bent.

REFERENCES

Anderson, R. C. 1925. "Italian Naval Architecture about 1445." *Mariner's Mirror.* 2: 135–63.

———. 1945. "Jal's 'Memoire no. 5' and the manuscript 'Fabbrica di Galere.'" *Mariner's Mirror.* 31.3: 161–67.

———. 1962. *Oared fighting ships.* London, England: Percival Marshall.

Bass, George Fletcher, and Frederick H. van Doorninck. 1982. *Yassi Ada: a seventh-century Byzantine shipwreck.* College Station: Texas A&M University Press.

Bathe, Basil W. 1978. *The visual encyclopedia of nautical terms under sail.* New York: Crown Publishers.

Bellabarba, Sergio. 1988. "The square-rigged ship of the *'Fabrica di Galere'* Manuscript." *Mariner's Mirror.* 74.2: 113–30 and 74.3: 225–40.

———. 1995. "Riddles: the enigmas of 'orza' and 'poggia.'" *Mariner's Mirror.* 81.2: 134–47.

Bettini, Sergio, et al. 1974. *Venezia e bisanzio.* Catalog for show at Ducal Palace, June 8–Sept. 30, 1974. Venice, Italy: Electa Editrice.

Bonino, Marco. 1978a. *Archeologia e tradizione navale tra la Romagna e il Po.* Ravenna, Italy: Longo Editore.

———. 1978b. "Lateen-rigged medieval ships. New evidence from wrecks in the Po Delta (Italy) and notes on pictorial and other documents." *International Journal of Nautical Archaeology* 7.1: 9–28.

———. 1988. Notes on the steering devices of ancient ships. In Tsalas, Harry (ed.). *Tropis II. Second international symposium on ship construction in antiquity.* Athens: Hellenic Institute for the Preservation of Nautical Tradition.

———. 1991. Archeologia navale. In *Storia di Ravenna II.* 1. *Dall'età bizantina all'età ottoniana territorio, economia e società.* Ravenna, Italy: Marsilio Editori.

Bovini, G. 1966. "Principali restauri compiuti nel secolo scorso da Felice Kibel nei mosaici di S. Apollinare Nuovo di Ravenna." *Corsi di cultura sull'arte ravennate e bizantina* 13. Ravenna, Italy.

———. 1971. *Ravenna.* New York: Harry N. Abrams, Inc., Publishers.

Bragadin, Marc'Antonio. 1974. *Le Repubbliche marinare.* Milan, Italy.

———. 1978. "Le navi, loro strutture e attrezzature nell'alto medioevo." *La navigazione mediterranea nell'alto medioevo* (Settimane di studio del centro italiano di studi sull'alto medioevo) 25.1: 389–412. Spoleto, Italy.

Carile, Antonio. 1976. "Episodi della IV crociata nel mosaico pavimentale di S. Giovanne Evangelista di Ravenna." In *Corsi di cultura sull'arte ravennate e bizantina.* Ravenna, Italy.

Casoni, Giovanni. 1847. Forze militari. pp. 193–250, in *Venezia e le sue lagune.* Venice, Italy: Nell'I.R. Privil. Stabilimento Antonelli.

Casson, Lionel. 1964a. *The illustrated history of ships and boats.* New York: Doubleday.

———. 1964b. *The great age of the sailing ship.* New York.

———. 1971. *Ships and seamanship in the ancient world.* Princeton, N.J.: Princeton University Press.

Cecchelli, Carlo, ed. 1932. *Catalogo delle cose d'arte e di antichità d'Italia (Zara).* Rome.

Chastel, Andre. 1963. *Italian art.* New York: T. Yoseloff.

Chiggiato, Alvise. 1987. "Le 'ragioni antique' dell'architettura navale." In *Ragioni antique spettanti all'arte del mare et fabriche de vasselli. Manoscritto nautico del sec. XV,* ed. Giorgetta Bonfiglio Dosio. Venice, Italy: Il Comitato Editore.

———. 1989. Unpublished line drawing of a galley, *galea rubea,* based on notarial document, 1275, *Registro Angioino* no. 24, Carol. 1275 B, Folio 351, Naples State Archives. Letter to author, April 12, 1989 (Private collection, Lillian Ray Martin).

———. 1991. "Contenuti delle architetture navali antiche." In *Rivista dell'Ateneo Veneto,* 178.

Christe, Yves, Tania Velmans, Hanna Losowska, and Roland Recht. 1982. *Art of the Christian world,* A.D. 200–1500*: A handbook of styles and forms.* New York: Rizzoli.

Ciciliot, Furio. 1996. "Sources for medieval nautical archaeology: Genoese notarial records." *International Journal of Nautical Archaeology* 25.3; 25.4: 239–42.

Concina, Ennio. 1988. *L'Arsenale della Repubblica di Venezia.* Milan, Italy: Electa Spa.

———. 1987. "Venezia: arsenale, spazio urbano, spazio marittimo. L'età del primato e l'età del confronto." In *Arsenali e città nell'Occidente Europeo.* Rome, Italy: La Nuova Italia Scientifica.

Corazzini, F. 1900. *Vocabulario nautico Italiano.* Turin, Italy: Tipografia San Giuseppe degli Artigianelli.

Delouka, Katerina. 1990. *Inventaire des graffiti navals des eglises Byzantines et post-Byzantines.* Master's thesis, under the direction of M. L. Pressouyre and M. E. Rieth, University of Paris, U.F.R. D'Archéologie, Paris, France.

Demus, Otto. 1984. *The mosaics of San Marco in Venice.* 2 vols. Chicago: University of Chicago Press.

———. 1988. *The mosaic decoration of San Marco, Venice.* Chicago: University of Chicago Press, published for Dumbarton Oaks, Washington, D.C.

Dolley, R. H. 1949. "The rig of early medieval warships." *Mariner's Mirror.* 35.1: 51–55.

Farrel, A. W. 1979." The use of iconographic material in medieval ship archaeology." Pp. 227–46 in *The archaeology of medieval ships and harbours in northern Europe,* ed. Sean McGrail. Greenwich, England: BAR International Series 66.

Fasoli, Gina. 1978. "Navigazione fluviale—Porte e navi sul Po." In *La navigazione Mediterranea nell'Alto Medieovo.* Spoleto, Italy: Settimane di studio del Centro Italiano di studi sull'Alto Medioevo.

Folda, Jaroslav. 1976. *Crusader manuscript illumination at Saint Jean d'Acre,* 1275–1291. Princeton: Princeton University Press.

Gauthier, Marie-Madeleine. 1972. *Emaux du moyen age occidental.* Fribourg, Switzerland: Office du Livre.

Gill, Claude S., ed. 1982. *Steel's elements of mastmaking, sailmaking, and rigging* (from the 1794 edition). Largo, Florida: Edward W. Sweetman Co.

Goodman, William Louis. 1964. *The history of woodworking tools.* New York: D. McKay.

Göttlicher, Arvid. 1985. *Die schiffe der antike: eine einfuhrung in die archaologie der wasserfahrzeuge.* Berlin, Germany: Gebr. Mann.

Guglielmotti, Alberto. 1889. *Vocabolario marino militare.* Rome, Italy: Voghera.

Gunda, Bela, ed. 1984. *The fishing culture of the world: studies in ethnology, cultural ecology, and folklore.* Budapest, Hungary: Akademiai Kiado.

Hahnloser, H. R. 1971. *Il Tesoro di San Marco.* Florence, Italy: Sansoni Editore Nuove, S.p.A.

Helms, S. W. 1975. "Ship graffiti in the church of San Marco in Venice." *International Journal of Nautical Archaeology,* 4.2: 229–36.

Herodotus. Fifth century B.C., *The Histories.* 1954. Reprinted 1964. Translated by Aubrey de Sélincourt. Baltimore, Md.: Penguin Books.

Hocker, F. 1987. "Sheets *(Poziae)* in the medieval lateen rig." *Mariner's Mirror.* 73.4: 367–68.

Jal, A. Augustin. 1840. *Archéologie navale.* 2 Vols. Paris, France: A. Bertrand.

Kaftal, George. 1978. *Iconography of the saints in northeast Italy.* Florence, Italy: Sansoni Editore Nuove, S.p.A.

Kapitän, Gerhard. 1984. Ancient anchors—technology and classification. *International Journal of Nautical Archaeology,* 13.1: 33–44.

Kedar, Benjamin Z. 1976. *Merchants in crisis: Genoese and Venetian men of affairs and the 14th-century depression.* New Haven, Conn., and London, England: Yale University Press.

Keith, Donald, H. 1988. "Anchors." Pp. 118–24 in *Archaeology in solution: The proceedings of the 17th annual conference on underwater archaeology,* edited by J. W. Foster and S. O. Smith. Salinas, Calif.: Coyote Press.

Kreutz, Barbara M. 1976. "Ships, shipping and the implications of change in the early medieval Mediterranean." *Viator* 7: 79–109.

Laughton, L. G. Carr. 1956. "The *Roccafortis* of Venice, 1268." *Mariner's Mirror.* 42.4: 267–78.

Landström, Björn. 1961. *The ship: an illustrated history.* Translated by Michael Phillips. Garden City, N.Y.: Doubleday. Reprint, 1968. London, England: Allen and Unwin.

Lane, Frederic Chapin. 1934. Reprint, 1976. *Venetian ships and shipbuilding of the Renaissance.* Baltimore, Md.: Johns Hopkins University Press. Reprinted by Greenwood Press.

———. 1963. "Venetian merchant galleys, 1300–1334: private and communal operation." *Speculum: a journal of mediaeval studies,* 38: 179–205.

———. 1973. *Venice, a maritime republic.* Baltimore, Md., and London, England: Johns Hopkins University Press.

Levi, Cesare Auguste. 1892. *Navi Veneti da codici, marmi e dipinti.* Venice, Italy: Filippi Editore.

Lewis, Archibald Ross. 1951. *Naval power and trade in the Mediterranean,* A.D. 500–1100. Princeton, N.J.: Princeton University Press.

L'Orange, Hans Peter, and P. J. Nordhagen. 1966. *Mosaics.* London: Methuen & Co. Ltd.

Lorenzetti, Giulio. 1982. *Venice and its lagoon.* Triest, Italy: Lint.

Luzzato, Gino. 1961. *Studi di Storia Economica Veneziana.* Padova: Casa Editrice Dott. Antonio Milani.

Martin, M. E. 1979. "The first Venetians in the Black Sea." *Archeion Pontou* 35.

Matthews, Sheila D. 1983. "The rig on the eleventh-century ship at Serçe Liman, Turkey." Master's thesis, Department of Nautical Archaeology, Texas A&M University.

McNeill, William H. 1974. *Venice: The hinge of Europe 1081–1797.* Chicago and London: University of Chicago Press.

Moll, F. 1927. "The history of the anchor." *Mariner's Mirror.* 13.4: 293–332.

———. 1929. *Das schiff in der bildenden kunst vom altertums bis zum ausgang des mittelalters.* Bonn, Germany: K. Schroeder.

Moriarty, James R., and Neil F. Marshal. 1965. "The history and evolution of anchors." Reprint, winter, 1971, *CEDAM International Bulletin* 4:3.

Mott, Lawrence. 1997. *The development of the rudder: a technological tale.* College Station: Studies in Nautical Archaeology 3, Texas A&M University Press, and Chatham Publishing, London.

———. 1994. "A three-masted ship depiction from 1409." *International Journal of Nautical Archaeology* 23.1: 39–40.

Muraro, Michelangelo. 1970. *Paolo da Venezia.* University Park: Pennsylvania State University Press.

———, and Andre Grabar. 1963. *Treasures of Venice: the Church of St. Mark's, the treasure of St. Mark's, the Ducal Palace, the Gallerie dell'Accademia.* Translated by James Emmons. Geneva, Switzerland: Skira.

Nebbia, Ugo. 1932. *Arte navale italiana: pagine di storia e d'estetica marinara.* Bergamo, Italy: Istituto italiano d'arti grafiche.

Nepoti, Sergio. 1973. "I bacini in maiolica arcaica della chiesa di S. Francesco in Bologna." Pp. 45 ff. in *Faenza* 59.

Newton, Eric, and William Neil. 1966. 2000 *years of Christian art.* New York: Harper & Row.

Norwich, John Julius. 1982. *A history of Venice.* Suffolk, England: The Chaucer Press; Penguin Books.

Nuovo archivio veneto, NS 4–5. Venice, Italy: Prem. Stab. Tip-lit. Visentini cav. Federico.

Pächt, Otto, and J. J. G. Alexander. 1970. "The Italian School." in *Illuminated manuscripts in the Bodleian Library, Oxford,* I. Oxford, England: Clarendon Press.

Pallucchini, Rodolfo. 1964. *La pittura Veneziano del Trecento.* Istituto per la collaborazione culture, Venice-Rome, Italy: Fratelli Fabbri Editori.

Pataky, Dénes, and Imre Marjai. 1973. *Ships in art.* Budapest, Hungary: Corvina Press.

Predelli, Ricc., and Adolfo Sacerdoti. 1903. *Gli statuti marittimi veneziani fino al* 1255.

Pryor, John H. 1982. "Transportation of horses by sea during the era of the Crusades: eighth century to 1285 A.D." *Mariner's Mirror.* 68.1: 9–27 and 68.2: 103–26.

———. 1984. "The naval architecture of Crusader transport ships: A reconstruction of some archetypes for round-hulled sailing ships." *Mariner's Mirror.* 70.2: 171–219; 70.3: 275–92; and 70.4: 363–87.

———. 1990. "The naval architecture of Crusader transport ships revisited." *Mariner's Mirror.* 76: 255–76.

———. 1992. Geography, technology, and war: studies in the maritime history of the Mediterranean 649–1571. Cambridge, England: Cambridge University Press.

Queller, Donald. 1977. *The Fourth Crusade: The Conquest of Constantinople* 1201–4. Philadelphia: University of Pennsylvania Press.

Relazione della Commissione elatta della R. Deputazione Veneta di Storia Patria. 1901. "Sulla scoperta di due barche antiche nel comune di Contarina (Rovigo)" in *Miscellanea di storia Veneta.* Second series, 7. Venice, Italy.

Robert of Clari. Twelfth–thirteenth century. *The conquest of Constantinople.*

Rubin de Cervin, G. B. 1985. *La flotta di Venezia—The Venetian fleet.* Milan, Italy: Automobilia. Sansoni Editore Nuove, S.p.A., ed. 1971. *Il tesoro e il museo.* Florence, Italy: Sansoni Editore Nuove, S.p.A.

Scandurra, E. 1972. "The maritime republics: medieval ships in Italy." pp. 206–24 in *A history of seafaring,* ed. G. Bass. London, England: Thames and Hudson.

Singer, Charles Joseph, and E. J. Holmyard, A. R. Hall, and Trevor Williams, eds. 1956. *A history of technology,* vol. 2. New York: Oxford University Press.

Steer, John. 1970. *A concise history of Venetian painting.* New York: Praeger.

Steffy, J. Richard. 1994. *Wooden ship building and the interpretation of shipwrecks.* College Station: Texas A&M University Press.

Stussi, Alfredo, ed. 1967. *Zibaldone da Canal, manoscritto mercantile del sec. XIV.* Venice, Italy.

Throckmorton, Peter and Joan. 1973. The Roman wreck at Pantano Longarini. *International Journal of Nautical Archaeology* 2.2: 243–66.

Thubrin, Colin. 1980. *The Venetians.* Alexandria, Va.: Time-Life Books.

Tinniswood, J. T. 1945. "Anchors and accessories, 1340–1640." *Mariner's Mirror.* 31.2: 84–105.

Umberto, Franzoi, and Dina Di Stefano. 1976. *Le Chiese di Venezia.* Venice, Italy: Alfieri (Fantonigrafica).

Unger, Richard W. 1980. *The ship in the medieval economy,* 600–1600. London, England: Croom Helm.

van Doorninck, Frederick H. 1984. "The fabrication of some medieval iron anchors at the Bodrum Museum in Turkey." Pp. 3–7 in *Underwater archaeology: The proceedings of the* 13*th annual conference on underwater*

archaeology, ed. Donald H. Keith. San Marino, Calif.: Fathom Eight Special Publication no. 5.
Vegas, Liana Castelfranchi. 1966. *Giusto de' Menabuoi.* Milan, Italy: Fratelli Fabbri Editori, Istituto per la collaborazione culture, Venice-Rome, Italy.
Venturi, Lionello. 1937. *Botticelli.* The Phaidon Press, Vienna. George Allen and Unwin, Ltd., London.
Villain-Gandossi, Christiane. 1979. "Le navire médiéval à travers les miniatures des manoscrits francais." Pp. 195–226 in *The archaeology of medieval ships and harbours in northern Europe,* Sean McGrail, ed. Greenwich, England: BAR International Series 66.
———. 1985. *Le navire médiéval à travers les miniatures.* Paris, France: Editions du Centre National de la Recherche Scientifique.
Villehardouin, Geffroi de, and Sire Jean de Joinville. 1204. *La conquête de Constantinople.* Paris, France. Published in the original French, 1969, with preface by Jean Dufournet, Paris, France: Garnier-Flammarion. 1957, translated by Sir Frank Marzials, *Memoirs of the Crusades.* London and New York: E. P. Dutton & Co, Inc.
Vocini, Michele. 1927. Reprint, 1950. *Le nave nel tempo. Iconografia della nave dalle origini ai nostri giorni.* Milan and Rome, Italy: Luigi Alfieri & C.
Weitzmann, Kurt. 1951. *Greek mythology in Byzantine art.* Princeton, N.J.: Princeton University Press.
Zampetti, Pietro. 1969. *A dictionary of Venetian painters: 14th and 15th centuries,* vol. 1. Leighton-On-Sea, England: F. Lewis, Publishers, Ltd.
Zanetti, Girolamo. 1841. *Della origine di alcune arti principali appresso i Veneziani.* Venice, Italy: A. Santini. Book available in library of Museo Storico Navale, Venice, Italy, and the National Gallery of Art, Washington, D.C.
Zorzi, Marino, ed. 1988. *Biblioteca Marciana-Venezia (The Great Libraries of Italy).* Italy: Nardi Editore.

Manuscripts and Archival Material

Arte de far vasselli. Material of manuscript dates to ca. 1400–20; this manuscript written late fifteenth or early sixteenth century. Vienna Osterreichische Nationalbibliothek, Cod. 6391, Vienna, Austria. Nearly identical copy of *Fabrica di galere* in Biblioteca Nazionale Centrale, Florence.
Baldassare Drachio. 1593. *La visione di Baldassarre Drachio.* Venice. Archivio proprio Contarini, b. 25, Provveditori all'Arsenale b.1, State Archives, Venice, Italy.
Capitolarium nauticum pro navis. 1255 copy of Zeno's Maritime Code, Biblioteca Querini Stampalia, Cl. IV Cod. I (=147), Venice, Italy.
Cinegetica dello Pseudo-Oppiano. Eleventh-century manuscript. Biblioteca Nazionale Marciana, Gr. Z.479, Venice, Italy.
Cronologia Magna. Fourteenth-century manuscript. Biblioteca Nazionale Marciana, ms LAT. Z 399 (=1610), folio 76v, 78v, Venice, Italy.
Fabrica di galere. Material of manuscript dates to ca. 1400–20; written at least seventy years later. Venice, Italy; now in the Biblioteca Nazionale Centrale, Coll. Magliabecchiano Cl XIX, cod. 7, Florence, Italy. Nearly identical copy of *Arte de far vasselli,* in Vienna Osterreichische Nationalbibliothek, Cod. 6391.
Ragioni antique spettanti all'arte del mare et fabriche de vasselli. 1480. Venice, Italy. Now original manuscript in National Maritime Museum, Greenwich, England, NVT 19. Transcription published in Dosio, G. Bonfiglio (ed.), 1987, *Ragioni antique spettanti all'arte del mare et fabriche de vasselli. Manoscritto nautico del sec. XV.* Venice, Italy: Il Comitato Editore.
Stefano di Zuanne. 1686. *La architectura navale.* Venice. Now kept at British Museum, Add. 38655, London, England.
Zibaldone da Canale. ca. 1310–50. *Zibaldone da Canale.* Original manuscript in State Archives, Venice, Italy. Transcription published in Stussi, Alfredo (ed.), 1967, *Zibaldone da Canale, manoscritto mercantile del sec. XIV.* Venice, Italy: Il Comitato Editore.
Zorzi da Modon, also called Giorgio Trombetta da Modon. 1444–49 manuscript, mistakenly referred to as "Timbotta" in past publications. *Book of Zorzi,* British Museum Library, MS.Cotton Titus, A. 26, London, England.

INDEX

Pages containing illustrations appear in *italics.*